# Napalm

# Napalm

## AN AMERICAN BIOGRAPHY

Robert M. Neer

The Belknap Press of Harvard University Press

Cambridge, Massachusetts · London, England

2013

Library of Congress Cataloging-in-Publication Data

Neer, Robert M., 1964–
Napalm : an American biography / Robert M. Neer.
p.   cm.
Includes bibliographical references and index.
ISBN 978-0-674-07301-2 (alk. paper)
1. Napalm—History.   2. Incendiary weapons—History.   3. Incendiary bombs—
Design and construction—History.   4. United States—Armed Forces—Weapons
systems—History.   I. Title.
UG447.65.N44  2013
355.8'245—dc23      2012034926

*For my father, a healer*

# Contents

## PARIAH

# Napalm

# Prologue

## Trang Bang Village, South Vietnam, June 8, 1972

Trang Bang, thirty miles northwest of Saigon, shuddered under artillery shells on the morning of June 8, 1972. It was the third day of a fierce battle between Viet Cong and North Vietnamese army infiltrators, who had seized the town, and South Vietnamese army units that had surrounded them. Rotors thumped. Propellers roared. Machine guns echoed in the streets. Smoke filled the air. Phan Thị Kim Phúc, nine years old, huddled with her mother and father, aunts, young brothers, cousins, and neighbors, about thirty villagers in all, in two outbuildings at a temple complex on the edge of town. A group of eight to ten South Vietnamese soldiers sheltered with them. Chips of masonry from nearby buildings rattled on their roof and clattered across the courtyard. On several occasions, napalm bombs filled the air outside with flames, and turned the insides of the buildings red. "Fire is falling from heaven!" the refugees lamented. A concertina wire roadblock on Route 1, the main national highway between Saigon and Cambodia which passed a few hundred yards to the south, had created a vast traffic jam. Journalists watched from just in front of the wire. A boy sold ice cones.[1]

Kim Phúc's family had fled to the temple three nights earlier, when Viet Cong soldiers took over their home and began to dig tunnels under

"The Terror of War." Nine-year-old Phan Thị Kim Phúc, stripped by flames and still burning with napalm, runs from her village followed by South Vietnamese soldiers on June 8, 1972. *AP Photo/Nick Ut*

their living room. Further retreat was impossible. She pulled her favorite cousin, a chubby three-year-old named Danh, close to her. A light rain began at lunch time.

At around 1:00 p.m. the rain cleared and a spotter airplane that had been circling the town dropped low and blasted two phosphorus rockets into an area behind the temple. White smoke rose to mark a suspected Viet Cong position. South Vietnamese troops near the front gate of the complex ran into the courtyard and tossed colored smoke grenades to indicate their own position. About 150 yards separated the two zones.

Suddenly, the soldiers decided an unreliable pilot might mark the temple outbuildings as a target. "Get out! Everybody get out! They are going to destroy everything!" they screamed. Kim Phúc's father and mother prepared the children for a dash to the roadblock. Slowest left first: Kim

Phúc's grandmother, her aunt and nine-month-old baby, and the aunt's two other children, including Danh. Children next: Kim Phúc and two of her brothers. Finally, the oldest siblings. "Run! Run fast, or you will die!" yelled the soldiers, who were themselves in motion. A woman grabbed a child frozen with fear. Sprinters made a rough line from the outbuildings, across the courtyard, through the gate, and onto Route 1.[2]

A slow-moving American-made South Vietnamese air force Skyraider propeller airplane appeared. It was badly off course and far from the white smoke. Nonetheless, it dropped its bombs. They were duds. A second plane appeared, even more off course. It too released its payload. A quartet of silver canisters filled with napalm jelly tumbled in silence toward the ground, then hit with unbelievable suddenness and vicious "pops." Giant welts of flame, speckled with brilliant phosphorus flares, and coils of thick white and black smoke covered the highway between temple and roadblock. A brutal wave of heat that felt like a giant had opened a furnace door swept over the journalists. A few seconds later, small figures began to appear from the smoke.[3]

Flames enveloped Kim Phúc. Biographer Denise Chong described what happened next: "Her first memory of the engulfing fires was the sight of flames licking her left arm, where there was an ugly brownish-black glob. She tried to brush it off, only to scream out at the pain of the burn that had now spread to the inside of her other hand." Napalm had caught her as she ran, and splattered over the upper left side of her body. It carbonized her pony tail, and seared her neck, back, and left arm. Chong continued, "[A] tremendous fatigue and weariness overtook her, and as an intense heat seemed to eat her from the inside out, she felt desperately thirsty." She screamed into the smoke: "Oh, Ma, it's too hot, too hot!'"[4]

Associated Press photographer Huynh Cong "Nick" Ut clicked off frame after frame as injured, terrified children ran to the checkpoint. Then he ran to help. Kim Phúc was burned naked. Chong wrote, "Her body radiated heat, and chunks of pink and black flesh were peeling off." Indeed, her skin was still burning in places. Soldiers and reporters gave her water to drink and poured more on her wounds. Tragically, the fluid reacted with the napalm and phosphorus on her skin, and injured the girl further. About one third of her body was seared raw: her back, continuing to her chest on her left side, the back of her neck into her hairline, and her left arm. Deep burns from jellied splashes cut into her right arm, buttocks, and stomach. Her right palm was an open wound from where she had smeared it with burning gel. Ut loaded Kim Phúc and her aunt, also scorched, into his van and drove them to a hospital in the nearby town of Cu Chi. "Please, help them," he said to the nurse, then continued to Saigon to deliver his film. Kim Phúc's photograph, titled "The Terror of War," appeared in newspapers around the world the next day, won Ut a Pulitzer Prize for best spot news photograph of the year, and has passed into legend as an iconic image of the twentieth century.[5]

Napalm was born a hero but lives a pariah. Its invention is a chronicle of scientific discovery as old as Yankee ingenuity and as modern as the military-academic complex. Its history illuminates America's story, from victory in World War II, through defeat in Vietnam, to its current position in a globalizing world.

# HERO

America's first Independence Day of World War II, July 4, 1942, was idyllic at Harvard University. On campus tennis courts nestled between the college soccer field's verdant green and the golden dome of the Business School library, players in whites gathered for morning games. They volleyed as university maintenance workers armed with shovels arrived, cut into the field, and built a circular parapet a foot tall and sixty yards in diameter. Fire trucks from the City of Cambridge rumbled up, and men flooded the circle to make a wide pool four to nine inches deep. Revelations 22.2—"On each side of the river stood the tree of life. . . . And the leaves of the tree are for the healing of the nations"—bore mute witness from a plaque on a nearby bridge across the Charles River. By mid-morning, all was ready for the arrival of Sheldon Emery Professor of Organic Chemistry Louis Fieser, one of the university's most brilliant scholars and head of "Anonymous Research Project No. 4," a top secret war research collaboration between the school and the government.[1]

Fieser arrived. He was forty-three-years-old, tall, bald, with traces of the Williams College varsity football lineman he once was still present in his bearing. An octet of assistants followed. He equipped four of the young men with boots, buckets, long sticks, and gloves, and positioned them around the pool. With assistance from the others, he gingerly lugged a live seventy-pound napalm bomb, bolted nose down on a metal stand, to the center of the lagoon. A wire ran to a control box on dry ground. Firemen and groundskeepers looked on. Players fifty feet away traded forehands.[2]

Fieser flipped a switch. High explosives blasted incendiary white phosphorus into forty-five pounds of jellied gasoline. A spectacular, billowing 2,100-degree-Farenheit fire cloud rose over the field. Lumps of searing, flaming napalm splashed into the water. Oily smoke filled the air. Assistants plunged into the muck, splashed water on burning blobs, and used their sticks to submerge and extinguish larger gobbets. They noted the location and size of chunks, and scooped salvageable jelly into buckets for weighing. Tennis players scattered.[3]

World War II was just seven months old for the United States: close, and far away. *Boston Globe* newspaper headlines that day announced desperate battles at El Alamein in Egypt and Sevastopol in the Crimea, an end to automobile and bicycle racing to conserve rubber, revised sugar rations, and the start of death penalty hearings for German saboteurs arrested on Long Island. Li'l Abner, in the comics section, explained what the struggle was about: "A world where a fella and his gal can look up at the moon just for the foolishness of it, and not because there may be planes up there coming to blast 'em both off the earth, a world where a fella is free to be as wise or as foolish as he pleases, but, mainly, a world where a fella is free! That world has disappeared, until we win this war."[4]

It had not completely disappeared. At 10:00 a.m. that morning a crowd gathered at Boston's City Hall, raised the Stars and Stripes, paraded to the Old Granary Burial Ground on Tremont Street, set flowers at the tombstones of John Hancock and Samuel Adams, and continued to the Old State House. On a tiny colonial balcony flanked by wood carvings of England's lion and unicorn, an orator read the Declaration of Independence, just as at the same spot in 1776.[5]

Professor Fieser's firestorm was over in seconds. Hunks of gel hissed, flickered, and died. A pungent aroma of phosphorus, like garlic or burning matches, mixed with the oily smell of gasoline, hung in the air over the flooded field and empty tennis courts.[6] Napalm bombs had arrived in the world.

# 1

## Harvard's Genius

Harvard's soccer-field test was one of the first progeny of the "military-academic" and "military-industrial" unions between academia, business, and the armed forces created after 1940 by the National Defense Research Committee (NDRC). Vannevar Bush, cofounder of armaments giant Raytheon and a Massachusetts Institute of Technology (MIT) electrical engineer, conceived the system. President Franklin D. Roosevelt established it on June 27, 1940, with a budget of about $100 million. In addition to napalm, the committee supervised creation of the atomic bomb, radar, sonar, proximity fuses, bazookas, amphibious landing craft, and some 200 other projects. By the war's end, five years later, Bush managed tens of thousands of scientists with practically unlimited funding.[1]

The "General of Physics," as *Time* magazine called him in an April 1944 cover story, was tall and thin, with a wry smile, close-cropped hair, and round rimless glasses. He was born in 1890 in Everett, Massachusetts, then as now a working-class town, and graduated from Tufts College in Medford in 1913. After he lost his job as a test engineer at General Electric—a fire shut down the facility where he worked—he taught elementary mathematics to women "not in the slightest degree interested," and a "somewhat absurd" physics course for premedical students, then enrolled in 1915 in a joint Harvard-MIT chemistry PhD program. He got married in 1916 and, under financial pressure, wrote his thesis in one year and received his PhD in 1917. During World War I, he worked with the National Research Council—a branch of the National Academy of Sciences and National Academy of Engineering established in 1916 to coordinate war research—to develop a magnetic submarine detector. Bush's group built a working device but bureaucratic mismanagement, in his estimation, prevented it from being used. "That experience forced into my mind pretty solidly the complete lack of proper liaison between the military and the civilian in the development of weapons in time of war, and what that lack meant," he wrote later. He taught at MIT after the war, made important breakthroughs related to the development of analog computers, and rose to become vice president of the institute from 1932–1938, a position roughly equivalent to chief operating officer. In 1939, he turned down an offer to be MIT's president to lead the Carnegie Institution of Washington, a research institute that made grants for basic scientific research.[2]

Adolf Hitler invaded Poland on September 1, 1939, and by mid-June 1940 German armies stood triumphant across an arc that stretched from northern France to the Soviet frontier. Bush gathered key leaders of the U.S. scientific research establishment, each of whom he had previously met individually or in small groups, for a collective lunch: Frank Jewett, newly elected president of the National Academy of Sciences and founding president of Bell Telephone Laboratories; James Bryant Conant, a chemist and president of Harvard University; Karl Compton, a physicist and president of MIT; and Richard Tolman, a physicist and professor at the California Institute of Technology. "We were agreed," he wrote, that America was sure to be drawn into the war, "that it would be a highly technical struggle, that we were by no means prepared in this regard, and finally and most importantly, that the military system as it existed . . . would never fully produce the new instrumentalities which we would certainly need." Universities, Bush believed, had to be integrated into the war effort. A coordinating committee was required.[3]

Bush brought this idea to Secretary of Commerce Harry Hopkins, who was one of Roosevelt's closest advisors and outspoken in his opposition to the Nazis. Hopkins was the fourth of five children of a peripatetic Grinnell, Iowa, harness store owner and his devoutly Methodist wife. He graduated in 1912 from Grinnell College. Mindful, perhaps, of town and college namesake Josiah Grinnell's adjuration to community service, Hopkins spent the early part of his career working in New York City for social welfare organizations including the Board of Child Welfare and the Tuberculosis Association. Later, he served the American Red Cross in New Orleans and Atlanta. In 1921, back in New York, he helped establish the American Association of Social Workers, and was elected its president in 1923. Hopkins came to the attention of Governor Franklin Roosevelt in 1931, when he directed New York's Temporary Emergency Relief Administration for unemployed workers. After FDR was elected president, the social worker rose through New Deal bureaucracies to head the Works Progress Administration, the nation's largest employer. Roosevelt appointed him secretary of commerce in 1938. He was sworn in on Christmas Eve.[4]

Hopkins immediately understood Bush's proposal for a military-academic partnership. "We found that we spoke the same language," the Carnegie Institute's director wrote. On June 12, 1940, the secretary arranged for Bush to meet Roosevelt. Britain's desperate evacuation of its army from Dunkirk was just eight days in the past. Italy declared war on France and Britain, and Norway's last division surrendered to the Wehrmacht two days before the meeting. The NDRC plan was in four paragraphs on a single sheet. "The whole audience lasted less than ten minutes (Harry had no doubt been there before me). I came out with my 'OK-F.D.R.' and all the wheels began to turn," Bush recalled.[5]

His remit was open-ended. "The Committee shall correlate and support scientific research on the mechanisms and devices of warfare . . . and may conduct research for the creation and improvement of instrumentalities, methods, and materials of warfare," read its establishing order. Ostensibly, the body reported to the Council of National Defense, an assembly created for a similar purpose in August 1916 and composed of the secretaries of war, navy, interior, agriculture, commerce, and labor. This designation made it part of the Executive Office of the President, which funded it. In practice, since the council's work had ended after World War I and few knew of its continued existence, the group reported directly to Roosevelt.[6]

"There were those who protested that the action of setting up N.D.R.C. was an end run, a grab by which a small company of scientists and engineers, acting outside established channels, got hold of the authority and money for the program of developing new weapons. That, in fact, is exactly what it was," Bush wrote.[7]

The founder chose executives in his own image. Conant, from Harvard, got responsibility for "Division B," in charge of bombs, fuels, gases, and chemical problems; Compton, from MIT, for detection, controls and instruments; and Tolman, from CalTech, for arms and ordnance. They served as volunteers, like Bush, and kept their existing jobs. Lyman J. Briggs, director of the National Bureau of Standards, added his Uranium Committee, which supervised atomic research, to the new organization. Bush eased him out of power over the following year, in favor of Conant, whom he thought was more competent, as the significance of this area became apparent. Additional committee members joined *ex officio:* Jewett from the National Academy; the commissioner of patents; the head of the Committee on Scientific Aids to Learning; and representatives from the army and navy.[8]

Perhaps the most extraordinary feature of the new committee was the way it planned to do its work. Rather than rely on government laboratories staffed by uniformed members of the military, or grants to individual researchers, as had been the practice for military research, the NDRC planned to contract its work to universities and private industry on a cost-plus basis. Bush conceived the new administrative structure. "We proposed to contract with the university itself, thus placing on it the responsibility for all such [business] matters, and also giving it the authority necessary for proper performance. In return we proposed to pay its overhead costs," he wrote. Harvard's president Conant explained the consequences: "Creation of the committee marked the beginning of a revolution . . . [and] has had a transforming effect on the relationship of the university to the federal government. . . . The essence of the revolution was the shift in 1940 from expanding research in government laboratories to private enterprise and the use of federal money to support work in universities and scientific institutes through contractual arrangements."[9]

Academic facilities were extensive and researchers did not require civil service certification, which allowed for fewer administrative restrictions and greater speed. University administrators responded with enthusiasm to the new structure, which allowed faculty members to work on military projects in their spare time and, in some cases, permitted students to submit NDRC projects as theses for advanced degrees. Private industry, the committee found, was less interested in cooperation in 1940, when budgets were tight, than after 1941 when funds flowed more freely. Nonetheless, many companies did important work even in the early days of the NDRC.[10]

Disbursements followed the institutional affiliations of committee leaders. In its first year, forty-one schools received 155 NDRC contracts. MIT led with twenty, followed by Harvard with thirteen and the University of California and Princeton with ten each. CalTech and the Carnegie Institute each received eight contracts. Division D, managed by Jewett at MIT, which was responsible for radar among other projects, received just over half of all funds: about $50 million in today's dollars. Division B under Conant was next with about $17 million. A total of twenty-two private businesses received fifty-two contracts. Uranium Committee projects got just $2.8 million in the first year.[11]

Conant leapt into action. Harvard's president was nothing if not ambitious. When he was twenty-seven, he told his wife that his life goals were to be the premier organic chemist in the United States, president of Harvard, and a cabinet member. He was born in Dorchester, Massachusetts, in 1893, graduated from Harvard College in 1914 after three years of study, completed the work for his PhD with a dual concentration in organic and electrochemistry in 1916, and received his doctorate in 1917. A foray with two friends into chemical manufacturing was unsuccessful: Conant and one of his partners started a fire that burned down the small building they had rented in Queens; a separate explosion later killed a third partner, and another man. In World War I, he led an army Chemical Warfare Service (CWS) research team that researched Lewisite, the "Dew of Death" poison gas, then returned to Harvard in 1919 as an assistant professor of chemistry. With respect to gas warfare, he wrote later, it was unclear "why tearing a man's guts out by a high-explosive shell is to be preferred to maiming him by attacking his lungs or skin." As to civilian casualties, they were "not only a necessary consequence of bombing, but one might almost say an objective of the fleets of bombers directed by the British, the Germans and the Russians, as well as by the Americans." This prodigy was appointed president of Harvard in 1933 at age forty and supervised sweeping reforms, from the use of standardized aptitude tests and an embrace of admissions based on merit rather than social standing, to modernization of the undergraduate curriculum away from Greek and Roman classics and toward the sciences.[12]

True to his penchant for fast action, by June 18, 1940—six days after Roosevelt's OK of the NDRC, and four days after his own appointment was made official—Conant recruited Roger Adams, chair of the Chemistry Department at the University of Illinois at Urbana-Champaign, and MIT professor Warren K. Lewis as vice chairmen of Division B. Adams was a fellow Bostonian, descendant of President John Adams, and a Harvard chemistry PhD and former professor at the university (his move to Illinois created the vacancy that Fieser filled). France capitulated one week later, and the Battle of Britain began two weeks after that.[13]

Conant and his colleagues spent the summer and early fall of 1940 recruiting chemists for the new organization. It was not easy. "Apparently there were very few chemists indeed in this country having a knowledge of military explosives, which is quite a different subject than commercial explosives. Hence it has been necessary for organic chemists to learn a somewhat new art," the NDRC explained in its first annual report. By mid-October, they had located enough to start. The Tripartite Pact launched the Axis alliance of Germany, Italy, and Japan at the end of September, and the United States began the first peacetime draft in its history in the second week of October. On October 23, Fieser and about twenty other top chemists gathered in Adams's Illinois living room to begin the work of Division B.[14]

Conant laid out the program. He described the NDRC, summarized its innovative contracting system, outlined the War Department's most pressing technical problems, and explained how each researcher might help. Enthusiasm ran high. Fieser agreed to synthesize new compounds for evaluation as possible explosives.[15]

Harvard assigned him two secret rooms in the basement of the Converse Chemistry Laboratory at 12 Oxford Street in Cambridge (off Divinity Avenue and within musket range of Memorial Hall, built to honor university graduates who fought for the Union in the Civil War). A quartet of his graduate students, all in their early twenties, joined the forty-one-year-old professor as assistants. By the spring of 1941, they had developed two new compounds more powerful than TNT.[16]

Louis Fieser was born on April 7, 1899, in Columbus, Ohio. His father was an engineer who traced his lineage to a village outside Heidelberg in Germany; his grandfather, a banker and one-time head of the Columbus school system, owned and published the first German-language newspaper in Ohio. Louis attended the public East High School and adopted two mottos there which, he wrote forty-two years later, summarized his life philosophy: *omnia possum* (anything is possible) and *labor omnia vincit* (work conquers all). This ambitious, industrious student graduated in 1916 and headed east to Williams College in northwestern Massachusetts. He lettered in football, basketball, and track, and in his senior year was a lineman on the unbeaten 1919 varsity football team. In 1920, he collected his college diploma and continued east to study chemistry at Harvard. His instructors included young professor James Conant. In 1922, the two published a collaborative paper. Fieser received his PhD for research on a related subject two years later. His eastern educational trajectory concluded with a postdoctoral year at Frankfurt and Oxford.[17]

Fieser began his career as an assistant professor of chemistry at Bryn Mawr College for women in 1925. "Girls can be very satisfactory students, or even superior ones; they also can have other qualities appealing to a 26-year-old male instructor. I fell in love with a member of my second class at Bryn Mawr," he wrote. He published some twenty academic papers during his years in Pennsylvania. In 1930, Harvard, where Conant was then a full professor, offered Fieser a position as an assistant professor. Mary Peters, his former student, enamored of both professor and profession, followed and enrolled in the university's chemistry PhD program. They were married in 1932. Peters, however, was stifled by the sexism of the Harvard department—she was not allowed in the laboratory with male students and forced to conduct her research, without supervision, in the deserted basement of a separate building—and left the program after she received her MA degree in 1936. She went to work as an assistant to her husband.[18]

At Harvard, Fieser concentrated on vitamin K, and developed a new interest in carcinogens. In the mid-1930s, with Mary's help, he published the first of a series of influential textbooks. In 1937, he became a full professor. In 1939, he was appointed to the prestigious Sheldon Emery Professorship, announced the first successful synthesis of vitamin K—a procedure that had important medical implications because of the role the vitamin plays in blood clotting—and received an honorary degree from his alma mater Williams. Fieser ultimately authored 341 research papers, including forty written as a sole author and thirty-six that he wrote with his wife, and thirteen books, many also written with his wife, of which five went through three editions. He was elected to the National Academy of Sciences in 1940. Many thousands of students took his classes during his almost four decades at Harvard.[19]

Fieser presented his work on explosives at an NDRC conference in Chicago on May 28. He then listened, intrigued, as Conant described a mysterious series of explosions at a DuPont paint factory. Workers there produced divinylacetylene, a liquid that could be mixed with paint pigment and which set to a tough, adhesive, protective film when exposed to air. Mishaps at the plant implied that the material was explosive and, since oxygen was excluded from the manufacturing process, perhaps spontaneously combustible. Military possibilities seemed obvious. Conant asked for an investigator. Fieser volunteered his laboratory for the task. He had just the man for the job.[20]

Emanuel Benjamin Hershberg drew his first breath on July 28, 1908, in Lynn, Massachusetts, north of Boston. His father was a shoemaker who later owned a tobacco shop on the Boston waterfront. E. B., as he came to be known, was a master of invention with a Da Vinci-esque range of mechanical ability: "A masterful experimentalist in organic chemistry, he was also versed in engineering, in mechanical drawing, in carpentry, in machining, in glass blowing, and in photography, and he had invented and constructed a number of laboratory devices which later found wide use, for example, the Hershberg stirrer, the Hershberg stirring motor, the Hershberg melting-pot apparatus," Fieser wrote. He received a degree in chemical engineering from MIT in 1929, and his PhD in chemistry from the institute in 1933, spent a year studying in Germany on a traveling fellowship, and joined Fieser's laboratory in 1934 in the depths of the depression.[21]

Fieser put E. B., who was also an Army Chemical Warfare Service reserve officer, to work in the Converse basement. He then traveled to DuPont headquarters in Wilmington, Delaware, where paint chemists briefed him on the explosions and their manufacturing processes. In Cambridge, the two researchers produced successive batches of divinyl-acetylene and exposed the liquid to air in pans placed in the window wells of their laboratory, shielded from wind and passersby. They watched as the material transformed into a gel that increased in viscosity over time. The experimenters poked at the pans with sticks, and dropped stones on them to try to produce an explosion or fire, but without encouraging results.[22]

Because they couldn't get the gels to explode or burn on their own, the scientists did it themselves. "At day's end we usually destroyed the gels . . . by setting fire to them with a match. . . . [T]hey burned with an impressive sputter and sparkle," Fieser wrote.[23]

This produced the crucial insight that led to napalm. Hershberg attributed their success to his mentor's inspiration. Fieser wrote that the men had the idea together. "We noticed also that when a viscous gel burns it does not become fluid, but retains its viscous, sticky consistency," Fieser wrote. "The experience suggested the idea of a bomb that would scatter large burning gobs of sticky gel."[24]

Hershberg made some improvised bombs from tin cans filled with divinylacetylene gel packed around gunpowder and the chemists tried them out in a remote section of Everett, "City of Pride, Progress and Possibilities," just up the Mystic River from Boston. Results were promising: the sticky gel ignited "with a sputtering, vicious-looking flame," Fieser remembered. "[T]hese probably were the first experiments on gelled fuels in this country," he wrote. As his colleague from the Harvard Chemistry Department Robert Woodward later observed of Fieser's scientific philosophy, "Louis, the prototypical man of action, was impatient of sustained abstract thought. Facing any problem or opportunity, his instinct was to dash into the laboratory, there to search for new facts, solidly based upon indefatigable experimentation—and Louis was par excellence a man to act without hesitation on his always superbly robust instincts."[25]

Napalm is a devastating weapon because it is sticky and burns at an extremely high temperature. Fire, in chemical terms, is the process of combustion, a complex and largely invisible sequence of events that occurs when molecules of oxygen combine with others. This releases heat and light in all directions. The most intense radiation takes place into whatever material the combustion occurs upon (which makes sticky incendiaries especially effective since they are in direct contact with whatever they burn), then upward, and finally, to the sides. Fire on a matchstick, for example, is hottest where the stick is burning, then above and to the sides of the flame, and finally below it. Molecules absorb radiated energy until they reach the temperature of the transmitting body or combust themselves, whichever comes first. If enough energy is released, visible flames appear and the material is said to burn. This process was first explained by the eighteenth-century French scientist Antoine-Laurent de Lavoisier who, as a result, is considered the founder of modern chemistry.[26]

Hotter things are more likely to combust. Molecules become agitated when heated, which causes a greater number to come into contact with the surface of the material they comprise and, in turn, heightens the probability they will combine with oxygen. As a general rule, an increase in temperature of eighteen degrees Fahrenheit doubles the chance of combustion. Coal, for example, will burn twice as fast at eighty-six degrees as at sixty-eight degrees—and 500,000 times faster at 400 degrees. To start a fire, place an incendiary in direct contact with whatever is to be burned—or below or next to it, in descending order of preference—and ensure there is plenty of oxygen. Thus, the best incendiaries ignite easily, burn hot, and stay close to their targets.[27]

A fearsome weapon results from this process. People and other animals dread fire, so it can induce panic: the flames of hell and fire-breathing monsters are common terrors. Almost everyone has experienced burns, so the pain of being burned to death is easy to imagine compared with less common injuries like a bullet wound. Most importantly, fire uses the energy contained in things themselves to destroy them. Larger targets mean greater potential devastation. Chicago's Great Fire of 1871 is illustrative: a conflagration that leveled much of a metropolis of approximately 324,000 people started, allegedly, when Mrs. Catherine O'Leary's cow knocked over a lamp. As Geoffrey Chaucer wrote with reference to ancient liquid incendiaries called "wildfire" in *The Canterbury Tales,* "Thou lykenest wommanes love . . . to wilde fyr/ The more it brenneth, the more it hath desyr." As a 1961 U.S. Air Force Air University textbook explained to Reserve Officer Training Corps students, in World War II "large targets (as an entire city) suffered more damage per ton of [incendiary] bombs than small targets, because fires had more opportunity to spread widely." Explosives, by contrast, carry all of their energy within themselves and seldom cause damage beyond the immediate area of impact. Nuclear weapons combine elements of both types of munitions but, arguably, inflict their greatest damage through heat. Explosives damage, fire annihilates: a shattered structure can perhaps be repaired, but an incinerated facility, its contents vaporized, melted, warped, or reduced to ash, is ruined.[28]

A few early examples give a sense of the antiquity and flexibility of this weapon. In 1400–1000 BC, the biblical hero Samson, angered to find that his father-in-law had given away his wife, "went and caught three hundred foxes, and took firebrands, and turned tail to tail, and put a firebrand in the midst between two tails. And when he had set the brands on fire, he let them go into the standing corn of the Philistines, and burnt up both the shocks, and also the standing corn, with the vineyards and olives" (the Philistines responded by burning Samson's wife and father-in-law alive). Ninth-century BC Assyrian reliefs show combatants fighting with flaming arrows and pots filled with blazing material. India's *Mahabharata* and *Ramayana* epics, probably initiated around 800–750 BC, describe the use of fire arrows, as does the myth of Hercules, who used burning arrows to kill the Hydra monster and complete the second of his twelve labors. Chinese theorist Sun Tzu listed five ways to attack with fire in his circa 500 BC *Art of War.* Thucydides described a flamethrower in 424 BC: engineers from Boeotia, he said, routed an Athenian garrison with a bellows-driven fire pot when they "sawed a great log in half, hollowed it out, and fitted [it] together again like a pipe. They suspended a cauldron from chains at one end, attached to an iron tube that projected from the beam, rolled it on carts to part of the wall made of vines and timber, inserted a huge bellows into their end of the beam, and blew. The blast passed into the cauldron filled with lighted coals, sulfur and pitch, made a great blaze, and set fire to the wall."[29]

Liquid and gel incendiaries have an equally ancient provenance. Hercules was consumed by a flaming shirt, woven with centaur blood by his deluded wife, that could not be extinguished or removed. Mythical Greek princess Glauke, popularized by Euripides in his 431 BC play *Medea*, suffered a similar fate. According to the story, Jason promised to marry Medea, a princess from Colchis, in modern Georgia, if she helped him win the Golden Fleece from her homeland. She did, and they wed, but he then abandoned her for Glauke. Medea sent her rival a beautiful crown and gown, perhaps impregnated with petroleum, which was common in surface deposits near Baku in the neighboring territory now known as Azerbaijan. When Glauke put on the garments and approached an altar— possibly illuminated by open flames—she ignited. "The chaplet of gold about her head [sent] forth a wondrous stream of ravening flame, from her bones the flesh kept peeling off beneath the gnawing of those secret drugs, e'en as when the pine-tree weeps its tears of pitch, a fearsome sight to see," Euripides wrote. More credibly, an Athenian attendant to Alexander the Great was severely burned during the Macedonian conquest of Mesopotamia when he agreed, at the suggestion of his inquisitive commander, to cover himself in *naptha*, or petroleum, in a bathhouse. The oil combusted—flames from nearby lamps, again, may have sparked volatile vapors—and the volunteer almost died.[30]

Romans suffered the first recorded military attack with liquid fire. In 69 BC, the army of consul Lucius Lucullus attacked the city of Samosata on the Euphrates in what is now southeastern Turkey. According to Pliny the Elder, residents of the city poured *maltha*—flaming mud—on the soldiers. This substance "adheres to every solid body which it touches, and moreover, when touched, it follows you, if you attempt to escape from it. . . . It is even set on fire in water. We learn by experience that it can be extinguished only by earth," he wrote. (Pliny distinguished *maltha* from *naphtha*, which he said was more liquid and used to treat Glauke's robe). Flames grilled the legionnaires in their armor, and broke the assault. Rome didn't capture Samosata for another 141 years.[31]

Legionnaires quickly incorporated incendiary liquids into their arsenal, and came to consider them divine in origin. In the tenth century, a millennium after Lucullus, Byzantine emperor Constantine Porphyrogenitus told his son that Constantine the Great, who ruled from 306 to 337 and moved the imperial capital from Rome to Constantinople, obtained the recipe for liquid fire directly from an angel. Flame weapons were holy, Porphyrogenitus explained, and it was anathema—punishable by a lightning strike—to disclose their secrets. Imperial armorers who produced incendiaries, he said, practiced a "divine art."[32]

Byzantine craftsmen developed a pump system that allowed their soldiers to shoot "Greek fire," so-called in their honor, onto their enemies. Constantinople was a center of mechanical innovation under the empire. Porphyrogenitus, for example, told of a golden tree with artificial birds that flapped their wings and sang, a model lion that moved and roared, and a jeweled lady who walked, powered by clockwork. Around 673, as the Muslim Arab armies of the Umayyad caliphate advanced from the south and west, a refugee named Kallinikos ("handsome winner") arrived in the capital from the Syrian town of Heliopolis. He adapted a pump, perhaps a double-action water pump, so that it could be mounted on a ship. A burning stream shot out through a moveable pipe, or "siphon," set into the bow—often decorated like the head of a monster. As the emperor Leo wrote later: "The front part of the ship had a bronze tube so arranged that the prepared fire could be projected forward to the left or right and also made to fall from above. This tube was mounted on a [platform] above the deck. . . . The fire was thrown either on the enemy's ships or in the faces of the attacking troops." This "sea-fire" of Kallinikos, which like its predecessors could not be extinguished with water (but apparently could be quenched with vinegar or urine), destroyed the Umayyad navy and saved the kingdom.[33]

Subsequent improvements miniaturized the technology so that it could be carried by soldiers in the field. Leo rhapsodized about "Small siphons discharged by hand from behind iron shields, which are called hand-siphons [and] have recently been manufactured in our dominions. For these can throw the prepared fire in the faces of the enemy." This allowed a variety of delivery options. "Flexible apparatus with [artificial] fire, siphons, hand-siphons . . . are to be used, if at hand, against any tower that may be advanced against the wall of a besieged town,"

Porphyrogenitus instructed. Commanders in the 1100s deployed a breath-powered system. Anna Komnene, daughter of the emperor Alexios I Komnenos, described a Byzantine incendiary attack in 1103 on a Pisan fleet near Rhodes: "This fire they made by the following arts. From the pine and certain such evergreen trees inflammable resin is collected. This is rubbed with sulphur and put into tubes of reed, and is blown by men using it with violent and continuous breath. Then in this manner it meets the fire on the tip and catches light and falls like a fiery whirlwind on the faces of the enemy." The canny princess in all likelihood omitted a key ingredient: petroleum. With this addition, her recipe is close to contemporary scholarly consensus about the composition of Greek fire: a "semi-liquid substance, composed of sulphur, pitch, dissolved nitre and petroleum boiled together and mixed with certain less important and more obscure substances," in the words of scholar C. W. C. Oman.[34]

Arab armies also made extensive use of liquid incendiaries but used soldiers, catapults, or trebuchets (slings powered by counterweights), rather than pump-powered jets, to deliver blazing munitions. Special "naphtha troops," called *naffatun*, protected by asbestos clothing and armed with copper *naffata* fire pots or ceramic hand grenades accompanied archer corps in Abbasid armies from 750. Arabs who besieged the Greek port of Salonika in 904 left numerous small ceramic pots believed to have been fire grenades. A 1200s workshop that manufactured similar devices was found at the city of Hama in Syria. Flamethrower technology spread east to China from Arabia around 919.[35]

Fire assaults created terror. The French crusader Jean de Joinville described an Arab *perronel* attack (literally, "stone thrower," probably a trebuchet), that hurled blazing tubs of Greek fire during the 1250 siege of a fortified camp near the Egyptian city of Al Mansura: "This was the fashion of the Greek fire: it came on as broad in front as a vinegar cask, and the tail of fire that trailed behind it was as big as a great spear; and it made such a noise as it came, that it sounded like the thunder of heaven. It looked like a dragon flying through the air. Such a bright light did it cast, that one could see all over the camp as though it were day, by reason of the great mass of fire, and the brilliance of the light that it shed," he wrote. That battle ended with the capture of the French king Louis

IX, the deaths of tens of thousands of Europeans, and the collapse of the Seventh Crusade.[36]

Liquid incendiaries declined in importance after the mid-1200s as gunpowder spread across the world from China. Explosives dramatically increased the range of projectile weapons and made it difficult or impossible to use traditional fire weapons, which had to be delivered at relatively close range. Heated shot, an ineffective incendiary compared to petroleum-based liquids, was the most gunnery officers could offer as an alternative. Rockets—used by Chinese and Mongolians from the mid-1200s—delivered burning materials from a distance, but were inaccurate and unreliable. Greek fire was not mentioned in Byzantine accounts after 1200, which has led some to speculate the recipe had been lost, perhaps because of excessive secrecy. This seems unlikely since the use of similar incendiary weapons decreased everywhere at about the same time.[37]

Engineers attempted to break this paradigm for half a millennium by increasing the range of fire weapons. It was not until 1805, however, that British designer William Congreve, inspired by Indian rockets encountered in the 1767–1799 Anglo-Mysore Wars, invented a circular iron shell mounted on a fifteen-foot wooden pole that could shoot a burning thirty-two-pound "carcass" warhead about a mile and a half, reliably and with some accuracy. For the first time in centuries, fire weapons had a greater range than artillery. England shot hundreds of fire missiles at the French port of Boulogne on October 8, 1806—their first such attack—but met with limited success. In 1807, however, Britain supplemented artillery and grenades with approximately 300 incendiary rockets during a three-day bombardment of Copenhagen that left thousands dead and one-third of the city in ashes. This forced the surrender of virtually the entire Danish Navy. Red glare from British rockets fired at Baltimore's Fort McHenry on September 13, 1814, inspired Francis Scott Key to compose what is now the U.S. national anthem. In the same year, also at Baltimore, Uriah Brown, one of the earliest American incendiary engineers, produced a steam-powered flamethrower—a modern version of the medieval Byzantine siphon—and demonstrated it to a "vast concourse" of citizens.[38]

Artillery, however, progressed even faster. Rifling inside gun barrels enhanced accuracy. Percussion caps, which spark on impact, eliminated ignition systems that relied on smoldering fuses, and improved reliability. Fire weapons, even those powered by rockets, couldn't keep up. Incendiary deployments remained rare.

America's Civil War spurred a flurry of flame research but a similar result: few deployments. President Abraham Lincoln urged aggressive research. In 1861, he ordered the army to help New York inventor Robert L. Fleming develop a proposed firebomb. On January 14, 1862, the president met with Levi Short of Buffalo, who claimed to have rediscovered the recipe for Greek fire. Short test-fired a pair of thirteen-inch shells later that month on the Ellipse, just south of the White House. They blew fire forty to fifty feet into the air, and covered a fifty-foot radius with flames for ten minutes.[39]

General George McClellan found the weapons barbaric—"Such means of destruction are hardly within the category of those recognized in civilized warfare," he wrote—but others thought more like Lincoln. General Benjamin Butler invited Short to display his devices over Boston Common, and subsequently purchased one hundred shells for use against New Orleans. Rear Admiral David D. Porter rented part of his family mansion on the Delaware River to Short to produce "Solidified Greek Fire" in tin cylinders three inches long and five-eighths of an inch in diameter. He then ordered ten gross (1,440) and used them to bombard Vicksburg, Mississippi, in May 1863. Defenders expressed outrage over this indiscriminate use of fire, despite the fact that just three significant conflagrations resulted. A "Greek fire" incendiary attack on Charleston on August 22–23, carried out on the direct order of Lincoln himself, produced similarly disappointing results. "My conscience will not permit me to recommend his greek fire, which I know to be good for nothing," Porter later wrote of Short's invention in a letter to his mother.[40]

World War I sustained the essential paradigm of the previous eight centuries, but offered a harbinger of things to come. German engineers introduced gas-powered *Flammenwerfer* (flamethrowers) that shot gasoline, or fuel oil, thickened with rubber about twenty yards. Artillery shells, now equipped with streamers to ensure a straight descent, continued in the tradition of U.S. Civil War fire experimenters. Zeppelin airships motored over London and launched incendiary bombardments. In all of these cases, however, principle was more impressive than practice: the weapons did relatively little damage.

Germany first attacked French troops with flamethrowers at Malencourt, in northeastern France north of Verdun, on February 26, 1915. An observer applauded "The fiery serpents which, as if rising out of the earth, fell roaring and hissing on the enemy's trenches and drove him to precipitate flight." That summer, British field marshal Sir John French reported "A new device has been adopted by the enemy for driving burning liquid into our trenches with a strong jet. . . . Most of the infantry occupying these trenches were driven back, but their retirement was due far more to the surprise and temporary confusion caused by the burning liquid than to the actual damage inflicted." A U.S. Chemical Warfare Service official history observed, "After the initial terror had subsided, however, Allied soldiers found that their own circuitous trenches provided them with adequate protection, since flame throwers at that time could not project fuel around corners or into most underground passages." It concluded, "The maximum range of the portable German weapon was 20 yards; its small tanks were quickly exhausted of fuel, and its operator, after firing, became a helpless target out in No Man's Land, defenseless and hampered with a heavy load." Over 90 percent of the fuel burned in vast clouds of black smoke before it reached its target.[41]

"Unthickened fuel made a great show," the NDRC wrote, "There were many who believed that the almost sole effect of the portable flame thrower was psychological." British, French, and U.S. engineers developed similar devices in response, but they were used on only a handful of occasions, and never by U.S. troops. After the war, the CWS abandoned the program and destroyed its stock of weapons. "In general, it was not considered a successful munition," the service concluded of these early flamethrowers.[42]

German Zeppelin airships firebombed London on May 31, 1915. Bombs, however, were few—ninety incendiaries and thirty explosives from a single dirigible in the first attack. Many did not ignite, and firefighters easily contained the conflagrations that did result. German engineers later produced a bucket-shaped bomb that contained a core of thermite (a mixture of powdered aluminum or magnesium and metal oxides, often iron, that burned white-hot at around 5,000 degrees) packed in cotton, doused with naptha and tar, and bound with tarred rope. Flaming bullets, invented in 1916 by the British in response to the air attacks, however, effectively defeated the dirigibles. British, French and U.S. scientists also developed firebombs—respectively the "Baby Incendiary" bomb filled with a "Thermalloy" blend of thermite and powdered aluminum; the Chanard dart, intended to be dropped from an airplane; and the Mark I and II bombs and darts—but the small devices played an insignificant role in the conflict.[43]

Airplanes restored incendiary weapons to their medieval pride of place. On April 26, 1937, the German Condor Legion, a volunteer force that supported fascist allies of the Nazis in the Spanish Civil War, demonstrated modern fire warfare when it deployed forty-three airplanes to drop fifty tons of thermite incendiaries and explosive bombs on the Basque town of Guernica. The municipality, jammed with people on a market day, was devastated: about three-quarters of its buildings burned, at least 300 people died, and thousands were injured. *Times of London* correspondent George Steer described the new kind of warfare: "First, small parties of aeroplanes threw heavy bombs and hand grenades all over the town, choosing area after area in orderly fashion. Next came fighting machines which swooped low to machine-gun those who ran in panic from dugouts, some of which had already been penetrated by 1,000 lb. bombs, which make a hole 25 ft. deep." He continued, "Many of these people were killed as they ran. A large herd of sheep being brought in to the market was also wiped out. The object of this move was apparently to drive the population under ground again, for next as many as 12 bombers appeared at a time dropping heavy and incendiary bombs upon the ruins." Japanese commanders underlined the point in August when they attacked Shanghai with firebombs and killed tens of thousands.[44]

Then, on September 7, 1940, Germany launched the first sustained incendiary bombing campaign in history: the London Blitz. During the Battle of Britain as a whole, the Luftwaffe dropped about 23,500 clusters of thirty-six one-kilogram magnesium shells packed with thermite. Bombs burned so hot they ignited their magnesium casings, which burned for up to fifteen minutes and threw lumps of molten metal up to fifty feet. They could not be extinguished with water. Larger German firebombs combined up to 500 pounds of thermite, oil, and magnesium shavings. Luftwaffe bombers attempted to do to cities with fire what many, after World War I, feared might be done with poison gas.[45]

A triptych of images from the period illustrate the new paradigm. Pablo Picasso painted *Guernica*, a grey-and-white vision of the disaster that befell the city, in June 1937. In Shanghai, rescuers plucked a burned baby from the rubble of the main railway station and set it, sobbing, by a track. H. S. Wong snapped a photo. Japanese authorities alleged that because the baby was placed in position the photo was not a faithful depiction of events. Its fame, however, was indisputable. In England, news cameras recorded a grim prime minister Winston Churchill in 1942 as he walked through the charred remains of Coventry Cathedral, gutted in November 1940 by an attack of over 1,000 firebombs. British analysis of the London Blitz concluded that a ton of the new incendiaries produced about five times more damage than the same amount of conventional high explosives. Churchill agreed about the potential for ruination from the air. "The Navy can lose us this war, but only the Air Force can win it," he said, just before German bombardments began.[46]

Given this history, the British were interested in Fieser's research on incendiary gels. In August 1941, two months after the Everett tin-can tests, Major Gerrard Rambaut of the Air Ministry, who helped develop the United Kingdom's magnesium incendiary, arrived at the Oxford Street laboratory for a visit. His key piece of advice was to establish a measurement system to allow quantitative comparisons between alternative gels. "An obviously sound suggestion," Fieser noted. Harvard's team built a structure with four upright pieces of wood attached to a wooden base and connected by two cross-pieces. Hemlock cured to a standard moisture content formed the upright pieces; they used tulipwood, which was easy to cut, for the base. Chemists dispensed a standard amount of gel from a modified grease gun, set the apparatus in one of their window-well testing areas, and lit the incendiary. After the fire stopped, the scientists scraped the fresh charcoal from each piece of wood with a wire

brush and weighed what remained. "I used to come home at night looking like a blackface comedian," Fieser recalled. The Converse Burning
Test was ready to evaluate incendiaries.[47]

Rambaut's presence at the top secret project was a small example of
the tight connections between British and U.S. scientists in the early
years of World War II. Britain moved first. In the desperate days after
Dunkirk when it appeared Germany might invade England, Churchill
approved a mission of seven scientists and military officers, led by chemist Henry Tizard, to pass the empire's greatest military secrets to the
United States. Researchers packed their treasures, including a stunning
innovation that vastly reduced the size of radar devices, in a black metal
deeds box purchased in an Army & Navy store. Physicist Edward Bowen,
a leading defense engineer, nearly lost this early "black box" in a crush at
Euston Station. "With my luggage, the box was more than I could han-
dle, so I called a porter and told him to head for the Liverpool train. He
grabbed the box, put it on his shoulder and headed off so fast that (an old
cross country runner and still pretty fit) I had great difficulty keeping up
with him," he recalled. "He got well ahead and the only way of keeping
track of him was to watch the box weaving its way through the mass of
heads in front." When it arrived in late September 1940, the mission
"carried the most valuable cargo ever brought to our shores," concluded
an official U.S. government history. America reciprocated in a fashion in
January 1941 when Conant traveled to London to open the only overseas
office of the NDRC. He was "hailed as a messenger of hope," he said,
and met with virtually all of the country's top leadership, including the
king and prime minister.[48]

America's Chemical Warfare Service (CWS), however, was slow to
recognize the return of incendiary bombardment as a devastating weapon
after its 800-year absence. Gas was its focus. At the end of August
1941—after a bureaucratic reorganization in June that created a new Office of Scientific Research and Development to manage all war-related
scientific research (Bush moved up to head the new group, and Conant
was promoted to the top job at its NDRC division)—administrators
abruptly told Fieser to stop his work on gels and start a new project devoted to blister agents, "vesicants" in chemical parlance: poison gas. A
1934 army Ordnance Department study explained consensus thinking:

"everything that can be accomplished by an incendiary bomb can, in most cases at least, be accomplished as well or better by either a smoke bomb loaded with white phosphorus (WP) or a demolition bomb loaded with high explosive." Planners ignored a 1936 warning by Columbia University professor of chemistry and CWS reserve officer Enrique Zanetti, who served as 1918 U.S. liaison to the French chemical branch: "The small size of these [incendiary] bombs may appear almost ridiculous, particularly after considering the tons of gas that are required to produce lethal concentrations; but here comes the essential difference between gas and incendiaries that makes fire far more dangerous to a large city. Gas dissipates while fire propagates. Each of these small bombs held within itself the devastating possibilities of Mrs. O'Leary's cow." [49]

"This reallocation did not please me," Fieser wrote. Gas was intended for use solely against people and banned under the Geneva Convention of 1929—although that treaty had been rejected by the United States and Japan, among others. It seemed inhumane. "Furthermore, I doubted very much that vesicants would be used in the war that seemed increasingly imminent, and I would much prefer to work on something of practical value to the war effort," he confided in his memoir. Nonetheless, the chemist swallowed his feelings and hired a team of Harvard researchers to begin poison gas studies. [50]

Fieser, however, was experienced in the ways of bureaucracies. Hazardous vesicant research required installation of ventilator hoods in his laboratory. He seized the opportunity created by this delay to initiate a survey of U.S. incendiary research. Other than his own project, he discovered, the NDRC had only four incendiary research programs: small efforts at Brown University and the University of Chicago, and contracts for improved flamethrower nozzle designs and fuel mixtures issued to MIT and the Associated Factory Mutual Fire Insurance Companies. None had made much progress. America had just two firebomb designs in 1941, both of which relied on British prototypes: a four-pound magnesium shell filled with thermite and a substitute made of steel, which did not ignite like magnesium but was cheaper and more readily available. Flamethrower technology was unchanged from 1918. When Fieser visited the headquarters of the CWS at Edgewood Arsenal near Edgewood, Maryland (now part of the Aberdeen Proving Ground), he learned that the government's entire incendiary research effort consisted of two men: one a former reservist and the other an air force pilot, assigned to improve the two existing bombs. A half-dozen civilian members of the CWS staff provided part-time support.[51]

Harvard's genius was not impressed. "I suspected from the start that the molten iron would have little power to start a fire and hence that the bomb was a flop," he wrote of the thermite designs. Moreover, "No burning tests had been applied and the only basis for evaluation was qualitative observation of the firing of bombs in the absence of combustible material." Edgewood's incendiary team expressed interest in his work on gels and a standardized fire measurement system, but said a shortage of manpower made it impossible for them to follow up on his research.[52]

Fieser telephoned Adams, his supervisor, in Illinois and implored the former member of his department to allow him to divert his poison gas budget to incendiary gel research: "I appealed . . . for permission to use the new manpower and funds for work on incendiaries rather than vesicants," he wrote. Adams, perhaps aware that Air Corps chief Henry "Hap" Arnold was concerned about possible magnesium shortages (and intrigued by the possibilities of gelled incendiaries after a briefing by Bush), approved the proposal on the spot.[53]

Bureaucrats caught up a few weeks later. On October 7, the CWS designated incendiary warfare an official project of the Department of War. Later that month, the NDRC awarded its first incendiary research contract—not counting Fieser's hijacked poison gas project—to the Standard Oil Development Company, a division of the oil giant. Its charge was to produce a small firebomb filled with a petroleum product.[54]

# 2

## Anonymous Research No. 4

Fieser's team was already off and running. The professor stopped teaching and threw himself full time into incendiary weapons development, listed as "Anonymous Research No. 4" in Harvard's ledger. University funds paid his salary. A $5.2-million NDRC grant, in today's dollars, covered research expenses.[1]

An improved metric was the first requirement for a comprehensive investigation. Researchers moved their burning-test apparatus out of the basement window wells and into a glass-walled room-within-a-room in the Gibbs Chemistry Laboratory on the third floor of the same building. Physicist Theodore W. Richards designed the facility to house precision balances for atomic weights—work for which he won the 1914 Nobel Prize in Chemistry. "Incendiary materials and bombs could be allowed to burn in the complete absence of drafts and the experiments could be viewed from all sides through the glass windows" that protected the scales, Fieser explained. Rather than the earlier charcoal-scraping procedure, scientists could now compare the weight of the entire testing structure before and after a fire with great precision. "The initial weight of the structure less the weight of the charred pieces gave a measure of the incendiary effectiveness of the sample tested. Results were reproducible with accuracy," the professor wrote. His team renamed their wooden frame the

"Gibbs Burning Test" in honor of its new home. Workers cut a large hole in the roof and installed a powerful ventilation fan.[2]

An intensive program of research on gelled incendiary weapons began. Scientists examined numerous compounds: rubber cements (raw rubber dissolved in nonflammable solvents), rubber dissolved in flammable liquids like benzene and gasoline (the former suggested by Major Rambaut), divinylacetylene, magnesium, thermite, and mixtures of other materials in various concentrations. Hershberg designed and built a special apparatus to measure the density and viscosity of thickened samples using a glass tube, centrifuge, and observation of the time required for a small steel ball to fall between upper and lower "viscosity marks." Magnesium, they concluded, was the best incendiary in an absolute sense, but not much better than rubber-gasoline gels, which had the added advantage of being sticky—and therefore more effective at starting fires—and in plentiful supply. Rubbers from what are now Malaysia, Indonesia, and Sri Lanka, the three primary sources of raw material, all worked equally well, although different concentrations of each variety produced best results. Vulcanized and recycled rubber, interestingly, proved unsatisfactory. Thermite performed relatively poorly.[3]

Field tests came next. CWS officials provided a truckload of M-47 bombshells designed for mustard gas. They were almost four feet tall, about eight inches wide, and made from thin steel that shattered easily. A metal burster tube about 1.5 inches in diameter filled with gunpowder ran through the center of the bomb and screwed into a hole in the top. An impact fuse screwed into the burster. The fuse ignited the burster, which exploded the shell and scattered the device's contents over a wide area.[4]

Fieser's team loaded shells with gel and gunpowder at the Gibbs Laboratory, replaced the impact fuses with electronic triggers, drove across the Charles River, and tested the bombs on athletic fields adjacent to the Harvard Stadium. They had an excellent view of the explosions from the top of the stadium and recorded the area of distribution, average size of the globs of gel, and estimated percentage burned at various formulations. It was, "an exciting line of experimentation," Fieser recalled. Security on the open fields in an urban neighborhood was nonchalant: "a film to be shown to the military had to be edited carefully for removal of an occasional small-boy spectator," the professor wrote.[5]

Researchers tinkered with optimal concentrations of rubber, gasoline, and gunpowder for a few weeks until they were satisfied. Then they recorded a final test on film, packed a demonstration seventy-pound M-47 in a box, and dispatched Fieser on the Federal Express train to the CWS headquarters in Maryland. When the professor handed his parcel to a station porter the man said, "It feels heavy enough to be a bomb."[6]

Chemical officers acted quickly. On November 27, Thanksgiving Day, Fieser received a call. Army officers wanted the recipe for his firebomb to fill an urgent shipment of 10,000 shells ordered for U.S. forces at Manila in the Philippines colony. His instructions were simple: cut rubber into strips and feed them through the hole in the nose of the bomb. Stand the shell on its end and fill it with gasoline until the liquid is 3 inches from the top. Screw in the burster tube and rest the bomb on its side. Rotate 180 degrees three times at one- to two-hour intervals.[7]

Events, however, moved even faster. On December 7, 1941, Japanese carrier-based aircraft attacked the U.S. Pacific Fleet at its primary base at Pearl Harbor in the Hawaii territory. Japanese troops quickly followed up with attacks on British, Dutch, and U.S. colonial possessions in present-day Malaysia, Indonesia, and the Philippines. A large fraction of the U.S. rubber supply was cut off. Manila's bombs never arrived.[8]

A few days after the surprise attack, Fieser attended the opening of a CWS laboratory at MIT. "Now find us something to use in place of rubber," said Colonel M. E. Barker, the chief of the Technical Service of the Chemical Warfare Service. Research began the next morning.[9]

CWS authorities set stringent requirements for the rubberless replacement incendiary gel. It had to be made from widely available, preferably inexpensive, materials, simple enough to be prepared in the field, tough enough to withstand an explosive blast without dissolving into a mist, stable enough to store for long periods, and able to withstand temperatures between the −40 degrees Fahrenheit chill of a high-altitude bomb bay and the 150 degree heat of a tropical storage facility.[10]

War brought a surge in the NDRC budget and a corresponding rush of interest in research opportunities from private businesses. In short order, chemists from the Arthur D. Little company in Cambridge, DuPont, the

Nuodex Products Company of Elizabeth, New Jersey, and others joined Standard Oil Development (SOD) as corporate incendiary researchers. Groups had frequent contact with each other and university investigators and exchanged some ideas and results.[11]

Fieser's team tried every available synthetic rubber. None produced an effective gel. Their only other clue was the knowledge that certain soaps derived from aluminum—as opposed to the sodium derivatives common in commercial products, and otherwise not too dissimilar from retail soaps—dissolved in lubricating oil to form grease. The slurry that formed was not tough enough, and it also was not sticky, but it established the principle that oil might be thickened in this way. And as Fieser wrote, "there are other metals and other acids."[12]

Arthur D. Little scientists suggested that Fieser's group experiment with aluminum naphthenate, a dark brown sticky byproduct of petroleum refining comprised of numerous elements. This tar could not be dissolved in gasoline at room temperature, but the Little researchers found that the two substances did form a tough gel if heat was applied or the aluminum naphthenate was washed with alcohol before being added to gasoline. Neither procedure met the field-filling requirement set by the CWS, but Fieser was impressed that the aluminum naphthenate complex produced a gel superior to any of the simpler soap mixtures his team had created. He suggested they try to mix multiple soaps with gasoline.[13]

Gibbs Laboratory filled with gels of various metal soaps and gasoline. A substance called aluminum palmitate, made by the Metasap Chemical Company of Harrison, New Jersey, produced the most intriguing result. On its own in gasoline, the chemical yielded a slushy gel. When aluminum naphthenate was added, however, a tough and sticky goo formed at room temperature. An early formula called for 5 percent aluminum naphthenate, 5 percent aluminum palmitate, 1 percent sawdust, and gasoline. Fieser combined the first two letters of naphthenate with the first four letters of palmitate and christened the mixture "napalm." He reported his findings to the NDRC on Valentine's Day 1942.[14]

Results from Cambridge captivated a chemical weapons conference held ten days later at the Edgewood Arsenal. When could the CWS see a demonstration? Tomorrow. Stearns Putnam, a twenty-five-year-old chemistry PhD student with close-trimmed brown hair and a wide smile, one of Fieser's "war boys," as the professor called his younger assistants, caught an afternoon Pullman from Boston. Metasap representatives brought twenty-five pounds of aluminum palmitate to the train when it stopped at Newark. Fieser and his acolyte filled ten M-47 shells the next day in the arsenal's Smoke Shop No. 2 workshop.[15]

They had competition. Next door, in Smoke Shop No. 3, SOD chemists loaded their own bombs with what they called Formula 122: a brew of stearic acid, rosin, castor oil, sodium hydroxide, water, kerosene, and gasoline. Harvard's men derisively nicknamed the rival gel "applesauce" because of its loose consistency. Airplanes dropped sample bombs from 10,000 feet onto Maryland mud the following day. Results were inconclusive. The teams returned home.[16]

Fieser intensified his focus on aluminum palmitate and asked every known manufacturer for samples, and a quote on 500 tons of the substance—a monthly minimum for bulk production. Metasap, American Cyanamid, Hershaw Chemical Company, Mallinckrodt Chemical Works, Armour and Company—a *Who's Who* of the U.S. chemical industry in 1942—responded. Jars of samples poured in. Scientists mixed batches from each. Metasap's powder, however, was the only one that produced a gel: aluminum palmitate from all of the other companies yielded only slurry.

Fieser headed to Harrison, just across the Passaic River from Newark. What was different about Metasap's aluminum palmitate, he asked company engineers? Their answer: it wasn't aluminum palmitate. Napalm was actually made from an aluminum soap derived from coconut oil that was 48 percent lauric acid and just 8.2 percent palmitic acid—assertions on packaging and invoices notwithstanding. Satisfactory alternatives, it transpired, could be produced from soaps obtained from palm kernel oil, and oil from common South American babassu palm trees.[17]

The term "napalm" thus had no chemical meaning. It was, Fieser wrote, "now seen to be nondescriptive": a generic for any incendiary made from thickened petroleum. "The name, coined by me, is derived from 'Aluminum napthenate-palmitate' and actually is a misnomer. Our initial experiments utilized a material marketed under the name aluminum palmitate but, as we later learned, this actually consisted of the soap of the total coconut oil fatty acids of high lauric content. . . . 'Nalaur' would have been a more accurate designation," he observed. Chief of the Stockpile and Shipping Branch of the government's War Production

Board, Harvard government professor William Elliot, issued an immediate order to freeze a supply of coconut oil sufficient for the foreseeable needs of the research team.[18]

Aluminum naphthenate and the Metasap coconut oil soap did not mix easily. Scientists requisitioned a meat grinder from a Harvard College dining hall to combine the chemicals with a small amount of kerosene. They mixed the spaghetti-like strands that resulted with gasoline, then ran the mixture through a pump to stir it. The army's field-filling requirement remained elusive.[19]

Nuodex Products, based outside Elizabeth, New Jersey, found the final piece to the puzzle. They manufactured aluminum naphthenate and advised Fieser it could be produced in powder form, rather than as tar. Their chemists suggested that all of the ingredients for napalm could be assembled as powders and then mixed with gasoline. Sample material arrived on April 13, 1942: dry brownish grains in a jar. Troops later dubbed it "fire roe" because of its resemblance to caviar. A 12 percent solution in gasoline, agitated with a single stir, produced a runny, pourable jelly. A few hours later, unattended, the material hardened into a tough, sticky gel. It kept these characteristics from −40 to 150 degrees Fahrenheit, was impervious to vibration, stable in storage, and produced excellent results in the burning test.[20] Napalm was born.

A weapon, however, is only as effective as its delivery system. Harvard's virtuosos made their second major contribution to modern warfare when they devised a way to scatter napalm in chunks over a wide area, and simultaneously ignite it in a cloud of fire.

Films of the field tests shot from the top of the Harvard stadium revealed that the M-47 bombs with gunpowder bursters often exploded in an irregular fashion. Much of the gel consequently failed to ignite. Some parts of the field became infernos, while other areas remained untouched. A significant amount of gel was often trapped in bombshell fragments.

Hershberg theorized that the gunpowder exploded too slowly. Rather than blowing the device apart in an instant, it allowed pressure to build up within the casing. Shells then ruptured along a seam and the napalm spurted out through the resulting tear, rather than in every direction. He proposed to fill the burster tube with TNT, or another high explosive, to produce a more violent and immediate explosion.[21]

TNT, however, produces no flame. Hershberg's solution was to surround the central tube with a container of white phosphorus, which ignites when it comes into contact with air. After consultations with experts at the U.S. Ballistics Research Laboratory in Aberdeen, Maryland, and Picatinny Arsenal in New Jersey, and manufacturing assistance from Noblitt-Sparks Industries in Columbus, Indiana, which made the bomb casings, a set of redesigned shells and bursters arrived on Oxford Street. "The performance, from the start, was most impressive," Fieser wrote, "The high explosive cuts the inner well into ribbons and opens the casing down the entire length. Pieces of phosphorus are driven into the gel, and large, burning globs are distributed evenly over a circular area about 50 yards in diameter. Extinguished with carbon dioxide or water, the phosphorus-containing gel may later reignite."[22]

Ultra slow-motion films shot at 1,000 frames per second by MIT electrical engineering professor Harold Edgerton (later famous for his work with stroboscopic photography that produced images of a balloon in mid-burst, and an apple being shot by a bullet) confirmed the superiority of Hershberg's design.[23]

Researchers tested four bombs on Independence Day 1942. "Bomb 1," equipped with a TNT-white phosphorus burster, squared off against "Bomb 2," using the old gunpowder-based system. Results proved unambiguous. Hershberg's shell threw about 96 percent of its gel compared to just 60 percent for the older design. Even better, about one-third of the napalm blasted by high explosives fell in large chunks that took the men around the pool a full minute to extinguish, even in water. The big sticky blobs were fearsome incendiaries. A gunpowder burster, by contrast, sprayed fine particles of gel that went out as soon as they hit the water.[24]

Not everyone was delighted by this triumph of chemical engineering. On July 30, 1942, H. C. McIntosh of the Navy Supply Corps School wrote to the dean of the Business School, "As you will recall, a few weeks ago some bomb experiments were carried out on the soccer field. A circular embankment approximately 175 feet in diameter was thrown up, which remained for about two days." It was most unsatisfactory: "This rendered about one-fourth of the drill area useless for that time.

Also, after the explosions, irritating vesicant fumes clung to that corner of the field for several days. Effects of these fumes were still visible in the eyes of one officer six days after exposure. In addition, some seventeen officers required treatment during the night." And against regulations: "The soccer field has been designated by the University as a drill field for the Navy Supply Corps School, and makes possible an important part of our indoctrination. In addition to a student body of approximately six hundred, two companies of Business School students start participation in our drill periods on August 3. This number cannot be accommodated on the field unless its entire extent is available, nor, except for Sundays, is the field left idle any day of the week." Research had to cease: "It has come to my attention that further experiments on this field are contemplated. If so, they will seriously hamper the training and athletic program at the Navy Supply Corps School. It is earnestly requested that another site for these tests be selected."

Fieser replied, "Dear Captain McIntosh: I greatly regret that the bomb firing experiments which we carried out on July 4th on a directive from the Chemical Warfare Service took up some of the space on the drill field area for a few days." He was skeptical: "Your comments on the effectiveness and persistence of fumes from the bomb may possibly represent an interesting commentary on the efficacy of this new munition, but I find it difficult to believe that there could have been a direct connection with the disabling of some of your personnel. There were eight men in all in my group of operators and we not only spent the day near the embankment but ran directly into the water-covered area immediately after each of the four explosions and spent practically the whole time making measurements and collections at the site of the bomb crater. A number of workers and firemen were exposed to some extent and there was no instance of any illness with any of these individuals or among my operators." In any event, the study was complete: "As for the future, we have no plans for further experiments calling for the soccer field and thus should cause you no further concern." Case closed.[25]


Fieser's men finished just in time. Administrators from the CWS scheduled final qualification trials for gelled incendiary weapons on July 11–

12, 1942, at the Jefferson Proving Ground in Madison, Indiana. Army Ordnance seized several farms and small villages and relocated residents so that their properties—a deconsecrated church, stores, a banker's large home, chicken coops, and pig pens . . . but no factories or commercial buildings—could be used as targets. Harvard's gel was to face off against an alternative made by DuPont from gasoline and a custom chemical cocktail. Fieser called it a "Fight to the Finish with the Industrialists." Hershberg's white phosphorus burster was also to be reviewed. Observers included representatives from the army, navy, and marines, the Office of the Chief of the CWS, the NDRC, including both Vannevar Bush and Roger Adams, and the British Air Commission, among others. Judges disqualified Standard Oil's "applesauce," and a late entry from Eastman Kodak based on ground-up newsprint, because of insufficient toughness.[26]

"We had some lucky hits and beautiful fires," Fieser reported of the Indiana tests. B-25 bombers scored numerous direct hits on the empty homes. In one case a direct hit on a large barn started a fire that also quickly destroyed two other buildings. In another, a napalm bomb placed by hand inside a house burned the building to the ground in less than three minutes. "It is difficult to imagine what happens when 42 lbs. of burning gel is plastered all over the inside of a sturdy wooden barn: flames bursting out of the windows, blasting open the door, belching forth at the eaves and then through the roof. In a matter of minutes what remained of the structure collapsed into a burning heap," the inventor wrote. In one test, the team drove twenty miles over rough roads to observe the two competing incendiaries torch two large barns located next to each other. Napalm destroyed its target, but the DuPont gel produced only a flash of light and a powerful blast. Officers concluded that someone had forgotten to add thickening agent and that the shell must have been filled with pure gasoline, which would account for the result.[27]

Despite this curious incident, assembled brass concluded that DuPont had the better product. Authorities also approved Standard Oil's bomb design, later known as the M-69, and Hershberg's phosphorus burster, for use in larger weapons. Procurement officers ordered several million shells, and millions of pounds of the DuPont incendiary to fill them. Napalm was out. Fieser packed his bags and returned to Cambridge.[28]

Standard's team took comfort in the knowledge that their design for a new incendiary gel bombshell was an uncontested masterpiece. This weapon was a hexagonal steel container nineteen inches long and just under three inches wide that held 2.6 pounds of jelly and weighed about six pounds in total. Its shape allowed "fierce fagots," as *Popular Science* described the bombs in 1945, to be stacked like cells in a honeycomb. When altimeters opened the clusters, plungers lifted to arm the weapons and gauze streamers unfolded from the backs of the shells. These stabilizing tails saved space and weight compared to metal fins. Impact activated a three- to five-second delay fuse that triggered an explosive charge, fortified with magnesium shavings, that lit the gel (theoretically after the bomb had come to rest on its side) and blasted it 150 feet from the tail of the bomb. This delayed ejection was considered a particular design masterstroke. "A horizontally moving flaming gob covered enormously more ground in search for a target than a stationary magnesium bomb," explained Hoyt Hottel, an MIT professor who directed NDRC incendiary weapons research after 1943. Some models included a small cup of white phosphorus to produce dense smoke and hamper firefighting. Wind tunnel experiments and 20,000 test shots from a mortar mounted on a crane onto three full-scale replica German houses at an SOD research facility—each with an attic and furnished bedroom, one built with a slate roof in the style of Rhineland residences, one with a Central German tile roof, and one of Eastern German design—allowed designers to perfect the thickness of the casing, streamer length, and similar details.[29]

Professionals at fire prevention and insurance specialist Factory Mutual Research Corporation in Norwood, Massachusetts, near Boston, focused additional incendiary bomb research specifically on bedrooms. Engineers bought as much appropriate secondhand furniture as they could find in Boston stores and furnished a test chamber approximately twelve feet by fifteen feet with a wool rug, bed and mattress, vanity with mirror and chair, dresser, and armchairs. They covered the walls and ceiling with gypsum board for easy replacement, and set fire bombs by the door, around the head and sides of the bed, and next to the arm chairs and vanity. "After 6 min elapsed, an experienced fire fighter and helper attacked the fire with a stirrup pump, approaching through the adjoining room, where he encountered heat and smoke from the bedroom. If he was unsuccessful in dealing with the fire it was judged out of control," an official history reported. Shaved white Cheshire pigs, whose skin was thought most closely to resemble that of humans, served as subjects in later stages of experimentation. As with the Indiana village tests conducted by the army, experimenters for Standard Oil and Factory Mutual do not appear to have modeled industrial or commercial buildings.[30]

Hershberg had an explanation for the failure of the DuPont incendiary at the remote farmhouse. He had discovered that if the rival gel was chilled and stirred with a paddle for a long period it underwent syneresis: gasoline separated from the gel like whey from yogurt left in a refrigerator. He speculated that vibration from the long trip over rough roads to the test site had produced this reaction, and that when the gasoline exploded it destroyed whatever weakened gel remained in the bomb.

This proved to be exactly the case. Toward the end of 1942, British officers reported that the gel in many of the U.S. incendiary bombs they received had started to "turn to water" and was no longer effective. Army procurement staff quickly switched production to napalm, which tolerated vibration, but not before many bombs filled with defective gel had been delivered by convoy across the perilous North Atlantic at the height of the German submarine war. This "inadequate production control," as an official NDRC history diplomatically explained the botch, delayed introduction of U.S. gelled fuel incendiary bombs to Europe.[31]

Japan's sole airplane attack on the contiguous United States, an incendiary strike, took place during this period, on September 9, 1942. A tiny Japanese bomber launched from a submarine dropped a single firebomb on a mountain slope near Brookings, Oregon, just north of the California state line. It kindled a small forest fire.

A separate Japanese "Fu-Go" or "windship weapon" balloon bombardment program between November 1944 and April 1945 released approximately 9,300 hydrogen balloons armed with small explosives into the jet stream that flowed toward North America. Japanese schoolgirls, with gloved hands and fingernails cut short, painstakingly fashioned the airships from hundreds of sheets of laminated paper, often handmade, in theaters and sumo wrestling halls requisitioned for the purpose. Completed balloons received a final lacquer derived from the fermented juice of green persimmons. Millions of people participated in the project. About 345 devices made it to the United States. They damaged power lines from the Bonneville Dam in Washington State, which disrupted plutonium production for three days at the Hanford Engineering Works, and killed six Oregonians on a Sunday school fishing trip: five children aged eleven to fourteen, and Elyse Mitchell, the pregnant twenty-six-year-old wife of a minister. Reverend Mitchell dropped off his party and went to park his car. While waiting, the children found and detonated a bomb. These appear to be the only deaths from enemy action in the continental United States during World War II. No German airplanes got within 1,000 miles of the country.[32]

British officers had another worry about U.S. incendiary bombs, aside from the inability of DuPont fillings to start fires: the M-69, they thought, notwithstanding 20,000 mortar tests, was too small to penetrate German roofs and upper floors and reach lower levels—a critical requirement for an incendiary bomb. Other specialists argued vociferously that the Indiana farm houses and barns were easier to ignite than actual enemy buildings.[33]

To resolve these concerns, the CWS decided to build and firebomb life-sized replica German and Japanese residences at its new Dugway Proving Ground in Utah, about seventy-five miles southwest of Salt Lake City. It was larger and had better weather than Edgewood in Maryland. Army officers contracted with SOD, which had experience with replica targets from their mortar research, to build the facility. Workers broke ground on March 29, 1943.[34]

A frenzied seven-week construction period followed during which engineers spared no effort or expense to achieve authenticity. Officers hired Erich Mendelsohn and Antonin Raymond, noted architects who had practiced for years in Germany and Japan, respectively, to design the homes down to the last detail. Traditional wooden pegs secured the Japanese structures. Logisticians located a shipment of Russian spruce, similar to hinoki wood used in Japan, headed for Portland. SOD diverted the boat to San Francisco, commandeered the cargo, and trucked it across the continent to Fort Dix in New Jersey. Technicians there conditioned timber for both sets of houses to a moisture content of about 15 percent, similar to that found in enemy homelands, then prefabricated the buildings. "[A] line of trucks from Dix in Jersey to the Utah Proving Grounds," carried the houses west, Raymond recalled. Esso employees across the country ensured that drivers, each of whom required a special wartime travel permit, received fuel and local assistance. Prisoners conscripted from the Utah State Prison helped build the villages, a five-mile access road, and a water tower in just forty-four days. Soldiers watered the putative homes with hoses to simulate the mists of Japan and winter rains of Germany.[35]

Researchers furnished the models with equal assiduousness. An SOD executive traveled to Hawaii, and logged thousands of miles driving along the Pacific Coast, to collect traditional tatami straw mat flooring from temples and private homes for the Japanese dwellings. Airplanes rushed the woven mats to Utah. Officials even built their own tatami factory, to cover their bets. Hollywood's RKO Studios provided designs for authentic German furnishings. CWS officials reopened a closed furniture factory in upstate New York to produce pieces to required specifications. A dozen fully furnished duplex Japanese houses in four units, typical of urban row house construction for workers, and a block of six urban German residential dwellings, three in Rhineland style with slate roofs and three of a Central German design topped with tiles, stood complete on May 15. As in earlier tests, the army did not model industrial or commercial buildings. All that was missing was people.[36]

Bombers pounded the houses with M-50 and M-52 thermite bombs, and M-69 bombs filled with napalm, throughout the summer. Trials necessitated three reconstructions of the villages to repair damage. Results were definitive. Napalm was a devastating weapon: a quantum improvement over thermite, lethal against dwellings, and particularly effective against Japanese homes. Uncontrollable fires started in more than one-third of German homes and more than two-thirds of Japanese houses spattered with gel. Officers invented a scale for incendiary effectiveness: "Any fire beyond control of the well-trained and properly equipped fire guards in 6 minutes was classified an A fire; a fire which was ultimately destructive if unattended was a B fire; and a fire judged nondestructive was a C fire," according to an official history. Final results from "functioning hits" were as follows:

*Table 1.* Results from 1943 Dugway Bombing Tests

| | German Houses | | | Japanese Houses | | |
|---|---|---|---|---|---|---|
| Fire Class | AN-M-50 (thermite) | AN-M-52 (thermite) | AN-M-69 (napalm) | AN-M-50 (thermite) | AN-M-52 (thermite) | AN-M-69 (napalm) |
| A—Uncontrollable within six minutes | 0% | 0% | 37% | 22% | 26% | 68% |
| B—Destructive if unattended | 26% | 18% | 16% | 20% | 14% | 13% |
| C—Nondestructive | 74% | 82% | 47% | 58% | 60% | 19% |

Source: National Defense Research Committee, U.S. Office of Scientific Research and Development, "Fire Warfare: Incendiaries and Flame Throwers," in *Summary Technical Report of Division 11, NDRC*, vol. 3 (Columbia University Press, 1946), 77.
Note: Dud bombs were excluded from these results.

Napalm was significantly more destructive than thermite, and Japanese homes almost twice as vulnerable to catastrophic fires from the gel than German structures. CWS historians explained the conclusion: "Using the results of the Dugway trials as a basis, plans for the bombing of Japan with the AN-M-69 were drawn up by the Army Air Forces in the fall of 1943." Follow-up research on existing factory structures at Eglin Field, near Valparaiso, Florida, which started in March 1944; experiments that autumn on specially constructed industrial target models at Edgewood Arsenal; and trials in early 1945 on a model Japanese room built in late 1944 at the Maryland facility, confirmed the Utah findings.[37]

Fieser and his team returned to Harvard and turned their secret laboratory on Oxford Street into a design center for special napalm weapons worthy of James Bond's Q Branch. Their clients were the Office of Strategic Services (OSS), predecessor of the Central Intelligence Agency, and the armed services.

An initial success came in November 1942 when the "Harvard Candle" personal napalm fire starter—intended for downed pilots or others who had to make fires in the wilderness—won an Army competition. The "candle" went into production as the M-1 Fire Starter. A "pocket incendiary" fashioned from napalm powder, kerosene, and a mechanical time-delay system, all packed into a box about the size of a deck of cards, emerged in the spring of 1943. Saboteurs could set it and walk away; the OSS ordered more than 400,000. In the spring of 1944, the chemists perfected the lunchbox-sized "City Slicker" oil slick igniter. OSS officers imagined partisans could release oil into a harbor then loose the devices like floating lanterns to ignite ships or other targets. Fieser and his wife traveled to California to supervise initial production. Subsequent modifications allowed use of the device on land as well as water and won it a new code name: the "Paul Revere."[38]

Additional inventions included a fourteen-gram pellet of napalm powder in a case that dissolved slowly in gasoline, and a glass napalm hand grenade that worked like a Molotov cocktail. Saboteur gas station attendants might slip the pellet into German tanks on their way to the Russian front, it was thought. Gasoline swelled the napalm over a few days and formed a blob that jammed the engine long after its placement. A safety device for the glass grenade was so ingenious the United States issued a patent for it in 1950. Nonetheless, the miniature firebomb was deemed too risky for battlefield use.

Independently, Fieser wrote *Arson: An Instruction Manual* for the OSS, and traveled to Europe as a member of the Alsos mission that scoured Germany for information about its nuclear bomb program in the last months before the Nazi surrender. He was armed for the trip, perhaps preposterously, with a swagger stick given to him by his wife and modified by an OSS friend to conceal a triangular dagger.[39]

A measure of the enthusiasm with which Fieser approached these projects can be seen in the name he gave a kitten acquired during his work on napalm. "We wanted to associate the new Siamese with this discovery, but the word Napalm was a classified military secret. So the pedigree name chosen was J. G. Pooh, which to us meant Jellied Gasoline Pooh. Before long J. G. became modified to Georgie," he wrote. Along similarly lighthearted lines, the professor explained napalm could be effective against crabgrass: he had sprinkled some on the lawn of his Belmont, Massachusetts home and ignited: Weeds burned away, and a few weeks later healthy grass grew back through the ashes, he asserted. Army officials subsequently attributed the genesis of napalm to this anecdote. A credulous Associated Press reporter swallowed the story. "If a Harvard chemistry professor hadn't battled with the crabgrass on the lawn of his suburban home, there might never have been the monster fire raids on Japan's great cities, an army officer disclosed today," he reported in April 1945.[40]

Harvard's team does not appear to have discussed the morality of firebomb attacks. "Our testing and our thinking were in terms of the burning of structures, not personnel," Fieser recalled in a autobiographical note written around 1970 for the fiftieth reunion of his Williams college class. He did not address the implications of the army's bombing experiments, and conceded only limited circumstances in which napalm might affect people, for example as an incidental consequence of an attack on a tank: "To be sure, there was our Antitank Grenade, a glass jar filled with Napalm gel and containing a vial of diethyl zinc, which takes fire when a steel ball crushes the vial and allows access of air. If the grenade strikes anywhere near the powerful air intake of a tank, combustion fumes will be drawn in to make the tank untenable."[41] With that, his introspective review ended.

# BIRTH

Byzantine naval troops in the 1100s deploy Greek fire against the fleet of Thomas the Slav.  Madrid Skylitzes/*Biblioteca Nacional de España*

A trebuchet of the 1200s equipped with defensive stockades hurls a fire pot over a castle wall. Harper's Magazine

Troops on the Western Front in World War I use flamethrowers to attack enemies in the forest to the left. New York Times/*Library of Congress*

A baby cries at Shanghai's South Station on August 28, 1937, after a Japanese incendiary bomb attack. *Office of War Information/National Archives*

Prime Minister Winston Churchill visits the ruins of Coventry Cathedral in September 1941, destroyed by incendiary bombardments in November 1940. *Imperial War Museum/Library of Congress*

"Goodness" surveys the ruins of Dresden after a British attack with magnesium incendiary bombs and explosives on Ash Wednesday, Valentine's Day, 1945. *AFP*

Harvard University's Sheldon Emery Professor of Organic Chemistry Louis Fieser, father of napalm. *Courtesy of the Harvard University Archives*

A Harvard College dining hall meat grinder slices napalm into strands before it is mixed with gasoline and siphoned to an M-47 bombshell, originally designed for mustard gas. *Louis Fieser,* The Scientific Method, *30*

A napalm bomb stands in a test pond on the Harvard College soccer field, behind the Business School, before its first trial on July 4, 1942. Tennis players in whites are in the background. *Louis Fieser,* The Scientific Method, *37*

First field test of a napalm bomb, Harvard University, Independence Day, July 4, 1942. *Louis Fieser,* The Scientific Method, *38*

Assistants extinguish gobs of burning napalm and collect samples approximately one minute after detonation (note empty tennis courts). *Louis Fieser,* The Scientific Method, *39*

White phosphorus ignites a napalm bomb and produces a smokescreen to hamper firefighters in a 1942 test. Harvard's football stadium is in the background. *Louis Fieser,* The Scientific Method, *48*

A contemporary view of the Harvard College soccer field. Tennis courts are in the background (the building in front of the Business School library's tower was built after 1942). *Photo by author*

# 3

## American Kamikazes

### Suicide Bomber Bats

A plan to turn millions of bats into suicide bombers bearing tiny na-palm time bombs was the most spectacular of the special projects at Louis Fieser's Harvard laboratory. Dr. Lytle S. Adams, a Pennsylva-nia dentist, pilot, and inventor conceived the idea when he heard about the Pearl Harbor attacks on his way home from a visit to the bat-filled Carlsbad Caverns in New Mexico. In the late 1920s, Adams patented a system for nonstop pickup of mail sacks by airplanes using a weighted cable and a special pickup rope. He organized the system as a business, and caught the attention of Eleanor Roosevelt in 1938 through work in ru-ral West Virginia. In January 1942, the entrepreneur called the First Lady and convinced her to pass a memo that described his bat plan to FDR.[1]

"[The] lowest form of life is the BAT, associated in history with the underworld and regions of darkness and evil," Adams wrote to the pres-ident. "Until now reasons for its creation have remained unexplained. As I vision it the millions of bats that have for ages inhabited our belfries, tunnels and caverns were placed there by God to await this hour to play their part in the scheme of free human existence, and to frustrate any at-tempt of those who dare desecrate our way of life." A fire attack by millions of bats, he continued, "Would render the Japanese people homeless and their industries useless, yet the innocent could escape with their lives."[2]

Roosevelt was intrigued. "This man is *not* a nut. It sounds like a perfectly wild idea but it is worth looking into," he wrote to Office of Strategic Services director Colonel William Donovan. "Wild Bill," as the director was known, referred the memo to the National Inventors Council (NIC), a commercial analog to the National Defense Research Committee (NDRC) established by Harry Hopkins at the Department of Commerce, the NDRC itself, and the Army Air Force. It wound up at the Chemical Warfare Service (CWS)—which dismissed it. White phosphorus was the only practical incendiary for such a task, Captain William G. Wiles, CWS liaison officer to the NIC, concluded in May 1942. That chemical had to be kept in an oxygen-free environment until ignition—but bats require oxygen to live. QED.[3]

Inventors Council director Thomas Taylor did not accept this rejection. He demanded that the CWS review their liaison's conclusion with the office of Army Air Force commanding general Hap Arnold. "It is requested that this office be informed if you see any possible use for such a munition," CWS technical director Colonel W. C. Kabrich dutifully wrote to Arnold on June 13. "Fantastic as the proposed plan appears, there might be a time in the future when it would be desirable to execute such harassing missions," Colonel H. A. Craig responded from the general's office on June 25. Senior NDRC chemistry administrator Earl Stevenson followed up in July with a suggestion to the navy that hibernating bats might be transported to Japan by submarine and released just off the coast. Summer turned to winter, however, and no chiropteran incendiary time bomb emerged from the CWS. Finally, in March 1943 officers at Edgewood appealed to the NDRC for assistance. Stevenson assigned Fieser to the project.[4]

Harvard's chemist had an immediate solution. A research team recruited by Adams from the Natural History Museum of Los Angeles County—the dentist headquartered his program in the City of Angels, where he had relatives—had determined that the best bat for the job was the ten- to eleven-gram Mexican free-tailed variety. The animals could carry a fifteen- to eighteen-gram payload; millions migrated to Texas each summer. Fieser drew on his pocket incendiary work to design a tiny napalm bomb and timer that weighed just 17.5 grams. "These were to be attached to hibernating bat vectors which would be flown over Japanese cities at night and parachuted down into warm-air, when the bats would awaken and carry the bombs onto or into highly combustible Japanese houses," he wrote.[5]

An initial test for the system was scheduled for May 1943 at the Muroc Army Air Base (now Edwards Air Force Base) outside Los Angeles. A large dry lake on the base, bleached white by the sun, would, it was thought, facilitate bat recovery. Standard Pyroxoloid, a firm based in western Massachusetts, prepared 3,000 tiny bombs and filled some with napalm. Technicians at the Gibbs Chemistry Laboratory loaded the rest with red phosphorus, which produces a dense smoke, to aid recovery. Connecticut toy company A. C. Gilbert, famous for its Erector Set building kits, manufactured the timers. An army team at Wright Field in Dayton, Ohio, built a special refrigerated truck to chill and transport hibernating bats, loaded it with bombs and timers, and drove it to Los Angeles. A B-25 bomber assigned to the test flew to California from Eglin Field in Florida. Fieser and two CWS officers from Edgewood arrived in Los Angeles on Monday, May 17, and proceeded to Adams's home for an evening review before the test scheduled for the next day.[6]

They discovered a large dinner party in progress at the dentist's residence. Adams had decided to celebrate progress on his top secret project by inviting a large collection of friends and associates. "We were horrified to find that Adams had invited a large company, including ladies, to a dinner party in celebration of the initiation of field tests on the Adams Plan, supposedly a highly secret project," Fieser recalled. Worse, from the perspective of the easterners, he had gathered only 150 test bats, rather than the agreed 3,000. It was mating season for bats in Los Angeles and they were hard to catch, the inventor explained.[7]

Improvisation followed. CWS lieutenant colonel R. Bruce Epler and some of Adams's staff from the Natural History Museum of Los Angeles made an emergency trip in the B-25 the next morning to Carlsbad in New Mexico—site of the project's initial inspiration. They landed at a nearby army air base, requisitioned a car, obtained a permit from the Parks Department, collected eight large crates of bats, and flew back to Muroc that evening. "Shortly after dinner the bomber flew in loaded with shrieking, kicking bats," Fieser recalled. Expeditionaries loaded the creatures into the refrigerated truck and turned on the cooling system full blast. When the cacophony did not diminish after a few hours, they wrapped blocks of ice in towels and tucked them in with the bats, and positioned fans to blow air over additional chunks of ice stacked around the mammals. Shrieks subsided around midnight.[8]

Researchers planned to pack the bats into five-foot-tall steel bombshells the size of a standard 500-pound bomb. Each shell was filled with circular steel trays about one and a half inches tall, subdivided into small rectangular bat-sized niches and fitted upside down one on top of the other. Hibernating bats with napalm bombs attached to their breasts with surgical clips—thought to simulate the teeth of a baby bat—were to be placed in each compartment. Timing and safety wires connected each bat to the tray above and to the compartment walls. Strings two- to three-inches long connected the trays. On release, a parachute deployed and a mechanical device jettisoned the casing. Trays fell to the bottom of their connecting strings like an accordion and released the timing wires. As the deployed bat bomb descended into warmer air, the bats were expected to wake up, wiggle or fall out of their cubicles, and fly away—in the process removing the safety wires and arming the bombs. Each shell could carry 1,030 bats. A twin-engined B-25 could carry twenty-five shells: almost 26,000 individual bat bombs. A Del Mar, California, company owned by entertainer Bing Crosby and his brother Larry was contracted to manufacture the devices.[9]

Adams produced only cardboard mockups, however, for the test. These disintegrated as soon as staff launched them from the B-25. Fieser, for his part, hadn't completed the safety mechanism for the miniature bombs, and the pilot refused to allow them on board. Team members clipped weights to the bats, in lieu of bombs, and threw them out of the bomber by hand. A ground crew raced after them in jeeps on the lake bed. Experimenters released an initial batch of test subjects at 2,000 feet. They plummeted straight to the ground in free fall. "Few if any of the bats had come out of hibernation," Fieser wrote. More altitude was required to give the animals enough time to wake up. The pilot circled higher and higher as the men performed tests at various heights. Ultimately, the plane was so high it was difficult to see from the ground. Results seemed to be the same no matter what the altitude. "Eventually it became clear that the bats were not in hibernation but dead," the Harvard professor wrote. "What had happened was that instead of freezing them to hibernation, we had frozen them to death the night before," he lamented. A second test was scheduled for the next month.[10]

Fieser and Epler decided that the air base at Carlsbad, close to the bat caves, was the best location for the next experiment. On his previous visit, Epler had noticed that a new auxiliary landing field, complete with control tower, barracks, offices, hangars, and outbuildings, had just been completed at a remote location on the base. Fieser and he visited the commander. They couldn't explain their mission, they said, but displayed their orders marked "Top Secret." The colonel agreed to delay inauguration of the auxiliary field, a flight training facility he had conceived and whose construction he had supervised, for a few days to allow their critical research.[11]

Their second effort was more successful. Team members collected a fresh set of bats, chilled them more gently, and loaded them into a completed Crosby company shell. Fieser's continued inability to perfect a safety mechanism, as well as judicious concern for local civilians, forced the use of dummy bombs rather than live incendiaries. Deployment took place over a group of observers that included Marine Corps general Louis DeHaven. Epler, notwithstanding his rank as a lieutenant colonel, insisted that the base commander, a full colonel, be excluded to maintain secrecy.[12]

The bat bomb dropped. Its parachute deployed at 4,000 feet. "Soon tiny motes began to flutter across the sky, flying in all directions, most borne northward in a fluttering clump by the breeze," recalled team member Jack Couffer, a junior chiroptologist from the Natural History Museum. Investigators leaped into jeeps and set off after the animals at high speed over rough country. They tracked a large group for miles to the barn of a local rancher, rushed onto his front porch, and asked if he had noticed anything unusual. "Like bats flyin' 'round in broad daylight? Unusual like that?" he answered. They begged for secrecy. "I got two sons somewhere in Europe fightin' the Hun. If you tell me that's what yer doin', however damned fool as it looks to me, is a military secret, nobody's goin' to get me to say a peep even by puttin' bamboo splinters under my fingernails and alightin' fire to 'em," he said. He gestured to a bat that peered down from a niche between ceiling boards just above them on the porch. It straddled a dummy bomb. The delivery system worked.[13]

That would have been a good place to end the day's research. Adams, however, wanted to conduct a second trial to confirm the first results. Fieser decided to take advantage of this opportunity to demonstrate his miniature napalm time bombs for motion picture and still photographers assigned to cover the event by the Army Signals Corps.

Assistants handed him six torpid chilled bats with bombs attached. Their delay device used corrosive copper chloride to dissolve a trigger wire. A thicker wire produced a longer delay. Demonstration units had fifteen-minute wires. Fieser ceremoniously injected chloride into one timer after another from a large steel and glass hypodermic syringe. As the cameras whirred and clicked, he carefully armed all six bat bombs.

Then, in an instant, the mammals woke up and took off. A hot New Mexico sun had revivified them with unexpected speed. Small shapes flapped away into the sky.

Couffer explained what happened next. "Exactly fifteen minutes after arming, a barracks burst into flames; minutes later the tall tower erupted into a huge candle visible for miles. Offices and hangars followed in order corresponding to the intervals between Fieser's chemical injections." A second confirmation of the bat plan's viability.[14]

Unfortunately, to preserve secrecy, and because the plan was to use dummy bombs, the team had deemed fire equipment unnecessary at the remote location. By the time the base commander—alerted by plumes of thick black smoke from his brand new facility—arrived with three fire engines, the time for remedial measures was past. Flames had jumped from building to building. Many structures lay in ashes. Moreover, the guards—under Epler's command during the test—refused to unlock the gates for their commander. A heated discussion ensued, with the fire trucks and base commander outside, and Lieutenant Colonel Epler inside. Not only did the junior CWS officer refuse to modify his secrecy requirements, he asked the colonel for a bulldozer to raze whatever might be left of his facility after the fires burned out. "We made a little mistake out there," Fieser said later in a talk to a group of engineers.[15]

Army officials decided they wanted no further part of the project. General DeHaven, however, was impressed by the evident destructive capability of napalm-armed bats. Marines took over the program in the autumn of 1943, renamed it "Project X-Ray," and put Colonel R. H. "Dusty" Rhoads in charge. Officers designated the Marine Air Station at El Centro, California, X-Ray headquarters, posted armed guards at the two largest bat caves in the United States (near San Antonio, Texas), and assigned a twin-engined Lockheed Lodestar airplane full time to the effort. Inventor Adams, who never had an official role, was forced out.[16]

Rhoads readied the system for deployment. On December 17–19, the marines tested the bat bombs at the Dugway Japanese and German villages. "The sterile towns stood several miles apart on the otherwise empty Utah plain, like abandoned movie sets picturing the aftermath of a devastating plague," Couffer recalled. Due caution was employed. Released bats carried dummy bombs, now glued directly to the animals. Researchers then placed tiny napalm bombs by hand in similar locations. Results proved positive, despite wet wood and cold temperatures. "The main advantage of the units would seem to be their placement (by the bats) within the enemy structures without the knowledge of the householder or fire watchers, thus allowing the fire to establish itself before being discovered," concluded Dugway's chief incendiary officer. Fieser attended this second Utah experiment and determined that napalm bombardment by bat was about 3.7 times more efficient than by gravity.[17]

Design and testing was complete by February 1944. Manufacturers and bat collection teams stood by to fulfill an expected initial order for 1 million bats, incendiaries, and timers. Then, suddenly and without definitive explanation—a historical mystery still to be resolved—the project was canceled after an expenditure of about $24 million in today's dollars. "Uncertainties involved in the behavior of the animal," NDRC chemist Harris M. Chadwell blandly wrote, created too many unknown variables.[18]

Napalm had to rely on more traditional vectors to reach its targets.

# 4

## We'll Fight Mercilessly

Amerian strategists had little interest in incendiary weapons after World War I. Gas, as Louis Fieser's research directives demonstrated, was deemed the weapon of the future. Flamethrowers seemed particularly problematic because operators ran terrible risks and most of their fuel burned before it hit its target. "Taken all in all, the flame thrower was one of the greatest failures among the many promising devices tried out on a large scale in the war," Chemical Warfare Service (CWS) chief Amos Fries wrote in 1921. "[I]t is easy to see how service in the [German] flaming gun regiments is apparently a form of punishment," he added. A 1934 index of army publications that discussed chemical weapons did not even mention flamethrowers.

Columbia professor Zanetti, a rare opposing voice on the matter, was ignored for years. In 1935, he mailed fragments of an Italian magnesium incendiary shell—recovered in Ethiopia by a *New York Times* correspondent and passed to him for analysis—to Edgewood Arsenal with commentary about its advanced characteristics. In 1936, he visited England, France, Germany, and Italy for the CWS and reported that the latter two countries had mounted flamethrowers on armored cars and light tanks. Nonetheless, "It is understood that the portable flame thrower will no longer be used in offensive operations, as it has been found that the casualties to flame thrower personnel have been excessive," concluded a comprehensive 1937 army review.[1]

Events prompted a change in policy. Portable flamethrowers played an important role in the stunning capture of the massive Belgian fort of Eben Emael by German paratroopers on May 10, 1940. "Those throwbacks to medieval war, the flamethrowers, opened up against the embrasures. The engineers moved forward, yelling, into their final assault," the army's *Infantry Journal* reported. Intelligence analysts described additional German flamethrower deployments in Poland and Holland. On August 12, newly installed Secretary of War Henry Stimson asked the chemical service to develop a portable flamethrower. Research started from zero, since none of the World War I devices had been saved. Officers hired the Kincaid Company of New York—ironically, a manufacturer of fire extinguishers—to design the weapon. After a few months, engineers produced a seventy-pound behemoth dubbed "E1," for experimental, that resembled a large oil drum with a hose and nozzle. It was mounted awkwardly on a simple harness and wobbled from side to side, which forced soldiers to move at a ponderous amble.[2]

Enter the NDRC. In February 1941 a team of MIT engineers with expertise in liquid jets improved the E1's nozzle. A separate CWS group, advised by incendiary experts from the Associated Factory Mutual Fire Insurance Companies, made the weapon lighter and stronger. "M1" flamethrowers arrived in the summer of 1941. Army officials ordered 1,000 just before Pearl Harbor. Systems had "two fuel tanks with a small cylinder of nitrogen fixed between them to provide projecting pressure. A hose from the tanks led to the barrel (or gun) which the operator held, and a small burst of flame released by a trigger ignited the fuel as it shot from the nozzle," the chemical specialists explained. Although it weighed about the same as its predecessor, it was easier to carry and significantly more reliable.[3]

Flamethrowers used by Japanese soldiers against GI's in the Philippines early in 1942 further focused U.S. attention. In March, Vannevar Bush created the Ad Hoc Committee on Flamethrowers with representatives from the NDRC, the CWS, the Corps of Engineers, and the army, navy, and Marine Corps. In the same month, the NDRC contracted with Standard Oil and the Gilbert and Barker Manufacturing Company to develop large flamethrowers that could be mounted on tanks or other vehicles.[4]

World War I's essential limiting factor, the flame filling, however, remained. CWS historians explained: "The fuel at the time was plain gasoline, which burst from the weapon as a great billow or fire-ball of flame and smoke. This was not considered very efficient since a stream of flaming gasoline was largely burned up on its way to the target and at best had only a limited range." Experts estimated the maximum effective range for operations against bunkers was a dispiriting five yards. Records of a U.S. attack on a Japanese position at Munda Airfield on New Georgia island in the South Pacific at 1:00 a.m. on July 26, 1942, demonstrated the dangerous tactics required to utilize this equipment. "With 60-pound fuel tanks on their backs, their faces blackened with dirt, and black tape covering all metal surfaces on the weapons which might reflect light and spot them to the enemy, the seven men crawled 75 yards from the battalion command post to a position in front of the Japanese bunkers," said an after-action report. It continued, "[S]upporting infantrymen moved up to within 20 yards of the bunkers, using small arms fire to keep the Japs bottled up while the seven men crawled five yards nearer." In unison, "Two of the flame operators facing the middle bunker fired first, crisscrossing their fire so as to burn out the underbrush and leave the gun port exposed. Then the officer between them sent a stream of flame through the narrow gun port into the bunker. At the same moment the men covering the other two bunkers fired their flame throwers and enemy resistance was at an end." A malfunction under such conditions was disastrous. On December 6, 1942, on New Guinea, for example, a team of U.S. soldiers stood up directly in front of a Japanese pillbox. Riflemen provided covering fire while a flamethrower operator pulled the trigger on his E1 device. A pitiful ten-foot sputter of oil emerged. Defenders killed most of the U.S. attackers. Remarkably, the flame operator survived.[5]

Napalm wrought a revolution. Fieser passed one of his earliest gel samples to the MIT NDRC lab working on flamethrowers. Institute engineers discovered that in addition to its other remarkable properties, the new gel liquefied at high pressure. Thus, it could be shot through a nozzle as a liquid, ignited, and then, like a science fiction monster, reform itself into a semi-solid as it traveled through the air. "Napalm gel is a non-

Newtonian material," explained army chemical engineer E. W. Hollingsworth. "This means that the viscosity of the gel varies with the rate of shear. . . . A napalm gel having jello-like consistency in a static state, has a viscosity almost comparable to that of lubricating oil when it is forced at high velocity through pipes or pumps." Even better for army purposes, flaming napalm traveled approximately twice as far through the air as unignited gel, probably because of the updrafts it generated and, perhaps, because of jet effects from burning gases. "It sure knocks the hell out of my ballistics training," said an artillery officer who transferred to the CWS.[6]

The result was "a phenomenal increase in range over ordinary fuels," according to Fieser, that tripled the range of portable flamethrowers to fifty- to seventy-five yards, and increased the amount of burning jelly delivered onto a target almost ten-fold, from just 10 to a full 90 percent of the material discharged. A spray of thickened oil was replaced by a rod of burning fuel that shot half the length of a football field or more, spattered onto whatever it hit, and stuck tight at over 2,000 degrees Fahrenheit. It was an application "of which we had not even dreamed," the Harvard chemist and his colleagues wrote later, and one which gasoline thickened with rubber, and DuPont's incendiary gel, could not match. "This 'dud' of World War I became one of the most potent weapons in the Pacific operations. . . . It was Napalm which did this," averred Harry Truman's secretary of war Robert Patterson. Within a month of this discovery, Standard Oil had adapted the M1 for napalm. It was standardized as the M1A1 in December 1942, ordered in bulk, and shipped to the landing teams for Operation HUSKY, the allied invasion of Sicily in July 1943.[7]

America's vast industrial machine went into action. Manufacturers from New Jersey, Ohio, and California experimented with various ways to produce incendiary gel, which was trickier than expected. "[C]ontractors almost invariably believed that the production of napalm would be a relatively simple matter, much like the manufacture of a commercial soap. In this they were mistaken . . . napalm had to have standard components and low moisture," an official history explained. Government administrators helped obtain crude oil from Venezuela and Aruba, which was particularly rich in napthenic acid, and ensured that producers received a sufficient supply of copra (boiled and dried coconut): a source of coconut fatty acid. This became hard to find as the war progressed since it was also used for civilian products, and many coconut plantations were in war zones. Workers at the United Wall Paper Company modified wallpaper conveyors to carry large quantities of napalm through heated drying rooms, calibrated to account for high summer humidity. Researchers at Columbia and Stanford Universities, and private businesses including Eastman Kodak, helped the CWS and NDRC solve last-minute production problems. In January 1943, only one production facility was in full operation, but by the end of the year nine factories made napalm. It arrived in tidy five and one-quarter, fifteen and three-quarters, and 100-pound hermetically sealed packages, the first two generally shipped overseas, and the latter delivered to arsenals and factories that manufactured incendiary bombs. Production increased from 500,000 pounds of powder in 1943 to 8 million in 1944 and 12 million in 1945.[8]

Napalm saw combat for the first time in Sicily in August 1943. American troops, in an action reminiscent of Samson's flaming foxes, incinerated a wheat field believed to shelter Germans. In the Pacific, the first napalm flamethrowers reached troops in July. Soldiers used them for the first time on December 15, 1943, when they burned defenders out of a cave on Pilelo, a tiny island off the coast of New Britain, northeast of Papua New Guinea.

Air bombardments followed in short order. Airmen mixed the powder with various combinations of oil and gasoline, wired white phosphorus incendiary grenades to barrels or auxiliary fuel tanks, and created "fire-bombs" (distinguished from later mass-produced "incendiary bombs"). These "gave great promise of success," recalled Rear Admiral Harry W. Hill. Standard Oil's M-69 napalm bombs saw Pacific combat for the first time on February 15, 1944, when the Seventh Air Force attacked the lush town of Pohnpei, capital of the eponymous Micronesian island. It lies 2,500 miles southwest of Hawaii and 1,800 miles northeast of Australia. A total of 118 tons of bombs hit the island, bypassed by U.S. troops as part of their "island hopping" strategy, over the next eleven days.[9]

Requests exploded as commanders observed napalm's effectiveness. Bombs quickly, and permanently, surpassed flamethrower requisitions. In Europe, 13,000 M-47 napalm bombs, mixed with explosives, gutted a Focke-Wulf aircraft plant at Marienburg in East Prussia in October 1943; another napalm attack the same month critically damaged ball-bearing plants at Schweinfurt. Ultimately, more than 500,000 of the bombshells tested at Harvard, each bearing about forty pounds of napalm, fell on Germany: perhaps 20,000 tons of incendiary gel. By December incendiaries, including napalm, accounted for 40 percent of all U.S. bombs dropped in Europe. Napalm firebombs fashioned from disposable auxiliary aircraft gasoline tanks, true to their promise, proved to be "an excellent tactical weapon to use against supply dumps, troop concentrations, convoys and vehicles," according to an official history.[10]

Demand proved so intense that by the summer of 1944, officers routed supplies of napalm powder directly from the United States to Normandy beachheads and ports to save time. Special "expediters" stationed at crucial points on the supply line ensured that gel kept moving to the front. Air chemical officers who sought supplies for the American Eighth Air Force in western Europe canvassed the Ninth Air Force in North Africa, and the Twelfth Air Force in the Mediterranean—only to discover that the former was already trying to get napalm from the latter. Supply officers diverted 50,000 gallons of flamethrower fuel to the air forces. Demand outstripped supply until the beginning of 1945 when expanded U.S. deliveries, combined with distribution of additional field mixing units, largely resolved the issue.[11]

Napalm strikes assisted the July breakout from the Normandy beaches, repeatedly hit German troops trapped at Falaise in early August, and spattered the headquarters of Field Marshal Guenther von Kluge at the end of the month at Verzey, among many other attacks. In August 1944, the CWS delivered 20,000 gallons, mixed at a British factory, to the Eighth Air Force. In September, commanders asked for 600,000 gallons. In November, they petitioned for 1 million gallons. U.S. planes dropped 157,000 gallons of napalm in Normandy between June and August 1944, and another 199,000 gallons over the next ten weeks on the Siegfried Line and other targets; 460,000 gallons later fell on the Gironde Estuary in France. Napalm "was extensively employed by tactical air forces in the European Theater and played an important role in the ultimate break through the western defenses of Germany," wrote historians at the Office of Scientific Research and Development.[12]

Commanders in the Pacific proved equally receptive to the new munition. On July 17, a navy officer visited recently conquered Saipan and showed a film of napalm firebombs to troops about to invade nearby

Tinian. "Enthusiasm for this new weapon was instantaneous," reported an official chronicler. Senior officers radioed an immediate request for almost four tons of napalm to Admiral Chester Nimitz, the commander in chief of all American forces in the Central Pacific. A few days later, a second navy officer arrived with some sample powder—but the wrong recipe. The simplicity of Fieser's invention stood the troops in good stead. "We tried using Jap aviation gasoline, but that gave too much fire effect. Then we tried Jap motor gas and oil, with the napalm powder, and it was quite successful," wrote a squadron commander. Ultimately, the men produced enough to fill ninety-one fuel tank bombs. Results at Tinian made believers of observers. "The first morning they put it down, I went up to the front line and those planes came in over our heads it seemed to me like about a hundred feet in the air. . . . [They] let go their napalm bombs right over our heads . . . maybe two or three hundred yards in front of us. It was a very devastating thing and particularly to the morale of the Japanese," recalled an invasion commander.[13]

By 1945, thousands of napalm bombs had exploded millions of gallons of the gel on Japanese troops from the South Pacific to the Philippines and Okinawa. In an assault on the strategic Ipo Dam outside Manila in May 1945, for example, hundreds of airplanes placed 50,000 gallons on defenders on one day, then returned the next with another 62,500 gallons. An observer described the attack: "200 to 250 5th AF fighters came in low, wave after wave, four to eight abreast . . . with each successive wave dropping its bombs on the near side of the bursts from the wave that preceded it. The fighter-bombers followed each other at 10- to 15-second intervals. A-20's then came in, showering the area with parafrags and winding up with a thorough strafing."[14]

Flamethrowers provided pinpoint delivery. Their precision proved invaluable against Japanese opponents who took refuge in caves and refused to surrender. "No weapon proved so effective against this type of target as the flamethrower," the chief engineer of the army's Maryland chemical center reported of such suicidal opponents. Portable flamethrowers allocated to each army division in the Pacific increased from 141 in June 1944 to 243 in February 1945.

European use of flamethrowers—limited, in contrast to Pacific islands, by terrain that favored a war of movement and defenders who frequently retreated when pressed—was sparing in comparison. Warm tropical climates, which made napalm relatively easier to ignite than in cooler latitudes, once engineers developed reliable lighting mechanisms, may have helped their relative popularity. Army administrators ultimately sent 4,769 portable flamethrowers to the Pacific—which shot over 1 million gallons of napalm—and 3,100 to Europe.[15]

Tanks proved a particularly devastating delivery system. Development of an American machine later nicknamed "Satan" started late in the war as awareness of napalm's qualities spread through the armed services. In Europe, U.S. troops relied on British and Canadian flame mountings that shot a variety of fuels up to 200 yards. These could be highly effective. In one spectacular assault reminiscent of an attack by fire-breathing dragons, a U.S. battalion led by a pair of Sherman tanks fitted with British "crocodile" flamethrowers captured a sixteenth-century citadel at Jülich, Germany. Attackers blasted napalm across the castle's moat and over the walls to force the defenders underground. They then demolished the main gate, made of steel, with high explosives and poured fire into the courtyard inside. A rearguard fled as U.S. troops entered the burning stronghold. A fortified house encountered on the way to the Rhine suffered a similar fate. "Turning off the road, the flame tank rumbled across the field and drew up close to the house. Here the gunner pointed the nozzle of his flame tank into the windows of the ground floor and sent in cloud after cloud of fire. That was all that was needed," related a Chemical Corps history.[16]

In the Pacific theater, the army, navy, and Marine Corps on Hawaii modified dozens of tanks to shoot napalm, based on a Canadian design. Mechanics completed a demonstration machine on April 15, 1944. It was "unanimously adopted," according to a colonel who helped supervise the project, and rushed to combat troops. A total of twenty-four napalm tanks attacked Saipan in June and July; many dozens more saw action on Iwo Jima and Okinawa. They were "the most important single weapon available to this Division," wrote the commander of the Fifth Marine Division, which sustained the highest casualty rate among U.S. forces on Iwo.[17]

There was no defense once this mythic terror came within range. "Though the laboratories at Edgewood Arsenal tried to develop some kind of defense against flame attack, none was found," U.S. experts wrote. "A hood-type mask was built, capable of withstanding 1,000 degrees Fahrenheit for one minute; a steel sliding door was designed for pillbox apertures; fireproof clothing and water fog and spray extinguishers were tried in the attempt to block the fiery liquid of the flame thrower. These measures, however, could reduce by only a small degree the effectiveness of the flame thrower. The weapon, once it reached its target, was almost invincible." A designer of the weapons concluded, "The only truly effective defense against flamethrowers is to prevent them from getting within range." Japanese troops, who largely lacked tanks, heavy artillery, and airplanes—equipment German soldiers could often summon—proved particularly vulnerable.[18]

This grim reality, combined with the appalling consequence of being burned alive, produced terror. "The Japanese on Tinian, after experiencing several fire bomb attacks, broke from their positions upon the approach of fighter planes with belly tanks and ran in a direction that was at right angles to the flight of the planes," noted an official history. "[W]hen the fires exploded near Japanese positions, the usually stoic occupants seemingly lost all caution and fled into the open, easy targets for other forms of attack," observed an army account of the Battle of Ipo Dam. After napalm attacks at Ipo, wrote an official U.S. history, "Positions in the area which had withstood infantry attacks for almost a week, were taken after only feeble resistance and minimal casualties."[19]

Flamethrowers had a similar effect. Infantry who assaulted a pillbox on Leyte Island in the Philippines with napalm and a bazooka found that "badly burned and demoralized Japanese offered little resistance." Napalm was "a very important factor in overcoming the enemy's inherent will to resist," troops reported of Japanese opponents. An anecdote from the 1944 campaign against the Siegfried Line in Germany, a heavily fortified defensive system, echoed these findings: "The fight over, Private Hansen casually sprayed the embrasures of the pillbox again in order to empty his flame thrower and reduce its weight. Smoke began to seep from the embrasures, and small arms ammunition to explode inside the pillbox. A moment later ten Germans pushed open the door to surrender."[20]

Incendiary war's brutality, which was the flip side of its effectiveness, elicited frequent comment. Robert Sherer, a veteran of the U.S. campaign on Okinawa, described one 1945 engagement: "The tank moved up to shoot streams of napalm into the cave. . . . Japanese soldiers who ran from the furnace were squirted with napalm—which, however, failed to ignite. One of the tankers saw to that with a tracer bullet, turning a fleeing man into a torch—which prompted a throaty cheer from the platoon. . . . [W]e cheered that incredibly horrible sight, the burning of another human. Whatever the justification, we'd become savages too."[21]

In total in World War II, U.S. forces dropped around 37,000 of the improvised fuel tank firebombs bearing millions of pounds of napalm. Of these, about two-thirds fell in the Pacific and the rest in Europe—an enormous preponderance for the eastern theatre given its significantly smaller scale than the war in Europe (Allied planes dropped 656,400 tons of bombs in the Pacific War, compared to 2.7 million tons of bombs in Europe).[22]

All of which was just a prelude, from the perspective of napalm's history, for the attacks on Japan that began in earnest in Tokyo late on the night of March 9, 1945.

America followed a strategy it called "precision bombing" for most of World War II. Airplanes attacked in daylight, to improve accuracy, from high altitude, to avoid defenders, and used a bombsight so advanced flyers vowed to protect it with their lives. Roosevelt defined the moral basis for this approach on September 1, 1939, when Germany invaded Poland and the Second World War began. "The ruthless bombing from the air of civilians in unfortified centres of population during the course of the hostilities which have raged in various quarters of the earth in the past few years, which have resulted in the maiming and death of thousands of defenseless women and children, has profoundly shocked the conscience of humanity," the president said. "If resort is had to this sort of inhuman barbarism during the period of tragic conflagration with which the world is now confronted, hundreds of thousands of innocent human beings, who have no responsibility for, and who are not even remotely participating in, the hostilities which have broken out, now will lose their lives," he continued. "I am therefore addressing this urgent appeal to every Government, which may be engaged in hostilities, publicly to affirm its determination that its armed forces shall in no event and under no circumstances undertake bombardment from the air of civilian populations or unfortified cities, upon the understanding that the same rules of warfare will be scrupulously observed by all their opponents," concluded America's commander in chief.[23]

Officers focused on practical justifications for the doctrine. "The nationwide reaction to the stunning discovery that the sources of the country's power to resist and sustain itself, are being relentlessly destroyed, can hardly fail to be decisive," air tactics and strategy director Muir Fairchild wrote in a 1939 strategic review. "It is generally accepted that bombing attacks on civil populace are uneconomical and unwise," and should be considered tactical errors, senior commanders Hap Arnold and Ira Eaker wrote in 1941. "The most economical way of reducing a large city to the point of surrender, of breaking its will to resistance," they added, "is not to drop bombs in its streets, but to destroy the power plants which supply light, the water supply, the sewer lines. . . . Human beings are not priority targets except in certain special situations." In practice, events demonstrated that U.S. bombing was precise relative only to even more indiscriminate forms of attack. As just one example, Hitler's personal Reich Chancellery headquarters—site of his private apartments and the underground *Führerbunker* where he committed suicide—remained standing until the end of the war, despite being specifically targeted by dozens of Allied bombing attacks.[24]

Japanese, German, and British air forces, by contrast, launched indiscriminate "area" attacks against urban centers with explosives and incendiaries, usually at night, from early in the war. British attackers in over 700 airplanes used magnesium incendiary bombs in Operation Gomorrah to incinerate eight square miles of Germany's second-largest city, Hamburg, on the night of July 27, 1943. A man-made fire hurricane, the world's first "firestorm," created a "blizzard of red snowflakes" that raised temperatures in the city to 1,500 degrees Fahrenheit, melted asphalt streets, generated winds of up to 150 miles per hour that blew out doors, smashed windows, and threw people to the ground, and killed an estimated 44,600 people. "One man was observed to fall. He was about to pull himself up with his hands when flames were seen to envelop his back and he was burned within five minutes without changing his position," reported a German doctor. Of shelters examined after the attack, he wrote, "Bodies were frequently found lying in a thick, greasy black mass, which was without a doubt melted fat tissue. . . . All were shrunken so that clothes appeared to be too large. These bodies were *Bombenbrand-schrumpfleichen* ('incendiary-bomb-shrunken bodies'). . . . Many basements contained only bits of ashes and in these cases the number of casualties could only be estimated." Approximately sixty-eight U.S. B-17s contributed two days of strikes against the city's huge shipyards, and a power plant.[25]

Royal Air Force (RAF) magnesium bombs produced a similar inferno in Dresden on Valentine's Day 1945—Ash Wednesday, as it happened. Germany's seventh-largest city was an important rail center and had thousands of workers at militarily significant factories, generally located in suburban areas. It was also a metropolis of extraordinary beauty and global cultural significance filled with refugees from Germany's collapsing eastern front. "Tally-ho!" the first British pilot called into his radio as he started the attack. A firestorm leveled thirteen square miles of the central city targeted by the British, and killed an estimated 25,000 people. Survivor Margaret Freyer recalled, "To my left I suddenly see a woman. I can see her to this day and shall never forget it. She carries a bundle in her arms. It is a baby. She runs, she falls, and the child flies in an arc into the fire." Rescuers confronted a grim scene. Freyer continued, "From some of the debris poked arms, heads, legs and shattered skulls. The static water-tanks were filled up to the top with dead human beings." Refugees who jumped into a firefighting reservoir near the city center discovered too late it had no exit ladder: hundreds clawed at each other until they suffocated or drowned, surrounded by flames. U.S. bombers targeted the central city, railroad yards, and industrial targets with explosives and incendiaries in two daylight attacks, the second a "blind" drop through thick clouds.[26]

Dresden's destruction, late in the war when the outcome seemed clear, prompted criticism of area incendiary bombing not heard at the time of Hamburg's incineration. "It seems to me that the moment has come when the question of bombing of German cities simply for the sake of increasing the terror, though under other pretexts, should be reviewed. . . . I am of the opinion that military objectives must henceforward be more strictly studied," Prime Minister Winston Churchill wrote in a secret staff memo a month later, as criticism of the attack roiled press and Parliament. "I do not personally regard the whole of the remaining cities of Germany as worth the bones of one British Grenadier," responded Air Chief Marshal Arthur Harris, head of the British Bomber Command. Churchill withdrew his comments two days later. In a reformulated note dated April 1, he concluded: "We must see to it that our attacks do no more harm to ourselves in the long run than they do to the enemy's war effort." Britain continued "area" attacks until the end of the war, and against Dresden in particular for two more months.[27]

Its "precision" strategy protected the United States from similar recriminations. In practice, however, bad weather, inaccurate radar systems, and vague targeting directives often made the policy more theoretical than real. "[R]adar bombing was better than no bombing," an official air force history tellingly stated. "Approximately 80 percent of all Eighth Air Force and 70 percent of Fifteenth Air Force missions during the last quarter of 1944 were characterized by some employment of blind-bombing devices," the history continued. "When cloud cover over Germany made precision bombing impossible (nearly half the time) the USAAF conducted area bombing rather than no bombing," summarized historian Thomas Searle. Only slightly more than one-third of all bombs dropped during this period by the U.S. Eighth and Fifteenth Air Forces, responsible for Northern Europe and the Mediterranean, respectively, fell within 1,000 feet of their target.[28]

Nevertheless, American commanders pugnaciously rejected any equivalence between "area" and "precision" bombing. In August 1944, for example, generals refused a British invitation to join a giant area attack on Berlin that could produce 275,000 casualties. Such "baby killing schemes" wrote Charles Cabell, a brigadier general and top advisor to Arnold, "would be a blot on the history of the Air Force and of the U.S. We should strongly resist being sucked in to any such venture. It gives full rein to the baser elements of our people. . . . [N]o man alive . . . can calculate or recognize a crumbling morale." Carl Spaatz, commander of U.S. Air Forces in Europe, agreed: "[T]here is no doubt in my mind that the R.A.F. want very much to have the U.S. Air Forces tarred with the morale bombing aftermath which we feel will be terrific," he wrote to

Arnold.[29] RAF leaders postponed the proposed THUNDERCLAP bombardment.

This argument grew harder to sustain as the war progressed. On January 28, 1945, Spaatz and British commanders announced new target priorities. Oil installations came first; "attack of Berlin, Leipzig, Dresden and associated cities where heavy attack will cause great confusion in civil population from the East" ranked second. On February 3, in a mission envisioned by Spaatz as a "blind" radar-guided attack and intended to "increas[e] existing pandemonium resulting from Soviet advances," according to Arnold's top assistant Laurence Kuter, more than 900 bombers assaulted Berlin. An estimated 25,000 civilians died. On February 22, Operation CLARION dispatched thousands of airplanes from the Eighth, Ninth, and Fifteenth Air Forces, and the RAF, to bomb and strafe transportation objectives and "targets of opportunity" across Germany, Austria, and Italy, including such small cities as Heidelberg, Göttingen, and Baden-Baden. "This is the same old baby killing plan of the get-rich quick psychological boys, dressed up in a new Kimono," Cabell wrote on his copy of the mission plan.[30]

American commanders strove to present their policies to the public as if nothing had changed. When Associated Press journalist Howard Cowan, for example, reported on February 18, 1945, after the Dresden firebombing, that "Allied air bosses have made the long-awaited decision to adopt deliberate terror bombing of the great German population centers as a ruthless expedient to hasten Hitler's doom," according to an RAF briefing officer, U.S. officials denied the assertion. An internal headquarters memorandum issued the day the story appeared, signed by Spaatz on behalf of Army Air Force commanding general Arnold, advised his staff: "(A) there had been no change in policy; (B) the United States Strategic Air Forces had always directed their attacks against military objectives and would continue to do so, and (C) the censor had passed the story erroneously." "Special care should be taken," Spaatz ordered his generals on February 21, with respect to CLARION, "against giving any impression that this operation is aimed, repeat aimed, at civilian populations or intended to terrorize them." Secretary of War Stimson told reporters on February 22, "our policy never has been to inflict terror bombing on civilian populations."[31]

Stimson's claim initially was as true in the Pacific as in Europe. Over time, however, U.S. commanders, frustrated by the inability of "precision" bombing to achieve results in the face of prolonged cloud cover and continuous jet stream winds over Japan; able to attack with increasing ease as Nippon's air defenses crumbled and gasoline shortages grounded its fighters; and fearful of the cost of an invasion, followed the "area" strategy used by the British and Germans. Napalm was their means to this end.

Japan's vulnerability to fire attack was well known to the U.S. military. "These towns are built largely of wood and paper to resist the devastations of earthquakes and form the greatest aerial targets the world has ever seen. . . . Incendiary projectiles would burn the cities to the ground in short order," army general Billy Mitchell, often considered the founding inspiration for the U.S. Air Force, had asserted in 1931. In the event of war, army chief of staff George Marshall told reporters in a secret briefing on November 15, 1941, "we'll fight mercilessly. Flying Fortresses will be dispatched immediately to set the paper cities of Japan on fire. . . . There won't be any hesitation about bombing civilians." A widely circulated 1942 article in *Harper's* magazine concluded, "In some of the slum sections of Kobe and Kyoto where there are no canals the suffering that an incendiary attack would cause is terrible to contemplate. But the fact remains that this is the cheapest possible way to cripple Japan. It would shorten the war by months or even years and reduce American and Allied losses by tens of thousands."[32]

In fact, despite Marshall's prophecy and the suggestion by *Harper's,* the United States initially used "precision" tactics against Japan. Bombing began in June 1944 from bases in China, and expanded in November when marines captured the islands of Saipan, Tinian, and Guam in the Marianas. Initial targets, according to the authoritative postwar United States Strategic Bombing Survey, were "aircraft factories, arsenals, electronics plants, oil refineries, and finished military goods, destruction of which could be expected to weaken the capabilities of the Japanese armed forces to resist at the Kyushu beachheads in November 1945." When massive B-29 Superfortress bombers attacked Tokyo for the first time on November 24, the Musashino aircraft plant was their primary objective.[33]

Japanese defenders attempted to resist but were overwhelmed as the war continued. Antiaircraft batteries protected major cities but proved less effective than comparable defenses in Germany. Fighters swarmed early in the conflict, but lack of fuel grounded many as time passed. As early as March 1945, pilots attempted the desperate expedient of kamikaze ramming. "[A] lone, laggard B-29 was dived on by a swarm of fighters. Suddenly, there was an explosion: a fighter had rammed the giant bomber's left wing head-on. The small plane, linked to its victim by a ribbon of white smoke, zigzagged down and crashed in the city; the big, flaming American bird lost altitude, made a few desperate tries to rise again, then suddenly heeled over and went down, probably in Tokyo Bay," French journalist Robert Guillain, who witnessed the end of the war in Tokyo, reported. Even this was insufficient to turn the tide of battle.[34]

Wind and clouds proved a far greater problem for the United States. "Over in [Europe] we hadn't known anything about jet streams, but now for the first time we ran into that ferocious jet stream of the Pacific. High winds, sometimes at two hundred m.p.h. You could go on forever, trying to get up to a target in such a wind. And if you went cross-wind, your bombsight wouldn't take care of the drift you had. If you came in down-wind, you didn't have time to get a proper run on the target. This was really a tough proposition to lick," wrote air force general Curtis LeMay, who directed the final attacks against Japan in 1945. Jet stream winds "scattered our bombs like confetti over the terrain," said the lead pilot of the November 24 attack. It failed.[35]

Worse than the wind, dense winter clouds shrouded the home islands three-quarters of the time. "When I spoke of seven days a month for bombing visually in Japan, that was a complete max. The average might have been three or four days a month," LeMay wrote after the war.

New B-29 bombers, deployed only in the Pacific, proved temperamental, especially under the strain of near-continuous high-altitude operations conducted over great distances. "B-29s had as many bugs as the entomological department of the Smithsonian Institution. Fast as they got the bugs licked, new ones crawled out from under the cowling," LeMay recalled. "There are something like 55,000 parts in a B-29; and frequently it seemed that maybe 50,000 of them were all going wrong at once."[36]

Napalm offered a solution. In the summer of 1944, the joint chiefs reconvened an "Incendiary Subcommittee" of fire experts, technologists, intelligence analysts, and service representatives to review the prospects for area incendiary bombing. In September, and again in later months, the group reiterated previous conclusions: Japan's cities were enormously vulnerable to fire.[37]

Napalm's effectiveness was by then well known. Its ability to incinerate a large city, however, had not been tested. At the end of 1944, Claire Chennault of "Flying Tigers" fame convinced U.S. commander for China Albert Wedemeyer to act against Hankow—modern Wuhan—a river port in the east-central part of the country. On December 18 LeMay, who at the time was responsible for air operations in India and China, sent ninety-four airplanes to attack the city's docks during the day with 511 tons of napalm bombs. Fire, in contrast to explosives, made imprecision unimportant. "Everything was fouled up there . . . people dropped in the wrong sequence, smoke obscured the primary areas, and so on. But that was an incendiary attack, and everything which was hit burned like crazy. And I think there was a vast similarity to the type of construction in Japan," he surmised. Success: Hankow burned, despite the haphazard targeting. America had an answer to the wind and clouds of Japan. Lauris Norstad, deputy chief of air staff at Army Air Force headquarters in Washington, and chief of staff for the Twentieth Air Force—a special unit under Arnold's direct command established to manage B-29 attacks on Japan—suggested a hundred-bomber area flame assault on the key industrial port city of Nagoya as an "urgent requirement" for future planning.[38]

Haywood Hansell, commander of the XXIst Bomber Command in 1944, the main operational unit of the Twentieth Air Force, however, remained committed to "precision" bombing. He had "with great difficulty implanted the principle that our mission is the destruction of primary targets by sustained and determined attacks using precision bombing methods both visual and radar," he protested to Arnold from Saipan. The policy was "beginning to get results" he continued, and he did not want to diverge from it. B-29s continued to aim "precision" attacks with high explosives and incendiary bombs through dense clouds and high winds. On December 22, Hansell ordered an incendiary attack on Nagoya—but targeted a specific Mitsubishi aircraft plant. Results disappointed. Losses mounted.[39]

Finally, on January 3, 1945, Hansell accepted Norstad's "area" proposal. Napalm was the tool he chose for the job. It was the munition's first large-scale use against Japan. Crews loaded ninety-seven B-29s with 237 tons of M-69 clusters and bombed Nagoya during the daytime from high altitude, without a specific target. Determined firefighters limited the blaze that resulted to an inconsequential three acres. Hansell returned to "precision" attacks focused on aircraft factories.[40]

In addition to its strategic implications, lack of bombing results had potentially dire bureaucratic consequences. "The Navy, never a fan of the B-29 program or the Army Air Forces in general, was finally on the verge of pouncing. Wasn't it time, the Admirals were saying, to face reality and turn the B-29s over to the Fleet as a tactical support arm?" wrote Robert Morgan, one of the most experienced and celebrated U.S. bomber pilots, who fought in both Europe and the Pacific.[41]

On January 7, Norstad met LeMay in Guam and ordered him to relieve Hansell as head of the XXIst Bomber Command. His message, according to LeMay: "You go ahead and get results with the B-29. If you don't get results, you'll be fired. If you don't get results, also, there'll never be any Strategic Air Forces of the Pacific. . . . If you don't get results, it will mean eventually a mass amphibious invasion of Japan, to cost probably half a million more American lives." On January 9, seventy-two B-29s armed with explosives failed for a fifth time to destroy the Musashino plant in Tokyo. America lost six airplanes; the Japanese, one warehouse. LeMay assumed command of air bombardment operations against Japan on January 19.[42]

The man who took the United States into a new era of war intimidated even those on his own side. "With his jowly, scowling face, his thick dark hair, and smoldering gaze, he gave many the impression that running a bombing campaign wasn't quite stimulating enough for him, that he wouldn't mind taking apart a few Quonset huts with his bare hands. His speaking style— barely audible sentence fragments murmured through clenched teeth— reinforced his aura as a borderline sociopath," Morgan recalled.[43]

America's new Pacific air commander was practical. His upbringing, like his bombing, drew a line between friends and adversaries, and while it acknowledged sympathy in the abstract allowed it no operational role. Curtis Emerson LeMay, oldest of seven children, was born in 1906 in a cottage in Columbus, Ohio—seven years after Louis Fieser was delivered in the same city. His father worked odd jobs—railroad worker in Ohio, and manager of a Montana fish hatchery, among other positions—and moved the family frequently. "Usually we had enough to eat," LeMay wrote in his memoir. A lesson from his early childhood: "It doesn't do any good to fake a thing, to fake an ill or a benefit. We have to face the facts the way they are, not the way we wish they were. . . . A clear concise awareness of the exact condition, the exact problem which faces an individual, is his best weapon for coping with it." In 1915, at age eight, he visited the Panama-Pacific Exhibition International Exposition in San Francisco and watched the stunt pilot Lincoln Beachy, famous for bombing the University of California at Berkeley stadium with a football while dressed in Stanford cardinal, and for flying while dressed as a woman. His life's course was set from that moment on, he said: he wanted to fly.[44]

In the meantime, however, the serious, industrious first son hunted sparrows with a BB gun and sold them to an elderly neighbor with a hungry cat at five cents a bird. LeMay purchased newspapers in bulk, resold them to paper boys, and invested the receipts in a bicycle, which he used to get work delivering packages and Western Union telegrams. He tinkered with sports equipment and guns, and filled his own ammunition in his spare time. When he got older, he worked as an ironworker during summer vacations. His mother worked as a housecleaner when the family's money got short.[45]

Ohio State offered a college education. LeMay worked nights, on occasion until 3:00 a.m., at the Buckeye Steel Casting Company to pay his tuition. When he discovered the Reserve Officers' Training Corps, he joined right away—and, after that, the National Guard—to finance his studies and gain an edge for a pilot's commission. "With me it was flying first and being in the Service second," he wrote. In 1928, he was approved as a flying cadet for the still-nascent Army Air Corps.[46]

World War II presented opportunities for leadership and advancement. Major LeMay threw himself into the task. He commanded a squadron of B-17 bombers over Germany, which made him familiar with every element of aerial attack from maintenance to defensive armaments and bomb bay operations. In March 1944, at age thirty-seven, he became the youngest major general in the U.S. Army. In August, he was given command of the XXth Bomber Command of the Twentieth Air Force, which flew B-29s from India over the Himalayas to China for attacks on Japanese targets there and in the southernmost part of Japan.

Conditions in India were difficult. In China, wracked by invasion and a barely suppressed civil war, and at the end of the longest supply line in history, they were even worse. LeMay rose to the challenge. Army crews had obtained 102 operational hours per bomber per month in the United States, and 81 hours per bomber overseas. In China, the young general achieved 92 operational hours per month on average for his Superfortresses.[47]

LeMay, however, did no better than Hansell with "precision" strikes on Japan. On January 23, he sent seventy-three B-29s to attack the same Mitsubishi plant at Nagoya his predecessor had failed to destroy. Only twenty-eight airplanes could find the target because of heavy clouds, and it was hit by no more than four bombs and a few incendiaries. Damage was slight. A strike on Tokyo four days later drew fierce resistance. Morgan remembered, "The Zeros [Japanese fighters] hit us like a rain of meteors. There must have been hundreds of them, swooping in wave after wave for close-encounter attacks. Our losses were the worst of the Pacific campaign to date—nine Superfortresses shot down and many more damaged. The Zeros followed us after we'd left the coast, staying on our tails fifty or sixty miles out over the ocean." By the third week of February, "U.S. pilots had flown more than 2,000 missions over Japan, with no decisive damage to any target," the veteran pilot reported. Pacific Island bomber bases, acquired at the cost of so many marine lives, appeared practically useless.[48]

Headquarters analysts concluded that Hansell's January napalm attack against Nagoya had failed because the bombs were not concentrated enough, and had not been aimed at the most flammable part of the city. On February 3, sixty-nine bombers attempted to focus almost 160 tons of incendiaries, plus several more tons of fragmentation bombs to deter firefighters, on the most combustible area of Japan's sixth-largest city,

Kobe: its residential district. Subsequent photos showed severe damage to both the target area and an adjacent industrial zone. In Washington, Arnold promoted urban-area incendiary attacks to second bombardment priority on February 19, surpassed only by aircraft engine plants. Six days later, 172 B-29s dropped more than 453 tons of napalm and explosives on snow-covered Tokyo. "Three to five seconds after the big firecrackers hit, they go off. An explosive charge violently ejects a sackful of gel which burns intensely," the air force reported in a confidential history. This time, a colossal fire started that burned one square mile of the city and destroyed almost 28,000 buildings. Snowflakes fell black with ash. An approach that worked was at hand. The hour for urban incendiary bombing, a form of warfare that has defined modernity—most recently through "mutually assured destruction" delivered by intercontinental ballistic missiles armed with hydrogen bombs—had arrived for the United States: LeMay and his staff resolved upon a massive napalm area attack against the enemy capital.[49]

To maximize his impact, "The Cigar," as LeMay was nicknamed, decided to attack at night at low altitude. He stripped defensive weapons and crews, except for a single tail gunner, from the Superfortresses to allow them to carry more bombs, and eliminated formations, which took time and fuel to coordinate. Japan's relatively inexperienced pilots—often poorly trained late in the war because of the shortage of gasoline—couldn't fight effectively at night, he gambled, and a surprise attack at an unexpected time might catch them on the ground. He also suspected that antiaircraft guns calibrated for high altitudes couldn't target low-level airplanes. An added benefit of an attack at 5,000 rather than 25,000 feet was that it saved fuel because less climbing was required; reduced engine strain because the air was thicker; and improved radar accuracy. These modifications increased payloads by one-third and allowed the 346 B-29s scheduled for the attack to carry more bombs than 1,000 of the B-17s used against Germany.[50]

Risks abounded in the new strategy. "The prospect gave me a feeling of dread. I remembered the low-level missions that had been tried out in Europe, and the results—whole squadrons of B-17s blown out of the sky," wrote veteran pilot Morgan. "Flak experts, almost to a man, told him he would lose seventy percent of his airplanes over Tokyo if he sent them in at that altitude," recollected XXIst Bomber Command public relations officer St. Clair McKelway: "at five to six thousand feet, the B-29 is a wonderfully big target." LeMay remembered: "I talked to a very few of the boys about this, and studied their reactions. Some of them thought it would be O.K. to revolutionize our whole process and go over Japanese targets at low altitudes. Others said, 'God. That would be slaughter,' and they were fully convinced that it would be." He imagined letters from the mothers of dead pilots. "The mother writes you a letter, and she says: 'Dear General. This is the anniversary of my son Nicky being killed over Tokyo. You killed him, General. I just want to remind you of it. I'm going to send you a letter each year on the same date, the anniversary of his death, to remind you.' "[51]

War orders explicitly envisioned civilian casualties: "Employment at scores of war plants throughout Tokyo and environs would be directly affected by casualties, movement of workers out of the area, use of manpower in reconstruction, and probably lowered worker morale," stated the target information sheet distributed to bomber crews. Japan's general mobilization to resist the expected U.S. invasion, which included women and children, and a theory that the enemy's industrial system relied on widely dispersed home manufacturing operations—judged incorrect by the postwar Strategic Bombing Survey—justified the plan for some. But it staggered even veterans. "The epicenter of this area was . . . an 11.8-square-mile melange of factories, houses, and shops," Morgan wrote. "If we succeeded, the devastation would beggar anything that had gone before. In human terms, the prospects were nearly unthinkable. Civilians were going to die on this run, die by the tens of thousands. Worse, they were going to be roasted en masse." As RAF air chief marshal Arthur Harris, commander in chief of British bombers from 1942–1945, later observed, "[A]lthough they had rigidly adhered to the theory, if not always to the practice, of precision bombing of factories in Europe, they used against Japan exactly the same method of devastating large industrial cities by incendiary bombs as was used in Europe by Bomber Command."[52]

LeMay welcomed the arrival of a more absolutist form of combat. "The whole purpose of strategic warfare is to destroy the enemy's potential to wage war. . . . If we didn't obliterate it, we would dwell subservient to it," he wrote. "I think now of that elderly wheeze about the stupid man who was not basically cruel—he was just well-meaning. The guy who cut off the dog's tail an inch at a time so that it wouldn't hurt so much," he joked. Less theoretically, he endorsed Harris's unforgiving assessment of the relative value of lives across battle lines: "[T]o worry about the *morality* of what we were doing—Nuts. A soldier has to fight. We fought. If we accomplished the job in any given battle without exterminating too many of our own folks, we considered that we'd had a pretty good day." Smoking a cigar and waiting for results in the operations control room at 2:00 a.m. on March 10, LeMay, speaking of Japan's generals, told McKelway, "I don't think he can keep his cities from being burned down—wiped right off the map."[53]

Organizational politics, however, was an area that did admit nuance. LeMay did not seek Arnold's advance approval for his radical shift in strategy. The reason, he said, was to protect his commander in case the mission failed. "[I]f I didn't tell him, and it's all a failure, and I don't produce any results, then he can fire me," he explained. "I made the decision. I weighed the odds. I knew the odds were in my favor. But still, it was something new. I could have lost a lot of people, appeared to be an idiot," he wrote. Nonetheless, the attack was hardly a secret: Twentieth Air Force chief of staff Norstad was on Guam when the bombers took off. It "may be an outstanding show," he cabled public relations staff in Washington.[54]

# 5

## The American Century

A windstorm ripped the skies over Tokyo on the night of March 9, 1945. Gusts of sixty miles per hour roared through narrow streets and over wooden houses that sheltered the city's millions. Blasts rose to eighty miles per hour as midnight approached.[1]

Far at sea, sentries on Japanese navy ships heard the roar of hundreds of U.S. bombers as they flew north at low altitudes. Radar stations on the Bonin Islands, 600 miles south of Tokyo, also detected the attackers. Warnings flashed, but it was unclear exactly where the airplanes were going. It was not until just after midnight that sentries on tiny islands near the capital heard the thunder of propellers and radioed "Major air raid on Tokyo."[2]

Pathfinder bombers reached the city minutes later, flying at about 5,000 feet: low enough to see individual buildings, parks, and streets. Searchlights flared, antiaircraft guns on ships in the harbor and land batteries boomed, and a few dozen fighters scrambled. Too late. The Pathfinders dropped hundred-pound M-47 bombs painted gray-blue and banded in purple to indicate their incendiary payloads—twins of the shells tested in Boston three years earlier—and burned a flaming cross about four miles by three into the heart of the city. "[W]ithin this target area of approximately 10 square miles, the average population

density is 103,000 people per square mile, an average probably not exceeded in any other modern industrial city in the world," reported crew
information sheets. Manhattan's Lower East Side immigrant neighborhood, by comparison, had a peak density of 106,240 people per square
mile in 1910. Commanding general Thomas Power steered his bomber
to 10,000 feet and circled as a "Master of Ceremonies" for Operation
MEETINGHOUSE, following a British technique developed in night
attacks on German metropolises.[3]

Silver bombers followed in a line that stretched for hundreds of miles
back over the sea. French journalist Robert Guillain wrote of the Superfortresses, "Their long, glinting wings, sharp as blades, could be seen
through the oblique columns of smoke rising from the city, suddenly reflecting the fire from the furnace below, black silhouettes gliding through
the fiery sky to reappear further on, shining golden against the dark roof
of heaven or glittering blue, like meteors, in the searchlight beams spraying the vault from horizon to horizon." As they passed, around 6,500
clusters of Standard Oil's M-69 bombs dropped from their bellies, burst
as they fell, and scattered around a quarter of a million individual "Molotov flower baskets," as the Japanese called them. Bright green forty-inch
streamers unfurled to point the bombs down headfirst. They smashed
through roofs to spatter blazing napalm and belch thick clouds of white
phosphorus. "[C]ylinders scattered a kind of flaming dew that skittered
along the roofs, setting fire to everything it splashed and spreading a
wash of dancing flames everywhere," Guillain recounted. About
690,000 pounds of napalm fell in less than an hour.[4]

Winds whipped and combined tens of thousands of fires. In less than
fifteen minutes, the flames began to coalesce in a rare event: a man-made
fire hurricane, or firestorm. A supernatural open chimney of flames and
smoke rose 18,000 feet over the city. Gale-force winds surged at ground
level as the flames and heat pulled oxygen up the column. Tokyo "caught
fire like a forest of pine trees" wrote U.S. observers, perched high above.
"The meager defenses of those thousands of amateur firemen—feeble
jets of hand-pumped water, wet mats and sand to be thrown on the bombs
when one could get close enough to their terrible heat—were completely
inadequate. Roofs collapsed under the bombs' impact and within minutes the frail houses of wood and paper were aflame, lighted from the

inside like paper lanterns," Guillain continued. "True there is no room for emotions in war," Power recalled later, "but the destruction I witnessed that night over Tokyo was so overwhelming that it left a tremendous and lasting impression on me."[5]

Survivor reports collected later by journalist Edwin Hoyt offer a vivid record of the night. Sumiko Morikawa was a twenty-four-year-old homemaker with a four-year-old son and twin eight-month-old girls. Her husband was posted somewhere in Japan. As the fires began, a neighbor helped them flee to a park. "Atsuko, Ryoko, have patience," she told the twins. "Kiichi, Mother will hold onto your hand and run," she said to her son. Houses and trees burned around them as they fled. In the park, they rushed to a pool. Sumiko ladled water onto the backs of the children. "It's hot!" shrieked Kiichi. His jacket and cotton air raid hood were burning. She doused them and huddled in the water with her children. The inferno drew closer. Flames poured from the windows of nearby buildings. People jammed into the pool, and filled the area around it. Fire and smoke grew still closer, thicker, and hotter. A ball of flames hit Kiichi in the head. "Mother, it's hot!" he screamed. She ladled water frantically. "Mother, it's hot!" Kiichi repeated, and closed his eyes. "Hang on, hang on. Don't go to sleep. We can see Father very soon," she implored. She tapped him frantically on the cheek. But he only rolled his eyes, then slumped over. The twins were dead. "Kiichi, Kiichi, don't leave me alone," she begged, and fainted. When she came to and looked around, the pool was dry. Kiichi was still breathing, but faintly. He shivered. She cradled him in her arms and walked to the side of the pool. Crying hysterically, she asked for forgiveness from her daughters, and covered them with her damp jacket. A friend's house was clogged with refugees, but they found a quilt for her. She wrapped Kiichi in it. A girl gave her a cup of hot tea. Sumiko took some in her mouth, cooled it and then, like a bird, trickled it into his mouth. Kiichi opened his eyes a little and said "Mama," then slumped over, dead.[6]

Toshiko Higashikawa was twelve and the oldest of five children. She had just returned to Tokyo to prepare for high school after eight months as an evacuee in the countryside. When the bombing began, her mother dressed the children in baggy trousers and air raid hoods and sent them to a shelter in the garden. These were usually shallow pits covered with bamboo rods and a thin layer of earth. As the napalm bombs fell and the buildings around them began to burn, her father decided they should head to a nearby school in the hope that the building would provide shelter. "We hurried through the streets, joining the fleeing crowd. Buildings were burning everywhere. . . . It was very scary and the hot wind from the fires burned our faces. . . . We could see the bombs coming out of the planes; sometimes they exploded in the street in front of us. There was fire everywhere," she remembered. "I saw one person caught by the claws of the fire dragon. . . . Her clothes just went up in flames. Another two people were caught, and burned up. The bombers just kept coming. Father was carrying my little brother and had my sister by the hand. We came to the school." It was hardly an improvement. "In the school's entryway waves of people, one after another, pushed and shoved. . . . No one could move, they were so tightly jammed in. Panic had developed." She could hear people shouting: "Gya. Help! It's hot! Mama! Uwa!" "Daddy! It hurts! Help!" Her hand fell off her father's backpack. Then, disaster: "Father's face got lost in the crowd." Her sister Utako and she "were drowning in the wave of people. Up above the fire was so bad you couldn't breathe. I don't know how long this went on. I felt faint." She heard her sister say, "Older sister. Ne chan," but could not see her. "Here! Here!" Utako cried. Toshiko thought, "I can't crawl out of here. I am resigned, my eyes are closing." Then, "I will try one more time to crawl out of here. . . . Ah! I have escaped!" "Ne chan," Utako called from under a mountain of bodies, "I am over here!" Toshiko reached her little sister, and rescued her.

They made their way through the burning city to an evacuation center. There, incredibly, the girls found their mother and third sister. Toshiko continued, "Mother and Sister Kazuyo were talking. Sister Kazuyo said, '[Baby] Katsubo is dead because of me. I am finished.' She said, 'Katsubo was screaming on my back when we were running away, but I couldn't do anything for him.' " Their mother said, "Kazuyo, you didn't kill Katsubo, don't feel guilty." Katsubo, who was just one year and seven months old, was dead. He lived a very short life, Toshiko reflected. Their father and brother also perished.[7]

No one was spared. Seizo Hashimoto was thirteen years old. He saw a woman, dressed in a red kimono with gold and silver threads and a gold *obi* sash, with a red lotus blossom in her hair, perhaps a geisha, seized by the firestorm, whipped and twisted in the air, and ignited: a human torch. A piece of her kimono swirled through the air and dropped at his feet. "In the dense smoke, where the wind was so hot it seared the lungs, people struggled, then burst into flames where they stood. The fiery air was blown down toward the ground and it was often the refugees' feet that began burning first: the men's puttees and the women's trousers caught fire and ignited the rest of their clothing," recounted Guillain. A neighbor of Chiyoko Sakamoto was in the last stages of pregnancy: "As they felt the fire the wife had gone into labor. Halfway through the birth process she began to die. She was terribly burned and crying out in a loud delirious voice before she died. The child was born filthy and burned in the face but alive; the father swept it up in an overcoat, clutched it to him, and saved it."[8]

Jammed bridges became funeral pyres. Civil guard commander Kinosuke Wakabayashi and his daughter, shielded by a concrete warehouse, saw thousands "streaming toward the Sumida River bridges, and leaping into the river, clothes and even their bodies aflame. Soon both banks of the river were clogged with bodies. The bridges were so hot that anyone who touched a bit of iron or steel was seared like bacon on a grill." On the Kototoi Bridge, another recalled, "The steel grew white-hot and people who touched the metal were seared like steaks on a barbeque."[9]

Water proved no friend. Rivers drowned refugees, killed them from hypothermia, or in some cases boiled them alive. "As panic brought ever fresh waves of people pressing into the narrow strips of [open] land, those in front were pushed irresistibly toward the river; whole walls of screaming humanity toppled over and disappeared into the deep water," Guillain reported. Fires sucked oxygen from the air, and suffocated some refugees as they swam. "[I]n some of the smaller canals the water was actually boiling from the intense heat," recounted a U.S. government after-action report. Pools and ponds vaporized.[10]

Some of the first reports about napalm's effects on human beings emerged from the historic night. Hoyt recorded the experience of air raid warden Masatake Obata when a cluster bomb hit about ten feet away: "[O]ne incendiary bomb tore loose from the cluster and was flung at him, exploding in his face. The helmet that was supposed to protect him funneled the force of the explosion directly against his jaw." Obata fell unconscious. Then, "He awoke, not knowing how long he had been out. His feet hurt, and he looked at them. His shoes had burned up and his toes had melted. His arms and hands hurt; they were burned black and he knew he had third-degree burns. His clothing was still burning in spots. He could not use his hands, and so he rolled over and over to put out the flames." Others were luckier. Neighborhood fire prevention officer Hiyoshi Inoue heard an airplane, then "felt something cold drop on his skin. It was not oil but it was oily." He was covered in unignited napalm.[11]

Bomber crews experienced their own terrors. On Guam their mission began at 4:36 p.m. when giant Superfortresses, three stories tall and almost one hundred feet long with a wingspan of 141 feet, began to roll down the runway every forty-five seconds. They kept taking off for almost an hour: fifty-four airplanes in total. As skies darkened, they met a second group of 121 airplanes from the U.S. base on Tinian. Finally, both groups lined up with 162 B-29s from Saipan to create a glimmering chain that headed north toward the imperial capital 1,500 miles away. Flyers saw orange flashes from fighting on Iwo Jima as they passed the island, and tuned in to a Japanese station that broadcast Western music when they approached Tokyo. "Smoke Gets in Your Eyes" followed by "My Old Flame" and "I Don't Want to Set the World on Fire," prompted nervous snickers from one crew.[12]

Ace pilot Robert Morgan described an inferno when his B-29 arrived over Tokyo: "Other B-29s around us were outlines in orange from the great groundfires. Hundreds of searchlights swept madly across the skies, the beams mostly eaten up by smoke, like some hellish Hollywood premiere night down there. . . . Debris, great jagged shapes of burning things, floated upward toward us along with the smoke. The smoke must have reached five miles into the stratosphere before it thinned out." A vast metropolis was prostrate: "Most of the Japanese Zeroes and Ginga fighters still sat, some of them melted, on their airstrips. Of those that had managed to get into the air, the thermal windstorms whipped up by the fires tossed them about the skies like helpless kites. As for the ground artillery fire, it was mostly inconsequential. . . . The guns were calibrated for the wrong altitudes." Thus, "We were bombing with damn near impunity."[13]

Updrafts flipped some of the giant airplanes, and bounced others up a third of a mile in seconds. "The updrafts brought with them a sickening odor, an odor that I will never be able to get completely out of my nostrils—the smell of roasting human flesh. I later learned that some pilots and crewmen gagged and vomited in reaction to this stench, and that a few had passed out," Morgan wrote.[14] Chester Marshall, another attack participant, confirmed that "At 5,000 feet you could smell the flesh burning. I couldn't eat anything for two or three days. You know it was nauseating, really. We just said 'What is that I smell?' And it's a kind of a sweet smell, and somebody said, 'Well that's flesh burning, had to be.' "[15]

Morgan saw the same scenes on the bridges from above as Japanese described below. "On a bridge spanning the Kokotoi River, a mob fleeing in one direction collided with a mob headed toward them. . . . Seven tons of fresh firebombs incinerated the whole vast horde," he wrote. "It was claimed, in later years, that screams could be heard aboard some of the B-29s trailing in at 7,000 feet," the veteran continued. Paint on airplane belly bomb bays blistered. Light from the flames was so bright it approached daylight, and pilots almost four miles in the air could read their watches. Tail gunners saw a red glow from the burning city 150 miles away on the flight home.[16]

Aircraft returned just after dawn. Of the 325 airplanes that started the mission, 279 made it to Tokyo. America lost fourteen, most from equipment failures. The balance returned to their bases. Enemy fighters did not shoot down any.[17]

Damage was apocalyptic. A total of fifteen square miles at the center of one of the world's largest cities lay in ashes, an area almost four times larger than that later destroyed by the first atomic bomb. Official tabulations recorded 87,793 people dead from the firestorm, 40,918 injured, over 1 million homeless in cold weather, 267,171 buildings wrecked, and 18 percent of Tokyo's industrial area and almost two-thirds of its commercial district destroyed. Tokyo's Fire Department estimated 97,000 killed, the Police 124,711 deaths. It took survivors twenty-five days to remove the dead from the rubble. If each word in this volume is imagined as a person, the book is roughly filled with dead from that night at Tokyo.[18]

Dr. Shigenori Kubota, a professor of medicine at the Imperial Army School of Medicine and director of Army Rescue Unit 1, responsible for all of Tokyo except the Imperial Palace, described his travels in freezing temperatures through the devastated area just before dawn on March 10: "There was no one to rescue. If you touched one of the roasted bodies, the flesh would crumble in your hand. Humanity was reduced to its chemical properties, turned into carbon." At the Sumida River, he recalled, "Burned bodies and logs blackened the surface of the river as far as the eye could see. . . . The bodies were nude, their clothes having been burned away, so there was no way to tell men from women and even children." As with later atomic attacks, diseases that resulted from the bombs ravaged survivors. Pneumonia, in particular, afflicted those with lung injuries caused by inhalation of smoke and superheated air. Radio Tokyo called the raid "slaughter bombing" and compared LeMay to the Roman emperor Nero.[19]

Guard commander Wakabayashi and his daughter walked home through ashes in the morning. When they got to the street where their house had stood, they saw only charred ruins. His daughter spotted her teddy bear lying face down, covered with charcoal, in a wasteland that had been her bedroom. She picked him up, and burst into tears: one paw was burned off.[20]

In Washington, General Arnold applauded. "Congratulations. This mission shows your crews have the guts for anything," he cabled LeMay. It was "the greatest single disaster incurred by an enemy in military history. . . . There were more casualties than in any other military action in the history of the world," concluded mission commander Power. "It is the most devastating raid in the history of aerial warfare," LeMay wrote in his diary. They knew their business: March 9 at Tokyo remains the single deadliest night in war's long history. Napalm's power was established.[21]

Initial public reports described devastation without death: there was no mention of casualties, only property damage. "More than 1,000 tons of incendiary bombs fell on the city's center in this all-out incendiary attack, and these rushed down on a section where the density of population is 100,000 to the square mile and where heavy industrial sections, residential neighborhoods, and wholesale and retail districts adjoin," *New*

*York Times* reporter Bruce Rae wrote on March 10. "CITY'S HEART GONE; Not a Building Is Left Intact in 15 Square Miles. Photos Show A MILLION HOMELESS," the newspaper headlined the next day. "Imagine Manhattan from Washington Square northward to Sixtieth Street plus the Borough Hall, Bay Ridge, Greenpoint, Williamsburg and Fulton Street sections of Brooklyn, add Long Island City and Astoria and Staten Island burned out so not a rooftop is visible and the picture becomes clearer of the area laid waste by the American bombers yesterday morning," explained correspondent Warren Moscow. Japan's government simply stated that all fires were out by 8:00 a.m. on the 10th.[22]

It took until May 30 for a complete picture of napalm's power to be revealed. On March 16, Japanese radio admitted that thousands of people had been burned alive in Tokyo, Nagoya, and Osaka. A week later, the empire reported immense damage to residential areas. "Domestic Broadcasts Reveal Refugees in Millions," read U.S. headlines. Finally, at a press briefing more than two months after his first great napalm attack, LeMay offered photographic proof: fifty-one square miles of Tokyo had been annihilated. "Approximately 4,500,000 of Tokyo's 7,000,000 people," once lived in the area, recounted reporter Moscow, "None of them could be living in that area now if the pictures tell the story. . . . [I]t is possible that 1,000,000, or maybe even twice that number of the Emperor's subjects, perished." America lost fifty-one planes in the twelve-week incendiary campaign.[23]

After Tokyo, American bombers attacked Japan's largest cities with napalm for ten days, beginning just twenty-nine hours after the last plane returned from the capital, until supplies ran out on March 19, 1945. After a three-week pause to restock, incendiary bombardments started again on April 13, and continued until the end of the war. "It would be possible, I thought, to knock out all of Japan's major industrial cities during the next ten nights," LeMay wrote after the March 9 Tokyo firestorm. "I told my wing commanders that I hoped they'd be able to start for Nagoya on the evening of March 10th." A mood of "Now we're in business," spread through the command, wrote public relations officer McKelway.[24]

As ordered, napalm bombs burned out two square miles in the center of Nagoya on March 12. Incendiary gel reduced eight square miles of

Osaka to smoking rubble two days later. In the ten days following March 9, 1,595 B-29 sorties dropped 18.7 million pounds of napalm and explosives on major Japanese cities, and reduced thirty-one square miles in the country's four largest conurbations to cinders. "We put down every M-47 and M-69 and M-76 we had left. Exactly eighteen hundred and fifty-eight tons of scalding chemicals. We couldn't mount another incendiary attack for almost four weeks," LeMay said.[25]

It was "nothing short of wonderful," Lauris Norstad wrote his general on April 3: probably the greatest damage ever "inflicted upon any people in a single eight-day period," he told the Washington press corps. When new napalm arrived, ordnance officers rushed it directly from supply ships to bombers, just as their counterparts had done in Europe. During the five months until the end of the war over 33 million pounds of napalm in about 13 million M-69 bombs, along with napalm in other bomb-shells, explosives, and other incendiaries, laid waste to 106 square miles in Japan's six largest cities, and destroyed or damaged 169 square miles in sixty of its largest metropolises.[26]

"[T]he present stage of development of the air war against Japan presents the AAF for the first time with the opportunity of proving the power of the strategic air arm. . . . [F]or the first time strategic air bombardment faces a situation in which its strength is proportionate to the magnitude of its task," LeMay wrote to Norstad on April 25. As each city ignited, Hollywood special effects engineers who produced pilot training films replaced tiny buildings with miniature ruins. "Our film then would always look exactly the way the target would appear to the crews going in on the next run," recalled voice-over narrator Ronald Reagan. Atom bombs, by comparison, incinerated 4.7 square miles in Hiroshima and 1.45 miles in Nagasaki, the equivalent of damage from 2,100 and 1,200 tons of napalm and explosives respectively, according to the Strategic Bombing Survey.[27]

By the time the war ended, around 42 percent of Japan's urban industrial area had been burned and 330,000 civilians killed. Being burned was the leading cause of death for civilians. Japan's sixty-six largest cities save Kyoto, spared for cultural and political reasons, ceased to exist as military objectives. After the napalm attacks began, about one-quarter of Japan's urban population, an estimated 8.5 million people, fled their homes. Leaflets dropped from the air by U.S. forces listed cities to be destroyed—emphasizing by implication the weakness of air defenses—and encouraged the migration. Tokyo shrank from over 5 million residents on January 1, 1945, to about 2.3 million on August 1.[28]

In addition to their effectiveness, incendiary area attacks proved far safer for U.S. forces than earlier bombardment strategies. Between June 1944 and March 9, 1945, the United States lost about one hundred B-29s, with little to show for the casualties. Napalm raids from March 9 to 19 had a devastating impact and cost America just twenty-four Superfortresses. On the last day of the war, in response to a call by Arnold for "as big a finale as possible," 1,014 aircraft—828 B-29s and 186 fighter escorts—pulverized Tokyo with napalm and explosives without a loss. In all, about half of the bombs dropped in July and August were M-69 shells filled with napalm. Other incendiaries, high explosives, and fragmentation bombs made up the balance. Japanese civil defense countermeasures such as the construction of fire lanes and emergency water reservoirs, and distribution of firefighting equipment to the general population, proved inadequate.[29]

"Fundamentally the thing that brought about the determination to make peace was the prolonged bombing by the B-29s," said former Japanese prime minister prince Fumimaro Konoye. He was not alone in his assessment. "I myself, on the basis of the B-29 raids, felt that the case was hopeless," said Admiral Kantaro Suzuki, who served as prime minister of Japan from April 7 to August 17, 1945, and negotiated the final surrender. U.S. experts agreed. "Japan would have surrendered even if the atomic bombs had not been dropped, even if Russia had not entered the war, and even if no invasion has been planned," wrote the authors of the U.S. Strategic Bombing Survey. "Indeed if the supply of incendiaries at the bases in the Marianas had not run short the 21st Bomber Command might possibly have brought Japan to surrender before the August raids on Hiroshima and Nagasaki," concluded the Office of Scientific Research and Development. "A great many writers recalled that they had thought war was somewhat beautiful and heroic. After the savage air raids, their ideas about war had changed," the Japanese newspaper *Nihon Dokusho Shimbun* reported of a 1956 reader survey about recollections of the war.[30]

U.S. factories produced about 80 million pounds of napalm by the end of the war. "With the exception of the atomic bomb, flame was the most effective weapon employed in Pacific warfare," wrote the chief chemical officer on supreme allied commander Douglas MacArthur's staff. "Filled with jellied gasoline, the AN-M69 incendiary was credited with the highest efficiency of any bomb against Japanese factories and dwellings," Vannevar Bush and James Bryant Conant concluded in a postwar summation. Most dramatically, Harvard's "Anonymous Research Project No. 4" development project, at $5.2 million, was over 5,000 times less costly than the $27 billion bill for the Manhattan Project's two bombs. Measured solely in terms of development expenses per Japanese city incinerated, napalm cost $83,000 per metropolis, compared with $13.5 billion for each atomic cataclysm.[31]

The Bomb got the press, but napalm did the work. Months before the *Enola Gay* departed for Hiroshima, Tokyo, Osaka, and dozens of other Japanese metropolises, along with many thousands of their inhabitants, lay in ashes. Its value proposition was irrefutable. For a relatively small investment, Armageddon greater than that achieved by atomic weapons was available to any country with an air force. Leaders everywhere took note.

# VICTORY

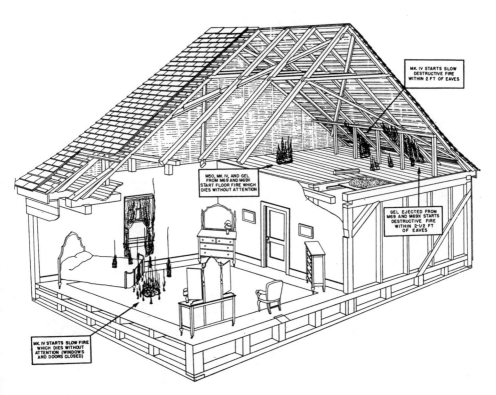

MK. IV STARTS SLOW
DESTRUCTIVE FIRE
WITHIN 2 FT OF EAVES

M50, MK. IV, AND GEL
FROM M69 AND M69X
START FLOOR FIRE WHICH
DIES WITHOUT ATTENTION

GEL EJECTED FROM
M69 AND M69X STARTS
DESTRUCTIVE FIRE
WITHIN 2-1/2 FT
OF EAVES

MK. IV STARTS SLOW FIRE
WHICH DIES WITHOUT
ATTENTION (WINDOWS
AND DOORS CLOSED)

Standard Oil's plan for a central German-style house used for 1942–1943 napalm bomb tests. Focus is on the bedroom and attic. Comments note the performance of various incendiary bomb designs.  *Standard Oil Development Company/National Defense Research Committee*

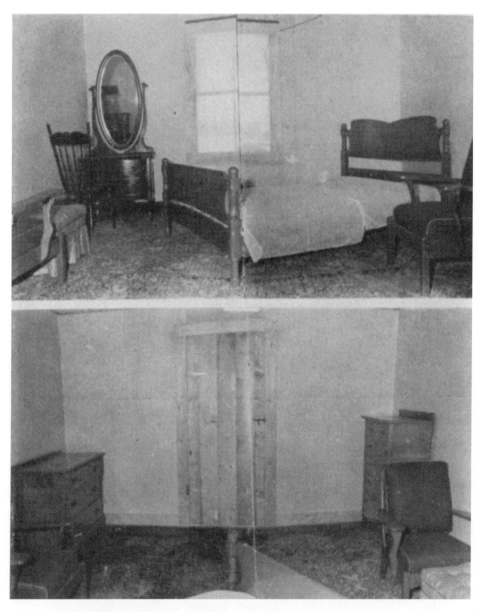

A German-style bedroom furnished for napalm and other incendiary bomb tests by the Factory Mutual Research Corporation in 1942–1943. The top shot shows the view from the door; the bottom the window view. *Factory Mutual Research Corporation/National Defense Research Committee*

Flames pour from the second-story window of a test structure as spectators observe an incendiary bomb test by Standard Oil researchers in 1942–1943.

*Standard Oil Development Company/National Defense Research Committee*

A model Japanese room created for incendiary bomb tests in late 1944 at Edgewood Arsenal, Maryland. Tatami mats, shoji screens, a low table with cushions, a storage chest, and bedding furnish the room. *National Defense Research Committee*

Views of German and Japanese residences in the 1943 incendiary bomb test villages at Dugway Proving Ground, Utah. *Chemical Warfare Service/National Defense Research Committee*

A ten- to eleven-gram Mexican free-tailed bat carries a 17.5 gram napalm time bomb designed in 1943 by Louis Fieser. *Harvard University Archives/HUGFP 20.3 Box 4*

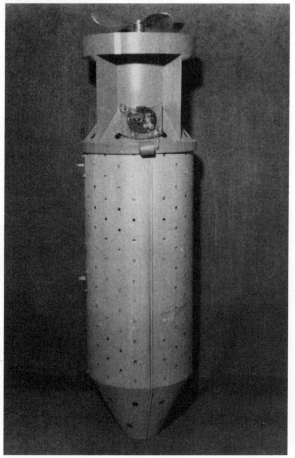

An early bat bombshell with a mechanical opening device. An altimeter switch improved later versions. *U.S. Navy*

"Egg-crate" trays in an opened bat bomb. Each bat, armed with napalm time bombs, dropped from its private compartment onto the roof of the tray below, which became its launching platform. Trays descended by parachute after the casing opened. *U.S. Navy*

Carlsbad Auxiliary Army Air Field, New Mexico, is accidentally destroyed in 1943 by escaped bats armed with napalm time bombs. *U.S. Air Force*

U.S. Marines attack Japanese positions protecting Mount Suribachi on Iwo Jima with flamethrowers on March 4, 1945. *Associated Press/U.S. Marine Corps*

A squadron of B-29 bombers heads toward cloud-covered Japan in 1945. *U.S. Air Force*

Curtis LeMay (with cigar) is briefed by a B-29 navigator about a fire attack on Nagoya, Japan on March 26, 1945. Thomas Power, who led the March 9 bombardment of Tokyo, is second from right. *Bettmann/Corbis*

Tokyo's Nihonbashi District after attacks with napalm and explosives. Concrete buildings are gutted. All other structures have been obliterated. *U.S. Army*

Osaka after napalm and explosives attacks.  *U.S. Army*

Hiroshima after atomic attack. *U.S. Army*

# SOLDIER

On Friday, June 2, 1967, as war loomed in the Middle East, the U.S. Navy spy ship *Liberty,* a grey warship jammed with electronic eavesdropping equipment and armed with four heavy-caliber machine guns on its deck, departed Spain for "Point Alpha." Her destination was a map coordinate in international waters about thirteen miles off the coast of Egypt's Sinai Peninsula, east of the city of el-Arīsh, and near the Egypt-Israel border. Orders from the Joint Chiefs of Staff, who controlled the intelligence vessel from above the normal chain of command, directed it to sail west along the coast toward the Egyptian city of Port Said near the Suez Canal. Listening equipment required the boat to remain close to shore, generally within sight of land. America's Sixth Fleet was prudently stationed more than 300 miles west.

At dawn on Monday, June 5, 1967, Israel locked in combat with Egypt, Jordan, and Syria. By Wednesday, the Jewish state had destroyed the air forces of its opponents and, aided by napalm bombs not least, seized the 60,000 square-kilometer Sinai Peninsula from Egypt, among other victories. Leaders signed a cease-fire on June 10, which gave the Six-Day War its name.

At 6:30 p.m. Washington time on June 7—12:30 a.m. on June 8 in the eastern Mediterranean, Day Four of the war—the Joint Chiefs sent the first of five messages ordering *Liberty* to stay well clear of combat. They were not sent by the highest "Flash" priority since the ship was not deemed to be in any imminent danger, and none arrived in a timely manner. At 8:49 a.m., *Liberty* reached Alpha, and began to cruise slowly west. At 9:30 a.m., an officer spotted a minaret in el-Arīsh, and noted it in the log. Technicians recorded information from nearby battlefields for the National Security Agency.[1]

A U.S. flag hung at the stern of the ship. Call letters stood out in white on its bow. Israeli pilots reconnoitered the vessel eight times between 5:58 a.m. and 12:45 p.m., in one case at masthead height. An initial report identified the ship as a U.S. Navy vessel and, later, specifically the *Liberty*. As the ship moved along the coast, however, subsequent pilots failed to see the flag or misread the call letters, and headquarters staff failed to note the earlier information. Officers judged later sightings to be of a different ship, and marked it unknown.[2]

At 11:24 a.m. explosions rocked areas west of el-Arīsh. By noon, *Liberty*'s captain noted thick black smoke that extended for miles from the city. Israeli Navy commanders, mindful of reports that the area had been shelled from the sea the previous day, determined they were under attack. They ordered torpedo boats to intercept the gray ship visible from the shore, and called for air support. Later investigations determined the reports of sea attacks were mistaken: the explosions originated on land. On the *Liberty*, off-duty Americans sunbathed on deck.[3]

Israeli Air Force pilots and a trio of air traffic controllers explain what happened just after 2:00 p.m., in translations released by the Israeli Air Force. At one minute past the hour, Menachem, the chief controller at Israeli Air Control South, near the Sinai border, radioed his colleagues, "We're sending in Royal," the code name for two French-made napalm-capable Dassault Super Mystère jets. "Kursa," code for a pair of Mirage jets equipped with rockets and machine guns, were already over the ship. "Menachem, if Royal has napalm, it will make things easier," the chief controller for the air force, Lieutenant Colonel Shmuel Kislev, observed just under a minute later from the Kirya, Israel's equivalent of the Pentagon, near Tel Aviv. "Is it permitted to go in?" Royal radioed. "Affirmative, you have permission Royal," Kursa confirmed.

"Sausages, in the middle and up . . . in one pass. Two together. We'll come in from the rear. Watch out for the masts. Don't hit the masts, careful of the masts. I'll come in from her left, you come behind me," Royal One said to his partner at 2:02:32 p.m. Servicemen on the *Liberty* saw the pair of warplanes fly over them, loop around, and then return with the sun at their backs.

"Authorized to sink," said Menachem's colleague Robert at Air Control Central, twenty-five miles south of Tel Aviv. "Menachem, is he blasting her?" Kislev asked. "He's going low with napalm," the chief controller replied. Then, dismay: "You've missed by an undershot," Royal lamented at 2:04 p.m. "I don't know. Number Two hit . . . and now he's strafing," an unidentified Israeli reported three minutes later. "The formation executed two attack runs with napalm, and one napalm bomb struck the ship," concluded an Israeli Defense Force history. In that instant, in a tragedy that to this day demonstrates napalm's power and the unpredictability of war, America suffered a foreign napalm bomb attack for the first time, and Israel, in an hour of need, inflicted a terrible wound on its staunchest ally.[4]

Kursa's napalm splashed over the ship's bridge, which had already been smashed by rockets and machine guns. "The jellied slop burst into furious flame on impact, coating everything, then surged through the fresh rocket holes to burn frantically among the men inside," recalled Officer of the Deck James Ennes. "I watched Captain McGonagle standing alone on the starboard wing of the bridge as the whole world suddenly caught fire. The deck below him, stanchions around him, even the overhead above him burned. The entire superstructure of the ship burst into a wall of flame from the main deck to the open bridge four levels above." He continued, "All burned with the peculiar fury of warfare while Old Shep [McGonagle], seemingly impervious to man-made flame and looking strangely like Satan himself, stepped calmly through the fire to order: 'Fire, fire, starboard side, oh-three level. Sound the fire alarm.'"[5]

"The pilothouse became a hopeless sea of wounded men, swollen fire hoses and discarded equipment. . . . In front of the helmsman a football-sized glob of napalm burned angrily, adding to the smoke and confusion. Smaller napalm globs burned in other parts of the room, refusing to be extinguished," Ennes observed. "My bare chest glowed with a hundred tiny fires as burning rocket fragments and napalm-coated particles fell on me like angry wasps. Desperately I brushed them away. As the tiny flames died, the hot metal continued to sear my chest," he recounted. "Through the fresh rocket holes I could see a tremendous fire raging on deck outside and I could hear the crackle of flames. The motor whaleboat burned furiously from a direct napalm hit while other fires engulfed the weather decks and bulkheads nearby," the officer of the deck remembered. Paint on interior bulkheads blistered from the intense heat of the jellied gasoline outside.[6]

A trio of Israeli torpedo boats approached, and began to signal. A machine gun, or guns, on the U.S. ship shot at the Israeli vessels—accidentally or on purpose is not clear. Disaster followed: the boats launched four torpedoes, one of which blasted a hole thirty-nine feet wide and twenty-four feel tall in the side of the *Liberty*, and strafed it. Nonetheless, the spy ship managed to sail away. A total of thirty-four sailors died and 171 suffered injuries: the deadliest attack on a U.S. warship since World War II.[7]

Israel, as it assessed events, quickly realized a mistake had been made. Its troops offered assistance, and its government provided a formal apology. It ultimately paid reparations to the United States and the families of those it had killed and wounded. America condemned the assault as "an act of military recklessness reflecting wanton disregard for human life."[8]

Napalm had turned upon its creator for the first time.

# 6

## Freedom's Furnace

Incendiary gel was a revelation embraced around the world after World War II. Louis Fieser's devastatingly simple chemistry was so obvious, once demonstrated, that the United States didn't even try to keep it secret. In 1946, the professor and his colleagues published a thorough discussion of their achievement in the journal *Industrial and Engineering Chemistry*. In 1952, as Julius and Ethel Rosenberg sat on death row for passing atomic secrets, the U.S. Patent Office issued certificate 2,606,107 for "Incendiary Gels" and made napalm's precise formula available worldwide.[1]

Governments wealthy enough to control air forces rushed to exploit the marvel. America and its Cold War clients were the greatest initial consumers. European imperial powers, themselves generally U.S. allies, also embraced it. Big nonaligned states made up a third major group of consumers. Napalm has been used in most significant military conflicts since 1945.[2]

Greece was the first country to deploy the gel after World War II. On June 20, 1948, the Royal Hellenic Air Force used napalm provided by the United States against communist positions in the Grammos Mountains. Dwight Griswold, the U.S. mission chief in Athens, was sensitive to potential criticisms. "We must expect propaganda agencies of Communist countries to . . . charge that the use of [the] fire bomb is unethical. . . .

[The] principal propaganda broadside will be directed against the United States, stressing that [the] fire bomb was made in America and used in Greece according to [the] plans of [the] American Army," he wrote. Not so sensitive, however, as to withhold the incendiary. In the event, just fourteen napalm bombs fell, to little effect and less criticism. In 1949, America vastly increased supplies, and on August 2 Operation Torch hurled hundreds of tons of napalm, high explosives, and rockets against rebel redoubts in the Grammos and Vitsi Mountains. This time, rebels took crushing losses: thousands surrendered or retreated north to Albania and other Balkan states, where authorities disarmed them. Victory for Athens. "American observers . . . believed that loss of life and great damage was caused in the rebel installations by the 500-pound bombs and charges of napalm incendiaries," the *New York Times* reported. Napalm had helped to win an early Cold War struggle.[3]

What worked well against thousands in Greece was even more effective against millions in Korea. At dawn on Sunday June 25, 1950, tens of thousands of North Korean troops, backed by numerous tanks and airplanes, crossed the thirty-eighth parallel into South Korea. Southerners had a far smaller force, virtually no tanks or airplanes, and about one-third of their army was on weekend leave. Officials abandoned the southern capital Seoul, thirty-one miles from the border, two days later. United Nations (UN) Security Council delegates—with the Republic of China based on Taiwan representing China, and Russia boycotting to protest the People's Republic of China's exclusion—resolved the same day to provide military assistance to South Korea.[4]

American napalm hit the ground within twenty-four hours of the UN vote. "Braumeister" Richard E. Smith, of Sacramento, California, was one of the few U.S. soldiers in Japan who remembered how to mix the gel. He prepared the first batches, and won himself the nickname "Napalm Smith." Crews loaded jelly into jettisonable fuel tanks, attached grenades as improvised igniters, and dispatched "hell bombs" across the Sea of Japan.[5] American troops followed within forty-eight hours. Fierce communist assaults, however, quickly forced them to join the retreat. Napalm covered their tracks, and protected their flanks. "Planes are taking off as opportunities permit to carry bombs, rockets and tanks of jellied gasoline (napalm) to throw at North Korean armored columns pressing southward against weary United States infantry detachments which have now been hammered by superior invading forces for five straight days," read a July 9, 1950, *Boston Herald* dispatch.

Outgunned ground troops found firebombs especially helpful against tanks. "The planes dive and release belly tanks filled with jellied gasoline both ahead and behind advancing armored vehicles, establishing a pattern not unlike the jig saw puzzle of depth charges which a surface vessel uses to surround a submarine. A direct hit, of course, permanently eliminates a tank. Even a near-miss, if close enough, generates enough heat from the jellied gas to fire a tank's fuel," the *Herald* continued. "With Napalm, it doesn't matter whether you hit the tank or not, so long as your bomb is in the general vicinity," Wes McPheron, an army combat radio reporter recently returned from the front, told a Washington press briefing in October 1950: "All that is necessary is for the spattering jellied gasoline to get on the tank and envelop it in flames. When the fire dies down and the smoke clears away, the black and gutted tank is as dead operationally as the crew aboard it." A pair of 110-gallon napalm tanks, army researchers reported, created a 15,000-square-foot blanket of fire with an "effective" area fifty-yards-square at the center.[6]

UN forces retreated to a perimeter around the southern port of Pusan and defended it against desperate attacks in August and early September. They counterattacked around September 15, 1950, in a breakout that coincided with U.S. Marine Corps amphibious landings 220 miles north at Inchon. Napalm led the charge. Fifth Air Force generals declared September 17 Napalm Day and organized 172 sorties to blanket the entire front line with liquid fire. "Napalm, the No. 1 Weapon in Korea," the *New York Herald Tribune* headlined on October 15. "Napalm had proven the most outstanding single weapon employed in the Korean operations," Earle Townsend, a staffer in the Office of the Chief Chemical Officer, wrote in January 1951. Marines nicknamed the gel "cooking oil."[7]

It was a devastating weapon. BBC correspondent René Cutforth described a typical attack: "[T]he Corsair, with the air of someone who has now finally lost all patience, came screaming in again, circled, slowed . . . and 'tossed,' as it were, negligently, a long, yellow, banana-shaped object over the knife-edge of the ridge." The bomb, he wrote, "fell slowly, turning over and over, and where it landed a dark red flame grew and spread outwards in waves until it covered a great area, Black smoke went up. The sound which came to us later was a sort of lax explosion. 'Floomf,' it said. 'That's napalm,' said the Colonel next to me, 'jellied petrol. It reaches a temperature of more than 1,000 degrees Centigrade in a few seconds. Horrible stuff.'" Skilled pilots placed flames just forty yards ahead of friendly positions. Strikes seemed to bewitch opponents. "Navy and Marine air squadrons blanketed both flanks with napalm, blossoming fires the full length of our six-mile column. That continuous air support finally so demoralized the enemy troops that they just wandered along our flanks in thinly scattered groups, seemingly more concerned with staying clear of the next napalm drop than with massing for an attack," wrote Marine combat historian John Patrick.[8]

On Valentine's Day 1951, napalm's ninth birthday, infantryman Paul Freeman watched strikes called to defend his encircled position. "The entire side or top of a hill would erupt in a big roiling ball of orange flames and thick black smoke," he wrote. Later, he walked the perimeter. "I went down a little draw, and I'll never forget the sight. There were hundreds of burned bodies in it. The snow was burned off the ground and Chinese bodies were lying in heaps, all scorched and burned from our napalm, their legs and arms frozen in grotesque angles. . . . But what I saw in that draw was only the beginning. We found hundreds and hundreds more, caught in draws and ravines where they'd been trying to hide," he said. Soldiers reported screams from burning enemies more than a mile away.[9]

Fear spread among northern forces. "The enemy didn't seem to mind being blown up or shot. However, as soon as we would start dropping thermite or napalm in their vicinity they would immediately scatter and break any forward movement," said the American commander of the first detachment of Mustang fighter-bombers to operate from a Korean airstrip. A pair of episodes from October 1950 are illustrative. In the first, four U.S. airplanes caught several hundred North Korean soldiers on a ridge, and attacked with napalm. Survivors hid in some buildings. As the aircraft returned for a second pass, white flags sprouted from the windows. In the second, two fighter pilots blasted a convoy with rockets and napalm, then headed for a small group of enemy soldiers who had observed the attack from a nearby hilltop. As the planes approached, white flags appeared. "Captured 12 North Korean prisoners while flying at 250 m.p.h. and without firing a shot," the pilots reported. UN troops made radio contact and disarmed the North Koreans.[10]

Ground forces deployed napalm as soon as equipment arrived. Marines landed fifteen "Tiger" flame tanks, emblazoned with images of the predators, at Inchon. They helped recapture Seoul ten days later. Fire had the same effect when shot from the ground as it did when dropped from the air. "After some of these 'Tiger' Tanks ran about 200 North Koreans up a ravine, and annihilated them, the North Koreans regarded these tanks with terror," wrote Gilman Wing, a staff member in the Chief Chemical Officer's Historical Office. "The psychological factor is tremendous," explained a U.S. officer. "One tank went into a valley recently and fired one burst, and at a distance of 1,000 yards all enemy ducked down in their foxholes and stopped firing. This included those way up on the sides of hills where we could not possibly have reached them."[11]

It was equally effective in large cities and small villages. At Seoul on September 22, the *New York Herald Tribune* wrote, "Planes dropped a fresh rain of napalm fire bombs on districts already consumed by yesterday's dropping of bombs." Fire tanks finished the job. "When they entered the streets in that place, it was like a firestorm, shooting napalm into those buildings," recalled U.S. veterans Jerry Ravino and Jack Carty. "The whole city was ablaze. . . . We (M26 Pershing tanks) would hit that building and keep on hitting it, but it wouldn't fall down. That's when we'd call in the Flame Tanks. They would just burn 'em out. They'd put their flames into the bottom floors and pretty soon that whole building was ablaze all the way to the top floor." Resistance ended quickly: "The railroad station was the last to get torched. . . . When the flame tanks started pouring napalm into the station, there was nothing but devastation, and panic . . . the NKPA were on fire, running out of the building."[12]

Portable flamethrowers delivered similarly unambiguous results on a smaller scale. Army historian Wing described the effect of incendiary gel on the mud basements of rural homes: "Ordinary burning had failed to deny the enemy the use of the house cellars because the mud walls would remain standing. The napalm from the flame throwers, however, generated enough heat to crumble the crude mud walls, causing them to collapse and fill the cellars." Flamethrowers scoured a mountainside in John Ford's 1951 navy documentary *This Is Korea* as its narrator intoned "Fry 'em out, burn 'em out, cook 'em." Napalm's efficacy, once again, was unsurpassed.[13]

United Nations troops fought back up the peninsula after the Inchon landings, and had almost reached the Chinese border by October 1950. Americans occupied Pyongyang, the northern capital, at the end of the month. China invaded to support its ally less than a week later, and their troops drove allied forces south. America evacuated Seoul and withdrew from Inchon on January 4, then counterattacked again and recaptured the southern capital. From mid-1951, the war settled into a stalemate.[14]

Napalm proved its worth as a defensive tool during this stage of the struggle. Troops filled large drums, or fougasses, with gel and placed them on explosives that launched them ten to twenty feet into the air. Secondary detonations then threw flames thirty yards in all directions, and silhouetted attackers against the blaze. Chief Chemical Officer E. F. Bullene described the effect at one outpost: "In the flash of exploding shells the whole mass of them could be seen a hundred yards below the line and coming fast. Suddenly geysers of flame erupted across the line, a flame so hot that American soldiers ducked to shield their faces. In just a few seconds, the flames billowed out, merged into a solid wall across the perimeter and engulfed the Reds." A silence, "The shooting halted abruptly, and, moments later when the flames died down, the enemy was gone. Soldiers turned to each other in wonderment." He concluded dryly, "The Chinese do not like to attack a position that has liquid fire."[15]

As impressive as napalm's tactical role was in Korea, however, its main use, as in World War II, was for strategic bombing. Initially, Washington returned to the "precision" strategy it followed before the napalm campaign against Japan. When China intervened, however, and the United States began to lose, generals returned to urban area bombardments.

President Harry Truman's June 1950 orders to his Pacific commanders specified that bombing must be "not indiscriminate." A targeting directive from Washington on June 30 required that attacks in North Korea be

limited to "purely military targets." Allegations of American barbarous-
ness and racism underlined the political value of this approach. In August
1950, for example, an Indian newspaper asserted "Americans and other
western people showed special solicitude toward the European enemy,
but adopted different codes of conduct in Japan and elsewhere in the
East, culminating in the choice of Japanese towns as targets for the first
atom bombs." Secretary of State Dean Acheson made an official request
that General Douglas MacArthur note the complaint.[16]

Air force generals in the Far East, however, pushed to burn cities from
the start of the war. "It was my intention and hope . . . [to] go to work
on burning five major cities in North Korea to the ground, and to destroy completely every one of about 18 major strategic targets," Emmett
"Rosie" O'Donnell, commander of bomber forces in Korea and a deputy
to Curtis LeMay during the attacks on Japan, later testified to Congress.
Warning leaflets, he said, "would take care of the humane aspects of the
problem."[17]

Washington, however, was firm. A plan at the end of September 1950
by MacArthur and Far East Air Forces commanding general George
Stratmeyer to send one hundred B-29s against Pyongyang was rejected
by the Joint Chiefs of Staff. "It is desired that you advise the Joint Chiefs
of Staff, for clearance with higher authority, of any plans you may have
before you order or authorize such an attack or attacks of a similar nature," they wrote. "As a matter of policy, the Joint Chiefs of Staff would
generally disapprove massed air attacks, even against military targets, if
such attacks could possibly be interpreted to be against the civilian
population of North Korea," Air force historian Robert Futrell observed
in an official history. This approach had domestic advantages, as well as
benefits to international relations. As air force chief of staff Hoyt Van-
denberg noted, "if Eighth Army did get clobbered and he was using the
mediums to bomb . . . [a] remote industrial area, it would have been
pretty unfavorable publicity for the Air Corps." In other words, the U.S.
public would object if airplanes on distant missions proved unable to
protect troops on the ground.[18]

Local commanders used their greater discretion over battlefield tactics to implement an absolutist strategy, based on incendiaries, however,
where possible. At a meeting on August 14, 1950, for example, MacArthur

went to his situation map, O'Donnell recalled, laid his hand flat over an area between the Naktong River and the Pusan perimeter, and said "Rosie, I want you to make a wilderness of this area." With ninety-eight B-29s, O'Donnell recalled, "I was supposed to make a wilderness out of 27 square miles, in which no one knew any whereabouts of an enemy, if indeed any enemy forces were there."[19] By the end of October, according to the general, that air mission and every other one was complete: "Just before the Chinese came in we were grounded. There were no more targets in Korea," he told Congress.[20]

China's entry ended the debate. On November 1, American forces traded fire with their World War II collaborators. On November 5, MacArthur ordered the destruction of every city, village, factory, installation, and means of communication, except for certain dams and hydroelectric plants, between the battle line and the border.[21] Shinŭiju, a major transportation center, was the first city to be incinerated. "You are authorized to go ahead with your planned bombing in Korea near the frontier including targets at Shinŭiju," the Joint Chiefs cabled. On November 8, B-29s dropped 85,000 incendiary bombs on the metropolis, "removing it off the map." Napalm hit Hoeryŏng a week later "to burn out the place." By the end of the month "a large part of [the] North West area between Yalu River and southwards to enemy lines . . . is more or less burning," the air force reported. It would soon be "a wilderness of scorched earth," authorities advised, in an echo of MacArthur's earlier order for territory farther south.[22]

Pyongyang was a top objective. After a preliminary attack on December 14, 1950, with explosives and incendiaries, General Matthew Ridgway launched B-29s armed with napalm on January 3 and 5, 1951, "with the goal of burning the city to the ground with incendiary bombs." North Korean state radio said the conurbation "burned like a furnace for two days." About one-third of the municipality was reduced to cinders. As in Japan, the air force used advance Pathfinder airplanes to mark Korean cities to be incinerated, followed by bombers that arrived at five-minute intervals to drop napalm from low levels around 4,000 feet. "Once the fire got going, each bomber added to the conflagration," Futrell explained. In a countervailing setback for the UN, North Korean and Chinese forces captured Seoul for a second time on the same day napalm made its northern counterpart a furnace.[23]

Periodic flame bombardments of the northern capital continued for almost two years. Operation Pressure Pump, an eleven-hour barrage on July 11, 1952, was one of the most remarkable. In a kind of merged area and "precision" approach, General Jacob Smart ordered that "Whenever possible attacks will be scheduled against targets of military significance so situated that their destruction will have a deleterious effect upon the morale of the civilian population actively engaged in the logistic support of the enemy forces." Leaflets warned residents to stay away from military facilities. On the day, American, South Korean, Australian, and British airplanes from airfields and aircraft carriers—virtually every unit available to the Far East command—flew 1,254 sorties and dropped 23,000 gallons of napalm on the capital. Follow-up leaflets reminded civilians of the earlier advice. When it resumed broadcasts two days later, Radio Pyongyang said 1,500 buildings had been leveled and 900 more damaged. After a few more assaults, commanders decided Pyongyang had no more targets worth attacking.[24]

Generals knew what worked. "Practically every U.S. fighter plane that has flown into Korean air carried at least two napalm bombs," chemical officer Townsend wrote in January 1951. About 21,000 gallons of napalm hit Korea every day in 1950. As combat intensified after China's intervention, that number more than tripled. On an "average good day," according to Eighth Army chemical officer Donald Bode, UN pilots dropped 70,000 gallons of napalm: 45,000 from the U.S. Air Force, 10,000–12,000 by its navy, and 4,000–5,000 by marines. Factories in Japan, risen like phoenixes, manufactured $40 plastic bombshells, which held ninety to one hundred gallons of gel, and much of the chemical fillings. Later in the war a pair of converted Korean artificial smoke plants made more. Troops mixed the rest. "It is a simple matter to mix some Napalm powder in with a barrel of gasoline, let it 'brew' for 24 hours, then pour it into a 150-gallon jettisonable fuel tank and head for any target that might present itself," Townsend wrote. A total of 32,357 tons of napalm fell on Korea, about double that dropped on Japan in 1945. Not only did the allies drop more bombs on Korea than in the Pacific theater during World

War II—635,000 tons, versus 503,000 tons—more of what fell was napalm, in both absolute and relative terms.[25]

Biblical devastation resulted. In May 1951, after President Truman relieved him from command, MacArthur testified to Congress that "The war in Korea has already almost destroyed that nation of 20,000,000 people. I have never seen such devastation. I have seen, I guess, as much blood and disaster as any living man, and it just curdled my stomach, the last time I was there. After I looked at that wreckage and those thousands of women and children and everything, I vomited." The former supreme commander continued, "If you go on indefinitely, you are perpetuating a slaughter such as I have never heard of in the history of mankind." War leveled at least half of eighteen of the North's twenty-two major cities. Pyongyang, a city of half a million people before 1950, was said to have had only two buildings left intact. LeMay, who went on to head the Strategic Air Command and became the youngest U.S. four-star general since Ulysses Grant, wrote "We burned down just about every city in North Korea and South Korea *both* . . . we killed off over a million civilian Koreans and drove several million more from their homes, with the inevitable additional tragedies bound to ensue." As O'Donnell, who had advocated early area attacks, told Congress on June 25, 1951, "Oh, yes: we did it all later anyhow . . . I would say that the entire, almost the entire Korean Peninsula is just a terrible mess. Everything is destroyed. There is nothing left standing worthy of the name."[26]

Observers noted napalm's harsh effects. Correspondent Cutforth described his arrival in a town twenty minutes after its capture by the UN in early 1951: "All around them stretched the still smoldering acres of ashes. . . . [A] corpse, bolt upright by some trick of contraction set up by the napalm which had killed him, sat hideously grinning, and smoldering all over." A few days later, a doctor at a British field hospital summoned him to complain about injuries caused by the new weapon. "In front of us a curious figure was standing a little crouched, legs straddled, arms held out from his sides. He had no eyes, and the whole of his body, nearly all of which was visible through the tatters of burned rags, was covered with a hard black crust speckled by yellow pus," the journalist wrote. "He had to stand because he was no longer covered with a skin, but with a crust-like crackling which broke easily." Pilots vomited at the effects of the munition. "Allied aviators reluctantly learned the nauseating lesson of indiscriminate slaughter," recounted a history drawn from official sources. "[W]e killed civilians, friendly civilians, and bombed their homes; fired whole villages with the occupants—women and children and 10 times as many hidden communist soldiers—under showers of napalm, and the pilots came back to their ships stinking of the vomit twisted from their vitals by the shock of what they had to do."[27]

People who survived napalm attacks bore horrified witness. On December 1, 1950, a marine pilot accidentally dropped his bomb in the middle of about one dozen U.S. soldiers surrounded by Chinese troops. Soldier James Ransone reported the results: "Men I knew, marched and fought with, begged me to shoot them. It was terrible. Where the napalm had burned the skin to a crisp, it would be peeled back from the face, arms, legs . . . like fried potato chips. Men begged to be shot. I couldn't." A few weeks later, on January 20, 1951, U.S. planes dropped napalm at the mouth of a cave in an area civilians had been told to evacuate. The cavern, as it happened, sheltered hundreds of refugees, including fifteen-year-old Eom Han-won. "When the napalm hit the entrance, the blast and smoke knocked out kerosene and castor-oil lamps we had in the cave. . . . It was a pitch-black chaos—people shouting for each other, stampeding, choking. Some said we should crawl in deeper, covering our faces with wet cloth. Some said we should rush out through the blaze. Those who were not burned to death suffocated," Eom recalled. The youth dodged machine-gun strafing from the airplanes, and escaped.[28]

In February, *New York Times* correspondent George Barrett described the haunting fate of a small village south of Seoul. "A napalm raid hit the village three or four days ago when Chinese were holding up the advance, and nowhere in the village have they buried the dead because there is nobody left to do so. This correspondent came across one old woman, the only one who seemed to be left alive, dazedly hanging up some clothes in a blackened courtyard filled with the bodies of four members of her family," he wrote, "The inhabitants throughout the village and in the fields were caught and killed and kept the exact postures they held when the napalm struck—a man about to get on his bicycle, fifty boys and girls playing in an orphanage, a housewife strangely un-marked, holding in her hand a page torn from a Sears-Roebuck cata-logue crayoned at Mail Order No. 3,811,294 for a $2.98 'bewitching bed jacket—coral.'" Barrett concluded, "There must be almost two hundred dead in the tiny hamlet."[29]

Such reports sparked some criticism outside the United States. In Britain, where memories of incendiary attacks by Germany during the Blitz remained fresh, members of Parliament (MPs) repeatedly protested civilian casualties from napalm in the spring of 1952. Opponents argued the gel was indiscriminate and cruel. Military forces should not use na-palm in "areas which are predominantly civilian," one MP argued. "It is a weapon which inflicts terrible and indiscriminate loss and suffering," said the archbishop of York, who demanded that it be outlawed. Cold War antagonists joined in, driven by principle, politics, or a combina-tion of both. Napalm "is a monstrous soul-destroying device that puts its user beyond the pale of human society," charged the Far East corre-spondent for the *London Daily Worker*, a publication associated with the USSR.[30]

Washington responded immediately, even though there was no com-parable domestic outcry. Pentagon officials denied that the air force tar-geted civilians, asserted it dropped warning leaflets before area attacks, claimed napalm burns were no different from any others, and maintained that similar weapons had been used since 360 BC. In private, Omar Bradley, general of the army and chairman of the Joint Chiefs of Staff, told the British that their objections "would harm Anglo-American rela-tions" if they continued. He requested permission to issue a statement that confirmed UK support for U.S. napalm attacks. Prime Minister Winston Churchill expressed misgivings, but did not stand in the way of agreement by Britain's commanders. Churchill recorded his medita-tions, if not his actions, in an August 22, 1952, file memorandum: "I do not like this napalm bombing at all. A fearful lot of people must be burned, not by ordinary fire, but by the contents of the bomb. We should make a great mistake to commit ourselves to approval of a very cruel form of warfare affecting the civilian populations." His record for his-tory continued, "Napalm in the war was devised by and used by fighting men in action against tanks and against heavily defended structures. No one ever thought of splashing it about all over the civilian population. I will take no responsibility for it. It is one thing to use napalm in close battle, or from the air in immediate aid of ground troops. It is quite another to torture great masses of people with it." Churchill's World War II memories evidently did not include, at least, the end of the war against Japan. In the end, Bradley never issued the statement.[31]

Napalm's most articulate defender in this period was British airpower theorist and law of war expert J. M. Spaight, former principal assistant secretary of the Air Ministry, festooned with honors and redoubtable at age seventy-six. In February 1953, writing in the impeccably establishment *Journal of the Royal United Services Institute for Defence Studies*, he argued the incendiary was precise rather than indiscriminate, effective in general and especially against objects, and impossible to regulate as matter of practice. "The bomb, it is evident, is not a weapon for strategic use . . . napalm was dropped with extraordinary precision, sometimes only 50 yards ahead of the American troops; it was also dropped on the sides of a hill while marines were all along the road directly beneath," he began. It had come into its own in Korea, he continued: "Napalm was one of the 'discoveries' of the Korean War. It had been used in the fighting in the Pacific in the 1939–45 War, but it was in Korea that its effectiveness as a stopping weapon was fully demonstrated." It fought effectively, in a noble cause. "If it is used to stop an enemy tank which is advancing and perhaps scrunching its way through the helpless wounded lying in its path, the sum of evil involved in its use is not all on one side of the account. . . . But for it the United Nations forces might have been bundled neck and crop out of Korea in 1950–51. That would have been an immeasurable calamity for humanity," he wrote. Moreover, "It is a particularly effective one against matériel; it is not primarily a weapon for use against personnel." Finally, Spaight maintained, its simplicity and low cost made it effectively uncontrollable. "The ingredients of napalm—jellied petrol—are common and universally available substances which could not possibly be controlled in the same way as uranium." Only better weapons, he concluded, would end napalm's reign—as only the long bow ended the utility of armored knights. "New weapons, horrible weapons maybe, will kill the new armour in due season," he concluded. Remarkably, Spaight did not discuss contemporaneous napalm bombardments of Korean cities in his article.[32]

Fighting slowed in Korea in mid-1953, and ended on July 27 with the Panmunjom armistice. As the ink dried, napalm, and the points of debate it inspired, disappeared almost entirely from public discourse.

America's Cold War clients in Asia, Latin America, and the Middle East used napalm frequently between the wars in Korea and Vietnam. U.S. advisors often supplied the gel directly. There do not appear to have been any significant objections. Its cost, always low, seems not to have even merited discussion. Philippine officers requested American napalm as early as November 1949 to use against communist Hukbalahap rebels. State Department officials rejected their petitions on the theory that napalm might create more enemies than it killed. Manila's engineers created a domestic alternative, but U.S. advisors reported it "did not give the desired effect because of inferior burning qualities." Finally, at the end of 1951, with napalm's results in both Greece and Korea an effective counter to diplomatic skepticism, supplies arrived in bulk. Airplanes dropped jelly bombs against guerrilla concentrations and agriculture in rebel areas until the end of the war in 1954.[33]

In Latin America, the first and most extensive use of napalm was in Cuba, where the United States hoped it could help Fulgencio Batista defeat Fidel Castro. On May 24, 1958, fortified with supplies of U.S. napalm, Batista launched Operation Verano, his first and only offensive. It failed. Pilots dropped burning gel on their own troops, as well as rebels, in the desperate retreat that concluded the operation. Castro declared victory seven months later. In 1961, the Central Intelligence Agency ordered napalm strikes to support the landing of its counterrevolutionary émigré army at Playa Girón in the Bay of Pigs on April 17. Individual B-26 bombers armed with machine guns and firebombs failed to have much impact that day, or on the morning of the next, according to invasion historian Howard Jones. The Agency then "stretched the rules of engagement by sending a half-dozen B-26s, two of them piloted by Americans and all under cover of U.S. Navy Combat Air Patrol planes," Jones wrote. Pilots "spotted a seven-mile-long convoy of tanks, trucks and militiamen," he continued. "Two of the planes peeled off in an attack, one hitting the lead vehicle with a rocket and the other destroying the last truck at the end of the line. The convoy immobilized, all six B-26s repeatedly battered the chaotic mass with bombs, rockets, machine guns and napalm, destroying seven tanks and twenty troop-filled trucks while inflicting eighteen hundred casualties and leaving two miles of smoke and fire churning upward." Despite this aid, the invasion collapsed on the afternoon of April 19.[34]

Washington backed at least two napalm strikes in Peru and Bolivia. On September 19, 1965, the Peruvian air force, assisted by U.S. Special Forces, firebombed a suspected communist guerrilla concentration near the Inca ruins of Machu Picchu.[35] Similarly, on March 31, 1967, the Bolivian air force attacked mountain guerrilla retreats with napalm in a campaign that ended with the capture, execution, and amputation of the hands of Argentine physician and revolutionary leader Ernesto "Che" Guevara.[36]

In the Middle East, Israel used napalm several times. In 1956, the new state deployed the gel against Egypt (in conjunction with French forces, and on its own); in 1964, against Syria; in 1967, against Egypt and again against Syria; in 1969, against Lebanon and Egypt; in 1970, in a raid on Egypt; in 1972, again in Lebanon; and in 1973, against Egypt and Syria during the Yom Kippur War. Egypt dropped napalm on Israeli forces in 1973.[37]

Turkey also occasionally used napalm, dropping gel bombs on Cypriot forces backed by NATO ally Greece in 1964, and again in 1974. "The planes fired rockets, cannon, incendiary bombs and napalm— jellied gasoline," Clyde Farnsworth reported for the *New York Times* in August 1964. "Hundreds of non-combatants have been killed in attacks on innocent people. The villages of Pomos and Pyrgos have been reduced to burning ruins, and a mass of humanity is aflame by the use of napalm bombs," asserted Zenon Rossides, the Cyprus representative to the United Nations. In a particularly awkward moment for the United States, a 750-pound napalm bomb manufactured by the American

Stove Company and marked "Property of U.S. Air Force" was recovered by Greek Cypriots. A photograph of the device was published in a 1966 pamphlet produced by the Union of Journalists of the Athens Daily Newspapers titled "Satan Storms Cyprus." In 1974, a Turkish airplane dropped a napalm bomb on three Austrian UN peacekeeping soldiers driving in their car, and burned the men alive.[38]

European air forces, similarly, relied extensively on napalm in the fighting that accompanied the end of colonialism. French forces led the way. On January 16, 1951, the first napalm bombs fell in Vietnam when L. M. Chassin, commander of the French air force in Indochina, used what he called "bombes spéciales" ("special bombs") for a last-ditch defense of the town of Vinh Yen near Hanoi. This largest aerial assault of the war to date was devastating. A rebel Viet Minh officer provided a vivid account: "[A]ll of a sudden, hell opens in front of my eyes. Hell comes in the form of large, egg-shaped containers, dropping from the first plane, followed by other eggs from the second and third plane[s]. Immense sheets of flames, extending over hundreds of meters, it seems, strike terror in the ranks of my soldiers. This is napalm, the fire which falls from the skies." Its effect was almost supernatural: "The bomb falls closely behind us and I feel its fiery breath touching my whole body. The men are now fleeing in all directions and I cannot hold them back. There is no way of holding out under this torrent of fire which flows in all directions and burns everything on its passage." One of the officer's soldiers ran up: "His eyes were wide with terror. 'What is this? The atomic bomb?' 'No, it is napalm.'" The new weapon won the battle for the French. Chassin reported that the enemy subsequently changed its tactics and hid from bombers under the jungle canopy. He recommended, therefore, that the gel be used to burn crops and forest cover rather than cities and the people in them.[39]

France also used napalm in northern Africa. On July 22, 1961, incendiary bombardments helped relieve a besieged military base in Bizerte, Tunisia. "Numerous victims died a terrible death by being burned alive by napalm bombs, despite the denial of the French delegation. My delegation has . . . photos showing the victims of napalm bombs," testified the Tunisian representative to the UN. Chassin's colleagues evidently heeded the general's advice about napalm: "Two-thirds of the French-planted forests that existed in eastern Algeria in 1954 were burned by French forces during the [1954–1962] guerrilla war for Algerian independence, because wooded land provided shelter for nationalist guerrillas. About one-half of the area was destroyed by napalm, according to [French engineer Jean] Carbonare," the *New York Times* reported in November 1962.

British and Portuguese armies likewise put the gel to work in Africa. "Napalm bombs were used to rout the terrorists," journalist Robert Conley explained of British tactics that ended the 1952–1960 Mau Mau Rebellion in Kenya. Portugal burned crops and devastated concentrations of Angolan guerrillas with napalm in 1961 and 1962. It was censured in 1972 by the UN 98 to 6 (Brazil, Portugal, white-ruled South Africa, Spain, the United Kingdom, and the United States in opposition) for "the ruthless use of napalm and chemical substances in Angola, Guinea (Bissau) and Cape Verde and Mozambique."[40]

Independence allowed former colonies to follow the example of their past masters. Egypt dispatched napalm bombs to support royalist allies in the Yemeni civil war that started in 1962. Bombardments forced villagers in contested areas to abandon their homes and live in caves. On September 24, 1965, and again in 1971, India dropped napalm on Pakistani troops. A reporter described charred vehicles along the Kashmir truce line. In 1969 and 1974, Kurdish residents of northern Iraq protested napalm attacks by the Baghdad government. Biafrans reported napalm use by Nigerian forces during the 1969 civil war. In Brazil, the military junta used napalm against Maoist rebels who tried to create a "liberated zone" in a remote part of the southeastern Amazon during the 1970–1974 Araguaian war.[41]

These widely dispersed conflicts drew extensive scrutiny from political leaders, lawyers, journalists, academics, and other commentators. Napalm specifically, however, was mentioned only in passing during this period, except for the scattered British objections in 1952. Britons did introduce words like "civilians," "cruel," "indiscriminate," and "illegal," into the discussion about incendiary bombardments—terms with significant legal relevance in later years—but their campaign largely ended with the Korean armistice. For much of the world in the years after World War II, napalm, in some respects like its creator America, was an innovation of awesome power available at low cost and in quantity: a new and unquestionable authority. Vietnam changed that.

# 7

# Vietnam Syndrome

American napalm's introduction to Vietnam was portentous. On February 27, 1962, two South Vietnamese air force pilots, trained by U.S. advisors, turned their Douglas A-1 Skyraiders and jelly bombs on the presidential palace of Washington's ally Ngo Dinh Diem in an attempted coup. "The planes made repeated passes over the Presidential Palace at low altitude, dropping napalm (jellied gasoline), firing rockets, strafing," the Associated Press reported. Officials initially denied the incendiary's involvement. "There is some sensitivity here on the subject of napalm, which was used against Vietnam by the French," explained *New York Times* reporter Homer Bigart. It proved hard to hide. "A check on the attack yesterday showed that the napalm bomb had engulfed the roof of the palace in a sea of flame," he continued. Damage was so extensive Diem ordered the entire palace, symbol of South Vietnamese executive authority, razed to the ground and replaced.[1]

Napalm's might was apparent to any observer. "A continuous sheet of flames a half mile wide was visible moving across one field," the Associated Press reported of a February 1963 strike by U.S. pilots against a South Vietnamese village. On May 1, as U.S. military commitments increased, Secretary of Defense Robert McNamara watched Vietnamese air force planes drop firebombs in an exercise. Just forty-eight hours later, reporters filed the first combat reports of napalm strikes by South Vietnamese forces. By the end of the year, its use was routine. "On clear days patrons lunching in the ninth-floor restaurant in the Caravelle Hotel [in Saigon] can watch Government planes dropping napalm on guerrillas across the Saigon River," Hedrick Smith wrote in the *New York Times*.[2]

In March 1964, publication in London of a photograph of a Vietnamese baby burned by napalm gave some pause, but did not produce nearly the reaction of later images. Washington issued an official statement of concern but denied its instructors had dropped the shell that caused the child's injury. On March 9, 1965, President Lyndon Johnson expanded napalm attacks to targets in North Vietnam. Gelled fire fell there eleven days later. "Napalm bombs are considered 'conventional ordnance,'" the *New York Times* explained to its readers when it reported the strike.[3]

Pentagon planners integrated napalm into America's military bureaucracy as its use expanded. In December 1963, the army and air force explained in an internal manual that thickened fuel "increases the range of flamethrowers, imparts slower burning properties, gives clinging qualities, and causes flame to rebound off walls or other surfaces and to go around corners." There were three kinds of napalm powder, the services advised: "M1" followed Louis Fieser's recipe of 50% coconut oil, 25% napthenic acids, and 25% oleic acid; "M2" added silica to increase stability; and M4, thickened with an aluminum soap derived from oxidized petroleum, mixed faster and yielded more gel. U.S. equipment included bombs up to 750 pounds in size, napalm land mines, and smaller canisters filled with the incendiary. E. B. Hershberg's white phosphorus burster design, tested on the Harvard College soccer field, was the incendiary ignition system of choice.[4]

Some observers applauded the ferocious effectiveness of sticky fire in terms reminiscent of World War II and the Korean War. Nobel laureate John Steinbeck was a particular enthusiast. In January 1966, he proposed the "Steinbeck super ball" in a letter to President Johnson's special assistant Jack Valenti, who forwarded it to Secretary of Defense Robert McNamara. "I think the most terrifying modern weapon is the napalm bomb. People who will charge rifle fire won't go through flames," the novelist wrote. "What I suggest is a napalm grenade, packed in a heavy plastic sphere almost the exact size and weight of a baseball. The detonator could be of very low power—just enough to break the plastic shell and ignite the inflammable. If the napalm is packed under pressure, it will spread itself when the shell breaks," the Nobel winner continued. "The detonator (a contact cap) should be carried separately and inserted or screwed in just before throwing. This would allow a man to carry a sack full of balls without danger to himself," he advised. America's national pastime prepared it perfectly for the weapon. "[T]here isn't an American boy over 13 who can't peg a baseball from infield to home plate with accuracy. And a grown man with sandlot experience can do much better. It is a natural weapon for the Americans," he explained. None appear to have been manufactured.[5]

By 1966, napalm was an integral part of the U.S. war effort in Vietnam. Fighter-bombers dropped perhaps 4,500 tons per month in Indochina overall: about 13 percent of the total weight of munitions delivered by air. The following year, the total approached 5,000 tons per month. It peaked in 1968 at an estimated 5,900 tons monthly. About 388,000 tons of U.S. napalm bombs fell on Indochina in the decade from 1963 to 1973, compared to 32,357 tons used on Korea in just over three years and 16,500 tons dropped on Japan in 1945. Why was the weapon so valuable? "People have this thing about being burned to death," a pilot said.[6]

New pilots often trained at Dixie Station, an area of the South China Sea off the coast of South Vietnam that hosted a rotating contingent of aircraft carriers. Here, according to military aviation specialist Frank Harvey, "He learns how it feels to drop bombs on human beings and watch huts go up in a boil of orange flame when his aluminum napalm tanks tumble into them." Tacticians considered napalm especially useful for close combat support. Pilots learned to drop 120-gallon tanks, which weighed 800 pounds and were ten feet long by three feet thick, from fifty feet in the air to within a hundred feet of targets. The thin tanks tumbled erratically as they fell, and blanketed an area about 150 feet long and fifty feet wide in flames. "Anyone who survives a napalm attack is apt to be dreadfully burned and, without first rate medical care, is condemned to a lingering, painful death or, at best, permanent disfigurement," the *New York Times* reported.[7]

Viet Cong troops, who had no access to combat airplanes, occasionally used napalm in hand-carried flamethrowers. "Spraying fire about in great whooshing arcs, the Viet Cong set everything afire. . . . Charred children were locked in ghastly embrace, infants welded to their mothers' breasts," *Time* reported of a 1967 atrocity. It was not, however, a large part of their arsenal.[8]

Pentagon manuals became more detailed as bombing increased. In 1966, the army's *Bombs and Bomb Components* distinguished "firebombs" from "incendiary bombs" primarily on the basis of shell thickness. "Fire bombs are usually thin-skinned," the document explained. Pages of schematic drawings detailed precisely what authors meant. By 1970, the service's *Combat Flame Operations Field Manual* specified "Firebombs are used primarily by elements of the tactical air force to support ground operations. Incendiary bombs are generally used by the strategic air force to attack strategic or deep targets." Both bombs were useful against combatants, the manual continued, but "incendiary" devices could be deployed against "Facilities that support enemy operations" which "include . . . urban areas." Here, army specialists wrote, notwithstanding J. M. Spaight's precision theories, area bombing was required: "To be effective as antipersonnel weapons, incendiary bombs must be used in sufficient quantities to overcome existing fire defense measures. Therefore, the object is to surround the personnel with a 'wall of fire' to create intense heat and to exhaust oxygen supplies in enclosed spaces. Area bombing must be used to accomplish this." Dreams of precision urban incendiary bombing died.[9]

Vietnam added an innovation to the tactics of aerial napalm delivery: barrel drops from helicopters, ignited by incendiary grenades. Veteran Bob Parker explained how it was done: "A 'Napalm Drop' was usually from a CH-47 Chinook cargo copter. [We] hung twenty or so fifty-five-gallon drums in cargo nets under the bird. . . . The pilot would dive on the target until it lined up with the bolts in the rudder pedals, and then release the hook. As the drums cascaded downward, a four-man crew would snatch the nets in through the floor and then stow them away." Then, Parker continued, "I would lean out the right side and drop a white phosphorus or thermite grenade to try to land with the napalm and ignite it. This sounds really simple, except that a normal drop was at max airspeed and less than 400 feet above the ground." Results from one such raid underlined the tactic's effectiveness: "The firing stopped and [a lieutenant] reported that several VC had decided to surrender. They came bursting out of their positions covered in jellied gasoline and ran into the arms of the American troops screaming 'Choi Hoi!' (in effect, 'I surrender!'). The others stayed in their bunkers and cooked in place."[10]

Even a massive commitment of this fearful weapon, however, was not enough for victory. In April 1972, the United States deployed napalm in the largest quantities ever seen in history to block a massive North Vietnamese offensive. *Time* described the frenzied effort. "When a flight of four Phantoms lands on the twin 10,000-ft. runways, the planes quickly taxi to rows of protective concrete revetments. Once a plane is safely parked, the pilot climbs out and is handed a cold can of Budweiser. While he sips the brew, a yellow forklift truck trundles up with armaments, and the ground crew hurriedly rearms the Phantom with an awesome array of weaponry—iron bombs, rockets and napalm canisters. Normally, the entire operation takes only 20 minutes. The beer never gets warm before the pilot climbs back into his Phantom to take off on another sortie." But the bombardments merely delayed defeat. In 1973, the United States withdrew its last troops. South Vietnam, despite the assistance of perhaps 400,000 tons of napalm dropped on its behalf, surrendered on April 30, 1975. Napalm, and with it America, had lost its first war.[11]

U.S. civilians responded to the use of napalm during the first years of the Vietnam War much as they had during the Korean War: it was not much discussed and, when it was, observers generally explained napalm's dire effects as an inevitable, if perhaps regrettable, element of war. As America's involvement expanded in 1965 and 1966, however, debate increased.

British commenters, as during the Korean War, voiced the first objections to American incendiary bombs. Graham Greene, in his 1955 novel *The Quiet American*, had one of his characters observe " 'What I detest is napalm bombing. From 3,000 feet, in safety.' He made a hopeless gesture. 'You see the forest catching fire. God knows what you would see from the ground. The poor devils are burnt alive, the flames go over them like water. They are wet through with fire.' " This was possibly the first criticism of napalm in English literature. Robert Davis, then chairman of the English Department at Smith College, dismissed the novel as fatuous in a review for the *New York Times:* "[Greene's] caricatures of

American types are often as crude and trite as those of Jean-Paul Sartre . . . a civilization composed exclusively of chewing gum, napalm bombs, deodorants, Congressional witch-hunts, celery wrapped in cellophane, and a naïve belief in one's own superior virtue."

Silence descended on napalm in Vietnam for almost a decade. Then, on April 8, 1963, as the United States expanded its use of the gel, Nobel laureate Bertrand Russell delivered a blistering critique in a letter to the *New York Times.* "[T]he war which is being conducted is an atrocity. Napalm jelly gasoline is being used against whole villages, without warning," he wrote. Editors offered a sharp rebuttal: "Napalm has been used by the South Vietnamese air force against real or imagined havens of Vietcong guerrillas. Its use has certainly killed innocent people—as other weapons have done in all wars. American advisors have opposed its employment, on both moral and practical grounds, against all except clearly identified military targets." Complaints of this nature about napalm, the editors concluded, reflected "An unfortunate and—despite his eminence as a philosopher—an unthinking receptivity to the most transparent Communist propaganda."[12]

Journalists struggled. To some, napalm's impact was an enigma. "Tactical air support is used extensively, but it often is difficult to ascertain whether the people killed by napalm or fragmentation bombs were guerrillas or merely farmers," an Associated Press reporter wrote on July 8, 1962. To others, the gel was counterproductive. French journalist Georges Penchenier, kidnapped and held near Saigon for sixteen days in 1964 by the Viet Cong, gave one of the earliest assessments of napalm's effectiveness, and its costs: "The destructive effects of American planes dropping napalm bombs—the Vietcong are terrified of them—are very great, and the insurgents have no answer to them. Every day, B-26's strafe the jungle, bombarding anything that looks suspicious and setting fire to what are presumed to be Vietcong crops." However, he continued, "Whenever a skirmish occurs, the Saigon air force intervenes and whole villages are burned down. How can one expect the countryside not to rally to the insurgents in such circumstances?" Local priest Augustine Nguyen Lac Hoa reached a similar conclusion. "How can we explain to a mother when her child is burned by napalm?" he asked the same year, when he accepted the Ramon Magsaysay Award for outstanding service to Asia. Impartiality, indeed, was difficult given the grievous injuries inflicted by the gel. "One distraught woman appeared at the field medical station holding a child whose legs had been horribly burned by napalm. The child is not expected to live," Neil Sheehan reported for the *New York Times* in February 1966.[13]

Pentagon officials, however, had no doubts about their gel's utility. They labeled critics naïve. "Restrictions on talk about the use of napalm came after the Vietcong gave particularly effective propaganda distribution to the photograph of a villager and his child after a raid. But the firebombs have been too valuable in penetrating caves and trenches to give up," an unidentified "senior American officer" told *New York Times* reporter Jack Langguth on March 7, 1965. "The public seems to have an aversion to napalm," the source continued, "because people think it's kinder to blast a man's head off than to fry him to death." The next day, 3,500 marines landed to defend a U.S. air base at Da Nang. By the end of the year, President Johnson had dedicated almost 200,000 U.S. troops to Vietnam.[14]

Objections and praise alternated as American commitments expanded. "I do not remember a single instance of a German military official (not even of an SS or Gestapo official) speaking as openly, callously and shamelessly of the German war crimes as your 'senior officer' speaks of the frying to death of women, children, helpless peasants, and other noncombatants in South Vietnam," World War II survivor Emily Rosdolsky of Detroit wrote to the editors of the *New York Times* on March 16, in response to the piece by Sheehan cited above. British parliamentarians compared napalm to poison gas weapons. On the other hand, thirty-three-year-old U.S. Army captain Joseph House of Birmingham observed of one battle, "If it hadn't been for the air strikes . . . there was a good chance we would have been overrun on our left flank." When helicopters and fighter-bombers began "pouring napalm over the Vietcong installations," a reporter recalled of the same clash, the enemy broke and ran. "[I]t was like shooting fish in a barrel" after that, House said.[15]

Correspondent Charles Mohr captured the nation's uncertainty in a September 1965 *New York Times* dispatch titled "Air Strikes Hit Vietcong—And South Vietnam Civilians." He began with an anecdote of "a woman who has both arms burned off by napalm and her eyelids so badly burned that she cannot close them. When it is time for her to sleep her family puts a blanket over her head." But, he continued, "No weapon is intrinsically bad in war (napalm is one of the very best)." He concluded with this exchange: " 'I wonder if any civilians were killed?' a pilot was asked. 'Who the hell knows?' was the answer."[16]

This was the uncertain context when the Stanford Committee for Peace in Vietnam, a group of about two dozen Stanford University students and faculty, bolstered by a few residents from nearby towns, began to meet. Committee members were "each more or less fitfully active against the war" recalled H. Bruce Franklin, then an assistant professor of English and American literature at the university. "It included a few people who called themselves pacifists, two who called themselves Marxists, and most who no longer knew what to call themselves," he wrote. This small group of thoughtful, committed citizens organized the first protests against the manufacture of napalm which, in turn, inspired a national movement against the Dow Chemical Corporation, the largest manufacturer of the gel.[17]

Conglomerate United Aircraft Corporation (now United Technologies) owned a firm called the United Technology Center (UTC) that manufactured napalm field mixing units at a rural plant in the small town of Coyote, fifteen miles south of San Jose. Stanford Committee members organized a leafleting campaign there in the winter of 1965. It had little effect: security guards intimidated workers who took flyers by ostentatiously photographing them, and there was scant publicity because of the facility's remote location. In January 1966, however, a worker at the firm's headquarters in Sunnyvale secretly told members of the group that the UTC had won a massive contract to produce napalm itself.[18]

"Napalm B," developed in 1964 by scientists at Eglin Air Force Base in Florida, burned hotter, stuck tighter, and ignited more reliably than earlier formulations. It was made with 50 percent polystyrene, a synthetic substance manufactured by Dow and sixteen other U.S. firms (Dow trademarked one variety as "Styrofoam"), 25 percent benzene, and 25 percent gasoline. In mid-1965, the Pentagon asked for production bids. A quintet of manufacturers stepped forward. Officers announced the winners in July 1965: an $11 million order for 100 million pounds of napalm to UTC, and contracts of up to $5 million for at least 25 million pounds each to runners-up Dow and Witco Chemical. Dow constructed a mixing line staffed by ten employees at a factory in Torrance, California, near Los Angeles.[19]

Activists saw an opportunity, and seized it. "[W]e thought we could at last do something concrete: stop local production. And practically all of us saw a great potential for some kind of mass campaign that would swiftly educate people about the 'immoral' nature of the war and the illusions of our government," Franklin wrote. Committee members decided to redouble their efforts in Coyote, expand the flyer campaign to the UTC's headquarters in Sunnyvale, and lobby corporate executives.[20]

Company chiefs agreed to a parley on January 25, 1966. A troika of military officers employed by the UTC—two retired generals and a retired admiral—flanked its president as he entered the conference room. Executives, Franklin wrote, invoked economic necessity, humanity, and patriotism to defend the company's work: "Even if we didn't want to work on napalm, we would have to just to stay in business. . . . Napalm will help shorten the war. . . . Besides, whatever our government asks us to do is right," the professor paraphrased their arguments. Committee members argued that international law prohibited war crimes, and claimed there was a close historical connection between Dow and Nazi chemical producers. They adjourned without a resolution.[21]

Security guards rebuffed the campaign against napalm itself as easily as they had blocked the mixing-machine protests. "That first day, most of them [plant workers] stopped to take the leaflet. Some went out of their way to be friendly. A few, though, tried to run us down. On the second day, the company posted plainclothes security guards and a photographer at the gate. Almost every worker driving through now pretended that we didn't exist, except for a few who again tried to run us down," Franklin recalled. A few workers stopped their cars a few miles down the road, where it met the main highway, and spoke with demonstrators. They said plainclothes security guards had been hired to watch them, and that they feared being fired if they showed any antiwar sympathies. A few employees did quit and, according to the academic, found themselves blacklisted by area employers.[22]

Stakes rose in March 1966, when the trade journal *Chemical and Engineering News* confirmed the UTC production contract. Not only had the firm agreed to manufacture napalm, it transpired, it had also agreed to deliver it ready to use, in bombshells. Executives announced their firm would sublease two "ugly, marshy" acres of a Standard Oil of California (now Chevron) storage facility for its bomb factory. This land, at the end of a causeway that jutted two miles into San Francisco Bay, was part of the port of the town of Redwood City, a municipality of 56,300 one town north of Stanford's campus in Palo Alto. Because public property was involved, the transaction required approval by the Redwood City Port Commission.[23]

Commissioners met to discuss the matter on the afternoon of March 21 at the port manager's office in an old frame building set amid unused oil storage tanks. It was immediately apparent this would not be a routine convocation: a dozen protestors jammed the manager's office and left barely enough space for the officials to gather. About seventy more filled a reception room and overflowed into a porch. Activists, accompanied by their children in some cases, had been organized by the Stanford Committee, a Palo Alto peace organization called Concerned Citizens, and a Redwood City Unitarian congregation.

A clerk asked for public comments. Napalm's public relations disaster began. "If you could actually see the bodies of men, women and children burned by this weapon, you would act to prevent Redwood City from becoming a name to go down in history with Buchenwald," declared one protester. "Redwood City will become known as a place where flaming death is manufactured," expostulated another. Dozens waited in line to comment. Board members decided to reconvene at the larger country office building in downtown Redwood City that afternoon.[24]

More than twice as many people, about 200, assembled when the hearing resumed at 5:00 p.m. Debate grew more heated. Olive Mayer, a local engineer who had inspected the ovens at the Belsen concentration camp, asserted that "Local government and professional people had to be involved in providing locations for the manufacture of those ovens, just as you commissioners are now called upon to make a decision concerning a napalm factory." Another resident, Elena Greene, berated the commissioners: "You are committing thousands of people to death. I don't know how you sleep at night." Franklin gave a speech about napalm's effects on civilians that caused the chairman to crack his gavel and roar: "Get that man out of here." A pair of policemen dragged the teacher out of the room, prompting his seven-year-old daughter to burst into tears. In the ensuing chaos, board members hastily voted to approve the sublease, and adjourned. Production was scheduled to begin on May 1, and to last for eight months. Redwood City had experienced its first antiwar protest.[25]

City regulations required a referendum on any vote by the port's board if requested within thirty days by 10 percent of registered voters. Activists formed the Redwood City Committee Against Napalm, sixty members strong, and launched a petition drive. They wrote a two-page *Napalm Newsletter* filled with information about the history of the weapon and its use in Vietnam—one of the first such compilations ever produced—and mailed a copy to every registered voter in the city. A large picture of a little girl with dreadful burns marked its cover. Leafleting redoubled at the UTC plant.[26]

Journalists found the conflict irresistible. "This is the first time since the start of the Vietnam War that the people will have an opportunity to express themselves at the ballot box on a specific issue connected to the war," Committee against Napalm chairman James F. Colaianni, also an attorney and managing editor of the strident five-year-old San Francisco political and literary journal *Ramparts*, told the *New York Times* on April 17. The newspaper's extensive coverage of the west coast protest stood in sharp contrast to its dismissal three years earlier of Bertrand Russell's complaints about napalm.

Some local newspapers supported the campaigners. One reported that the UTC had harassed protestors, and published a transcript of a call to a local business: "This is United Technology Center calling. We wondered if you knew where your employee _____, was yesterday. Did he tell you he was taking time off to picket our plant?" Others opposed the drive. "While there may be some question about the use of napalm in warfare, it is not a question to be decided by the voters of Redwood City or any other municipality. . . . It is easy to see what would happen if every city were to be allowed to make its own decisions as to what war material is acceptable to its own citizens," editorialized the *Palo Alto Times:* "the result would be chaos." NBC and CBS gave the debate national prominence when they featured it on their network news broadcasts. Letters, mostly favorable, streamed in to the committee from across the country.[27]

Passions ran high. "It will put us on the map," a port commissioner said of the planned factory. A councilman spoke of an "economic boom" that might follow. Others disagreed. "The good name of Redwood City with its old slogan 'Climate Best by Government Test' appeals far more to me than 'Napalm City by the Dead Bay'!" one resident wrote in a letter to the editor of the *Redwood City News*. Stanford Committee members produced an "Emergency Report on the Manufacture and Use of Napalm," a more extreme, if less widely distributed, variant of the *Napalm Newsletter*. It laid out the history of the weapon, alleged that the United States had caused 300,000–400,000 civilian casualties to date in Vietnam, and concluded, "Those killed by napalm are literally roasted alive."[28]

On April 20, 1966, the Committee against Napalm submitted a petition signed by 3,761 Redwood City voters—well over the 2,416 required. Officials claimed the sublease decision was not a matter subject to a referendum rules, and refused to accept the petition. Committee members sued.[29]

Napalm production started while the parties waited for their case to come to trial. Acres of stacked crates of 500- and 750-pound bombshells, delivered by a subcontractor, lined the causeway that led to the plant. Activists organized vigils. "In the mild California climate, the protesters could watch [the plant] from the other side of the wire-mesh fence which separated it from the road," recalled Eric Prokosch, then a graduate student, "The empty aluminum bomb shells were brought in by truck (thoughtfully marked 'Do Not Drop'); the polystyrene powder, used to thicken the napalm, came in by train and was mixed with the incendiary fuel in vats. The mixture was then piped into bomb cases through a tube, and the filled bombs were loaded on barges, to be towed across the San Francisco Bay to a naval storage site from which they would be shipped to Vietnam." Franklin remembered, "You could even stand at the high chain-link fence and watch as the empty bomb casings were swung over to a raised platform and pumped full of napalm." Protesters hectored workers through megaphones. Managers ostentatiously photographed demonstrators, and their car license plates, and blasted recorded music at them—Tchaikovsky's Symphony *Pathétique* was a favorite. On May 16 and 17, in the first acts of civil disobedience against napalm, jazz musician Aaron Manganiello, joined by a Palo Alto psychiatrist and, a day later, two Stanford students, lay down in front of trucks delivering empty bomb shells. Police arrested them.[30]

Leaders of the Redwood City committee summarized their case to a crowd of 400 people who gathered in the auditorium of the local Sequoia High School in mid-May, just before the judge's ruling on their suit to force a referendum. Napalm, they argued, was indiscriminate, cruel, and racist. "We're talking about a systematic planned murder of tens of thousands of civilians who have nothing to do with the war," Colaianni said. "Imagine the terror of not knowing when the next airplane, flying at speeds greater than the speed of sound, will drop two acres of flame on the place where you live," observed Unitarian minister and committee vice-chair William Hough. "Except for a few raids against the Germans in World War II, it [napalm] has been used only against nonwhite people in Japan, Korea and Vietnam," Franklin maintained.[31]

On May 20, 1966, Judge Melvin E. Cohn rejected the committee's filing. The Redwood City lease to Standard Oil, he informed the courtroom, had actually expired on May 1. A new lease, he reported, had been signed on 26 April between Standard, the UTC, and the port—six days after the petition by the protesters was submitted. That agreement, he ruled, now governed the property. If the plaintiffs wanted to challenge it, they had six days left to draft a new petition and collect new signatures. Moreover, the judge said, "I have no intention of trying to decide whether the United States should be fighting a war in Vietnam. Nor do I intend to try to decide whether the armed forces should be dropping napalm bombs in that fighting." With those words, in an irony of history, Judge Cohn launched the campaign against napalm that swept the country over the next three years.[32]

Cohn's decision infuriated activists, super-charged the local anti-napalm movement, and attracted attention from national anti-war leaders. On May 28, 1966, a Sunday, 1,200 people packed the Sequoia High School's football stadium to launch a national campaign against napalm, beginning with a boycott of Dow. The national consumer goods company, Prokosch explained, was an attractive target: "Its best-known product was Saran Wrap, a clear plastic tissue which clung to the food it enclosed, as Dow's jellied fuel clung to the skin. Saran Wrap was to be found in households across the country; any local antiwar group could go to the nearest supermarket and call for a boycott." And, he added, "Further opportunities for protest were afforded by the frequent visits of Dow recruiters to university campuses." Rhetoric was strong. "Peasants burned—profits up," "Napalm kills democracy here too," and "Would You Want Your Daughter to Marry a Napalm Producer," read signs at the event.

After the stadium meeting, participants marched to the UTC napalm plant for a rally. Vietnam War opponent Senator Wayne Morse of Oregon and progressive Congressional candidate Robert Scheer, later a *Ramparts* managing editor, addressed the crowd. Redwood City spent $9,000 to manage the event. "Broadway in Redwood City is not a bright modern thoroughfare, but the merchants have always made a valiant effort to keep it neat and it is always cheerful and clean. . . . Suddenly the street took on a dirty, grey and sombre look," a resident complained in a subsequent letter to the *Redwood City Tribune*. "The citizens of Redwood City must, in some way, repaint the tarnished and desecrated picture of this fair city, previously considered the jewel of the Peninsular Pendant," the missive continued.[33]

Protests took place the same Sunday in New York City, and in Torrance. In Manhattan, about seventy-five people organized by the fifteen-member Brooklyn-based Citizens Campaign against Napalm—supported by the antiwar groups Women Strike for Peace, Youth against War and Fascism, and the United States Committee to Aid the National Front—rallied at Dow's Rockefeller Center offices. "Napalm Burns Babies, Dow Makes Money," read one sign, in an echo of the California placards. Another, pitched more directly at New York's Jewish population, warned "Nazi Ovens in '44, U.S. Napalm in '66." Newspapers, television news networks, and wire services covered the protest. In Torrance, about one hundred people organized by Students for a Democratic Society (SDS) and Freedom Now activists picketed Dow's facility. Counter-demonstrators from the Victory in Vietnam Association shouted support for the factory.[34]

Rallies spread during the summer of 1966. In August, students from the University of Michigan, Wayne State University in Detroit, and the

University of Toledo, joined by members of a dozen Detroit anti-war groups, converged on Dow's headquarters in Midland, Michigan, population 27,000, 128 miles northwest of Detroit, for "August Days of Protest." Representatives won a meeting with H. D. (Ted) Doan, the middle-aged president of the firm, and grandson of the its founder, followed by another on the 22nd by a quartet of SDS activists. Their discussions, however, produced no change in corporate policies. A *Detroit Free Press* article dubbed the effort "a flop." At the end of the month, dissidents gathered again in Manhattan and Torrance. Police at Rockefeller Center arrested twenty-nine who attempted to reach Dow's thirty-seventh-floor offices. Protests that autumn greeted Dow recruiters at Wayne State, Cornell, the University of South Florida, the University of California, Los Angeles, and the University of California, Berkeley.[35]

Awareness of napalm grew. When the Johnson administration dispatched "truth teams" across the country to explain Vietnam policy as the semester began, war opponents put napalm front and center. Paul Soglin, a student leader, recalled the discussions at the University of Wisconsin–Madison: "The representative of the Defense Department was asked, 'What does napalm do.' So he gave a technical description of napalm, being a gel and so on. The crowd was rumbling." Students repeated the question. "He says, 'Well, it can catch you on fire.'" Finally, "The General said, 'Well, you really want to know what it does. It burns. It burns people.'" Truth was served.[36]

Dow did not underestimate the potential threat represented by the protest movement. "I would hate for Dow to come out of Vietnam with the 'Merchants of Death' label that was pinned on du Pont after the First World War; and yet, unless we come to grips with this problem, it is likely to happen," an internal company memo warned in December 1966. Public relations staff met frequently, developed a coordinated corporation-wide response, circulated a standard statement to local managers, and ensured that spokesmen stuck to it religiously. Executives used measured language, stressed respect for the free expression of ideas, and built their case around arguments similar to those used by the Sunnyvale UTC executives: duty, humanitarianism, and patriotism.

"Aside from our duty to do this, we might add that we would feel deeply gratified if what we're able to provide helps to protect our fighting men or to speed the day when fighting will end," Dow's eastern public relations manager, Dean M. Wakefield, said in response to the first Rockefeller Center pickets. "We're a supplier of goods to the Defense Department and not a policy maker," he added, and noted "Fourteen GIs signed a letter including this statement: 'The effectiveness of napalm in saving U.S. lives is overwhelming.'" Ted Doan reiterated these points in a *Wall Street Journal* op-ed the following year: "[W]e feel that our company should produce those items which our fighting men need in time of war when we have the ability to do so . . . we reject the validity of comparing our government with Hitler's Nazi Germany." He concluded, "Basically, the debate over Vietnam, as long as it remains peaceful and honest debate, is a healthy thing." As to economic necessity, Dow stressed the opposite: napalm, officials said, was a minuscule part of its business.[37]

Pentagon representatives stayed equally true to their argument that napalm affected few civilians. In response to a 1966 query from New York senator Robert F. Kennedy, the Department of Defense asserted "Napalm is used against selected targets, such as caves and reinforced supply areas. Casualties in attacks against targets of this type are predominantly persons involved in Communist military operations." Chairman of the Joint Chiefs of Staff Earle Wheeler explained to reporters in February 1967: "Napalm, by virtue of its splashing and spreading, can get into defensive positions. It's also especially effective against antiaircraft positions . . . the napalm splashes in and incapacitates the crew and sometimes destroys the weapon."[38]

Initially, Dow's strategy appeared to work. Boycott calls accomplished little—only about 8 percent of Dow's sales, in any event, came from products sold directly to consumers—and the campus protests subsided as the year drew to a close. A September 1966 position paper for the National Coordinating Committee to End the War in Vietnam shows the extreme actions frustrated protesters felt might be necessary: "Carry South Vietnamese victims of napalm and strafing—dead or alive—through white suburbs. If they cannot be smuggled into the country, obtain napalm in sufficient quantities to roast unquenchable pigs and cows in suburban streets. Or drop it from small airplanes on white suburban schoolyards on the opening day of school." Of course, the paper noted, "Whether this would raise *anti*-war sentiment would have to be considered."[39]

Relief programs for those hurt by napalm emerged as a positive alternative for activist efforts. The most highly publicized program was the Committee of Responsibility for Treatment in the United States of War-Burned Vietnamese Children started by Helen Frumin of Scarsdale that summer. Promises of hospital beds and convalescent care from doctors and citizens across the country poured in during the autumn. At the same time, news reports suggested the impact of napalm might be less than imagined. "[T]here are about two patients with serious napalm burns each week," Neil Sheehan reported after a visit to one of the largest regional hospitals, located eighty miles south of Saigon. Accurate or not, this kind of report dampened criticism further. As early as August 6, only a few people stopped when a large New York peace march, organized to mark the twenty-first anniversary of the Hiroshima bombing, passed right by Dow's midtown offices.[40]

# 8

## Seeing Is Believing

A trio of articles published in January 1967 described napalm's effects on South Vietnamese civilians, especially children, to a mass U.S. audience for the first time. They reenergized the movement. Magazines at opposite ends of U.S. journalism, geographically, historically, and demographically, broke the story: on the one hand, five-year-old *Ramparts,* from the West Coast, with an audience of about 100,000; on the other, the eighty-four-year-old *Ladies Home Journal* and sixty-four-year-old *Redbook* women's periodicals, edited in New York, with circulations of 6.8 million and almost five million, respectively. All concluded that napalm, far from the modern marvel described by earlier correspondents, was a diabolically cruel, child-seeking killer.[1]

*Ramparts* offered the most detailed report and included fifteen full-color pages of burn victims and jammed hospitals: the first such catalog of civilian napalm casualties in a national American periodical. "Torn flesh, splintered bones, screaming agony are bad enough. But perhaps most heart-rending of all are the tiny faces and bodies scorched and seared by fire," wrote author William F. Pepper, director of the Mercy College Children's Institute for Advanced Study and Research in New York. "Napalm and its more horrible companion, white phosphorus, liquidize young flesh and carve it into grotesque forms. The little figures are afterward often scarcely human in appearance, and one cannot be confronted with the monstrous effects of the burning without being totally shaken," he reported, "The initial urge to reach out and soothe the hurt was restrained by the fear that the ash-like skin would crumble in my fingers." He cited a report by the Swiss relief organization *Terre des Hommes* on hospital conditions: "In places with the atmosphere of slaughter houses for people, where flies circulate freely on children who have been skinned alive, there are no facilities for hygiene, no fans, and no air conditioning."

Pepper asserted that napalm hurt children most severely, laid responsibility for the injuries directly on the United States, rejected claims of military necessity, and ended with a call for action. "A burn is especially critical in a child because the area of destruction relative to total body surface is proportionately greater than that of an adult," he wrote, "The tragedy that is befalling children in Vietnam is all the more our responsibility where children burned by napalm are concerned; only the United States is using this weapon, and it is fitting that we should provide the care for the mutilated children." As to the Pentagon's assertions to Robert Kennedy, Pepper retorted, "I am compelled to wonder what military functions were being performed by the thousands of infants and small children, many of whom I saw sharing hospital beds in Vietnam, and a few of whom appear in photographs accompanying this article." He concluded, "Every sickening, frightening scar is a silent cry to Americans to begin to restore their childhood for those whom we are compelled to call our own because of what has been done in our name."[2]

Renowned war correspondent Martha Gellhorn's article in *The Ladies Home Journal* was equally heartrending. "In the children's ward of the Qui Nhon province I saw for the first time what napalm does. A child of seven, the size of our four-year-olds, lay in the cot by the door. Napalm had burned his face and back and one hand. The burned skin looked like swollen, raw meat; the fingers of his hand were stretched out, burned rigid. A scrap of cheesecloth covered him, for weight is intolerable, but so is air. His grandfather, an emaciated old man half blind with cataract, was tending the child," she wrote. "A week ago, napalm bombs were dropped on their hamlet. . . . All week, the little boy cried with pain, but now he was better. He was only twisting his body, as if trying to dodge his incomprehensible torture," Gellhorn witnessed. She concluded with white-knuckle prose: "Farther down the ward, another child, also seven years old, moaned like a mourning dove; he was still crying. He had been burned by napalm, too, in the same village. His mother stood over his cot, fanning the little body, in a helpless effort to cool that wet, red skin. Whatever she said, in Vietnamese, I did not understand, but her eyes and her voice revealed how gladly she would have taken for herself the child's suffering."[3]

Gellhorn used a metaphor of instant familiarity to drive home her point. She recounted the observation of a New Jersey housewife and mother of six who had adopted three Vietnamese children, and traveled to the country to see conditions firsthand. "Before I went to Saigon, I had heard and read that napalm melts the flesh, and I thought that's nonsense, because I can put a roast in the oven and the fat will melt but the meat stays there," the American mother said. "Well, I went and I saw these children burned by napalm and it is absolutely true. The chemical reaction of this napalm does melt the flesh, and the flesh runs right down their faces onto their chests and it sits there and it grows there. . . . These children can't turn their heads, they were so thick with flesh. . . . And when gangrene sets in, they cut off their hands or fingers or their feet; the only thing they cannot cut off is their head," she testified.[4]

Napalm affected women, children and the elderly disproportionately, the celebrity correspondent asserted. She agreed with *Ramparts* that children suffered particular harm: "Children are killed or wounded by napalm because of the nature of the bombings. Close air support for infantry is one thing. The day and night bombings of hamlets, filled with women, children and the old, is another."[5]

Physician Richard Perry's *Redbook* article, written with Robert Levin, was perhaps the most poignant. The experienced orthopedic surgeon spent years in Vietnam treating civilian victims of the war. His words carried the passion of personal experience: "[N]othing could have prepared me for my encounters with Vietnamese women and children burned by napalm. It was shocking and sickening, even for a physician, to see and smell the blackened flesh. One continues for days afterward getting sick when he looks at a piece of meat on his plate because the odor of burning flesh lingers so long in the memory. And one never forgets the bewildered eyes of the silent, suffering, napalm-burned child. What could anyone possibly say to such a child?" His conclusion was devastating: "The Vietcong do not use napalm, we do."[6]

A rebuttal of sorts by physician Howard Rusk, a renowned medical rehabilitation expert and part-time columnist for the *New York Times*, appeared two months later. An "intensive tour of 20 Vietnamese civilian hospitals from the 17th Parallel in the North to the Gulf of Siam in the South," Rusk reported, found not one case of burns due to napalm. "There have been cases of severe burns from napalm but the numbers are not large in comparison to burns due to accidents," he wrote. Rusk said he saw every burn case at the hospitals, and attributed the vast majority to cooking accidents, in particular the use of relatively inexpensive gasoline in stoves designed for kerosene. Just 15 percent of overall hospital admissions in South Vietnam, the physician asserted, came from war-related injuries. "[T]he picture that has been painted by some in the United States of large numbers of children burned by napalm is grossly exaggerated," he concluded. Rusk's lightning tour and summary findings, however, whatever their accuracy, were no match for the vivid testimony and scorching photographs in the January articles. His two-part report was buried on pages 84 and 30 of successive Sunday editions, and got relatively little notice. Later observers attributed findings of few injuries to napalm's lethality: "this is an all-or-nothing weapon" an Australian medical team reported in 1968.[7]

After the *Ramparts, Redbook,* and *Ladies Home Journal* articles, and the photographs, napalm was no longer just a bright flash in the jungle: it was a painful fact, marked by scarred children.

Martin Luther King Jr. was one of the first to respond. The Nobel Peace Prize recipient flipped through a stack of magazines at a restaurant in the Miami airport on January 14, 1967, while waiting for an airplane. He froze, according to companion Bernard Lee, when he reached Pepper's piece in *Ramparts:* "Martin just pushed the plate of food away from him. I looked up and said, 'Doesn't it taste any good?' and he answered, 'Nothing will ever taste any good for me until I do everything I can to end that war." Lee continued, "That's when the decision was made. Martin had known about the war before then, of course, and had spoken out against it. But it was then that he decided to commit himself to oppose it."

Within a month, in February 1967, 2,500 members of the Women Strike for Peace group paraded posters of the *Ramparts* pictures at a demonstration outside Secretary of Defense Robert McNamara's Pentagon office. Napalm's victims had become real.[8]

Scattered campus demonstrations against Dow recruiters resumed in mid-winter as students returned from vacation. These actions proved more confrontational than those of the previous fall, and received proportionately more media coverage, but were muted in comparison with those that followed that autumn: a harbinger, but not yet a national movement. At the University of Wisconsin–Madison on February 21, 1967, for example, about one hundred students refused to leave a hallway outside interview rooms used by Dow recruiters in Commerce Hall at the center of campus. "What we had was these pictures from *Ramparts* magazine of napalmed kids. Almost everybody had a picket sign like that. . . . The idea was to confront people and make them face up to what was going on," explained protester Henry Haslach. Students shouted "baby killers" and "good Germans" at representatives of the chemical company, chanted and sang, and refused to clear the area. Police made nineteen arrests. The next day, 200 protesters blocked the university chancellor's office to challenge the incarcerations. Administrators bailed out the student prisoners in a gesture of sympathy, and the crisis passed. "Dow I," as the event came to be called in Wisconsin, pushed the number of stories around the country about Dow and napalm over 1,000 for the first time.[9]

Some students supported the use of napalm in Vietnam and came to Dow's defense. A January demonstration by twenty Students for a Democratic Society (SDS) members at Pennsylvania State University produced weeks of angry letters to the *Daily Collegian*. As one correspondent wrote, "[T]he purpose of the Viet Cong is strictly terror; whereas the purpose of the bombing—of the napalm—is to flush out the VC and thus rid the country of terror." The author continued, "The Viet Cong have showed their mettle by taking the leader of each village they terrorize and splitting his legs like we would a wishbone . . . how do you fight that kind of ungodly savageness? . . . with the same type of warfare that they are using—because it is the only thing these animals understand." Responses like these received less attention as the year continued, and perhaps fewer adherents, but did not entirely fade away. In Madison, counterprotesters at the Commerce Hall rally, many drawn from the local Reserve Officers' Training Corps program, shouted support for Dow. "Napalm is good for V.C. acne," read one placard.[10]

New York peace activists continued actions through the winter and spring of 1967 that made impacts large and small. Sunday March 19 was designated "Napalm Sunday" by a group of about seventy-five protesters who marched from the Metropolitan Museum of Art to St. Patrick's Cathedral. A triptych that read "Napalm Burns People," later adopted as a leitmotif by protesters across the country, made its first appearance here. "We marched in threes, and each trio had signs that, when combined, read 'Napalm Burns People,' supplied to us by the Village Peace Center," explained organizer Jack McGuire.[11]

A few weeks later, on April 4, 1967, King called for a revolution in American values, and set napalm at the center of his argument. In the spectacular main hall of the Riverside Church on Manhattan's Upper West Side, modeled on France's Chartres Cathedral, he declared, "A true revolution of values will lay hand on the world order and say of war, 'This way of settling differences is not just.' This business of burning human beings with napalm . . . cannot be reconciled with wisdom, justice, and love." He concluded, "A nation that continues year after year to spend more money on military defense than on programs of social uplift is approaching spiritual death." President Ulysses S. Grant's granite mausoleum, chiseled with his epitaph "Let Us Have Peace," stood stolidly across the street. A chorus of 168 newspapers denounced King's comments.

Less eloquently, but to the reverend's point, activists gathered in New York's Central Park for the "Spring Mobilization" on April 15 distributed fortune cookies that read " 'Help! I'm a prisoner in a US peasant-cooking facility'—anonymous Dow employee."[12]

A sit-in on March 20, 1967, at Pomona College north of Los Angeles, the first in the school's history, exemplified the whimsicality, and even good humor, that was an element of student anti-napalm protests during this period. Dow representative Hans Beetz arrived a bit before 9:00 a.m. and was escorted to the campus music room, which had been reserved for his interviews. When administrators opened the locked door, however, they found twenty-five SDS members jammed inside. A large poster on a tripod displayed photographs of people burned by napalm. Occupiers demanded that two representatives from their group be allowed to attend the interviews, to present their side of the matter. "Pomona College was not founded for the purpose of training people to burn children," a demonstrator told the dean of students.[13]

Determined, Beetz prepared to conduct interviews despite the crowd. A pair of applicants arrived, collected forms, and dropped off their resumes. Beetz attempted to interview them remotely by telephone, but was forced to quit when protesters clustered around to eavesdrop. Exasperated, he got into his car and drove away. Activists raced after him in a trio of vehicles to make sure he left. Student government representatives adopted a resolution the following week that condemned Dow for its production of napalm and urged students to "carefully consider those activities before consenting to be interviewed by the company." The *Los Angeles Times* reported that this was the first criticism of Dow by a student government in Southern California. Company executives told the school they would not be back that year.[14]

Through it all, Dow stood firm. In early 1967, United Technologies quietly stopped napalm production at its Redwood City facility when it delivered its 100-millionth pound to the government. Witco, the second of three military suppliers, also ended its manufacturing operations at about the same time. In March 1967, at a two-day board meeting devoted to napalm policy, however, Dow resolved to "stand up for what it believed in," according to board chairman Carl Gerstacker. "Our sons were serving in that war," he recalled in an oral history interview, and "we felt a strong obligation to support them." Dow thus became the only U.S. napalm manufacturer.[15]

Academia added to the growing public awareness of napalm in July 1967 when *The New England Journal of Medicine* published the first clinical review of the weapon's effect on people under the auspices of Physicians for Social Responsibility, an international nongovernmental organization of doctors established in 1961 to examine the medical and public health effects of nuclear war. Author Peter Reich was an instructor at Harvard Medical School; coauthor Victor Sidel was a senior physician at Massachusetts General Hospital: credentials that warranted attention.[16]

Reich and Sidel characterized napalm as a "chemical weapon," confirmed the horrific nature of the burns it caused and the particular risks to children, emphasized the special psychological power of the weapon, and concluded that doctors should familiarize themselves with the subject as part of their public health responsibilities. "Napalm burns are likely to be deep and extensive. The adhesiveness, prolonged burning time and high burning temperatures of napalm favor third degree burns in all affected areas, with coagulation of muscle, fat and other deep tissue likely. Burns of this depth will probably result in severe scar contractures and deformities, especially when they occur under conditions making early skin grafting difficult," the doctors wrote. Moreover, they added, "Napalm wounds contaminated with white phosphorus may continue smoldering long after the initial trauma." Children, the physicians explained, "will suffer a disproportionately high mortality and morbidity because of special problems, acute and chronic, presented by the burned child." Panic, they advised, was "more likely to be observed among napalm victims than among those wounded by other agents."[17]

Sidel explained later that the primary purpose of the piece was informational, given the paucity of knowledge about napalm in the civilian medical community. Antipathy to the Vietnam conflict, however, ensured an immediate audience. "People were not aware of the use of napalm in previous wars, but because the opposition to the war in Vietnam was so widespread and so vehement there was interest. This was picked up as an example of the ways in which this war was being fought," he observed years later.[18]

# 9

# Indicted

Towering political thunderheads had gathered above napalm by the end of the summer of 1967. Its effect on civilians was increasingly widely understood. The war was burning hotter: draft boards pulled in 119,265 inductees in 1963; 112,386 in 1964; 230,991 in 1965; and 382,010 in 1966, the most since the Korean War. Dow Chemical was as close as a campus recruiting visit or, as Eric Prokosch noted, local supermarkets. Ferocious clips of combat appeared nightly on television. Passions ran high. "Perhaps if you accept the war, all can be justified—the free strike zones, the refugees, the spraying of herbicide on crops, the napalm," four staff members, who resigned in September from the International Voluntary Service Vietnamese humanitarian relief organization, wrote in an open letter to President Lyndon Johnson. Protests the previous autumn and spring proved to be like raindrops that herald a deluge.[1]

The tempest broke at the University of Wisconsin–Madison on October 18, when Dow executives again advertised interviews at Commerce Hall. As in the February "Dow I" action, students jammed the hallway outside the conference rooms and prevented would-be candidates from entering. This time, however, more than a thousand protesters and observers crowded around the building; Madison police officers in riot gear, summoned by university authorities, clubbed dozens of students inside the hall, and many more outside the building (the first extensive violence at a rally against the Vietnam War); an activist cut down the U.S. flag on top of the building where the demonstration occurred, and set off fire-crackers in the midst of the melee; a thrown brick smashed the face of a policeman, broke his nose, and knocked him out; protesters rocked a police wagon so violently they forced the release of several prisoners held inside; and, as classes changed at the end of the hour and the crowd swelled to around 4,000–5,000 students, tear gas was used for the first time on an American campus. Police arrested thirteen people, and sixty-five students and officers ended up in the hospital. Television broadcast images of the violent confrontation coast to coast, and triggered almost 2,000 newspaper articles and editorials about Dow and napalm: almost double the total number of articles about the firm and its controversial product published to that date.[2]

Comments by participants illustrate how attitudes had hardened to-ward the "Best Weapon Used in Pacific" since 1945. "Napalm was this hideous, jellied gas burning at 2,000 degrees Fahrenheit. It didn't just kill you; it tortured you. It has a complete reference to Zyklon B, the gas they used in the concentration camps. It felt like chemical warfare at its worst," explained Mark Greenside, one of the student protesters. "To use the University buildings to, in effect, provide a subsidy to Dow, by pro-viding them the space, we thought was absolutely wrong," student leader Paul Soglin said. "The horror of napalm made an indelible impression on all of us and especially on students," recalled Professor Maurice Zeit-lin. "I didn't want to see any more Vietnamese children running around with their clothes burned off. There were millions of us who thought if we put in enough time and made enough noise that it would be impossi-ble for the government to keep sending young men to Vietnam," con-firmed activist Jim Rowen.[3]

Headlines from Madison spurred protests against Dow and napalm at campuses across the country. By the end of December students at the Universities of Illinois and Michigan, Boston College, the University of Minnesota, Harvard, Columbia, Brandeis, Boston University, several branches of the University of California, the University of Chicago, the City College of New York, Indiana University, New York University, the University of Pennsylvania, and numerous others had rallied against the incendiary. Dow reported confrontations at forty-six of the 178 colleges recruiters visited that autumn, and 133 of the 339 schools they interviewed at in the 1967–1968 academic year—more than double the fifty-five anti-Dow protests of the 1966–1967 school year.[4]

Executives put on a brave face and attempted to follow the same public relations strategy that had served them well the previous spring. "Spokesmen for the Dow Chemical Company, a napalm manufacturer, said yesterday that campus demonstrations against the company had not hurt its recruitment drive at universities. They said the company had no intention of curtailing the drive or changing it," the *New York Times* reported in October 1967. "The United States is involved in Vietnam. As long as we are involved we believe in fulfilling our responsibility to this national commitment of a democratic society. And we do this because we believe in the long-term goals of our country. . . . [O]ur company has made the decision to continue to produce napalm B and other materials as long as they are needed by our Government," read a condensed version of the company's policy statement distributed to staff members. "[E]ffective weapons such as napalm are saving the lives of American men," Dow president Herbert Doan told *Time*.[5]

A spokesman plaintively repeated earlier assertions about the minimal importance of napalm relative to Dow's total business. Annual sales of the incendiary to the U.S. government were just $6.5 million: less than one-half percent of gross revenue. "Looming larger in the company's marketing list of more than 800 products are water-purifying chemicals, cold medicines, insecticides and anesthetics—many of which are also used in Viet Nam," *Time* observed. This argument, if it had ever been dispositive, now swayed no one: napalm was not comparable to cold medicine. Dow's absolute production—54,620 tons delivered to the military in 1966 alone, and over 22,000 tons produced in the first six months of 1967—justified condemnation in the minds of opponents.[6]

Harvard's confrontation on October 25, 1967, one week after the violence at Madison, was especially wrenching. Rhetoric was heated from the outset. "Is it in the interests of chemistry students—or of any students—that war profiteers like Dow prostitute science for repression and murder?" asked advance leaflets. A sit-in started at 9:30 a.m. in the James Bryant Conant Laboratory at 12 Oxford Street, where director of

Dow Labs Frederick Leavitt planned to interview recruits. "The demonstrators argued that any corporation guilty of war crimes and partner to genocide—in this case, Dow—had no right to come on the Harvard campus," the *Harvard Crimson* student newspaper reported. Conant Laboratory, named to honor the former National Defense Research Committee head and Harvard president, was attached to the rear of the Converse Chemistry Laboratory building: the very place where Louis Fieser and E. B. Hershberg conducted their window-well experiments. It is unclear if protesters knew its history. At 11:00 a.m., activists discovered Leavitt had relocated to nearby Mallinckrodt Hall and was conducting interviews—a decoy businessman remained at 12 Oxford Street. Students ran to the new location. Director of the laboratories Ronald Vanelli, the *Crimson* recounted, "immediately attempted unsuccessfully to escort [Leavitt] through the crowd which by then had grown to over 100. They stepped on and over three tiers of seated demonstrators but were then met by rows of students standing, with arms linked." Michael S. Ansara, class of 1968, told Leavitt he could leave only "after he signed a yellow sheet of paper bearing the hand-scrawled pledge: 'I agree to stop interviewing on the Harvard campus and not to return for that purpose.'" Activists questioned the businessman aggressively on napalm, Dow, and the war for about five minutes, the *Crimson* continued, and then he and Vanelli disappeared back into the conference room. They remained there until about 6:00 p.m., when students voted to end the protest. Leavitt's ordeal was the longest of any Dow recruiter during the anti-napalm campaign. "Napalm—and the company that makes it—have become symbolic of a war that tries to destroy communism by bombing people," *Crimson* writers editorialized the next day.[7]

Fieser, who had retired a few months earlier, was a "bystander," in his words, at the protest. He declined to receive a student delegation that visited his office, which was also located in Mallinckrodt Hall. Leaflets handed out a few blocks away in Harvard Square showed a picture of a child with terrible burns. "CAN YOU SUPPORT NAPALM used against CHILDREN?" asked the text. "If you met the mother and father whose 10-year-old daughter you see here, they would want you to explain why SHE is a victim of NAPALM. Dropped from American planes, this jellied gasoline roasts to death or maims countless other children every day," it asserted. Signatories—the Citizens Campaign against Napalm, Student Nonviolent Coordinating Committee, Massachusetts Political Action for Peace, and Students for a Democratic Society (SDS)—urged "Don't buy Dow products."[8]

After World War II, Fieser returned to his interest in public health and carcinogens. His academic accomplishments were extraordinary: 284 research papers; more than twenty books, including the nation's most widely used basic organic chemistry text; the prestigious Judd prize for cancer research, and the Nichols Medal from the American Chemical Society; numerous teaching awards; membership in the American Academy of Arts and Sciences, and the National Academy of Sciences; the only chemist on the groundbreaking 1963 Surgeon General's Advisory Committee on Smoking and Health that established a link between cigarette smoking and lung disease; and honorary degrees from Williams College and the University of Paris.[9]

Until Vietnam, the professor reported, nothing but congratulations followed his work on napalm. President Harry Truman awarded him a Certificate of Merit in 1948 for his invention. Letters rolled in from soldiers who said his gel saved their lives. Then, in 1966–1967, everything changed. His mailbox was filled with vitriol. "He said some of the writers were saying, in effect, 'We thought you were a great guy, and now you're a bum,'" the *New York Times* reported.[10]

When questioned, Fieser drew a bright line between his research and actual deployments of napalm. "I couldn't foresee that this stuff was going to be used against babies and Buddhists. The person who makes a rifle . . . he isn't responsible if it is used to shoot the President," he told journalist John Lannan in November 1967. "You don't know what's coming. That wasn't my business. That was for other people. I was working on a technical problem that was considered pressing," he told another reporter one month later. More generally, he added, "It's not my business to deal with the political or moral questions. . . . Just because I played a role in the technological development of napalm doesn't mean I'm any more qualified to comment on the moral aspects of it." In 1968, he said at the end of an interview with *Time*, "I have no right to judge the morality of napalm just because I invented it."

To Fieser, napalm was interesting primarily as a chemical innovation. As he said at his retirement party, held just three weeks after student demonstrations wracked his laboratory building at Harvard: "Until the day before the lecture, I had planned to demonstrate the interesting and completely non-personal uses of Napalm to be culminated by the burning of a handsome $7 box from the Harvard Coop. . . . Mary talked me out of even mentioning Napalm." None of the other speakers at the dinner mentioned the infamous incendiary. Hoyt Hottel, an MIT professor and former NDRC Division 11 colleague of Fieser's, confirmed how attitudes changed in Cambridge, Massachusetts. In a 1995 interview he recalled, "There was a postwar period in which I would not dare say publicly that I had been involved during the war in the use of napalm, because that was such an ugly thing."[11]

As if by unstated agreement, Fieser's work on napalm, which had held a prominent place in his biography prior to 1967, was metaphorically airbrushed out of his record after the campus protests. His hometown newspaper did not mention the munition in its report on his retirement celebration. The *Williams Alumni Review* was equally discreet when it announced his appointment in 1968 as a research professor at Smith College. Napalm received scant, if any, mention in the many eulogies published after his death, from pneumonia, on July 28, 1977. At his memorial service, the closest anyone came to a mention of the gel was when associate Robert Woodward described World War II as the "Great Conflagration." Colleague E. J. Corey marveled, in a characteristic assessment, "One remembers him for the delight he took in his work. . . . He approached each task with boundless energy, great zest and relentless efficiency." A 1977 compendium of member biographies, published by the National Academy of Sciences, wrote of his war work, "With the approach of World War II, Fieser was drawn increasingly into war-related projects. A brief excursion into the area of mixed aliphatic-aromatic polynitro compounds for possible use as exotic explosives was followed by studies of alkali salts of long chain fatty acids as incendiaries, but by far the most important of his war-related work was his long and intensive study of the quinone antimalarials." Academicians did not include Fieser's patent on napalm, or the technical paper he wrote about its production, in their extensive bibliography of his publications. In the spring of 1996, Mary Fieser dedicated the Louis and Mary Fieser Laboratory for Undergraduate Organic Chemistry at the university. Harvard's official *Gazette* did not mention napalm when it lauded the namesakes at year end: "Louis Fieser was a distinguished researcher whose career included work on antimalarial agents, cortisone, and vitamin K-1."[12]

Dow could not distance itself as easily. By the end of 1967, the firm was besieged. Knowledge about the way napalm killed was now widespread. Opponents turned the company's argument that the gel was a small part of its operations on its head, and asserted that Dow's insistence on keeping business it didn't need made the firm especially culpable. Palo Alto activists returned to the fore when they published a call for petition signatures against napalm in newspapers nationwide, and submitted the massive document that resulted to the House Armed Services Committee. Students called on their schools to divest from Dow, and routinely blockaded recruiters in interview offices. There was so much activity that on November 8 the firm's public relations staff began to circulate an internal *Napalm News* about the latest trouble spots.[13]

Rhetoric was searing. "We are not, then, dealing with trivialities, but with monstrous deeds," Boston University history professor Howard Zinn wrote in his autumn 1967 pamphlet *Dow Shalt Not Kill*. Napalm bombing "ranks with the destruction of Lidice by the Germans, the crushing of the Hungarian rebellion by the Russians, or the recent mass slaughter in Indonesia," he asserted. "The fact that there is only an indirect connection between Dow recruiting students and napalm dropped on Vietnamese villages, does not vitiate the moral issue. It is precisely the nature of modern mass murder that it is not visibly direct like individual murder, but takes on a corporate character, where every participant has limited liability," he argued. "The use of napalm is bringing shame upon our nation throughout the world. Its use is wholly unworthy of the ideals for which this nation stands. We demand that our President and the Members of our Congress take immediate steps to stop the manufacture and use of this barbarous weapon," read the Palo Alto petition.[14]

Market-based arguments made little headway against such impassioned assertions. President of IBM Thomas Watson Jr., for example, in a letter to the student newspaper at his alma mater Brown University, said it was "ridiculous in the extreme" to expect a company to "subvert the democratic process" and refuse to sell one of its products to its own government. He noted there was almost no major U.S. corporation that was not contributing in some way to the war. Students brushed his justifications aside, however, and urged alumni to withhold donations under all circumstances until Brown divested from Dow. Pickets reappeared at the chemical giant's Rockefeller Center offices.[15]

A December 18 protest at California State University, Los Angeles, showed how fully anti-napalm forces controlled the field by the end of 1967. The demonstration, the first ever organized by the local SDS chapter, began with a rally and march to the school's main administration building, then continued to the recruiting office housed in an old trailer. Dow recruiters locked themselves inside when the students arrived, so demonstrators pummeled it, and left it "dented, though not destroyed," in the words of a SDS newsletter. The protesters burned a dummy with homemade napalm and tossed a stink bomb into the trailer, which forced the recruiters out. They hurried to another building, which was promptly occupied by students. Campus police, backed by 350 City of Los Angeles officers stationed about 300 yards away behind a small hill, announced that everyone was under arrest. The harried recruiters seized advantage of a break in the action, jumped out a back window, and raced to their car. "The students chased them, and looked at them through the car windows as they sped away," SDS said. The executives told a tale of horror on local evening radio shows, according to the newsletter.[16]

Dow felt the pressure. "[I]ts image is suffering. Next to LBJ, Dean Rusk and Hubert Humphrey, Dow, the manufacturer of napalm, has become the most popular target for campus anti-war protests," *Science* magazine reported. Second-guessing began inside the firm. "Creative men," might be more difficult to attract as a result of the demonstrations, Doan fretted. "You just don't know what it is doing to the quality of students we're talking to," said Director of Corporate Recruiting Raymond F. Rolf. "It was very disheartening," recruiter George Allen recalled of a visit to San Jose State College. "One of the fellows I was interviewing I had to talk to in the washroom because we were both so blinded by the tear gas." Executives began to assess their options. "There is certainly a possibility of our not bidding or bidding high," for a renewal of the napalm contract, board chairman Carl Gerstacker told the *Los Angeles Times* on November 23. A spokesman, however, quickly backtracked, and Gerstacker clarified the next day, "My remarks were intended to mean only that I cannot commit my company at this time to a course of action for the indefinite future."[17]

By 1968, napalm's identification with the horrors of the Vietnam War, and by extension Dow Chemical, was complete. Protests moved off campuses and activist clergy joined students as principal organizers. On May 7, the New York-based group Clergy and Laymen Concerned about Vietnam (CALCAV) assembled hundreds of protesters for a rally at the University of Michigan at Ann Arbor followed by an overnight "March on Midland" caravan to Dow's annual meeting, which was to be held at Midland's Central Intermediate School. About 500 clergy and students, many wearing black armbands, crowded the school's lawn the next morning. "Genocide via napalm," "The war is wrong—so is Dow," and "Dow Know-How In Every Drop of Napalm," read signs. "[I]t will cost Dow hundreds and hundreds of millions of dollars to rebuild its image as a maker of chemicals for progress instead of chemicals of destruction," Scarsdale stockbroker Daniel J. Bernstein remonstrated with shareholders. "We must not surrender to government the right to make moral choices," preached Quaker clergyman Rev. James Laird.[18]

Dow denied corporate responsibility for the Vietnam War, and again pleaded duty and patriotism. Humanitarianism and commerce had been dropped from its list of arguments. "Companies don't start wars, and companies can't end them . . . if you want to stop the war why aren't you talking to legislators?" Gerstacker lectured CALCAV leader Rev. Richard Fernandez in a public discussion before the shareholders meeting. A group of seventeen counterdemonstrators may have increased the discomfort of corporate officers with their supportive messages: "I Back Dow, I Like My V.C. (Vietcong) Well-Done," read one.[19]

Corporate authority prevailed. Bernstein's nomination of war opponent and former Federal Reserve board chairman Marriner Eccles to the Dow board was defeated by 25 million votes to 1,212. A show of hands soundly rejected a resolution to end Dow's production of napalm. "You can harass us. You can hurt us—and we have been hurt. . . . But as long as our democratically elected government sends draftees to die in Vietnam, we're going to support those men," Gerstacker said in closing remarks. Attendees adjourned to the strains of "We Shall Overcome" from demonstrators.[20]

A few days later, nine committed Catholics led by brothers Daniel and Philip Berrigan—both priests, and dressed in clerical collars—broke into the Catonsville, Maryland, draft board office, removed between 378 and 600 files for prospective draftees, covered them with homemade napalm made from gasoline and soap flakes, and burned them in front of waiting news cameras. The action took less than fifteen minutes. "We felt it was fitting that this agent which had burned human flesh in the war in Vietnam and in many other places should now be poured on the records which gave war and violence their cruel legitimacy," David Darst, a Jesuit who was one of the participants, said at his subsequent trial. "We used a contemporary symbol napalm to destroy records which are potential death certificates," said Thomas Lewis, another of the so-called Catonsville Nine. Mary Moylan, a nun and former nurse-midwife told the court: "To a nurse the effect of napalm on human beings is apparent. I think of children and women bombed by napalm, burned alive by a substance which does not roll off. It is a jelly. It adheres. It continues burning. This is inhuman, absolutely. To pour napalm on pieces of paper is certainly preferable to using napalm on human beings. By pouring napalm on draft files I wish to celebrate life, not to engage in a dance of death." Vietnam, Daniel Berrigan wrote in a meditation distributed to media at the event, was the "Land of Burning Children." Copycat actions followed in New York, Milwaukee, Boston, Chicago, and other cities. Similarly, on March 22, 1969, a different set of nine Catholics, including six priests, broke into Dow's Washington, D.C., office, wrecked office equipment, spattered human blood over the walls, ceilings and floors, put up photos of napalmed children, and threw documents into the street where they formed piles four inches deep. Whereas in 1965 just 38 percent of Americans were familiar with Dow according to a survey, by 1969 no less than 91 percent of the public "knew something about" the firm.[21]

Even the company's Canadian subsidiary felt the heat. In November 1968, a time bomb exploded in front of the home of general counsel Len

Weldon at 5:00 a.m. "It scared the devil out of my family," the lawyer recalled. In early 1969, a trio of protesters threatened to blow up the firm's Toronto sales office unless its manager signed a pledge to stop napalm production.[22]

Dow had had enough. In October 1969, when its Pentagon contract came up for renewal, the corporation resubmitted its 1968 bid without adjustment—and lost the contract to arms manufacturer American Electric Inc. of La Mirada, California, southeast of Los Angeles. It announced the development on November 14. Its rival manufactured bombshells, and had been filling them with napalm from Dow's Torrance facility since 1967 at its plant in Long Beach, south of Los Angeles. American Electric had built a polystyrene plant just that year, possibly with the napalm contract in mind. Napalm's new manufacturer was a subsidiary of the City Investing conglomerate, produced no consumer products, and had no plans to recruit on college campuses. Dow denied it had deliberately overbid, and reaffirmed its commitment to provide whatever products the government required.[23]

Absolution proved harder to obtain, however, perhaps because of the manufacturer's lack of contrition. Days after Dow announced it had lost its contract, students at Notre Dame University locked up a company recruiter to protest the firm's previous work on napalm. National attention followed the university's decision to suspend or expel ten students in response. Dow's continued production of the Agent Orange herbicide added to its infamy. Even though anti-napalm campus protests largely ended with Dow's napalm production—the firm recorded twenty-nine demonstrations in the 1968–1969 school year, and just four in 1969–1970: "no one talks about it anymore," a reporter at the Harvard *Crimson* student newspaper said of the incendiary in June 1970—the company was fused as tightly in the public's mind to napalm as the gel was to the skin of its victims. "[W]e have in effect been cut off from a segment of society, the size of which is indeterminate, which has blocked us out emotionally because they see us as a symbol of the hated war in Vietnam," Gerstacker admitted in June 1970. Dow shareholders fell from 95,000 to 90,000 during the years of campus protests. "We suspect a good many of the 5,000 we lost reacted at least in part to the napalm stories," the chairman said ruefully.[24]

Dow's record as a manufacturer of napalm remains an important part of the company's public identity. In 1987, for example, almost two decades after it had stopped producing napalm, *Time* magazine reported on the launch of a national public relations campaign as follows: "Dow Chemical, vilified on college campuses during the Viet Nam War for manufacturing napalm, is reaching out to young people in television commercials that show freshly minted college graduates signing on to help feed the world." In 2005, almost forty years after the heroic effort by recruiter Hans Beetz to interview candidates by telephone from the occupied music room at Pomona College, the *Economist* magazine, in an article titled "America's most-hated companies: a roll-call of commercial vilification," awarded Dow a satirical "lifetime achievement award for the courting of controversy," in part because of its work on napalm. Dow's president, chief executive officer, and chairman Andrew Liveris observed at a 2006 conference on Ethics and Compliance: "Believe me, we have had our share of ethical challenges, most of them very public . . . starting with the manufacture of Napalm during the Vietnam War . . . when suddenly we went from being a company that made Saran Wrap to keep food fresh to a kind of war machine . . . at least, according to the characterizations of the time." Dow remains a defense contractor, but appears not to manufacture weapons.[25]

Protests aimed specifically at napalm faded back into the broader antiwar movement from which they initially sprang after Dow left the business. American Electric's Long Beach plant never attracted sustained opposition, although it took some time for this denouement to become clear: on December 1, 1969, the *New York Times* dubbed Long Beach "napalm capital of the world"—and reported that local protests had started. Activism in Southern California, however, came largely from local homeowners concerned about safety and property values, rather than war protesters, as in Redwood City. On June 25, 1969, an explosion at the plant rained hot molten plastic on the adjoining Cherry Manor community of 226 homes. A truck spilled seven shipping containers filled with napalm onto the Long Beach Freeway the following week. No one was hurt, but tempers frayed. Another explosion on October 2 sprayed hot plastic on the lawns of homes that adjoined the plant and a dozen cars and trucks owned by a neighborhood business. Representatives of the city manager moved to stop production and the Cherry Manor Homeowners Association sued the city for negligence. But accidents ended when the plant resolved its start-up difficulties, and with them most objections.[26]

Civilian injuries caused by napalm, however, remained an element of protests against U.S. involvement in Vietnam until the war ended. A series of December 1971 "napalm" attacks against Christmas trees decorated with war toys and medals in several cities, organized by Vietnam Veterans against the War, was typical in its use of the gel to draw attention to the broader movement. Posters of napalm victims remained a fixture at antiwar demonstrations.[27]

Thus, by the time Kim Phúc and little Danh began their run from the temple on June 8, 1972, napalm was closely associated with the war in Vietnam in the minds of millions. Moreover, as a result of the nationwide education program that was one result of the anti-napalm campaign, accounts like that of reporter Fox Butterfield for the *New York Times* could be comprehended at a level of detail hard to conceive before 1966: "Sgt. Nguyen Van Hai watched incredulously as a South Vietnamese plane mistakenly dropped flaming napalm right on his troops and a cluster of civilians. In an instant five women and children and half a dozen Vietnamese soldiers were badly burned, their skin peeling off in huge pink and black chunks. 'This is terrible, the worst I've ever seen!' said Sergeant Hai."[28]

Danh's three-year-old legs proved too slow to escape the fire cloud. A soldier scooped him up as he ran through the temple gate, but was himself incinerated. His grandmother, who avoided the worst of the flames, gathered his mutilated body, and arrived at the checkpoint a few moments after Kim. Sheaths of skin dangled from the boy's small feet, and flapped with her steps. He died within the hour.[29]

After the fog of war cleared, Kim's parents began a desperate search for their daughter. Nearby Cu Chi town yielded no trace of her. Impecunious, the couple, who made their living as proprietors of a roadside noodle stand, walked thirty miles to the capital Saigon. They searched the city's hospitals for three days, and slept in the open each night. Clerks at the last institution they visited, Saigon's First Children's Hospital, denied that any child of Kim's description had been admitted. Her parents checked every bed in the eight-story institution. Then, overwhelmed and exhausted, they slumped together in the lobby. A cleaner passed with his mop. Kim's father approached him. "Excuse me, did you see a young girl brought here who was burned very badly? It would have been three days ago. . . . Maybe she did not survive?" he asked. The cleaner led them outside and pointed to a small building with peeling clapboards and large windows covered by shutters. "That room is for children who will die," he said.

When her parents arrived, Kim's biographer Denise Chong wrote, "Their daughter lay on a cot in a fetal position. A gray-brown gob matted her burnt hair, her face was badly swollen, and the bandages on her wounds were fetid with infection and stuck with charred and dead skin."[30] She moaned. She lived. Her parents rushed to the only doctor they had met at the hospital, and clung to him in desperation. "Please, our daughter has been left to die," implored her father. A glimmer of recognition passed between physician and parent: they later recalled being students together in Saigon. In twenty minutes, an ambulance arrived to take Kim to the National Center for Plastic and Reconstructive Surgery, a special clinic founded in 1968 by a pair of New Yorkers: plastic surgeon Arthur Barsky and attorney Thomas Miller. It was perhaps the only civilian facility in South Vietnam that could have treated her.[31]

Recovery from burn injuries can be excruciatingly painful. A doctor at Kim's hospital compared the experience to being flayed alive: suffering so severe it constituted a "wound to the soul." Each morning, after an examination, nurses took Kim to a special bathtub filled with surgical soap and warm water and removed her dressings. Then, in a process called debridement, they used a handheld shower to peel away dead and infected skin. Scissors supplemented the water jets when necessary. Nine-year-old Kim received no anesthetic. When her sister came to visit, she fainted at her screams.[32]

Skin grafts began once the infections had been healed and Kim's strength had somewhat returned. Doctors used a special knife called a dermatome to shave swathes of skin from healthy areas of her body and affix them to the deepest wounds. Donor sites suffered an injury comparable to a serious burn, and required careful treatment. Finally, to ensure that her new skin grew back without fusing to itself, Kim Phúc was sealed in a body cast and placed in traction. She began physiotherapy, which introduced new odysseys of suffering, when the cast was removed. In November 1972, after almost six months at the clinic, the longest stay in the history of the facility, the little girl was discharged. "Napalm is the most terrible pain you can imagine," she told an interviewer years later.[33]

The Vietnam War, in turn, was increasingly associated with U.S. failure by the summer of 1972. South Vietnam's military struggled to contain a major enemy offensive, its government wobbled, and preparations for an American withdrawal became more apparent by the day. What was symbolic in 1962, when U.S.-made napalm devastated President Diem's Saigon palace was, increasingly, reality. Authorities did not censor "The Terror of War," as they did comparable images from Japan during World War II and the Korean War, and the photograph captured a moment of high drama, but it was far from unique: photographs of children injured by napalm in Vietnam had circulated in the United States for years. Rather, the napalm that hit Kim Phúc was an intimation of national defeat, as much as a record of individual tragedy. It lashed a wound and hardened, like a scar, into certainty.[34]

America's last combat troops left Vietnam in March 1973. Most of their napalm went with them: 23 million pounds in 34,653 ten-foot-long, cigar-shaped, army-green aluminum canisters, each packed in an individual wooden crate, returned to California. Troops stacked the bombs on sixty-seven open acres at the Seal Beach weapons station in the Fallbrook weapons facility next to the Camp Pendleton Marine Corps Base between Los Angeles and San Diego. Final defeat for the United States came on April 30, 1975, when its last helicopter left the U.S. embassy in Saigon. In Southern California, the nation's napalm arsenal sat in the sun and waited to hear its fate. Gradually, over the next almost quarter century America, and the world, came to a condemnatory judgment.[35]

# STALEMATE, TO DEFEAT

U.S. Air Force P-51 Mustang "Sexy Sally" illustrates a low-level "nape scrape" napalm attack on a Korean town on August 1, 1951. *U.S. Air Force*

Pyongyang after United Nations attacks with napalm and explosives.
*Vitalii S. Latov*

A trio of South Korean women, burned by U.S. napalm bombs, at an aid station near Suwon, South Korea, on February 4, 1951. *AP Photo/Eugene Fox, U.S. National Archives, File*

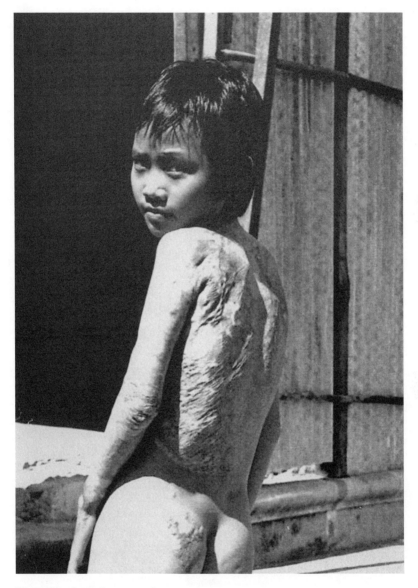

Kim Phúc shows her wounds. *Perry Kretz*

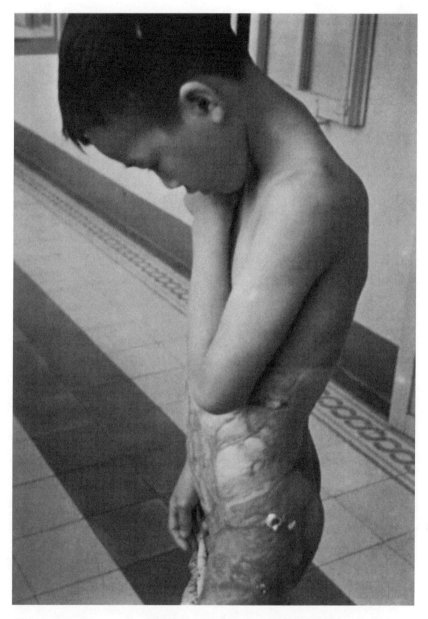

A picture of a Vietnamese child burned by napalm, published in January 1967 by *Ramparts* magazine: one of the first photographs of a civilian napalm casualty widely distributed in the United States. *William F. Pepper*

A New York rally against U.S. involvement in the Vietnam War on March 16, 1967, led by Dr. Benjamin Spock (second from left) and Martin Luther King Jr. (center). *AFP*

View of the October 18, 1967, protest against Dow Chemical at the University of Wisconsin–Madison, from a broken window in the Commerce Building. *Image courtesy of the UW-Madison Archives*

# PARIAH

Napalm made its mass-market screen debut in the 1979 blockbuster *Apocalypse Now,* the first film to show a napalm strike to a global audience. Its power was undeniable, but the results it achieved proved illusory on examination, or even counterproductive. Lieutenant Colonel Bill Kilgore, played by Robert Duvall, ordered a daybreak assault on Charlie's Point at the mouth of the fictional Nung River. His objective was to secure a famous "point break" wave formation, where currents met the land, for champion surfer and patrol boat crewman Lance Johnson. A secret mission by Special Forces captain Benjamin Willard, played by Martin Sheen, which required securing the promontory so his boat could voyage up river, was incidental. Millions saw the movie, which won two Academy Awards, including Best Picture, and had gross receipts of about $160 million.[1]

Napalm's moment came as day broke. A vast field of helicopters churned the air. American soldiers from the First Cavalry Division (Airmobile), toughest in Vietnam, sat in Kilgore's helicopter as orderlies loaded ammunition. A trio of surfboards was strapped to the skids. Liftoff came, and as waves rushed by below, loudspeakers suddenly blared out Richard Wagner's "Ride of the Valkyries." Ominous and lethal, the machines swept low over the shore, devastated a village and its defenders with rockets and machine guns, then settled on the beach amid explosions and billowing smoke. Kilgore, Johnson, and Willard jumped out. A pair of surfers swam toward the break.

Incoming shells and machine gun fire, however, made riding waves impossible. Kilgore barked into an RT, or Radio Telephone, "Big Duke Six. Goddamit, I want that treeline bombed. Bomb it into the Stone Age, son." A trio of needle-nosed silver Phantom jets descended from the clouds and dropped a colossal load of napalm on the jungle. Flames turned the screen red and orange. Silence followed.

"You smell that?" Kilgore said, almost to himself. Then, louder, "You smell that?" Lance, the champion surfer, asked "What?" Kilgore, lit by the glow of burning trees, retorted, "Napalm, son—nothing else in the world smells like that. I love the smell of napalm in the morning. You know, one time we had a hill bombed for 12 hours, and when it was all over I walked up; we didn't find one of 'em . . . not one stinking dink body. But the smell—you know, that gasoline smell—the whole hill—it smelled like . . . victory." He looked off, nostalgically, then said, "Some day this war's gonna end."[2]

In an extended version of the picture, Kilgore licked his fingers and lifted his arms as he walked along the shore. "Lance, the wind," he said. A rushing breeze was building. "The wind—it's blowin' on shore . . . it's gonna blow this place out . . . it's gonna ruin it!" He waved his arms in circles. "It's the god damned napalm, that's what's doing it." Lance and Willard prepared to leave. "It was the bombs causing a vortex with the wind," the colonel protested. As they ran for their boat, he bellowed through an electronic bullhorn, "It's just the fucking napalm."[3]

While the spectacular sequence left little doubt about napalm's destructive capabilities, it recorded only frustration. Kilgore's speech described a bombardment that left just the smell of victory. Napalm ruined even the wave formation it was intended to secure.[4]

# 10

Baby Burners

During and immediately after the Vietnam War, U.S. writers, artists, musicians, and many leading politicians, adopted the thesis first articulated by the Redwood City protesters: napalm was cruel, lamentably American, and a metaphor for defeat in Vietnam. Arbiters of popular culture, led by Hollywood, developed this message about weapon, country, and conclusion in the late 1970s and early 1980s, and sold it to hundreds of millions of people worldwide. By the mid-1980s "napalm" had acquired a slang meaning that connoted almost anything extreme—with an underlying implication of violence. After September 11, 2001, as demands for vengeance swept the country, admiration for the incendiary in some pockets of U.S. culture rose to heights not seen since the Korean War: film directors used it as a form of entertainment, marketers found advantage in its fame, and fan communities formed on the Internet. This countertrend, however, was limited and thus ultimately highlighted the condemnatory paradigm for napalm that has remained largely unchanged for decades.

Criticism by artists started in the late 1960s. Novelist J. G. Ballard picked up in 1969 where his fellow Englishman Graham Greene left off in *The Quiet American* in 1955. In *Love and Napalm: Export U.S.A.*, published in New York, Ballard cited the incendiary as emblematic of American perversions and a key element in "optimum child-mutilation film" production. "Using assembly kits of atrocity photographs, groups of housewives, students and psychotic patients selected the optimum child-torture victim. Rape and napalm burns remained constant preoccupations, and a wound profile of maximum arousal was constructed," he recounted. "Despite the revulsion expressed by the panels, follow-up surveys of work-proficiency and health patterns indicate substantial benefits. The effects of atrocity films on disturbed children were found to have positive results that indicate similar benefits for the TV public at large." In conclusion, "These studies confirm that it is only in terms of a psycho-sexual model such as provided by the Vietnam war that the United States public can enter into a relationship with the world generally characterized by the term 'love.'"[1]

Painter Leon Golub agreed. His 1969 New York *Napalm* series depicted the gel as an obscenity. Critic Grace Glueck, in her *New York Times* review headlined "A Hostile Witness to the Inhumanity of the Human Condition," wrote that Golub offered, "A view of history as a panorama of unending, unresolvable conflict." *Napalm I,* she continued, "depict[ed] a pair of flayed men, one gesturing in defiance, the other in agony." Rudolf Baranik's 1967–1974 *Napalm Elegies,* a collection of thirty interpretations of a photograph of a brutally burned Cambodian child, conveyed a similar message.[2]

Musicians far from the nation's cultural capital, however, produced the most widely publicized artistic commentary on napalm during the war. A dozen or so antiwar active-duty soldiers stationed at the Mountain Home Air Force Base in the town of Mountain Home near Boise, Idaho, opened a coffee house and musicians' collective in 1971 called the Covered Wagon (an air force security code for "sabotage.") Local critics in the settlement of 7,000 made death threats, urged attacks on the coffee shop and its members, broke the building's doors and windows on numerous occasions, and even lit it on fire, but the collective persevered. In 1972, the men released *We Say No to Your War! Songs Written and Sung by the Covered Wagon Musicians Active-Duty Air Force People, Mountain Home AFB, Idaho,* which included "Napalm Sticks to Kids," a biting parody of a call-and-response training cadence.[3]

Member John Boychuk explained the song's history: "A group of Air Force and Army GIs assigned to the 1st Air Cavalry sat down one night in a hootch in Vietnam to write these words. Each person made a verse about an incident in which he had taken part." The reminiscences, he wrote, have "been reprinted in GI newspapers all over the world, [and are] probably the most widely quoted poem to come from the GI movement." Indeed, although producers sold only a relatively small number of albums, "Napalm Sticks to Kids" became a nationwide anthem for antiwar protestors. A typical verse: "A baby sucking on his mother's tit/ Children cowering in a pit/ Dow Chemical doesn't give a shit/ Napalm sticks to kids."[4]

Antiwar politicians seized on the gel's rising celebrity. Minnesota senator and 1968 Democratic presidential candidate Eugene McCarthy, for example, wrote in his poem "Vietnam Message," "We will take our napalm and flame throwers/ out of the land that scarcely knows the use of matches." In the final days of the 1972 presidential campaign, South Dakota senator George McGovern reduced an audience at the University of Minnesota to stunned silence, and then tears, when he played a veteran's description of a napalm strike called in to Boston radio talk show host Jerry Williams: "We went into villages after they dropped napalm, and the human beings were fused together like pieces of metal that had been soldered. Sometimes you couldn't tell if they were people or animals."[5]

Veterans often felt the force of the powerful emotions stirred by such testimony. Helicopter trooper Bob Parker, for example, returned from Vietnam in 1971. On his first day back in the United States he and his wife "drove to the nearest shopping mall to buy me some civilian clothes." There, he later reminisced, "A college-aged fellow noticed my flame-thrower qualification badge and made some remarks about me being a baby-burner." Parker continued, "I got used to people walking away when they figured that I was in the army. . . . I was an outsider in my own country, and in many ways, have stayed that way ever since."[6]

This paradigm accelerated after 1975: napalm became a manifestation of the pathos, cruelty, and futility of America's greatest defeat. Novelist and veteran Philip Caputo captured an early stage of the process when he wrote in his 1977 autobiography *A Rumor of War*, "A man saw the heights and depths of human behavior in Vietnam, all manner of violence and horrors so grotesque they evoked more fascination than disgust. Once I had seen pigs eating napalm-charred corpses—a memorable sight, pigs eating roast people." Singaporean intellectual Robert Yeo drew broad social implications from the gel in his volume of poetry published the same year *And Napalm Does Not Help:* "[D]emocracy is a wind-blown seed and the land/ is now too soiled for any sprig to grow/ but the hardiest; and napalm does not help."[7]

Artists in the 1980s built on these early expressions. They commented more frequently on napalm, and in a wider range of media, than in any previous period, and made the gel a proxy for brutality and oppression. In 1981, British musicians Nicholas Bullen and Miles Ratledge created the band Napalm Death and established grindcore punk as an internationally popular genre with performances in thousands of venues worldwide and over thirty albums. Its name stands as a "direct, literal and stark anti-war reference—napalm as a combustible substance being a particularly hideous element of warfare," according to band member Barney Greenway. Complete lyrics to the first track on their 1987 debut album offer a taste of this ideology in practice: "Multinational corporations/ Genocide of the starving nations." Wehrmacht, another punk band with a substantial following, was established in 1985 in Portland, Oregon, and has invoked napalm along similar lines to criticize authority. Chorus lyrics for its 1987 song "Napalm Shower" read: "Napalm spreads on, our city is gone. . . . Our governments fucked . . ." Napalm Records, established in Austria in 1992, is the world's largest distributor of death metal punk recordings.[8]

With respect to Vietnam in particular, views of napalm grew harsher as awareness of its effects spread and the reality of U.S. defeat sank in. In 1981, Scottish novelist William Boyd updated Greene's elegiac flames that "go over them like water," and Ballard's fantasies, with a notably unflinching exposition of napalm burns on a Vietnamese girl. In his short story "On the Yankee Station" he wrote of a young prostitute, "She turned abruptly to reveal her back. . . . When he saw her back, Lydecker's brain screamed in silent horror. His hands rose involuntarily to his mouth. The girl looked at him over her shoulder. 'Nay-pom,' she said quietly in explanation. 'Nay-pom, G.I.' . . . Her back was a broad stripe, a swath of purpled shiny skin where static waves of silvery scar tissue and blistered burn weals tossed in a horrifying flesh-sea." Poet Bruce Weigl was equally blunt in "Song of Napalm," his 1988 ode: "[T]he girl runs only as far/ as the napalm allows/ until her burning tendons and crackling/ muscles draw her up/ into that final position/ burning bodies so perfectly assume. Nothing/ can change that, she is burned behind my eyes/ and not your good love and not the rain-swept air/ and not the jungle-green/ pasture unfolding before us can deny it."[9]

Newspapers played relatively little role in this aspect of napalm's story: coverage was almost entirely documentary rather than analytical. Industry bellwether the *New York Times* set a record for annual mentions of napalm in 1951, the first full year of the Korean War, for example, when it published 232 pieces that mentioned the gel. Coverage plunged to 146 mentions the following year, and just forty-five in 1953. In 1967, as U.S. involvement expanded in Vietnam, the periodical's napalm reports hit a second peak, with 187 citations. Coverage declined from there: 120 stories in 1968, about eighty-three mentions each year from 1969 to 1972, forty-nine in 1973, and not more than thirty-six citations in any subsequent year—many just terse summaries buried deep in the journal. The year 2001, when America invaded Iraq, was the only exception: coverage more than doubled, from fourteen mentions in 2000 to thirty-seven references, but trailed off after that. The *Los Angeles Times* followed a similar pattern, with less coverage of napalm in the Korean War than its East Coast counterpart, but comparable attention from 1955 on. An analysis of publications cataloged by Google Books shows a similar spike in interest in the late 1960s, with a high point in 1970. This lag relative to newspapers likely reflects the longer publication lead-time for materials in that database.[10]

Mass market films more than compensated for print's peacetime neglect. *Apocalypse Now,* which featured Colonel Kilgore's crazed soliloquy, and opened with a napalm strike set to the song "The End" by The Doors, set the standard in 1979. *An Officer and a Gentleman,* released in 1982, gave "Napalm Sticks to Kids" international fame: "Flying low and feeling mean/ Spot a family by a stream/ Pickle a pear and hear 'em scream/ 'Cause napalm sticks to kids," Navy recruits chanted as they trained. "Eighteen kids in a free fire zone/ Books under arms, just walking on home/ Last kid walks home alone/ 'Cause napalm sticks to kids," they yelled. A pair of Academy Awards helped the film gross $130 million domestically, and perhaps twice that internationally, from a worldwide audience of tens of millions.

*Running on Empty,* a 1988 film that grossed just $2.8 million in domestic revenues, showed that Hollywood's image of napalm was consistent across the commercial spectrum, from large releases to small films. "The laboratory is credited with the development of *(mispronounces)* nap-palm, used extensively in the Vietnam War," one young son of anti-war fugitives read in a newspaper report on his parents. "[W]hy'd they have to blow it up?" he asked his brother. "Because they didn't stop making it when they asked 'em politely. . . . They were dropping that stuff on people," the teenager replied.[11]

As time passed, popular portrayals emphasized napalm's destructive power and, simultaneously, the gel's inability to change the outcome in Indochina. *Platoon,* a hit 1986 film written and directed by Oliver Stone and set in 1967 "somewhere near the Cambodian border," presented the gel as a creation of almost supernatural might. In a climactic final scene, a desperate U.S. officer radioed the air force to "expend all remaining" on his overrun outpost. A cataclysm followed that killed friend and foe, left a ruined, charcoaled world, and allowed two American rivals to come to grips: a confrontation that left one dead and the other profoundly damaged. It was the first depiction of a napalm strike at ground level in a major Hollywood release. An Academy Award for Best Picture and three other Oscars helped push gross domestic revenues to $139 million, and global receipts to perhaps $280 million from tens of millions of viewers.[12]

*Forrest Gump,* released in 1994, and even more watched and lauded, offered similarly abstracted violence. In a dramatic finale to the film's Vietnam segment, napalm fire clouds chased the hero out of the jungle with a wounded companion in his arms. Flames destroyed everything, but didn't hurt anyone visible. The film then jumped immediately to the United States: "That's all I have to say about that," Gump averred. An Academy Award for Best Picture and five other Oscars followed. *Forrest Gump* had gross revenues of over $677 million, which suggested maybe 100 million cinema viewers.[13]

Napalm was now better known by more people in more places around the world than ever before and, arguably, depicted with less basis in reality than at any time since the 1967 *Ramparts* photographs. *USA Today* journalist Jack Kelley, subsequently fired for inventing stories, caught the *zeitgeist* when he ascribed Shiva-like destructive powers to "napalm-tipped matches" ostensibly produced at a former Cold War munitions plant in the Ukraine. In a 1993 "exclusive" of doubtful veracity he wrote, "The new 3-inch-long, napalm-tipped matches—yes, napalm . . . light when wet and stay lighted—or give off an eerie red, nuclear-like glow—for one minute." The napalm fire, he continued, "is so intense it instantly burned through a half-inch glass ashtray and a quarter-inch-thick wooden table under it, then set a rug on fire. . . . The matches, like trick birthday candles, can't be extinguished by persistent blowing. Dousing them with water usually doesn't work, either. Stepping on them only breaks the matches into little pieces, which continue to glow."[14]

*Fight Club,* a film released in 1996, took the conception of napalm as a supernatural force to an end point of sorts. Hero Tyler Durden, a soap salesman (perhaps a genuflection to the early role of chemical soaps in napalm's manufacture), introduced himself with a do-it-yourself recipe for the gel: "Did you know if you mixed equal parts of gasoline and frozen orange juice concentrate you can make napalm? . . . One can make all kinds of explosives using simple household items, if one were so inclined." Violence trailed Durden throughout the film. Chuck Palahniuk was even more explicit in the novel that inspired the picture. His story opened on the roof of the world's tallest building, with a gun pressed to the back of the narrator's throat. Unseen protagonists below hurled desks and filing cabinets through shattered windows onto a distant street. In the context of this mayhem, the narrator introduced himself with napalm recipes: "The three ways to make napalm: One, you can mix equal parts of gasoline and frozen orange juice concentrate. Two, you can mix equal parts of gasoline and diet cola. Three, you can dissolve crumbled cat litter in gasoline until the mixture is thick."[15]

Napalm was an abstraction, even an emotion for some, by the turn of the millennium: a signifier for violence. Author David Schickler, for example, saw the gel in 2001 as a metaphor for passion. "Some fiber of her

soul longed to kill . . . to cleanse countries with napalm, or to be taken
viciously by a man on the steps of a church," he wrote in his story "Kissing in Manhattan." "It sounded sexy, shiny, and explosive, like the music I wanted to make," New York musician Tim Stegall recalled of the
name he chose for his start-up punk band Napalm Stars.[16]

After 9/11, America's gloves came off and napalm returned to earth as a
patriotic, if imperfect, fighter with a job to do. *We Were Soldiers,* a dra-
matization of the 1965 Battle of Ia Drang in Vietnam, set the new tone on
March 1, 2002. For the first time in a cinema, audiences came face to face
with the effects of napalm on people. As in *Platoon,* a U.S. commander
called in an incendiary strike on his own overrun position. Unlike *Platoon,* flames marked the beginning rather than the end of the story. Fire
first caught a squadron of Vietnamese troops, who collapsed with night-
marish screams. Then, a pair of silver bombs tumbled onto a U.S. position. Hal Moore, commander of U.S. forces, wrote in the memoir of
the battle he co-authored with journalist Joe Galloway that served as the
basis for the film, "I jerked my head around and looked straight into the
noses of two F-100 Super Sabre jet fighters aiming directly at us. At that
moment, the lead aircraft released two shiny, six-foot-long napalm canisters, which slowly began loblollying end over end toward us." When the
napalm hit American troops, Moore and Galloway continued, "Their
hair was burned off in an instant. Their clothes were incinerated. One
was a mass of blisters; the other not quite so bad, but he had breathed the
fire into his lungs." Rescue attempts exposed the full horror. "Somebody yelled at me to grab the feet of one of the charred soldiers," Galloway remembered, "When I got them, the boots crumbled and the flesh
came off and I could feel the bare bones of his ankles in the palms of my
hands. We carried him into the aid station. I can still hear their screams."
Movie cameras captured the agony of twenty-two-year-old U.S. soldier,
and new father, Jimmy Nakayama in grisly detail. A final shot focused on
his scorched face as a rescue helicopter lifted off. "Tell my wife and baby
I love them," he screamed, from half a mouth.[17]

Friendly fire tragedies notwithstanding, *We Were Soldiers* captured
the mood of the times when it gave napalm much of the credit for the

eventual U.S. victory at Ia Drang: the incendiary's end was just, however brutal its means. Reconnaissance platoon leader Pat Payne, interviewed by Moore and Galloway, explained that the planes "were a sight for sore eyes, and the cheers rang out as they made their first runs." For the soldier, napalm was the same battlefield hero it had been since World War II: "You could see a large number of North Vietnamese, fifty or a hundred, quite a number, within fifty or seventy-five yards of us—massing to attack—when one of the Air Force planes dropped the napalm on a direct hit on them. We began to cheer." Millions watched the motion picture, which grossed $115 million worldwide.[18]

In a poignant sidelight, the Center of the Tokyo Raid and War Damages, a Tokyo museum organized by survivors of the 1945 napalm attacks and dedicated to their memory, opened eight days after *We Were Soldiers* was released. Attention was insignificant compared to the multimillion dollar Hollywood picture: $828,000 in private donations funded the memorial, and a few thousand visitors arrived for opening day. A short *New York Times* note did not even mention the facility's name, and drew a sharp distinction, however opaque to the burned, between destruction by conventional flames and atomic fires. "Japan's cities were incinerated after similar Allied firebombing of German cities, whereas the atomic attacks even now remain unique in history," asserted reporter Howard French. A teacup melted into a lump was one of the Center's memorials.[19]

Special Forces veteran John Mullins restored napalm to its former glory as an American hero in his niche market 2004 novel *Napalm Dreams*. It was characteristic of some post-9/11 attitudes. Green Berets reinforced an isolated Special Forces base and discovered a lost group of U.S. troops and their Montagnard tribal allies: "They still sat at their last recorded position, the four Montagnards lying in a semicircle around the three Americans. Almost as if they had been placed there for some barbaric religious ceremony," reported Sergeant First Class Walter "Spearchucker" Washington. "One of the U.S. soldiers had been shot, the other killed with more than 100 cuts. The other sat against a tree, sightless eyes staring out into the jungle. His pants had been pulled down around his ankles, and his genitals were missing. There were no other wounds. The claw marks on the trunk of the tree to which his hands had been tied were mute witness to his suffering." Mullins was blunt: "While Washington had a grudging admiration for his adversaries, he didn't have much sympathy."

Napalm was, without debate, the correct tool for retaliation. "The Montagnard soldiers unquestioningly flattened themselves against the clay, one so close to Washington his merry brown eyes were staring into his own. The expression changed when the first whoosh of a napalm canister struck just outside the wire," the Special Forces veteran wrote. "Glad I'm wearing a hat, Washington thought as the blast of searing heat struck them. It was like opening the door to a furnace, the heat seeming to penetrate to the bone." Sympathy was the soldier's first reaction: "The shifting valley winds brought back to him the smells: burning gasoline, woodsmoke, and underlying it the unmistakable stench of charred flesh. Someone was out there, he thought. Poor bastards." Reflection, however, produced wrath: "'Burn, you cocksuckers,' he said as another flight of Phantoms came in."[20]

Closer to home, by 2007 homemade napalm had passed from *Fight Club* fantasy to everyday necessity. In the Paramount Pictures thriller *Shooter,* framed former military sniper Bob Lee Swagger started his quest for redemption with his assistant, renegade Federal Bureau of Investigation special agent Nick Memphis, in a suburban hardware store. "You got your list, right?" the sharpshooter asked. "Yeah," Memphis responded. They loaded spray paint, small cans of propane, pipes, and clothes line into their carts. In the next scene, a dry gravel riverbank in the middle of the woods, the men worked on the open rear panel of a dusty pick-up truck. Swagger picked up a propane tank with small bottles taped to it: "All right. Tear gas is going to be on my remote." He handled a plastic bottle filled with yellow gel: "Napalm on the first four." Memphis asked, "What exactly are we getting ready for?" Swagger answered, "As much as we can be." They later used their gel to dispatch a small army of guards: victims flailed, screamed, and died covered in flames; no noncombatants suffered. *Shooter* grossed $96 million in theaters around the world, and was the best-selling DVD in the United States for the week after its release.[21]

Businesses saw opportunity in napalm's new respectability. The first napalm-branded consumer product, a skin cream, appeared on November

15, 2007. Avant Research, "the newest, most dynamic, most innovative, and the most cutting-edge brand in the dietary supplement industry," introduced Napalm™, a "unique and 'explosive' mixture of ingredients that is sure to help you make quick work of enemy fat cells dug in deep on the battlefield of your body." Promotional materials promised, "By applying it to specific areas of your body, such as your abdominals, glutes, or thighs, the scientific concoction of glycyrrhetinic acid, raspberry ketones, SesaThin™, yohimbine HCl, and synephrine HCl, all work together through different physiological pathways to help you take out stubborn body fat that doesn't go away fast enough." Application was simple: "As explained in the Performance Pyramids, rub gel into skin, twice daily, where fat loss effects are desired." A panel assembled by the BodyBuilding.com website nominated Avant for 2008 New Brand of the Year.[22]

Napalm Orange hair dye, which glows in the dark, debuted the next year from Melbourne, Florida, dye specialist Special Effects. The color joined Blue Haired Freak, Blue Mayhem, Bright as F#$% Yellow, and others in the company's lineup. A pair of testimonials from customers gives a sense of napalm's meaning to some younger Americans: "I did it while my family was away for christmas, and they came home expecting me to look terrifyingly wierd [*sic*], but had nothing but good things to say to me when they finally saw it. The lighting in the first photo does not even do justice to how ungodly bright it actually was. Not only that, but it looked absolutely mindblowing under blacklight." A second: "i recently bleached my hair to platinum blonde—almost white and then dyed napalm orange special effects dye. it is actually as bright as the picture shows!! people are amazed when they see how crazy bright my hair is."[23]

By 2008, napalm was just good clean fun for some. In *Death Race*, an August release from Universal Pictures, prison island inmates competed to the death in customized cars. In the final turns of one race hero Jensen Ames, nicknamed "Frankenstein" and played by British martial artist Jason Statham, found himself pursued by an enemy pounding his vehicle with a heavy machine gun as they hurtled through an abandoned warehouse. "Get on my lap!" he barked to Case, his navigator, played by model Natalie Martinez. His mechanic and an assistant, listening by radio, exchanged speculative glances. Case settled herself on Ames, cleavage jutting against her tight t-shirt. Cut to a canister: "NAPALM" stenciled across it in red. Case parted her lips, reached between Ames's legs, and pulled a thick black and yellow shaft. The napalm shell ejected, smashed into the roof of the building, and spattered gel over the pursuit car. "Fuck. What the hell?" yelled their rival. Case pulled a glowing cigarette lighter from its socket, stood up in the car's open roof, and looked back. Windblown hair framed her face. "Merry Christmas, asshole!" she shouted. "Aww, shit!" their pursuer howled as the lighter spun toward him. It hit with a massive explosion. Close up shots caught their opponent's screams of agony, and his attempts to brush off the gel as he burned alive. His car swerved, hit another, and flipped high into the air, covered in flames, in a spinning, slow-motion wreck. "Nice work," Case smiled at Frankenstein as she dropped back into her seat. *Death Race* received weak reviews—"an assault on all the senses, including common," according to Roger Ebert of the *Chicago Sun-Times;* "as hard as metal and just as dumb" averred Robert Koehler of *Variety;* and "an ill-advised and severely wussified remake" in the opinion of *San Francisco Chronicle* critic Peter Hartlaub—but grossed $76 million and was seen by a vast audience.[24]

Computer games and the Internet allow napalm aficionados who see the gel primarily as a form of entertainment to find each other. Napalm.net offers gel for sale ("Napalm.Net has bought 5,000 pounds of weapons grade Napalm and has individually packaged it in safe, attractive, displayable canisters. Each canister holds one liter of actual Napalm which you can ONLY purchase through Napalm.Net.") but is actually a hoax website that sells t-shirts. ("HA!!! Did you actually think that we would sell YOU napalm? You were BURNED by Napalm.Net! On this joyous occasion, we are offering a personalized 'i got burned @ napalm.net' T-Shirts.") "Napalm" freeware from Firestarter lets users write notes in burning letters on their computer desktops. Video games routinely offer napalm armaments. Sony gamers, for example, can buy a "Napalm and Cordite" PlayStation expansion pack for *Killzone 2* by Guerrilla Games: "use the Flamethrower and Boltgun to lay waste to your enemies with the Napalm & Cordite Pack!" *Mercenaries 2: World in Flames* for Xbox offers napalm airstrikes to obliterate enemies.[25]

Social networks facilitate napalm fan clubs. The most popular, "NA-PALM Fun Club" on Facebook, has about 4,100 "likes"; a smaller one boasts around 1,700 "likes." Users comment on videos of napalm strikes and discuss the munition. YouTube offers many instructional videos that explain how to make napalm by dissolving Styrofoam in gasoline. These attract tens of thousands or even over 100,000 viewers in the case of the most popular presentations. *VICE* magazine researchers testified in 2009 to the flammability of this formula. A lighter applied to a small piece of napalm concocted from Styrofoam, they reported, "immediately produced a high-temperature flame and, shortly after, began to drip apart into tiny pools of fire that stayed lit for a good five minutes. Stepping on these puddles will just transfer the napalm to your shoe, so letting them burn out is really the only viable option." Experimenters daubed their gel on a television: "Upon ignition, the set immediately went up in an inferno and smoke billowed toward the roof."[26]

"Napalm" is contemporary slang for any extreme behavior. Singer John Mayer summed up his relationship with pop star Jessica Simpson as follows in an interview with *Playboy:* "Sexually it was crazy. That's all I'll say. It was like napalm, sexual napalm." Twitter commenters often use the word in a similar manner. "Any long term deficit plans will require some tax increases and cuts to defense and Medicare all of which are political napalm," user CowboyKush, for example, tweeted in 2010.[27]

Although notable, the reach of this post-9/11 change in public opinion should not be exaggerated. *Death Race*'s cultural impact, measured by the film's revenues, reviews, and subsequent influence, was far smaller than, for example, *Apocalypse Now*. Napalm's Facebook fan groups and YouTube home chemists have audiences of only a few thousand: infinitesimal in the context of the millions who watch hit movies. Avant's skin care product, Special Effect's hair dye, and Firestarter's freeware are obscure products. *Napalm Dreams* is ranked 1,790,678 in Books on Amazon.com.[28]

"The Terror of War" photograph better captures napalm's contemporary popular identity. Kim Phúc, age nine, is a cultural icon cited by editorialists to illustrate commentary on everything from labor rights to land use. In a 1994 cartoon about plans to build a Disney theme park near a Civil War battlefield, for example, Goofy raced her down Highway

One. Kim Phúc illustrated a sign that said "Just Do It!," the Nike slogan, in a 1997 cartoon about working conditions in Vietnamese factories owned by subcontractors to the athletics firm. She stood behind an American suburban home in a 2001 illustration for a *Boston Globe* book review, and ran with a hooded prisoner in a 2004 cartoon about the Abu Ghraib prisoner-abuse scandal. Kim Phúc burned by napalm remains a synonym for America's defeat in Vietnam and, more generally, civilian tragedy in modern war.[29]

Most unequivocally in popular culture, napalm is American. From novels like *The Quiet American* to *Napalm Dreams,* poems "Vietnam Message" to "Song of Napalm," and films *Apocalypse Now* to *Death Race,* U.S. commanders are the ones who order death by liquid fire. Even in cases where America was not immediately responsible—the bomb that burned Kim Phúc, for example, was dropped by a South Vietnamese air force pilot—its culpability is inferred. As *New York Times* reviewer Walter Goodman wrote of Dutch filmmaker Manus van der Kamp's 1985 polemic documentary *Kim Phuc,* "The powerful pictures of the little girl running in pain and panic are shown over and over. They are offered as representing the sufferings of the Vietnamese people—and the blame, we are given to understand, is all America's."[30]

A result of this near-universal correspondence between popular presentation and historical record is a politically devastating message that ties America in general, and its government and military in particular, to napalm and the suffering it carries. British graffiti artist Banksy summarized this conclusion in his 2004 *Can't Beat the Feeling* tableau: Kim Phúc, naked and in agony, runs while American icons Mickey Mouse and Ronald McDonald hold her forearms.[31]

# 11

# Trial of Fire

International lawyers largely ignored napalm until the Vietnam War began to turn against the United States. As it became clear, however, that the war would end in an American defeat, or even debacle, a global effort to regulate the gel so intimately associated with U.S. involvement in Indochina gathered strength. Initial legal criticisms came in 1965 from Soviet Bloc countries. American diplomats dismissed them as propaganda. Investigations under the broader auspices of the United Nations, however, began in 1968 and 1969. Groups of government experts met to discuss napalm from 1972. North Vietnamese attacks intensified, U.S. withdrawals accelerated, and "The Terror of War" photograph hit front pages as they worked. Multinational conferences convened in 1974 and 1976—bracketing North Vietnam's 1975 victory—produced draft regulatory codes. Finally, in 1980, the UN adopted its Convention on Certain Conventional Weapons (CCW). Protocol III made incendiary weapons use against a "concentration of civilians" a war crime. Initially, only a few dozen states accepted this judgment. But successive decades added dozens of additional nations to the list, including the United States in 2009. At the time of writing, 106 states are parties to Protocol III. Napalm is now on probation, as it were, in much of the world.[1]

The road to current law was long. It began in 1859, improbably, in Sétif, Algeria, a leafy town 190 miles east of Algiers. This was the centerpiece
of a 20,000-hectare concession granted by French emperor Napoleon III
to a Genevan colonial venture. Jean-Henri Dunant, thirty-one-year-old
scion of one of the Swiss city's wealthiest families, proposed a massive
real estate development project in the territory. To succeed, he needed
water rights controlled by the emperor. Napoleon was battling Austria in
northern Italy at the time, so the perspicacious entrepreneur traveled to
the front lines to plead his case. He arrived at Castiglione delle Stiviere,
west of Verona, on June 24, 1859, just as cannons at the Battle of Solferino, one of the largest military engagements in European history, began
to thunder seven kilometers to the east.[2]

It was an eye-opening experience for Dunant. "More than 300,000
men stood facing each other; the battle line was five leagues long, and the
fighting continued for more than fifteen hours," he observed in a memoir
he published three years later. "Here is a hand-to-hand struggle in all its
horror and frightfulness . . . crushing skulls, ripping bellies open with
sabre and bayonet. No quarter is given; it is a sheer butchery; a struggle
between savage beasts, maddened with blood and fury. Even the wounded
fight to the last gasp. When they have no weapon left, they seize their
enemies by the throat and tear them with their teeth." Things got worse
the next day, "When the sun came up on the twenty-fifth, it disclosed the
most dreadful sights imaginable. Bodies of men and horses covered the
battlefield; corpses were strewn over roads, ditches, ravines, thickets
and fields; the approaches of Solferino were literally thick with dead."
Then, "Scenes as tragic as those of the day before, though of a very different sort, began to take place. . . . With faces black with the flies that
swarmed about their wounds, men gazed around them, wild-eyed and
helpless. Others were no more than a worm-ridden, inextricable com-
pound of coat and shirt and flesh and blood." Dunant deferred his commercial ambitions and helped organize a volunteer corps. Local women,
girls, and boys distributed water, soup, and tea. Passers-by, including a
pair of English tourists and a Parisian writer, bathed the wounded and
changed their dressings. Local leaders organized thousands of beds
across the region.[3]

Enthusiasm ebbed, however, after about a week. "With a few most
honourable exceptions, the people grew tired and weary," the Genevan

wrote. And care was limited. "It must not be thought that the lovely girls and kind women of Castiglione, devoted as they were, saved from death many of the wounded and disfigured, but still curable, soldiers to whom they gave their help. All they could do was to bring a little relief to a few of them," he cautioned. Stricken, Dunant proposed an international voluntary organization to organize relief efforts for future wars. A global conclave, he proposed, could enunciate universal principles to guide the program.[4]

On February 7, 1863, the Société Génévoise d'Utilité Publique, or Geneva Society for Public Welfare, endorsed his call for an international conference. Swiss federal officials backed the idea. Dunant crisscrossed Europe, at his own expense, to obtain commitments to attend. In October, delegates from sixteen states approved sweeping resolutions that laid the groundwork for a gathering of plenipotentiaries. On August 22, 1864, a dozen nations signed an agreement for "Amelioration of the Condition of the Wounded in Armies in the Field," and agreed to guarantee neutrality to relief personnel and expedite supplies for their use. To honor Switzerland, the conferees chose its national flag, reversed, for a logo: a red cross on a white field. This was the first "Geneva Convention." An international law of war was born.[5]

Treaties adopted in Europe between 1868 and 1907 established an initial consensus about principles of legal warfare and the illegality of most incendiaries, especially fire bombs. Russian chancellor prince Alexander Gorchakov, a veteran diplomat, took a foundational step in 1868 when he invited the world's greatest powers to an International Military Commission at St. Petersburg "to examine the expediency of forbidding the use of certain projectiles in time of war between civilized nations." On December 11, 1868, four years after the Red Cross was established, seventeen of the world's strongest states, including the United Kingdom, France, Prussia, Austria-Hungary, Turkey, and Russia, agreed to "technical limits at which the necessities of war ought to yield to the requirements of humanity." Diplomats established a distinction between combatants and noncombatants, and asserted that only the former are legitimate military targets: "[T]he only legitimate object which States should endeavour to accomplish during war is to weaken the military forces of the enemy." Delegates judged illegal weapons that "uselessly aggravate" suffering: "[I]t is sufficient to disable the greatest possible number of men; That this object would be exceeded by the employment of arms which uselessly aggravate the sufferings of disabled men, or render their death inevitable; That the employment of such arms would, therefore, be contrary to the laws of humanity." Finally, among numerous other conclusions, the assembly declared it a crime to use incendiary projectiles that weighed less than four kilograms (deemed the dividing line between bullets and artillery shells): "The Contracting Parties engage mutually to renounce, in case of war among themselves, the employment by their military or naval troops of any projectile of a weight below 400 grammes, which is either explosive or charged with fulminating or inflammable substances."[6]

America came late to the discussion. Although the United States, wracked by civil war, attended the Geneva Convention of 1864, it did not ratify the pact that resulted, and was not invited to the St. Petersburg commission. On May 21, 1881, Clara Barton and a group of supporters established the American Red Cross in Washington, D.C. Due in large part to their lobbying efforts, the United States ratified the First Geneva Convention in 1882, and began to participate in international law of war discussions.[7]

Subsequent multilateral agreements reaffirmed the basic findings at St. Petersburg. In 1899, the First Hague Peace Conference, proposed by Tsar Nicholas II, convened in the Netherlands. Among other statements, delegates agreed categorically that the "right of belligerents to adopt means of injuring the enemy is not unlimited"; clarified the 1868 "useless aggravation" concept (*propres à causer des maux superflus,* in the definitive French text) as "superfluous injury"; asserted that "The attack or bombardment, by whatever means, of towns, villages, dwellings, or buildings which are undefended is prohibited"; and banned for five years "the launching of projectiles and explosives from balloons, or by other new methods of similar nature." A total of forty-nine countries, including the United States and major European powers, signed the agreement, which was limited to wars between signatories and revocable if a nonsignatory joined the fight.[8]

A follow-up Second Hague Peace Conference in 1907 retranslated *maux superflus* or "useless aggravation" as "unnecessary suffering" (the two translations are now judged synonymous), and renewed the ban on "discharge of projectiles and explosives from balloons or by other new methods of a similar nature," until such time as a third peace conference might be convened. Great Britain and the United States, China, the Netherlands, Belgium, and Norway, and several other smaller powers, ratified the document. France, Germany, Italy, Japan, and Russia, which together controlled most of the world's military forces, did not.[9]

World War I put the strength of the St. Petersburg covenant to the test. In 1916, British scientists developed the world's first incendiary bullet: a forbidden munition because it weighed less than 400 grams. Attorneys in the United Kingdom determined the weapon could legally be used against balloons—deployed at the time to drop fire bombs on London—so long as pilots followed special procedures. Royal Air Force lieutenant Walter Noble explained: "This special ammunition is not used against enemy aeroplanes; and when taken up for use against balloons a card, signed by the G.O.C. [of] the R.A.F. in the Field, is pinned to the cockpit of the user, certifying that it is for use against balloons only. There is no doubt as to the necessity for this. One of these bullets if lodged in one's flesh would, it is said, proceed to burn away all flesh and blood in its vicinity." Enforcement was swift and harsh for those deemed to have broken international rules. "The thought came to me," a U.S. officer wrote after he crashed in no-man's-land in June 1918, "that if I were nearer the German lines than the French, I had better get rid of the incendiary balls in my machine. If you are captured with incendiaries they shoot you without trial." That the United States was not a party to the St. Petersburg Declaration was a subtlety evidently too fine for the battlefield. The officer secreted his incendiaries under the body of a dead German soldier, and escaped.[10]

Superficial progress and fundamental decay in international regulation of incendiary weapons marked the period between the world wars. Treaties that ended the Great War stripped fire weapons from members of the defeated powers but did not affect arsenals of the winners. An agreement to rule poison gas illegal was adopted, but comparable efforts for incendiary munitions did not advance beyond drafts. Simultaneously, developments in bomber technology expanded the size of battlefields to entire countries, and undermined the distinction between combatants and civilians. Attorneys offered no new constructs to respond to these changes. Thus, by the late 1930s, although in theory a case could be made that some forms of incendiary warfare, especially the use of incendiary bullets, were illegal, in practice, given the fragmented state of international law, the argument was hard to sustain.

Armistice agreements left little room for debate: the Central Powers could not have incendiary weapons. The Treaty of Peace between the Allied and Associated Powers and Germany, signed at Versailles, precluded ownership of incendiary weapons by German forces with comprehensive restrictions on their manufacture, importation, and storage. "The use of flame throwers, asphyxiating, poisonous or other gases, and all similar liquids, materials or devices being prohibited, their manufacture and importation are strictly forbidden in Austria. Material specially intended for the manufacture, storage or use of the said products or devices is equally forbidden," read Article 135 of the Treaty of Saint-Germain-en-Laye, which ended hostilities between the Entente and Vienna. Article 82 of the Treaty of Neuilly-sur-Seine, which brought peace to Bulgaria, and Article 119 of the Treaty of Trianon, which ended hostilities with Hungary, contained almost identical language.[11]

Diplomats discussed changes to international law during this period that might have significantly limited deployments of incendiary weapons, but in the end made no changes. An early effort was a 1923 attempt to legalize and regulate incendiary bullets. A conference of jurists dispatched by the governments of the United States, Britain, France, Italy, Holland, and Japan suggested that such munitions should be allowed against aircraft, but not against civilians under most circumstances. "The use of tracer, incendiary, or explosive projectiles by or against air, is not prohibited. This provision applies equally to States which are parties to the Declaration of St. Petersburg, 1868, and to those which are not," read one proposed protocol. "Aerial bombardment for the purpose of terrorizing the civilian population, of destroying or damaging private property not of a military character, or of injuring non-combatants is prohibited," stipulated another. No states adopted the proposal.[12]

League of Nations emissaries made a more determined effort at regulation during the General Conference for the Limitation and Reduction of Armaments, the world's first global disarmament conference, convened at Geneva in February 1932. Every member of the international body, plus the United States and the USSR, attended: sixty nations in all. A Special Committee established to review incendiaries concluded they should be banned. When used against cities, the committee wrote, fire weapons are "particularly threatening to civilians," and when used in flamethrowers against combatants, "the cruelty inherent in the use of these appliances causes suffering that cannot be regarded as necessary from the military point of view." Thus, they should be forbidden. A majority of the committee added that incendiary weapons were inherently weapons of offense and thus warranted additional limitations. On July 23, diplomats agreed without dissent that "incendiary weapons shall be prohibited under the conditions unanimously recommended by the Special Committee." By March 1933, it was "An established rule of international law" that incendiary weapons should not be used as projectiles, "flame projectors" or in any other way except for defense against airplanes, as the British government wrote in a draft convention submitted to the disarmament conclave. On September 22, 1933, delegates unanimously adopted this language as the basis for a future legal code.[13]

All for naught. Germany withdrew from the disarmament conference on October 14, 1933, at Adolf Hitler's order. The summit limped along, with long recesses, until May 1, 1937, when it was abandoned. No binding treaties resulted.[14]

Outside the conference rooms, a new military paradigm approached from above. Prior to the airplane, as legal scholar Julius Stone has written, "[A]rmies did the fighting while in their rear civilians (or noncombatants) worked, if male, or wept, if female. Only professional soldiers came to grips with one another." It became axiomatic, he continued, that war should be waged only against armed men—the "only legitimate object," in the words of the St. Petersburg Declaration. "It was a praiseworthy principle in the circumstances of the pre-air age in war, but it was not one which could survive the arrival of the bombing aircraft," Stone observed. "For, objectively considered, it was not a logical principle. By no process of reasoning could a belligerent be persuaded that the manufacturers of armaments in his enemy's country were less active enemies than the men who wore uniforms and opposed him in the field. They had been spared so far because they could not be got at and for no other reason at all. They can be got at now." The international law of war for incendiary weapons, scanty though it was, was about to be swept away entirely.[15]

Early incendiary bombardments made possible by technological developments drew legal protests. Britain, for example, proposed an inquiry into Germany's 1937 attacks on Guernica, and the United Kingdom, the United States, and France all complained to Japan about its fire attacks on Chinese cities in the same year. As World War II progressed, however, allegations of criminality disappeared in the face of military determination. "It may well be, and I personally do not blink at the fact, that these great German war industries can only be paralysed by bringing the whole life of the cities in which they are situated to a standstill, making it quite impossible for the workmen to carry on their work. That is a fact we may have to face and I do face it. It is, I suggest, a full justification for our present bombing campaign," British lord Cranborne told the House of Lords on February 9, 1944. "If the town also suffered," German general Karl Bodenschatz testified of devastated Coventry at the postwar Nuremberg Tribunal, "that is comprehensible in view of the navigation facilities available at that period of the war." Concerns about the legality of incendiary weapons like those that produced the Great War's cockpit notecards disappeared. "[T]he degree of each side's confidence in its air superiority was the main factor controlling its determination to destroy enemy military objectives at all costs," Stone summarized.[16]

To victors, however, belong spoils, history, and, apparently, international law. After World War II established the effectiveness of incendiary bombardments—in particular, napalm attacks—lawyers used a two-step process to legalize them. First, postwar attorneys defined the key issue for incendiaries as precision, rather than cruelty. As Article 14 of the first major project to address the subject, "Draft Rules for the Limitation of the Dangers Incurred by the Civilian Population in Time of War," produced in 1956 by the International Committee of the Red Cross (ICRC), phrased the issue, legal prohibitions properly applied only to "weapons whose harmful effects—resulting in particular from the dissemination of incendiary, chemical, bacteriological, radioactive or other agents—could spread to an unforeseen degree or escape, either in space or time, from the control of those who employ them, thus endangering the civilian population." Second, counselors defined napalm as a precision weapon in most cases. International law largely followed the argument advanced by British authorities in response to Korean War complaints about napalm's inhumane and indiscriminate qualities: almost all weapons create terrible suffering but napalm was, at least, more discriminating than high explosives. Incendiaries, ICRC commentators wrote in their analysis of the 1956 Draft Rules, "are sometimes limited in their effects e.g. the flame-thrower or napalm when used against a tank, but sometimes have uncontrollable consequences as in the case of certain bombs scattering inflammable material over a considerable distance." As the UN Secretariat concluded in a 1973 review: "It would appear that the I.C.R.C. was attempting in article 14 to deal with incendiaries other than napalm and flame-throwers, which were then seen as having limited effect."[17]

Napalm reigned unchallenged. Commanders used it extensively, in Korea and elsewhere, and for more than two decades after 1945 no international code was even proposed to regulate it.[18]

# 12

## The Third Protocol

Vietnam shattered this postwar consensus, and ushered in years of wrangling that ended in the world's first treaty to criminalize napalm deployments under particular circumstances.

Soviet Bloc countries, arrayed against the United States and its allies in Vietnam, raised the first objections. In April 1965, as napalm bombing increased dramatically in Indochina, a joint communiqué issued by the USSR and the Democratic Republic of Vietnam, or North Vietnam, condemned "the use of barbarous weapons of annihilation, including napalm bombs, against the peaceful population." A few months later, on January 24, 1966, the president of North Vietnam specifically protested napalm attacks against his county. Finally, on July 6, 1966, Warsaw Pact nations collectively decried the munition that clung to flesh and burned to the bone. These protests dragged napalm onto the world stage.[1]

Publicity increased on May 13, 1968, when eighty-four states, including the United States, assembled under United Nations (UN) auspices at Teheran for the first International Conference on Human Rights ("We pledge ourselves once again to the holy struggle for human dignity," U.S. president Lyndon Johnson wrote in his benediction). Delegates singled out napalm bombardments as one of the modern world's worst practices: "[T]he widespread violence and brutality of our times, including massacres, summary executions, tortures, inhuman treatment of prisoners, killing of civilians in armed conflicts and the use of chemical and biological means of warfare, including napalm bombing, erode human rights and engender counter-brutality," asserted Conference Resolution XXIII. A detailed review of the munition, attendees resolved, was warranted: General Assembly delegates should ask the secretary-general to study "The need for additional humanitarian international conventions or for possible revision of existing Conventions to ensure the better protection of civilians, prisoners and combatants in all armed conflicts and the prohibition and limitation of the use of certain methods and means of warfare." Law of war consultant to the UN Secretariat and professor of law at Harvard Richard Baxter commented, "The stimulus to renewed thought about the prohibition or restriction of use of certain conventional weapons was, not surprisingly, the war in Vietnam, coupled with a renewed concern with the humanitarian law of war in general." On December 19, 1968, as campuses across its host country reverberated with anti-napalm protests, the General Assembly affirmed the Teheran Conference's Resolution XXIII.[2]

A curtain began to lift on napalm. UN secretary-general U Thant's office switched on a spotlight. In its report released on November 20, 1969, staffers made explicit what Resolution XXIII implied: napalm deserved special scrutiny. "[I]n view of the reference to napalm in the Teheran Conference resolution, the legality or otherwise of the use of napalm would seem to be a question which would call for study and might be eventually resolved in an international document which would clarify the situation," read the first of five *Respect for Human Rights in Armed Conflict* reports prepared for the General Assembly between 1969 and 1973. In 1970, after no action was taken, the secretary-general repeated his call: "The contemplated report on the question of napalm which might be prepared by the Secretary-General could facilitate subsequent action by the United Nations with a view to curtailing or abolishing such uses of the weapons in question as might be established as inhumane," reiterated that year's *Respect* review.[3]

Results came as the United States advanced plans for a military drawdown in Vietnam. On December 20, 1971, the nations of the world, gathered at the UN, declared napalm "cruel" and affirmed the need for a comprehensive study of it and other incendiaries. Existing surveys, the General Assembly resolved, "do not deal with the question of prohibiting or restricting the use of other methods of warfare that are cruel, such as napalm, or that indiscriminately affect civilians and combatants." Assembly members requested the secretary-general "to prepare as soon as possible, with the help of qualified governmental consultant experts, a report on napalm and other incendiary weapons and all aspects of their possible use."[4]

Consultant experts, seven in total, set to work on May 15, 1972, in New York. Military, medical, chemical, and diplomatic authorities from Nigeria, Romania, Czechoslovakia, Sweden, the USSR, Peru, and Mexico, supported by members of the UN Secretariat, the World Health Organization, and the International Committee of the Red Cross (ICRC), examined the nature, history, and use of napalm and other incendiary weapons. America, still fighting in Vietnam, declined to participate on the grounds that the UN was not an appropriate forum for what it called arms control negotiations. On June 9, while the team was in recess, "The Terror of War" photograph of Kim Phúc ran on front-pages around the world. Protests against the Vietnam War and napalm deployments there rocked New York throughout the summer. On September 22, 1972, after a final group conclave in Geneva, the UN received *Napalm and Other Incendiary Weapons and All Aspects of Their Possible Use: Report of the Secretary-General.*[5]

Expert opinion was unequivocal: incendiary weapons were powerful, cruel, and indiscriminate, impossible to protect against, proliferating quickly, and largely lawless. Napalm was an exceptional munition within this category and especially in need of regulation. "[I]ncendiaries are among the most powerful means of destruction in existence; they characterize the savage and cruel consequences of total war," the authorities wrote. "Except for nuclear weapons, and perhaps also certain biological and chemical weapons, no other armament places such destructive power in the hands of military commanders," they emphasized. As to cruelty, they started with the observation that "Burn injuries . . . are intensely painful and, compared with the injuries caused by most other categories of weapon, require exceptional resources for their medical treatment." Thus, "When judged against what is required to put a soldier out of military action, much of the injury caused by incendiary weapons is [therefore] likely to be superfluous." And correspondingly, for civilians "incendiaries are particularly cruel in their effects."[6]

Panelists dismissed arguments that incendiaries could be precisely targeted: "Even when they are used as individual weapons, they may still strike over a considerable area, or initiate fires that spread far beyond their immediate targets." Relatively speaking, "The element of control which can be exercised over the effects of such weapons as bullets, or even high explosive bombs, is lacking in the case of most incendiary weapons, and like all area weapons they are essentially indiscriminate," they continued. "They may bring uncontrollable destruction of the lives, possessions and habitations of combatants and non-combatants alike," the group counseled.[7]

That protection from napalm and incendiary weapons was almost impossible highlighted their indiscriminate nature. In the case of area attacks, "Although it is possible to conceive of a shelter programme of sufficient quality to enable a city population to survive a conflagration or even a fire-storm, such a programme would be very expensive, both economically and in terms of changes in the society, and would take many years to establish. Few if any countries have undertaken such a programme." For tactical strikes, "local non-combatants are, as a rule, much more vulnerable than the combatants, who are familiar with the destructive properties of incendiary weapons, and trained in the various counter-measures." Therefore, "The indiscriminate nature of the effects of incendiary weapons is thus further underlined by the difficulties of providing adequate protection for the civilian population," the panel concluded.[8]

Napalm—which the experts defined as "any gelled-hydrocarbon incendiary," following Louis Fieser—was worst of all. First, it was particularly prone to misuse. "Because of the considerable area covered by each napalm bomb and often great inaccuracy of its delivery, and because also of the frequently close proximity of military and civilian objects, firebombs may cause severe damage in the civilian sector even when, ostensibly, the targets of attack are military," the authorities advised. Second, it was especially easy to produce: "Many of these weapons are extremely simple to manufacture, and the necessary raw materials are readily available the world over. This is particularly true of napalm weapons."[9]

Regulation, the advisors concluded, was urgently needed. Progress produced proliferation: "The rapid increase in the military use of incendiary weapons, especially napalm, during the past 30 years is but one aspect of the more general phenomenon of the increasing mobilization of science and technology for war purposes." Napalm had a high profile: "Incendiary weapons, in particular napalm, are already the subject of widespread revulsion and anxiety." General Assembly delegates, the experts wrote, should devise measures "for the prohibition of the use, production, development and stockpiling of napalm and other incendiary weapons." Napalm stood publicly accused.[10]

Countries around the world embraced the report. On November 16, 1972, one hundred states backed a draft resolution approved by the Political Committee of the General Assembly that deplored napalm's use in combat. No countries opposed the measure. America and fourteen other members abstained. Advocates of regulation decried their refusal to endorse the experts' conclusions. "The United States' use of napalm in Vietnam was attacked during the committee debate, which focused on a report by a group of experts calling napalm one of the most destructive weapons known," the *New York Times* reported.[11]

Further evidence for changing views on napalm came at the end of the month, when General Assembly Resolution 2932 affirmed the Political Committee's conclusion that napalm's use was deplorable "in all armed conflicts." General Assembly members described incendiary weapons—a category of arms, they forcefully asserted, always "viewed with horror"—as "largely indiscriminate," and urged that the secretary-general's report be published "for wide circulation." This meant it would be sold to the public in bookstores, rather than buried as an administrative filing. Reports from Vietnam informed debate. "As a result of the use of napalm in the war in Viet-Nam, a number of persons writing on the subject have stated that the weapon has been used so indiscriminately and causes such suffering that it belongs in the category of weapons which are forbidden on those accounts," the secretary-general's office observed in its 1973 *Respect for Human Rights* report. As a matter of law, however,

"Those delegations speaking in support of the resolution did so in terms suggesting that the use of napalm—for it was to this weapon that attention was principally given—ought to be forbidden but was not yet prohibited by general international law," the secretary-general's staff continued.[12]

There was a deafening legal silence. No conferences convened. No treaties emerged. A fundamental weakness, some scholars asserted, had been revealed in a core principle of the international law of war: "unnecessary suffering" and "superfluous injury" could not be defined. No scale of values could determine the appropriate amount of suffering for a specific military gain, Harvard's Baxter wrote. "And if one adopts a somewhat impressionistic approach to the question, then it would seem that the more effective a weapon is in disabling and killing, the more likely it is to be 'unlawful' because of the suffering it causes." Precision, he argued, was a more workable standard. He proposed as a principle: "If a weapon directed against military personnel or against military objectives indiscriminately harms civilians because there is no possibility of confining its effects to the military target, the weapon might be stigmatized as unlawful on that account."[13]

Stymied, napalm's opponents attempted to open a second front in 1972: the gel, they argued, should be banned as a gas weapon. Napalm "gives off large quantities of carbon monoxide, which may cause poisoning and death. In other words, the use of napalm for military purposes is regarded as particularly cruel because its victims, besides being burnt alive, are asphyxiated and poisoned. Such a use is therefore considered to be a violation of the 1907 Hague Convention and the 1925 Geneva Protocol for the prohibition of the use of chemical and bacteriological (biological) weapons," the secretary-general's 1973 *Respect for Human Rights in Armed Conflict* report observed when it documented this line of reasoning. This argument never advanced beyond preliminary stages, however, likely because advocates could not conclusively establish the frequency with which napalm acted through gas effects rather than burns.[14]

Changes at the Red Cross advanced worldwide debate. At its XXII International Conference in November 1973, the Geneva-based International Committee and ninety-eight national societies, joined by representatives from seventy-eight governments and twenty intergovernmental and non-governmental organizations—over 500 delegates in all—agreed to expand the organization's mandate from humanitarian law to the law of war. "An organization that had over the years acquired very great expertise in the protection of such war victims as civilians and prisoners of war was now called upon to assist in the assessment of weapons and their effects—to move from humanitarian law to the law of combat," Baxter explained.[15]

Not without controversy. As Pentagon law of war expert W. Hays Parks recounted in 2006, "The fact that the I.C.R.C. sought and gained a mandate to pursue the conventional weapons issue . . . gave pause within and outside the I.C.R.C. Historically, the I.C.R.C.'s role has been protection of war victims: military wounded, sick, and shipwrecked on the battlefield; prisoners of war; and civilians in enemy hands. Some within the I.C.R.C. believed that assuming a role with regard to the legality of weapons would detract from its long-time humanitarian mission." Nonetheless, the XXIInd conference resolved to convene its own group of government experts to advise a Diplomatic Conference on the Reaffirmation and Development of International Humanitarian Law Applicable in Armed Conflicts (the "Diplomatic Conference") about a possible expansion of the 1949 Geneva Conventions to cover conventional weapons. Swiss officials set February 1974 as the date for the convocation.[16]

In New York, General Assembly delegates maintained pressure. On December 6, 1973, the UN adopted Resolution 3076 (XXVIII) "Napalm and Other Incendiary Weapons and All Aspects of Their Possible Use." World representatives invited Diplomatic Conference delegates to consider "the question of the use of napalm and other incendiary weapons . . . and to seek agreement on rules prohibiting or restricting the use of such weapons."[17]

Experts assembled by the Red Cross to assist the Diplomatic Conference did their part to keep attention focused on napalm. Over the next twenty-seven months, these advisors produced two extensive reports on the law of war and legality of specific weapons. Each contained an extensive review of napalm. Ultimately, the Diplomatic Conference, which finalized proposed revisions to the Geneva Conventions in 1977, did not produce specific rules for napalm. It did, however, resolve on a "Follow-Up regarding Prohibition or Restriction of Use of Certain Conventional Weapons" that included napalm by name and drew heavily on the expert reports. These findings, along with an additional General Assembly resolution in 1974 that again condemned napalm and urged a code to govern its use, set the stage for adoption in 1980 of Protocol III of the United Nations Convention on Certain Conventional Weapons.[18]

The first ICRC expert gathering met in September and October 1974 at the Swiss lakeside town of Lucerne, near Zurich. Members, including a U.S. delegation, agreed unanimously that burns are the most painful kind of injury, saturation incendiary bombardment of cities was a war crime, and public opinion plays an important role in the formulation of international law. As the final report stated: "All experts agreed that . . . generally speaking, severe burn wounds were probably the most painful type of wound and frequently remained so for long periods of time . . . and that they may result in permanent disability, including physical, functional, cosmetic, social and psychological disability."[19]

Specific rules for napalm, however, foundered on the now-familiar definitional shoals of suffering and precision. One group of experts (cloaked in anonymity by conference rapporteurs) asserted that incendiary weapons were inhumane. They argued from "such factors as the nature of the wounds inflicted, the degree of pain which victims of war burns had to suffer, and the difficulty and prolonged duration of medical treatment. In all these respects, they were convinced that the suffering due to severe burns caused by incendiary weapons was considerably worse than that resulting from other war wounds." A second unidentified group denied it: "While admitting that, generally speaking, severe burn wounds were probably the worst possible type of wound, these experts were not convinced that the use of incendiary weapons resulted in all cases in an exceptionally high incidence of casualties, let alone of gravely wounded; on the contrary, they thought that in certain situations these figures might even be significantly lower than those resulting from the use of other weapons." Banning incendiary weapons, the skeptics argued, "even if militarily feasible, might well result in an increased number of casualties and of severely injured in particular."[20]

Similar paralysis gripped specialists on the subject of precision. "According to a number of experts, incendiary weapons are unquestionably indiscriminate in that they exert their primary effect over a certain area, while moreover the secondary effect they often have and which is due to the self-propagating character of fire is beyond the control of the user of the weapons," wrote authors of the final conference report. However, they continued, other experts, "while conceding that incendiary weapons, like most other weapons, could be used without discrimination, denied that they were indiscriminate in all cases, or by their nature. In the view of these experts, modern incendiary weapons are as accurate as other weapons and are, indeed, at times even more discriminate than other weapons that might be used in their stead; their primary effect can be confined to a strictly limited area, and the spread of the fire, as with many alternative weapons, depends upon the nature of the target." Area attacks like those of World War II, members of the latter group maintained, were obsolete and, since they could only be mounted by a few countries, unlikely to the point of irrelevance. "It was stated by some experts that large-scale incendiary attacks on urban or rural areas were no longer considered important in military doctrine. It was also pointed out that the capacity for mounting and conducting fire-raid attacks on cities, such as those of World War II, was today at the disposal of only a very few States, if any at all. In the opinion of these experts, therefore, large incendiary area attacks were a thing of the past," the Red Cross report observed. As a practical matter, the latter group of analysts concluded, "In more recent armed conflicts, while incendiary weapons might at times have been used indiscriminately, in other instances they had proved their capacity for discriminate use." Specialists proved similarly divided over whether a general rule was sufficient to prevent saturation firebombing of cities, or if a specific legal prohibition against urban area attacks was necessary.[21]

In the end, there was no consensus about the best legal standard. Some experts called for a complete prohibition on incendiary weapons and napalm. Others urged proscription of "indiscriminate attacks against civilian population centres." A final group recommended that laws control specific weapons, rather than assert broad principles.[22]

Experts did appear to agree, however, that public opinion worldwide militated against the use of incendiary weapons—although they split as to the importance of that observation as a matter of law. "In the eyes of some, public opinion concerning the use of incendiary weapons provided yet another argument for the illegality of the use of those weapons," the Lucerne report advised. Others, it continued, "who could not accept the public conscience as an independent source of international law, were prepared to admit that existing public opinion with respect to incendiary weapons provided a strong political factor for governments to take into account."[23]

The UN General Assembly was more unified. On December 9, 1974, the world body sounded yet another clarion about napalm. Resolution 3255 (XXIX) seized on the unanimity of the ICRC's Lucerne experts about the pain of burn injuries to condemn the gel and urge its abolition. Delegates pushed the ongoing Diplomatic Conference to write these recommendations into international law. In a relatively rare recorded vote, ninety-eight states approved the resolution and twenty-six, including the United States, its North Atlantic Treaty Organization (NATO) allies, the USSR, and members of the Warsaw Pact, abstained. "[S]evere burn wounds are probably the most painful type of wound and frequently remain so for long periods of time," the UN resolution observed. "Emphasizing the consensus of the Conference of Government Experts," the statement continued, the world body "Condemns the use of napalm and other incendiary weapons in armed conflicts in circumstances where it may affect human beings or may cause damage to the environment and/or natural resources," and "Urges all States to refrain from the production, stockpiling, proliferation and use of such weapons, pending the conclusion of agreements on the prohibition of these weapons." The global assembly invited governments, the ICRC, specialized agencies, and other international organizations to transmit to the secretary-general "all information about the use of napalm and other incendiary weapons in armed conflicts"; requested a follow-up report from the secretary-general; and encouraged the "Diplomatic Conference on the Reaffirmation and Development of International Humanitarian Law Applicable in Armed Conflicts to continue its consideration of the question of the use of napalm . . . and its search for agreement on possible rules prohibiting or restricting the use of such weapons."[24]

Red Cross officials resumed their deliberations in January 1976. In coordination with an ad hoc committee assembled by the Diplomatic Conference, the group gathered a second collection of specialists, again with U.S. representatives, at a different Swiss lakeside resort: Lugano, thirty kilometers east of historic Solferino. Napalm was still center stage. "Of all incendiary weapons, it is napalm which has aroused the greatest public concern," the experts stated.[25]

Advocates for regulation of incendiary weapons, aware of the divisions at Lucerne, offered three main proposals. All cited precision, rather than suffering, as their legal basis. "All of these proposals have one thing in common, in that they consider solely the protection of civilians, that is to say, they take account only of the propensity of those weapons for producing indiscriminate effects," the experts advised. Mexico suggested a complete ban of incendiaries. Sweden proposed a ban with limited exceptions (for example, fire weapons specifically designed for use against armored vehicles). The Netherlands, with Australia, advanced a simple rule: "[I]t is prohibited to make any city, town, village or other area containing a concentration of civilians the object of attack by any incendiary munition."[26]

Group members discussed research findings for the first time. A Canadian expert described experiments on goats that suggested little risk to the animals from napalm: "Goats had been clipped and then tethered in the open or in narrow slit trenches. Each one was covered with a single army blanket. A standard napalm bomb was dropped on the animals, completely enveloping 30 goats in its fireball. One goat was severely injured by a direct hit from the bomb casing. Two goats had slightly reddened skin, and six had singed hairs. No goat was asphyxiated or displayed signs of carbon monoxide poisoning." Canada also reported results from experiments on people that suggested *homo sapiens* might be more at risk from napalm than *capra aegagrus hircus:* "A burning blob of napalm on the bare skin became intolerable after one second. The size of the blob had no impact on the pain threshold. A single layer of cotton protected the skin against burning for 6–7 seconds, and a second layer for 30 seconds. Of the thickened-napalm blobs striking an individual in a simulated hit, 69% could be extinguished with the bare hands."[27]

Results from Korean War studies presented at Lugano underlined humanity's vulnerability to napalm: "it was to be expected that about 35% of those caught by a firebomb would be killed, and of the survivors 25–30% would need to be evacuated by other people and 50–55% would be *hors de combat.*" Striking though these figures were, U.S. Army weapons design specialist Wayne Copes reported that results from war-game simulations showed "general purpose bombs and bomblets-dispenser munitions would cause, respectively, 1.5 and more than 5 times as many incapacitating wounds to enemy troops as would napalm." Other experts attacked these conclusions for not considering alternate weapons such as aircraft guns, rockets and smart bombs, and ignoring complicating factors like weather, battlefield illumination, and the psychological effect of napalm.[28]

Opponents of regulation advanced arguments similar to those made at Lucerne. They revisited the inconclusive debate over suffering ("There is no consensus on whether injuries from incendiary weapons are likely to impose more suffering either than other war burn injuries or than any other type of traumatic injury"), asserted napalm might be a blessing ("the military value of napalm could perhaps be considered to reside more in its psychological effects than in its physical ones; and since it thereby achieved its desired results more by stimulating flight than by direct casualty-production, a case could be made that it was likely to cause less overall suffering than alternative types of weapon"), and simultaneously maintained incendiary weapons were uniquely valuable ("represent an important element in the military arsenals of some States, and the security of those States would be weakened by a general prohibition of use") and that napalm in particular didn't warrant special scrutiny because it probably could be replaced ("it would be unduly short-sighted to concentrate on napalm for it was readily conceivable that other incendiary agents, perhaps more destructive ones, could be used in place of it").[29]

Unsurprisingly, the experts again failed to achieve consensus. Nonetheless, under the glare of relentless publicity, international law, now with precision as its guiding principle, appeared to have drawn its net tighter than ever before around napalm. "[S]erious attempts were made to reduce the distance between opposing views, to explore the middle ground lying between them and to show more flexibility," Austrian head of the General Working Group Erich Kussbach observed with diplomatic blandness. "This attitude has to be welcomed even though for the time being it did not succeed in achieving any conclusive agreement on the subject," he asserted.[30]

After this lengthy lead-in, the Diplomatic Conference itself side-stepped incendiary weapons. Delegates from the Soviet Union, Italy, and Germany, among others, echoed the 1972 U.S. argument that arms control was distinct from international law. The former, they said, had no place at such a conference. Diplomats acceded to what is perhaps, in practice, a distinction without a difference: Additional Protocols I and II to the Geneva Convention of 1949—130 articles adopted on June 8, 1977—cover care for the wounded, prisoners, and the sick, and provide rules to reduce unnecessary suffering and protect civilians, but say nothing about incendiary weapons.[31]

Napalm appeared to have escaped the law. On the final day of the almost two-and-one-half-year diplomatic conclave, however, attorneys opened a pursuit route that ultimately led to its capture under international jurisprudence. Resolution 22, "Follow-Up regarding Prohibition or Restriction of Use of Certain Conventional Weapons," identified a rogues' gallery of weapons delegates believed deserved special scrutiny: bombs that splintered into plastic fragments invisible to X-rays, land mines, booby traps, and incendiary weapons—including napalm, specified by name. A conference was to be convened not later than 1979 to promulgate "prohibitions or restrictions" on these and other devices. Napalm's court date was set.[32]

Pentagon authorities, with their napalm-drenched Vietnam debacle in its final throes, and well aware of the burgeoning interest in conventional weapons among international groups in general and the ICRC in particular, started a continuous process of legal review for new weapons in 1974 to ensure they met America's legal obligations. As the 1970s continued, and the reality of defeat in Vietnam and its unfolding consequences sank in, U.S. policy makers for the first time stepped back diplomatically, commercially, and operationally from napalm.[33]

Defense Department attorneys produced a standard statement of the U.S. understanding of law of war principles to guide their review. Their language was so carefully hedged, it seems unlikely to have imposed much practical limitation on action. Its existence, however, shows that policy makers acknowledged international law and saw value in genuflection, at least, to its principles. Of "unnecessary suffering," the lawyers wrote, "There is no agreed international definition. . . . A weapon or munition would be deemed to cause unnecessary suffering only if it inevitably or in its normal use has a particular effect, and the injury caused is considered by governments as disproportionate to the military necessity for it." As if that wasn't opaque enough, they added, "This balancing test cannot be conducted in isolation. A weapon's or munition's effects must be weighed in light of comparable, lawful weapons or munitions in use on the modern battlefield." Despite the ambiguity of this benchmark, certainty, attorneys stated, was required for a determination of illegality: "A weapon is not unlawful merely because it may cause severe suffering or injury. . . . The correct criterion is whether the employment of a weapon for its normal or expected use inevitably would cause injury or suffering manifestly disproportionate to its military effectiveness."

Motivations of individual soldiers, moreover, trumped the characteristics of particular weapons. Pentagon lawyers continued, "In determining legality, a State is not required to foresee or anticipate all possible uses or misuses of a weapon, for almost any weapon can be misused in ways that might be prohibited. A soldier armed with a handgun may murder an innocent civilian or a prisoner of war in his or her custody. The soldier has committed a violation of the law of war for which he or she should be brought to trial and, if convicted, punished. The fact that a pistol was used to perpetrate the crime does not transform an otherwise lawful weapon into an illegal weapon." Extending the principle, "The same may be said of an aircraft attack on a civilian object, or indiscriminate attacks by ground or air forces. A lawful weapon used to commit a crime makes the act criminal but does not make the weapon system or weapon illegal."

Finally, with respect to targeting, the United States eschewed general principles in favor of a case-by-case approach. "Law of war issues related to lawful targeting are addressed at the time of employment, to be determined by the on-scene commander under the circumstances ruling at the time," America's attorneys wrote. "The commander authorizing a weapon's use should consider its characteristics where innocent civilians are present in order to ensure consistency with mission rules of engagement and law of war proscriptions on the directing of attacks at civilians not taking an active part in hostilities, or who otherwise do not pose a threat to friendly forces." [34]

Politicians, diplomats, and operational military commanders were less circumspect. Jimmy Carter charged in the 1976 presidential campaign that "moral bankruptcy" had turned the United States into "an arsenal" for the world, and hurt the country. In 1977, after his election, he endorsed Presidential Review Memorandum 12, produced by the State Department's Bureau of Political-Military Affairs, which ordered the United States to stop exports of "brutalizing" weapons such as napalm bombs. On May 9, the administration leaked this new policy at a summit with Britain, France, West Germany, Italy, Japan, and Canada. Napalm was now a forbidden weapon whose export was prohibited along with nuclear, chemical, and biological munitions. It remained, however, in the U.S. arsenal.[35]

Traditional flamethrowers went next. In 1978, the U.S. Army declared these Iwo Jima heroes obsolete. FLASH, the Flame Assault Shoulder Weapon, a shoulder-mounted rocket launcher that shot 1.3-pound rockets filled with thickened triethylaluminum (a liquid that burns at 1,400–2,200 degrees Fahrenheit when exposed to air) took their place. In an echo of the range limitations that made Greek Fire obsolete after cannons appeared, rockets traveled five times farther than portable flamethrowers could shoot, weighed half as much per system, and required less maintenance, according to FLASH's Army Training Circular. When set to semiautomatic, the device delivered one rocket per second. For the first time in history, America's commitment to napalm was less at the end of a decade than at its start.[36]

The UN Conference on Certain Conventional Weapons (CCW) opened as proposed in Diplomatic Conference Resolution 22 on September 10,

1979. Representatives from eighty-two nations convened at the Palais des Nations in Geneva. Incendiary weapons drove the debate. "The prohibition or regulation of incendiary weapons was for many the *raison d'être* for the C.C.W., given the extensive and widespread destruction resulting from their use in World War II and, to a lesser degree, in post-World War II conflicts," observed U.S. delegation member Parks. "Many felt that any agreement on conventional weapons which did not include a Protocol on incendiary weapons would have the distressing appearance of a fire-brigade which had forgotten to bring the hose-pipe. If nothing had been achieved on this subject, it is likely that all the work of the Conference would have been wasted," agreed professor of international humanitarian law Yves Sandoz, who was employed at ICRC headquarters during the period. To make the overall treaty easier for states to accept, drafters segregated rules for specific weapons in individual protocols, linked by a core treaty document that specified general administrative procedures. This allowed governments to subscribe to regulatory regimes à la carte: devices that produced nondetectable fragments (Protocol I); mines, booby traps, and other devices (Protocol II); and incendiary weapons (Protocol III). States had to endorse the basic treaty and at least two protocols to become parties to the agreement.[37]

Lawyers at two preparatory conferences, and at the CCW's two formal negotiating sessions, reviewed familiar arguments about napalm: its lethality, military efficacy, and the proper scope of international law. Medical debates again proved inconclusive. Opponents of a blanket prohibition repeated the argument, advanced at Lucerne, that area incendiary attacks were militarily obsolete, given the improved accuracy of modern aircraft and delivery systems. Moreover, they noted, massive bomber fleets like those of 1945 no longer existed. Rebutters asserted that sufficient capacity remained for devastating attacks. A study submitted without attribution by one of the principal delegations presented the value of incendiaries versus high explosives down to the decimal: to achieve a 50 percent destruction of petroleum storage facilities, the anonymous authors asserted, required eighty-nine sorties with high explosives compared to just thirteen with incendiary weapons; ammunition depots necessitated 996 explosive attacks compared to 456 strikes with mixed payloads of incendiaries and explosives. Just seventeen sorties with mixed armaments accomplished results comparable to fifty-eight attacks with explosives alone against aircraft manufacturing plants. Incendiary weapons cut risks for attackers and civilians near target sites, the analysis concluded, insofar as they reduced the number of attacks required to destroy targets.[38]

Diplomats ultimately rejected finely calibrated arguments like these in favor of a simple standard for incendiary weapons: no attacks under any circumstances against "the civilian population as such" or "concentrations of civilians." As Parks, who negotiated the protocol for the United States, wrote, "[N]otwithstanding rules of engagement [for napalm] drawn up by a number of nations in recent conflicts to limit the employment of incendiary munitions in proximity to inhabited urban areas, mistakes of combat had frequently led to suffering of innocent civilians. The distinction between intentional and unintentional injury or death is lost on the civilian who suffers that injury."[39]

Lawyers made a number of important exclusions. Combatants received no protection. "Munitions which may have incidental incendiary effects, such as illuminants, tracers, smoke or signaling systems," including widely used white phosphorus, negotiators decided, did not count as incendiary weapons, and thus were not subject to the protocol. In a nod to Sweden's 1976 proposal at Lugano for a ban with exceptions, "Munitions designed to combine penetration, blast or fragmentation effects with an additional incendiary effect—such as armour-piercing projectiles, fragmentation shells, explosive bombs and similar combined-effects munitions in which the incendiary effect is not specifically designed to cause burn injury to persons, but to be used against military objectives, such as armoured vehicles, aircraft and installations or facilities," were also excluded from the definition of an "incendiary weapon."[40]

A positive result of these restrictions was an easily comprehensible standard for napalm and other incendiaries. "Incendiary weapon" meant "any weapon or munition which is primarily designed to set fire to objects or to cause burn injury to persons through the action of flame, heat, or combination thereof." These "can take the form of, for example, flame throwers, fougasses, shells, rockets, grenades, mines, bombs and other containers of incendiary substances," according to Protocol III. "Concentration of civilians" meant "any concentration of civilians, be it permanent or temporary, such as in inhabited parts of cities, or inhabited towns or villages, or as in camps or columns of refugees or evacuees, or groups of nomads." A "Military objective" was "any object which by its nature, location, purpose or use makes an effective contribution to military action and whose total or partial destruction, capture or neutralization, in the circumstances ruling at the time, offers a definite military advantage."[41]

In addition to protection for civilian populations "as such," it was "prohibited in all circumstances to make any military objective located within a concentration of civilians the object of attack by air-delivered incendiary weapons." Incendiary weapons that were not air-delivered, such as for example flamethrowers, might only be used "when such military objective is clearly separated from the concentration of civilians and all feasible precautions are taken with a view to limiting the incendiary effects to the military objective and to avoiding, and in any event to minimizing, incidental loss of civilian life, injury to civilians and damage to civilian objects." There was even protection for natural resources, proposed by the USSR: "It is prohibited to make forests or other kinds of plant cover the object of attack by incendiary weapons except when such natural elements are used to cover, conceal or camouflage combatants or other military objectives, or are themselves military objectives."[42]

These restrictions on napalm proved the most difficult hurdle for the Convention on Certain Conventional Weapons. The Soviet Union, less than one year into its invasion of Afghanistan, balked at Protocol III. The United States, with no comparable military engagements, initially proved more amenable, and accepted the proposal in the first days of October 1980. Moscow could not stand alone: on October 7, the *New York Times* reported "The Soviet delegation was the last to approve a ban on using napalm or similar flame-spreading substances in air strikes against military objectives near civilian concentrations. Moscow was left isolated when the United States last week approved the ban." Delegates finalized the convention on October 10, 1980. A total of thirty-five states signed it at the UN on April 10, 1981. It came into force with fifty signatories on December 2, 1983.[43]

And just like that, napalm bombs became criminal when used against civilians "as such" or "concentrations of civilians" under any circumstances. "Delegates said the most important achievement was the banning of the incendiary bombing of cities and other areas where civilians are concentrated even if military objectives are present," the *New York Times* noted at the end of the drafting process. Protocol III "would appear to prohibit the starting of fire storms in cities or dropping napalm on villages or towns," correspondent Bernard Nossiter explained in April.[44]

America, however, proved unwilling to accept this global paradigm. Despite its reported promise, the United States ultimately decided to preserve its freedom of action with respect to napalm and other incendiary weapons: U.S. diplomats left Protocol III blank when they eventually signed the CCW on April 8, 1982. Washington under President Ronald Reagan stood alone against all of its NATO allies, except Turkey; every Warsaw Pact state, except Romania; and the People's Republic of China. All of these states approved Protocol III in relatively short order.[45]

# 13

## Judgment Day

It took about two decades after America's defeat in Vietnam for the arguments advanced by protesters in the late 1960s to percolate around the world and coalesce into a near-universal antipathy to napalm backed by international law. During that time, military forces deployed the incendiary on every continent except North America, Australia, and demilitarized Antarctica: jelly bombs fell in Africa, Asia, the Middle East, Latin America, and Europe. Gradually, however, what started as articles, artworks, and protest signs in Redwood City, New York; Madison, Wisconsin; and napalm's birthplace Cambridge, Massachusetts, spread throughout popular culture and became a consensus—a kind of social echo to napalm's global embrace by political and military commanders. Civilians in the United States came to see napalm, eventually with near-hysterical intensity, as a monster. Combat deployments worldwide produced vituperation that increasingly outweighed tactical benefits. Napalm became a public relations problem for officers and politicians. Development of alternate weapons technologies, including smart bombs and improved cluster munitions, highlighted the weapon's relative costs. In response, military tactics started to change.

Ultimately, the U.S. government severed some of its public ties to its remarkable creation. On April 4, 2001, in a well publicized "last canister ceremony" at the Fallbrook Naval Weapons Station between Los Angeles and San Diego, navy officials bade a loud farewell to napalm. Presidents Bill Clinton and George W. Bush both recommended that the U.S. Senate ratify Protocol III to the Convention on Certain Conventional Weapons (CCW). On September 23, 2008, it finally did. President Barack Obama signed it on his first full day in office. In sixty-seven years, napalm has moved from a position of heroic omnipotence to one of global infamy and international legal regulation.

This is far from an American abandonment of napalm. Obama appended a diplomatic reservation to his signature of Protocol III that arguably rendered his commitment meaningless. Napalm remains legal to use in combat under international law, and American forces deployed it during the 2003 invasion of Iraq—but, in sharp contrast to previous wars, they denied it.[1]

Africa was the most common region for confirmed napalm attacks in the years after the Vietnam War. In Ethiopia, the Dergue, or "shadow" junta, backed by the USSR, dropped gel bombs repeatedly on Eritrean rebels and Somali forces from at least 1976 to 1985. "Whole villages have been devastated by saturation bombing raids—sometimes involving napalm," *Time* reported in 1976. "We walked across an acre of charred ruins and ashes," British *Sunday Telegraph* journalist Norman Kirkham recounted of a 1978 visit to the town of Garbo attacked by Ethiopian and Cuban troops. At breakfast time, he wrote, "the green-and-brown camouflaged jet turned and began to descend again, this time followed by a MiG-21 loaded with napalm. . . . [It] dived on the four corners of the village, dropping its deadly napalm in a neat rectangle. Within ten minutes, Garbo had been turned into an inferno." More than ninety people died in the flames or were killed by the strafing; others suffered hideous burns, according to Kirkham. A decade later, risks remained from firebombs: "Civilians are regularly lectured on how to wipe burning napalm jelly from their skin," *Time* advised in 1985. Farther south, news reports mentioned napalm bombings by Rhodesian aircraft in 1977, and Cuban and Soviet attacks on pro-Western forces in Angola in 1978.[2]

Napalm bombs fell in west, central, and east Asia in the 1970s and 1980s. U.S. sources reported frequent use of napalm by Soviet troops in Afghanistan during the 1979–1989 invasion and occupation. In 1983, in a more limited example, Thai troops dropped napalm on 150 Vietnamese soldiers entrenched along the Cambodian border—perhaps the first use of napalm in Indochina since 1975. Iraqi forces used napalm extensively against Kurdish citizens in the 1986–1989 Anfal extermination campaign.[3]

Latin America saw at least two post-Vietnam deployments. In 1980, El Salvador's government used napalm against domestic insurgents. "Before the U.S. started helping us, we had to use napalm, because we didn't have any other equipment. We bought it from Israel several years ago, and used it until 1981. If we hadn't done that, I might not be sitting here today," Colonel Juan Rafael Bustillo, head of the Salvadoran air force, told a 1983 U.S. fact-finding mission. In 1982, during the Falklands War, Argentine Pucara aircraft dropped two napalm bombs on British troops. Both missed. UK troops discovered 9,000 gallons of the gel in field mixing units when they captured the Goose Green Airfield on East Falkland, and additional stocks at the airfield near the capital city, Stanley.[4]

As napalm's disrepute grew, combatants around the world frequently alleged its use by opponents. Those accused almost inevitably denied the charges: testimony to the weapon's notoriety. Thus, in 1977, Polisario guerrillas claimed French forces had used napalm in Western Sahara. "Largely in the domain of fiction," French foreign minister Louis de Guiringaud promptly, and carefully, commented in a parliamentary address a few days later. Fretilin, the East Timorese independence movement, asserted in 1980 that Indonesia used napalm to burn crops. Jakarta denied the charge. In January 2006, president of newly independent East Timor Xanana Gusmao repeated the contention in a report to the United Nations, and added that civilians had been targeted. A *Washington Post* reporter recorded a categorical denial: "Indonesia's defense minister, Juwono Sudarsono, challenged the report's accuracy Friday, denying the country used napalm." Chad made repeated claims that Libyan forces used napalm during fighting in the Sahara. In 1983, officials presented a forty-three-year-old man they identified as a captured Libyan air force pilot to reporters to lend credence to their charges. "We were dropping napalm as well," the man said. "Outside, a crowd of 5,000 people surged towards him, hissing, shouting and calling for his execution. The guards, one of them holding a grenade launcher inches from the Libyan's head, fought back the crowd before bundling him into a truck," Alan Cowell reported for the *New York Times*. Libya denied the attacks even took place, let alone that napalm was used. South Africa denied that it had used napalm against Angolan rebels. Russia denounced 1995 Chechen claims, repeated in a *Washington Post* editorial by a member of the newspaper's controlling family, that it used napalm against civilians in the rebellious province.[5]

By 1991, with the notoriety of napalm established, and Protocol III more than a decade old, British commanders planning Operation Desert Storm against Iraq concluded napalm's reputation was tarnished to a point that trumped its military utility. American officials rejected this assessment. "British officials say that in light of its infamous reputation the allies do not intend to use it against Saddam's troops. But napalm, which is most effective against massed troops out in the open, is among allied weapons stockpiled in the gulf, and U.S. officials do not rule out its use," *Time* reported. In the event, U.S. pilots dropped napalm bombs only to burn Iraqi defensive trenches filled with oil. "Much had been written about the inferno the Iraqis would create by filling trenches with burning oil. But in the Marines' sector, U.S. planes had burned off the oil prematurely by dropping napalm," George Church reported in *Time*. After the war, Iraqi authorities used napalm extensively to suppress a Shiite uprising in the south of the country.[6]

Judgment Day for napalm came on November 18, 1994, when Serbian commanders dropped a gelled incendiary bomb on the town of Bihać in northwest Bosnia and started a chain of events that confirmed the judgment of Britain's Desert Storm planners. It was the second strike on Bihać, located in a UN-declared "safe zone," in ten days, and far from the first Serbian challenge to the global body in the two-year-old conflict. But it was the first time napalm had been used. "Serb forces, defying stern United Nations warnings, today crossed a deadly threshold in the Bosnian struggle by dropping napalm on a 'safe area' designated by the U.N. The incident in northwest Bosnia was the first confirmed use of napalm in the 2½-year war," *Time* reported. "Many hot greetings. HOT. This is the beginning," read a message found on a shell fragment, handwritten in the Cyrillic alphabet used by Serbians. It appeared immaterial that the solitary firebomb did not explode, and no one was injured in the attack. Napalm, a fiend whose very name now invoked images of barbarism, had slouched back onto the world stage in a theater of war that was a center of global attention.[7]

World leaders responded immediately, and without equivocation. A UN Security Council vote the next day authorized expansion of the war into Croatia so that Serb air bases could be targeted. "We face a new threshold" that might "spawn a new spiral of war," declared U.S. secretary of state Madeline Albright. "The flames of war in the Balkans have been fanned even more," observed even Russian delegate Sergei Lavrov, a traditional ally of Serbia. Sir David Hannay, the British UN representative, called the attacks "totally unacceptable." Just three days later—it would have been sooner but for bad weather—jets from the United States, Britain, France, and the Netherlands joined in "the largest air raid in Europe since the end of World War II and the biggest mounted by the NATO [North Atlantic Treaty Organization] alliance since it was established in 1949 to counter Soviet military power," the *New York Times* reported. "NATO Punishes Serbs for Napalm Attack," *Time* headlined. Alliance warplanes, the magazine wrote, bombed "a base where Serbs equipped planes with napalm bombs used last week against the Bosnians in Bihac." Napalm, and the reaction to it, took "the Western alliance's political involvement in the Bosnian war to a new level," in the estimation of *New York Times* reporter Roger Cohen.[8]

Public opinion about civilian uses for napalm in the United States experienced a similar hardening as the twentieth century progressed. Initially, many had high hopes that peaceful functions might be found for the incendiary gel. Gardeners, the Forest Service, civil aviation authorities, and soap manufacturers, some thought, might be particular beneficiaries. "The deadly flamethrower, already nemesis of the Jap fighter at Okinawa, is already in peacetime use, attacking water vegetation which impedes navigation. A special mixture . . . is destroying clogging alligator grass and water hyacinth," a reporter recounted at the end of World War II. "The U.S. Forest Service has suggested using the flamegun for backfiring forest fires. Agriculturalists expect to employ it in modified form for burning over areas. The Pittsburgh municipal airport contemplates use of the flamethrower to remove hard-packed ice and snow on runways," the article continued. "Napalm, that spelled death and destruction as an incendiary ingredient in wartime flame-throwers, will soon be used by the Army as a G-I liquid soap," the *Science News-Letter* advised in 1946. "Within a few months, the War Department states, 50,000 gallons of a new quick-suds soap made of napalm will be available for everything from scrubbing barracks floors to G-I shampoos," the periodical continued. "Napalm is also reported to have a limited use in some hospital applications," it concluded, without elaboration.[9]

Napalm was indeed used to fight forest fires in remote areas after Japan's defeat. In 1982, for example, Forest Service helicopters dropped gel bombs to control a fire that had jumped into "wilderness so rugged that bulldozers could not be used," according to an Associated Press report datelined Happy Camp, California. Rangers have also used napalm to help regenerate Colorado forests. A 1989 attempt to use "small bags of napalm" dropped from a boat to burn oil spilled from the *Exxon Valdez* tanker in Alaska, however, was unsuccessful. Pittsburgh airport administrators resisted temptation and chose more traditional sweeping and blowing machines.[10]

Use of the weapon in proximity to civilians, however, has generated intensifying resistance. In 1992, for example, opponents of a navy firing range on the island of Vieques in Puerto Rico seized on reports of a napalm test—the first use of the gel at the range in a decade—as a reason to relaunch anti-base protests dormant since the early 1980s. Critics cited napalm's environmental toxicity, its brutal effects, and its use in

Vietnam. "Napalm contains an incendiary material and gelatinous phosphorous that burns everything around it and adheres to skin. Between 1963 and 1968, the United States dropped nearly one hundred thousand tons of napalm on Vietnam. Just one ton of this combustible gelatin will burn a surface area equivalent to one and a half football fields in seconds," opposition activist Robert Rabin wrote in a pamphlet produced by protesters. "The U.S. military has also tested napalm in Vieques. Napalm is jellied gasoline that sticks to human skin. Thousands of civilians were killed or maimed for life in Vietnam by Washington's use of napalm," base critics Rolland Girard and Ron Richards asserted in a 1998 piece in *The Militant,* the International Socialist Workers Party magazine. A 1999 report by a Special Commission on Vieques, appointed by Puerto Rico's governor, documented numerous findings that lessened support for the base, "in particular its disclosure that U.S. forces training in Vieques have used napalm and uranium-laced munitions during war games," according to the *Washington Post.* Protests, including civil disobedience, forced the navy to withdraw from the facility and close the nearby Roosevelt Roads Naval Base on May 1, 2003.[11]

Residents of Coos Bay, the largest city on Oregon's coast, reacted with a frenzy in 1999 when navy officials announced plans to use napalm to burn fuel oil on a freighter grounded at a local beach. Japanese freighter *New Carissa,* steaming to collect a load of wood chips on February 4, hit a sand bank about one mile from the town and just 150 yards from the Oregon Dunes National Recreation Area. Fuel tanks loaded with 359,000 gallons of tar-like bunker oil used to power the ship began to leak four days later. Authorities declared an emergency and closed local oyster beds. Multitudes of seals, sea lions, otters, birds, and other wildlife, and Oregon's $24 million-a-year Dungeness crab industry, faced disaster. An attempt to ignite the oil with hand grenades and buckets of gasoline failed. Navy and coast guard officials announced a second try with 400 pounds of C-4 plastic explosives and 600 gallons of napalm: the largest planned burn of a waterborne oil spill in U.S. history.[12]

Townspeople panicked. "You think napalm, and you think of Vietnam and half the country being burned up," said Joyce Jansen, a City Hall secretary. "People were afraid for their children." Residents flooded the police and fire departments with phone calls: more than one hundred to police alone from a community of perhaps 4,000 families. Some wondered whether they should flee to a larger town eighty miles inland, others asked if their children could be hit by flying debris as they walked home from school. "It is incredible, the rumors that are going around," said police chief Chuck Knight. Of course, terror was not universal: a few brave souls gathered at the beach with shirts that read "I got burned in Coos Bay."[13]

Just after sunset on February 11, 1999, a spectacular series of explosions, visible for twenty-five miles, shot flames hundreds of feet high over the ship, and rocked the town. "We've got a good hot fire going," reported a command center spokesman. Ultimately, the decision to use napalm proved a mixed blessing: about 90 percent of the oil burned, but the ten percent that escaped produced one of the worst oil spills in Oregon's history. Moreover, the fire was so hot it split the ship in two and created a salvage problem that took almost a decade to resolve.[14]

Similar community agita blocked proposals to use napalm to incinerate mountains of dead animals collected by health officials in the United States and the United Kingdom after disease outbreaks. Napalm applied with a retail "Terra Torch" flamethrower could reduce an adult livestock carcass to ash in about an hour, Nevada Department of Agriculture employee Ron Anderson reported after an anthrax epidemic in 2000. "It works very nice for diseases such as anthrax, because you get this bloody discharge which can have the spores in it. . . . When you are done burning the carcass, then the area (with spores) around the carcass can be torched," he advised. Traditional pyres made of surplus lumber, railroad ties, coal and tires required up to three days to burn animals and cost far more, the United Kingdom's *New Scientist* magazine reported during a 2001 foot and mouth disease epidemic that left up to 60,000 dead animals rotting in fields and barns. "Should not the use of napalm be considered urgently? Is the reason why it is not being considered . . . the fact that there are overtones of Vietnam that might not be acceptable to the public?" Labour member of Parliament Tam Dalyell, representative of Linlithgow in Scotland's central lowlands agricultural district, demanded of Environment Minister Michael Meacher in the midst of the crisis. Meacher denied napalm's public image dissuaded him from considering it. "I have no Vietnam-related inhibitions about napalm and I am perfectly prepared to look at its use. If it can make a contribution to the—I hope—rapidly decreasing number of fires in open fields, I am happy to take it on board," he responded.[15]

Scientists made a case on the merits. "Napalm sounds dangerous, but it is actually relatively easy and safe to use, and probably safer than either petrol or diesel alone," Martin Hugh-Jones of the School of Veterinary Medicine at Louisiana State University in Baton Rouge, who also conducted carcass incineration experiments, told the *New Scientist* reporter. "There's nothing mysterious about napalm," Nevada official Anderson told veterinary trade magazine *DVM* the next month: "It is the same equipment (and substance) they use in the U.S. Forest Service and the Bureau of Land Management when they want to control prescribed burning (wildfires)." As *Carcass Disposal: A Comprehensive Review,* produced in 2004 by the U.S. National Agricultural Biosecurity Center Consortium observed, "For most people, napalm conjures up images of warfare, destruction, and horrific human casualties. However, napalm has been used in a variety of peace-time applications, including the break up of oil spills and the destruction of anthrax-infected cattle carcasses in the US."[16]

Historical imagery, however, and the views of "most people," to use the National Agricultural Biosecurity Center's assessment, trumped the technocrats. Coverage of Anderson's research in the British *Independent* newspaper tellingly misidentified his "Terra Torch" suggestion as a "terror torch" proposal: "Mr. Anderson said the terror torches came in various sizes and would be effective on sheep carcasses." A BBC report on the debate chose "The Terror of War" photograph and an image of a soldier fleeing a giant fireball as its illustrations for the agricultural discussion. "Mention of napalm immediately conjures images of jungle warfare, destruction and horrific human casualties. The photograph of a naked young girl fleeing a napalm attack became one of the most poignant images of the Vietnam War," the BBC began. It concluded, "[T]he chemical's devastating wartime history and its public perception that [*sic*] may put ministers off using napalm. A spokesman for the Department of the Environment, Transport and the Regions said the use of napalm was unlikely." In the United States, *Carcass Disposal: A*

*Comprehensive Review* appears to have been the last serious consideration given to a civilian application for napalm.[17]

As public opinion evolved, America's napalm arsenal rusted in California. Eventually, some of the canisters spread over sixty-seven acres—dubbed "Napalm Park" by base operatives—started to leak. Environmentalists worried that carcinogens in the gel, now described by the navy as "honey-like" after years in storage, might seep into the soil. A population of Stephens' kangaroo rats, a protected endangered species, took up residence in some of the tens of thousands of wooden crates, and added to the complexity of the situation. Politicians began to make inquiries. In 1982, navy officers decided to dispose of the stockpile.[18]

Destroying the gel proved exceptionally difficult. Officers tried to sell the 23 million-pound reserve, but all three potential buyers located by the Defense Reutilization Marketing Office fell through. An on-site processing system built in 1988, the Palm Enterprises Treatment Facility, had to be abandoned the next year when distillation equipment proved unable to separate benzene and polystyrene from gasoline in sufficient quantities—a necessary precursor to disposal. Neighbors protested incineration proposals. "Burning this stuff and sending it up in the air is like getting bombed with napalm. . . . The one thing you don't want to do with this stuff is to hurt any more people," Stormy Williams, cofounder of local group Desert Citizens against Pollution, told a local newspaper in 1995. "What we're talking about here basically is just gasoline and plastic," said navy spokesman Richard Williamson; however, he acknowledged, "there is an emotional element involved because of its association with the Vietnam War." Finally, the navy awarded the nonprofit Battelle Memorial Institute, administrator of seven national research laboratories, a $28 million contract to do the job. Engineers built a $5 million processing facility at Fallbrook and, in 1997, signed a $2.5 million contract with Pollution Control Industries (PCI) in East Chicago, Indiana, to destroy the napalm, fittingly enough, by fire. "The napalm was to be squeezed out of the aging canisters like toothpaste and placed inside 6,000-gallon isocontainers aboard railroad cars. . . . Pollution Control would accept the isocontainers, blend the napalm with a solvent so it would burn at a lower and more predictable heat level, and then ship it to a cement kiln, where it could be burned as fuel, or to another site like a toxic waste disposal incinerator," Rick Lyman reported for the *New York Times*. A train loaded with 12,000 gallons of napalm was to depart California every weekday for two years.[19]

Then came a political reaction that made the engineering challenges appear inconsequential. A few days before Christmas, Representative Rod Blagojevich, a freshman Democrat from Chicago, learned about the navy's contract with PCI. A storm of protest erupted. "My first objection was why wasn't there public disclosure and why send it two-thirds of the way across the country and through a heavily populated area like Chicago?" Blagojevich told the *New York Times*. He hinted at environmental racism, because the train would pass near Chicago and end in poor, largely black and Hispanic, East Chicago. Blagojevich noted recent chemical fires at PCI's plant and a recent $80,000 fine for state environmental and safety violations, and observed that the firm's chairman, Kevin Prunsky, had pleaded guilty to providing false information to federal officials in a case involving the disposal of hazardous waste in a Chicago neighborhood.[20]

Napalm's reputation, however, was the essential problem. "At the root of the controversy, most of those involved agree, was the ghastly image of napalm, symbolized for many Americans during the Vietnam War by the specter of flaming jungles and a photograph of a Vietnamese girl in naked panic after napalm bombs burned the clothes off her body," reporter Pam Belluck wrote in the *New York Times*. "Ah, napalm. Lt. Col. Kilgore, the crazed character played by Robert Duvall in 'Apocalypse Now,' just loved the smell of the stuff in the morning," began a story on the controversy in the *Chicago Tribune*. Blagojevich, wrote reporter Mike Dorning, had "issued denunciations and summoned images of Hiroshima-scale explosions." Betty Balanoff, a leader of Northwest Indiana Residents for Clean Air, which opposed the plan, told Dorning "This is like the straw that broke the camel's back. . . . We've been talking to the Government about cleaning the place up and then they go and dump napalm here."[21]

Navy officers and PCI executives fought back with community meetings, school visits, and press briefings, and attempted to reroute the proposed train through the district of Republican congressman Jerry

Weller. He immediately objected. "Despite its reputation, napalm is safe to transport and more stable and less volatile than gasoline, which is commonly sent by railroad," defense officials told the *Chicago Tribune*. Company president Robert Campbell showed reporters a jar of napalm he kept on his desk. Thomas McGillis, materials manager for the firm, made a batch of napalm from "household items," including Styrofoam cups, and set it on fire to prove it was less flammable than gasoline. A Navy Inspector General review found no irregularities that warranted breaking the contract. Nonetheless, controversy became so intense that when Ku Klux Klan members applied to hold an unrelated rally in Cicero, Illinois, officials initially denied the request partly because of rumors a napalm train was scheduled to pass nearby on the same day. For their part, Southern California congressmen Randy (Duke) Cunningham and Ron Packard pressed the navy to begin shipments as soon as possible.[22]

It was too much for PCI. On Friday April 10, 1998, at the start of an Easter weekend, attorneys for the firm faxed a letter to Battelle asking that it not send any napalm until "all matters are resolved." On Monday, company lawyers complained that "the gantlet which P.C.I. has been forced through is beyond its contemplation of the project." They requested that the navy and Battelle "cease making further shipments and [to] recall all shipments already made." PCI wanted out. "We have been subject to an emotionally charged political confrontation that has toyed with the facts. . . . [Given] a negative connotation about napalm and its role in the Vietnam War, we at PCI were fighting an uphill battle," president Campbell told the *Chicago Tribune*. Public hysteria, he said, was to blame. "To us, it's the same old, same old. . . . It just happens to be that word and that picture of that 9-year-old Vietnamese," the businessman protested to the *New York Times*.[23]

But the napalm train had left the station: the first tank of incendiary gel departed for Indiana on Holy Saturday. "What we have here is one tank car of napalm carrying 12,000 pounds of napalm from a place in California to a place in Indiana. This is a carefully worked out plan by the Navy," Assistant Secretary of Defense for Public Affairs Kenneth Bacon told reporters at a Tuesday afternoon briefing. Congressmen from Illinois and Indiana accused the service of trying to sneak napalm through their states during the holiday. "I think it was absolutely inappropriate for the United States Navy in the dead of night over this holiday weekend to begin the shipment of napalm," said Indiana congressman Pete Visclosky. When the train eventually returned to southern California, however, Congressmen Cunningham and Packard reacted with outrage, and demanded an investigation by the General Accounting Office.[24]

Battelle upped the value of the contract to $10 million and reassigned it in July to the GNI Group of Deer Park, Texas—an industrial city on Houston's Ship Channel with many petrochemical installations. Before they received the contract, GNI officials organized a public meeting for Battelle and navy officers to assess community sentiment. Texas congressman and House whip Tom DeLay visited Fallbrook to satisfy himself, he said, that the shipments were safe.[25]

About 10,000 gallons of napalm arrived two weeks later with "only the briefest flurry of complaint," the *New York Times* recounted. Californians were glad to see it go. "I'll believe it when it actually gets there, and we don't see it returning," one told CBS News. Navy officials kept the precise date of departure and route of the shipment a secret. "In light of the clamor sparked by the April shipment, neither the Navy, the prime contractor, GNI, nor the Burlington Northern Santa Fe railroad would specify what time the first train was scheduled to depart or what route it would take," CBS reported. "We took a lesson from what happened in Indiana," said GNI vice president for regulatory affairs Bill Reeves. "We saw the politicians come out, saw the misinformation of what went around. We just felt that if we got this out to the public, quickly, it would be understood and, by and large, it was," he continued. "We did as much as we could this time around to educate and inform the public and to make sure that any questions were answered in advance," agreed Lee Saunders, a navy environmental affairs spokesperson. "The people of Houston deal with this kind of stuff all the time," explained Robin Yocum, Battelle's manager of media relations: "You say napalm to most people, and they picture the image of that little girl running down the road. But you explain to people in Houston that it's just gasoline mixed with benzene and styrene and they know right away what you're talking about and what you're dealing with."[26]

Residents said they simply had no choice. "People along the Ship Channel don't feel they can do anything about it," said LaNell Anderson, a Houston real estate agent and member of Grandparents of East Harris County. "They feel powerless, as though they've been designed [*sic*] as a national sacrifice zone. You know, these toxic companies looked for the place with the least resistance and that's why they came here." Judy Starns, who lived in the working-class community of Channel View, just across the water from the napalm processing facility, told the *New York Times,* "We've already got a toxic soup around here. . . . We've breathed, choked and slurped enough of that stuff that we're wise and we're fed up. California didn't want it. Indiana didn't want it. Just leave it to Texas." As Deer Park city manager Ron Crabtree observed dryly, "there's an understanding here that this is a part of our economic base."[27]

Whatever the cost to Texas, napalm disposal proved a rich prize for GNI. "The increase in the revenues for the waste management services segment was primarily attributable to a major increase in the service provided to the U.S. Navy for the treatment of Napalm," the company reported in a February 2000 Securities and Exchange Commission filing. In May, GNI reported an additional $1.2 million government payment. By 2001, the overall cost for the disposal project had almost doubled from its original budget to $48 million. Processed material was delivered to the Baton Rouge, Louisiana, plant of French chemical firm Rhodia to fuel industrial furnaces that required "high quality" fuel.[28]

On April 4, 2001, acting secretary of the navy Robert Pirie Jr. declared an end to U.S. napalm. "At a low-key ceremony this morning at the Fallbrook Naval Weapons Station in San Diego County, the final two canisters of Vietnam-era napalm will be recycled and sent on their way to Texas and Louisiana," reported the *San Francisco Chronicle.* "Acres and acres of napalm bombs, gone. Recycled into fuel (and) aluminum casings," Captain Thomas Boothe, who oversaw the project, told guests. Officials said the site would be restored to its native state: a habitat for kangaroo rats and California gnatcatchers. "Napalm, as a weapon, is now gone," said Seal Beach commander Paul Bruno. "We can now say it is a part of history," asserted Fallbrook Chamber of Commerce executive director Bob Leonard. "Good riddance," said Pirie, "the public should be elated."[29]

Perhaps the public would have been pleased if the United States really had eliminated napalm from its arsenal. In fact, it only erased the word from official discourse. After 2001, although American forces used napalm, officers no longer called it by that name. When questioned about the December 2001 Battle of Tora Bora in Afghanistan, for example, General Tommy Franks replied, "We're not using—we're not using the old napalm in Tora Bora." Ferocious denials by U.S. officials during the 2003 invasion of Iraq, even in the face of bluntly contradictory reports by journalists, underlined the potency of the charge and echoed the vituperative reactions of governments elsewhere accused of napalm deployments.[30]

# 14

## The Weapon That Dare Not
## Speak Its Name

On January 6, 2003, the American modular cargo delivery system ship S.S. *Cape Jacob* docked in Kuwait. U.S. sailors and civilian contractors boarded and began a series of twenty-four-hour shifts to unload napalm, hand grenades, and bombs for the Third Marine Air Wing (MAW). By early February, as Secretary of State Colin Powell reviewed his speech on Iraqi weapons of mass destruction for the United Nations Security Council, and Pentagon planners announced that a bombing wave could quickly break the Iraqi army, the work was almost complete. "Everything from hand grenades to 2,000-pound bombs and napalm are shipped, ready for use whenever 3rd MAW needs them," the Department of Defense's *Defend America* newsletter reported on January 12. Morale was high. "We've had no mishaps—that's what you look for in ordnance," said officer-in-charge Marty Groover. "This is motivating," enthused Pennsylvania native Jim Brown, "It's exciting to know the work we're doing here is supporting . . . Marine aviation units."[1]

At 10:16 p.m. on Wednesday, March 19, President George W. Bush announced, "The people of the United States and our friends and allies will not live at the mercy of an outlaw regime that threatens the peace with weapons of mass murder. We will meet that threat now, with our Army, Air Force, Navy, Coast Guard and Marines, so that we do not have to meet it later with armies of fire fighters and police and doctors on the streets of our cities." American bombs had already fallen on Baghdad.[2]

Safwan Hill, a few kilometers north of the Kuwait border in southern Iraq, looms over the main road that runs from Kuwait to Basra, and on to Baghdad. In 1991, U.S. and Iraqi officers finalized cease-fire terms at an airfield near its base. In 2003, marines picked up where their predecessors left off: their howitzers rolled into place along the Kuwaiti frontier on Thursday March 20 and took aim at a summit observation post bristling with soldiers, weapons, and communications gear. Behind the lines, navy technicians loaded airplanes with Mark-77 firebombs, each packed with hundreds of pounds of napalm.[3]

America attacked the hill on Friday morning. "Marine Cobra helicopter gunships firing Hellfire missiles swept in low from the south. Then the marine howitzers, with a range of 30 kilometers, opened a sustained barrage over the next eight hours. They were supported by US Navy aircraft which dropped 40,000 pounds of explosives and napalm," reporter Lindsay Murdoch wrote in the Australian *Sydney Morning Herald* newspaper. "Anything that was up there that was left after all the explosions was then hit with napalm. And that pretty much put an end to any Iraqi operations up on that hill," CNN confirmed. Dawn on the 22nd showed just a single antenna where the observation post had been, wreathed in smoke. "Dead bodies are everywhere," a U.S. officer reported by radio. "I pity anybody who's in there," said a marine sergeant. "We told them to surrender."[4]

A navy spokesman in Washington immediately denied napalm had been deployed. "We don't even have that in our arsenal," Lieutenant Commander Danny Hernandez said the day the stories appeared. A subsequent statement from the Pentagon to the *Herald* asserted, "Your story claiming US forces are using napalm in Iraq is patently false. The US took napalm out of service in the early 1970s. We completed destruction of our last batch of napalm on April 4, 2001, and no longer maintain any stocks of napalm."[5]

Sensational news, however, spreads like wildfire. Salon.com reprinted Murdoch's report the day it was published, and immediately raised the issue of international law and potential war crimes. "A legal expert at the International Committee of the Red Cross in Geneva said the use of napalm or fuel air bombs was not illegal 'per se' because the United States was not a signatory to the 1980 weapons convention that prohibits and restricts certain weapons," the website explained. However, it continued, quoting Red Cross advisor on weapons and international humanitarian law Dominique Loye, "[T]he United States has to apply the basic principles of International Humanitarian Law (IHL) and take all precautions to protect civilians. In the case of napalm and fuel air bombs, these are special precautions because these are area weapons, not specific weapons." In turn, the *New York Times* noted Salon's coverage as "the first to highlight an item from the *Sydney Morning Herald* that reported the use of napalm by United States troops." *Times* editors published an additional navy denial, and their own correction, the next day.[6]

American troops advanced quickly toward Baghdad, but bridges caused delays. In late March, a crossing at the Saddam Canal in central Iraq proved especially problematic. Passage across the Tigris River north of the city of Numaniyah in April was also difficult. Napalm cleared both obstacles. "We napalmed both those (bridge) approaches," Colonel Randolph Alles, commander of Marine Air Group 11, told *San Diego Union-Tribune* reporter James Crawley on August 5, 2003, five months after the events. "Unfortunately, there were people there because you could see them in the (cockpit) video. They were Iraqi soldiers there. It's no great way to die," he added. "The generals love napalm," Alles observed: "It has a big psychological effect." Marine Corps major general Jim Amos, who commanded marine jet and helicopter units in the Iraq War and led the Third Marine Air Wing, "confirmed aircraft dropped what he and other Marines continue to call napalm on Iraqi troops on several occasions," according to Crawley.[7]

Navy officials, confronted with this additional evidence, admitted in August 2003 that firebombs filled with a "fuel-gel mixture" had been used in Iraq, but distinguished them from napalm. "During the war, Pentagon spokesmen disputed reports that napalm was being used, saying the Pentagon's stockpile had been destroyed two years ago. Apparently the spokesmen were drawing a distinction between the terms 'firebomb' and 'napalm,'" Crawley explained: "If reporters had asked about firebombs, officials said yesterday they would have confirmed their use." He continued, "What the Marines dropped, the spokesmen said yesterday, were 'Mark-77 firebombs.' They acknowledged those are incendiary devices with a function 'remarkably similar' to napalm weapons. Rather than using gasoline and benzene as the fuel, the firebombs use kerosene-based jet fuel, which has a smaller concentration of benzene." Marine spokesman Colonel Michael Daily was sympathetic. "Many folks (out of habit) refer to the Mark-77 as 'napalm' because its effect upon the target is remarkably similar," he said. Indeed, Public Affairs spokesman for Twenty-Nine Palms Marine Base captain Robert Crum told the *Sydney Morning Herald* a few days later, "The average young Marine may be unfamiliar with the technical nomenclature, and probably does refer to this munition [Mark-77] by the vernacular 'napalm.'" The difference, Daily asserted, was that the newer formulation had "significantly less of an impact on the environment."[8]

Informed observers rejected the distinction. "You can call it something other than napalm but it is still napalm. It has been reformulated in the sense that they now use a different petroleum distillate, but that is it," said John Pike, founder of the award-winning GlobalSecurity.org website, former director of the Federation of American Scientists Military Analysis program, and one of the world's top experts on security issues. "It's Orwellian. They do not want the public to know. It's a lie," maintained Robert Musil, executive director of Physicians for Social Responsibility—an institution still expert on napalm thirty-six years after Peter Reich and Victor Sidel's groundbreaking article in the *New England Journal of Medicine*. It "fits a pattern of deception" by U.S. authorities, Musil added.[9]

European media organizations concurred. "Heavy Reproaches Against US Pentagon: Napalm Bombs In The Iraq War," headlined German state broadcaster ARD on its 7 August *Monitor* news program. "Napalm. The Horror-weapon from the Vietnam-war. It is internationally banned and outlawed, its use is forbidden by the Geneva-Conventions. But nevertheless, it was used in the Iraq-war by the U.S. army," intoned an announcer. British reporter Andrew Buncombe's coverage in the United Kingdom's national *Independent* newspaper was equally pointed: "US admits it used napalm bombs in Iraq" blared the headline. "American pilots dropped the controversial incendiary agent napalm on Iraqi troops during the advance on Baghdad," the journalist charged. "The

Pentagon denied using napalm at the time, but Marine pilots and their commanders have confirmed that they used an upgraded version of the weapon against dug-in positions. They said napalm, which has a distinctive smell, was used because of its psychological effect on an enemy," he asserted.[10]

Buncombe bore down on America's exceptional dedication to napalm, and its defeat in Vietnam. First, he used Protocol III to define a global paradigm: "A 1980 UN convention banned the use against civilian targets of napalm, a terrifying mixture of jet fuel and polystyrene that sticks to skin as it burns." Next, he highlighted American exceptionalism: "The US, which did not sign the treaty, is one of the few countries that makes use of the weapon." Finally, he drew a line twenty-eight years long from Vietnam to napalm: "It was employed notoriously against both civilian and military targets in the Vietnam war." Buncombe reiterated the prevarication offered to *San Diego Union-Tribune* reporter Crawley: "Officials said that if journalists had asked about the firebombs their use would have been confirmed. A spokesman admitted they were 'remarkably similar' to napalm but said they caused less environmental damage." He concluded, "The revelation that napalm was used in the war against Iraq, while the Pentagon denied it, has outraged opponents of the war."[11]

America's attempt to hide its napalm in plain sight by changing the meaning of the word produced an international political incident that embarrassed the government of its closest ally, Great Britain, in relatively short order. Over a longer period of time, the practice created public confusion that played into the hands of critics.

In January 2005, expectation mounted in the United Kingdom that Prime Minister Tony Blair would soon call an election. Labour member of Parliament Harry Cohen, an early and vociferous opponent of Blair's Iraq War policy, chose that time to ask Armed Forces Minister Adam Ingram if Mark-77 firebombs had been used by Coalition forces, and if the weapon was comparable to napalm. Politics appeared to be a primary motivation for the question since U.S. Navy officers had stated in interviews seventeen months earlier that their forces had used Mark-77s.

Ingram confirmed the firebombs were comparable to napalm but, remarkably, denied they had been used: "The United States have confirmed to us that they have not used Mark 77 firebombs, which are essentially napalm canisters, in Iraq at any time. No other coalition member has Mark 77 firebombs in their inventory."[12]

There the sensitive matter rested as British politics swirled. Blair announced on April 5 that a general election would be held on May 5. On April 20, as Ingram later testified, he was "made aware" of evidence Mark-77s had indeed been used in Iraq. The armed forces minister did not publicize the information, however, but "sought clarification from the Pentagon." Blair was reelected fifteen days later with 35.3 percent of the popular vote to 32.3 for his opponents, a scant 3 percent margin. He lost much of his majority in Parliament. Iraq War policy was a key issue.[13]

Ingram reversed both elements of his January answer on June 13, 2005, six weeks after the May vote. In a letter to Labour member of Parliament Linda Riordan, he now confirmed firebombs had been used in Iraq—but this time denied they were comparable to napalm. First, Mark-77s: "The U.S. destroyed its remaining Vietnam era napalm in 2001 but, according to the reports for I Marine Expeditionary Force (I MEF) serving in Iraq in 2003, they used a total of 30 MK 77 weapons in Iraq between 31 March and 2 April 2003, against military targets away from civilian areas." Second, napalm: "The MK 77 firebomb does not have the same composition as napalm, although it has similar destructive characteristics. The Pentagon has told us that owing to the limited accuracy of the MK 77, it is not generally used in urban terrain or in areas where civilians are congregated."[14]

An uproar ensued. War opponents, and foes of Blair in general, charged conspiracy. Officials pleaded incompetence, and bad information from their American ally. Recriminations flew. On June 24, the BBC reported "Defence Secretary John Reid said American officials in Baghdad had given the wrong information. He claimed it was 'cock up' not conspiracy. He told ITV's Jonathan Dimbleby programme: 'First of all, they didn't use napalm. They used a firebomb. It doesn't stick to your skin like napalm, it doesn't have the horrible effects of that. Secondly, we have never used anything that even approximates to what they were using.' "[15]

Labour member of Parliament Alice Mahon, who submitted the initial question jointly with Cohen, was outraged. "It is a 'disgrace' that British ministers say they did not know US forces had used napalm-style fire bombs in Iraq," she told the BBC. "She said Mark 77 bombs were simply a more sophisticated version of napalm bombs which still 'melt people,' " the broadcaster reported. That the deployment was minuscule compared to previous wars—thirty bombs that weighed about 15,000 pounds in total, versus hundreds of thousands of tons of napalm in, for example, Indochina—seemed immaterial: mere mention of Vietnam's jelly bombs conjured a terrifying bogey.[16]

If "napalm" had no definition, its meaning could expand as well as contract. An extended debate over weapons used by U.S. troops during attacks on the Iraqi city of Fallujah in 2004 was a case in point. In 2007, UK playwright Jonathan Holmes extrapolated from the media reports reviewed above to assert in his antiwar drama *Fallujah* that U.S. troops, in addition to the engagements at Safwan Hill and against bridges, had also used napalm in his play's eponymous city. This spectacular claim, combined with a celebrity cast, helped garner enormous publicity for the play during its London run. "The denunciations of the United States are severe, particularly in the scenes that deal with the use of napalm in Falluja, an allegation made by left-wing critics of the war but never substantiated," reviewer Jane Perlez wrote in the *New York Times*.[17]

"Incendiary Weapons Are No 'Allegation,' " New York-based media monitor Fairness & Accuracy in Reporting (FAIR) responded to Perlez a few weeks later in an Action Alert to its members. Their analysis conflated napalm, white phosphorus, and incendiary weapons in general. FAIR wrote, "If Perlez meant to say that the U.S. military had only confirmed the use of a napalm-like weapon elsewhere in Iraq, not in Fallujah, while the only incendiary weapon admitted to have been used in Fallujah was white phosphorus, then that's a very slender technicality." A 2005 documentary broadcast on Italian state broadcaster RAI Television News mixed clips of napalm bombardments in Vietnam—including the attack that wounded Kim Phúc—with testimony about white phosphorus attacks in Fallujah, and echoed FAIR's sweeping conclusion about napalm use. "Calling what was used in Fallujah 'napalm' may have greater emotional impact than calling it WP [white phosphorus]. Napalm raises images of Vietnam and, especially, that tragic 1972 photograph of a naked little girl, running down a street, screaming in agony from napalm burns," observed *New York Times* public editor Clark Hoyt.

His review of the controversy required two lengthy columns to clarify it, even in part. "The war in Iraq has stirred up such passion that something very valuable is in danger of getting lost—facts," Hoyt concluded.[18]

Extraordinary publicity still accompanies the barest mention of "napalm." When an obscure "jihadist" group posted a crude "napalm recipe" on its website in May 2009, for example, CBS News highlighted the story on its "Internet Terror Monitor" service: "A group linked to the 'Global Islamic Resistance' called the 'Abu Mus'ab al Suri Brigades,' distributed a new seven-page illustrated document that suggested an easy recipe for the making of Napalm. The recipe says it can be produced using common household items, such as soap and sugar. The manual was distributed on several jihadi Internet forums today along with videos showing the kind of damage this destructive substance can cause." In an example from local U.S. television news, a 2012 Florida methamphetamine-laboratory arrest became the "napalm case" and the talk of local news for days when a half-full Mason jar of the gel was discovered in the backyard of the suspect, who worked for a defense contractor.[19]

Less visibly, American military officials continue to acquire napalm weapons, and manufacturers advertise napalm delivery capabilities to buyers in the know. A January 13, 2004, army procurement solicitation, for example, sought manufacturers for MK-77 firebomb shells. "Firebombs rupture upon impact and spread burning fuel gel on surrounding objects," U.S. Army Field Support Command official Mary Hill explained to prospective suppliers. Specifications stipulated "Cigar-shaped, non-stabilized" bombs that "tumble end over end when released from the aircraft." All "Fuel gelling mixture beads," Hill continued, "will be government furnished material." Providence, Rhode Island–based Textron Corporation's Bell AH-1Z Zulu attack helicopter, "the ultimate in attack helicopters," as another example, advertises "Mk 77 fire bombs" among its weapons capabilities.[20]

America ultimately determined its interest lay with the world, at least in theory, insofar as regulation of napalm and incendiary weapons was concerned. Its chief diplomat called the country to this judgment on December 7, 1996, a full fifty-five years after Japan's attack on Pearl

Harbor drew the nation into World War II and helped create napalm. "Certain military concerns" about Protocol III which had necessitated "further study by the interagency community" for fourteen years, President Bill Clinton's secretary of state Warren Christopher announced, had been resolved.[21]

Clinton and Christopher's resolution was for the United States to sign the protocol, but reserve the right to ignore it. "Incendiary weapons have significant military value, particularly with respect to flammable targets that cannot so readily be destroyed with conventional explosives," Clinton wrote in his Letter of Transmittal to the Senate, perhaps with an eye on ongoing UN inspections for weapons of mass destruction in Iraq. "At the same time, these weapons can be misused in a manner that could cause heavy civilian casualties. In particular, the Protocol prohibits the use of air-delivered incendiary weapons against targets located in a city, town, village, or other concentration of civilians, a practice that caused very heavy civilian casualties in past conflicts," he continued. Therefore, the president suggested America "reserve the right to use incendiaries against military targets located in concentrations of civilians where it is judged that such use would cause fewer casualties and less collateral damage than alternative weapons." A good example of this, he wrote, "would be the hypothetical use of incendiaries to destroy biological agents in an enemy storage facility where explosive devices might simply spread the agents with disastrous consequences for the civilian population."[22]

Defense Department attorneys suggested in accompanying commentary that efficiency, echoing arguments at the 1979 CCW conference, might also be an appropriate reason to evade the law: "Certain flammable military targets are also more rapidly destroyed by incendiaries," they wrote. For example, "a fuel depot could require up to eight times the bombs and sorties to destroy using only high explosives rather than incendiaries." And, they concluded, "Such an increase means a significantly greater humanitarian risk of collateral damage."[23]

Senators remained unconvinced. Protocol III languished before the Committee on Foreign Relations for the next decade. Republican George W. Bush followed the policy of his Democratic predecessor and supported ratification when he took office in 2001. Committee members, however, remained bipartisan in opposition: Chairman Joe Biden of Delaware, a Democrat, made no more progress on incendiary weapons regulation when he led the committee from 2001 to 2003 than Republicans Jesse Helms of North Carolina or Richard Lugar of Indiana, who held the gavel for the rest of the period from 1997 to 2007. Barack Obama's committee membership after January 2005, following his election as senator from Illinois, also made no apparent difference.[24]

As Washington meditated, the world moved. No fewer than ninety-nine states had endorsed Protocol III by 1999. American diplomats found it increasingly difficult to negotiate within the Convention on Certain Conventional Weapons (CCW) framework because they had not committed to its most important provision.[25]

Moreover, vast coalitions of states and nongovernmental organizations bypassed the UN entirely at the turn of the millennium to enact worldwide bans on land mines and cluster weapons. These agreements stood in pointed contrast to the inability of CCW signatories to devise comprehensive regulatory regimes for these munitions. An International Campaign to Ban Landmines, established in 1992, united international advocacy groups Handicap International, Human Rights Watch, Medico International, the Mines Advisory Group, Physicians for Human Rights, and the Vietnam Veterans of America Foundation, and linked them to supportive governments. Just five years later, 156 countries—not including the United States—signed the 1997 Mine Ban Treaty. Protocol II of the CCW had been superseded, as a practical matter, for signatories. Campaigners shared the 1997 Nobel Peace Prize.[26]

In the summer of 2006, news reports about fighting between Israel and its opponents in southern Lebanon drew attention to the dangers of cluster munitions: weapons that scatter hundreds, or thousands, of bomblets or grenades over vast areas. Many do not explode until years later. A global coalition similar to that organized against land mines produced an even more rapid response than the landmines campaign. In 2007, at a summit in Oslo, Norway and forty-six other states, supported by a Cluster Munitions Coalition of more than 350 nongovernmental organizations, called for a treaty to ban the weapons. A remarkable 107 states—again, not including the U.S.—signed the Convention on Cluster Munitions in Dublin on May 30, 2008. UN secretary-general Ban Ki-moon called it "a major advance for the global disarmament and humanitarian agendas."

This convention came into force under international law on August 1, 2010. CCW negotiators, who had not even managed to draft a protocol to regulate cluster munitions, had again been preempted.[27]

U.S. politicians rediscovered an interest in Protocol III as the campaign against cluster weapons accelerated. In February 2007, the same month cluster coalition leaders gathered in Oslo, President Bush placed the incendiary protocol on his administration's annual treaty priority list. In August, the American Bar Association, voice of the U.S. legal establishment, elevated passage of the provision to official policy, and threw its lobbying weight behind it. "U.S. ratification would further the United States' humanitarian objectives without compromising the appropriate use of important military technologies," the lawyers wrote. Finally, on April 15, 2008, more than a decade after Clinton first submitted the protocol to the Senate, and as representatives from across the globe prepared to depart for the cluster weapons signing ceremony in Dublin, Foreign Relations Committee staffers convened the first U.S. hearings on statutory controls for incendiary weapons.[28]

Testimony was a legalistic marvel. On the one hand, participants asserted Protocol III would have no immediate impact because America already complied with its terms. "U.S. ratification of these treaties will not change U.S. military practice in any way, shape, or form. Let me repeat that. Our military already complies in practice with all five treaties before this committee today. Formal U.S. ratification of these treaties would do nothing—nothing to change or alter our current military practices," Pennsylvania senator Robert Casey, who chaired the hearing and was the only senator to attend in person, said in his opening statement. "[T]hese measures are already consistent with U.S. practice," agreed State Department legal advisor John Bellinger. Indeed, observed Charles Allen, Department of Defense deputy general counsel for international affairs, Protocol III "reconfirms the legality of military use of incendiary weapons for targeting specific types of military objectives." Ratification, he suggested, would "provide clearer support for U.S. practice, given past controversies surrounding incendiary weapon use." Moreover, any potential future impact, witnesses asserted, could be circumvented by the reservation suggested by Clinton and Christopher. America would "reserve the right to use incendiary weapons against military objectives located in concentrations of civilians where it is judged that such use would cause fewer civilian and friendly force casualties and less collateral damage than alternative weapons, such as high-explosive bombs or artillery," Allen testified.[29]

On the other hand, witnesses argued ratification would realign the United States with global norms, strengthen its international relations, and improve the prospect for regulation of cluster weapons under the CCW—rather than their prohibition under the Convention on Cluster Munitions. "[F]ormal Senate approval and entry into force by the United States will set an important example and bolster U.S. leadership when it comes to promulgating universal adherence to law of war treaties. It is difficult for the United States to persuade other nations to adhere to humanitarian and cultural practices when we refuse to formally join the types of treaties that are before the committee today," lectured Senator Casey. Ratification "will allow us to participate fully in relevant international meetings on the implementation of these treaties," he prognosticated. "Becoming a party to these treaties also will significantly strengthen our negotiating leverage and our credibility in our work on other law of war treaties, to the extent that other States ask why they should cede to U.S. positions if we do not ratify those treaties after they do so," attorney Bellinger agreed. He elaborated, "[W]e go into these negotiations, people listen to us, they change their positions in response to the United States because they think we're doing the right thing. But if we then never ratify, ourselves, they sort of feel we've pulled the football away and it does mean that, the next go-round, they are going to be less likely to compromise."[30] Bellinger and Allen disparaged the Oslo initiative for cluster munitions, and expressed high hopes for a future CCW Protocol VI to regulate the weapons. "[T]he current draft of the Oslo text would significantly complicate cooperation between the militaries of State Parties and non-State Parties in missions in which the use of cluster munitions may be effective and appropriate," they warned in a joint response to questions submitted by Casey. "Regardless of the outcome of the Oslo process, the C.C.W. is better positioned to take effective steps to address the humanitarian concerns associated with the use of cluster munitions in a context that recognizes their military value," they advised. Allen reiterated, "The CCW framework is advantageous to the United States because it balances humanitarian and military interests; the alternative to CCW is an effort by some other countries to achieve a ban on the use, production, and transfer of these weapons without recognizing their military utility in some circumstances." Joint Chiefs of Staff senior strategist Brigadier General Michelle Johnson summed it up: "America stands for something."[31]

Committee members agreed. They voted without dissent to report Protocol III favorably to the Senate, subject to Clinton's reservation, on July 29, 2008. Their report to the full Senate, echoing Bellinger's testimony, stressed the importance of U.S. credibility in a global community: "Joining these treaties would put the United States in a better position, however, to persuade other countries to adhere to humanitarian practices in armed conflict. Moreover, U.S. ratification is important because the United States loses credibility when it does not formally become a party to the very treaties it has championed," advised the Foreign Relations Committee. Ratification, the senators and their staffs wrote, "would set an important example and would make it possible for U.S. officials to participate fully in relevant international meetings regarding, for example, the implementation of these treaties."[32]

Senators ratified Protocol III, unanimously and without debate, on September 23, 2008, along with seventy-seven other treaties—the largest number of international accords approved by the body on a single day since 1910. Law of war pacts in the group, including Protocol III, represented "a renewed effort to assert U.S. leadership in the international community on law of war matters," Special Assistant to the Army Judge Advocate General for Law of War Matters Dick Jackson declared in the *Army Lawyer* journal, "They are also an example of the U.S. Government's public diplomacy efforts to portray the U.S. military as a law-abiding member of the international community." Ratification, he wrote, "helps restore U.S. leadership in the law of war."[33]

President Obama signed Protocol III into law on January 21, 2009, his first full day in office. He offered no comment, and traditional news outlets did not report the event. Perhaps the highest-profile mention of the new law was on the *Undiplomatic* blog of former diplomat and human rights worker Charles J. Brown. He echoed Special Assistant Jackson's assessment, albeit in far more pointed language. In a post appropriately titled "Most Underreported Story of the Week: CCW," Brown wrote "[T]his is yet another repudiation of Bush. The Convention is an annex to the Geneva Convention, one largely uncontroversial outside of the Cheney-Bolton-Whack-job wing of the Republican Party. This represents not merely a willingness to work within existing international norms, but also a promise to adhere to the laws of war—a view with which the Bushies were [*sic*] vehemently (and notoriously) disagreed. Somewhere, John Bolton and David Addington are developing facial tics." A total of 106 countries were States Parties to Protocol III in late 2012.[34]

Law had finally caught up with napalm in the country of its birth, at the age of sixty-six.

Or had it? After an initial period of silence, perhaps a result of the lack of news coverage, the European Union body charged with overseeing CCW issues raised concerns in December about the U.S. "reservation and understanding" attached to Protocol III. Under the 1969 Vienna Convention on the Law of Treaties, nations are deemed to have accepted reservations if they do not object to them within twelve months. The UN depositary's notification of America's reservation was dated February 5, 2009. After a "whirlwind of correspondence," according to one European diplomat, seventeen states, including France, Germany, Spain, and the United Kingdom, filed objections to America's unilateral declaration between February 1 and 5, 2010.[35]

Complaints asserted a range of legal and diplomatic principles. France observed that because of the reservation, "despite the assurances given by the United States of America, it cannot guarantee the protection of civilians, which is the *raison d'être* of the Protocol." Germany objected to the understanding that "would leave the decision of whether or not the respective norms of the Protocol should be applied to the discretion of a military commander." Britain offered only "to consider the U.S. position as not counter to the object and purpose of the treaty if it could be interpreted narrowly enough."

Nonetheless, all of the European nations, with the exception of Denmark, allowed Protocol III to come into effect between themselves and the United States, subject to their objections. Denmark's ambassador commented only that her country, despite its complaints, "has not expressed any intention precluding the entry into force of Protocol III."

Thus, international law is debatable. Some states assert that America is bound by the terms of Protocol III as written, whatever its unique national caveats. Others maintain that the U.S. interpretation of the treaty will be adopted more broadly over time, and therefore "that use of incendiary weapons in civilian areas is not completely forbidden anymore." Judgment remains elusive.[36]

In the court of worldwide public opinion, however, a verdict appears to have been rendered: napalm violates the spirit of contemporary civilization. America's military spokespeople testify to this reality with their punctilious parsing of "napalm" from "firebombs." American legislators, despite gestures of acceptance, have not yet fully acknowledged either the letter or the spirit of global law.

# INFAMY

About 23 million pounds of Vietnam War-era napalm bombs cover sixty-seven acres at Fallbrook Naval Weapons Station, between Los Angeles and San Diego, in 1998. *Bettmann/Corbis*

U.S. Navy napalm and explosives create a giant fireball over the grounded freighter *New Carissa* near Coos Bay, Oregon, on February 11, 1999.
*Brandon Brewer/U.S. Coast Guard Digital*

"Abu Ghraib 'Nam," a 2004 cartoon in *The Scranton Times* compares Iraqi prisoners mistreated by U.S. forces at Abu Ghraib prison in Iraq to the 1972 *Terror of War* napalm victims. *Dennis Draughton*

Napalm Topical Fat Loss Matrix skin cream by Avant Research. *Caleb Stone/Avant Labs*

"Can't Beat the Feelin'," 2004. Screen Print. *Banksy*

# Epilogue

## The Whole World Is Watching

Napalm was conceived in truth, the motto of America's oldest university, and born in Boston, the cradle of liberty. Its nationality is American. Although it has fought under many flags in most of the world's major military conflicts since its invention, it has burned more people, across more of the earth's surface and over a longer period of time, in the name of the United States than in that of any other nation.

"Wee shall be as a citty upon a hill. The eies of all people are uppon us," John Winthrop, another famous Bostonian, prophesied in 1630.[1] His prediction, vouchsafed by events, has been especially relevant for napalm: print, then photographs, and finally motion pictures have documented the incendiary's workings in ever greater detail. Initially, this worked to the gel's advantage. Americans applauded front-page stories on the incineration of Tokyo and the firebombing of other Japanese cities—although Fat Man and Little Boy emerged as the most famous weapons of the war. During the Korean War, the *New York Times* and other newspapers printed hundreds of articles that mentioned napalm. Governments in Greece, Cuba, Israel, Peru, Bolivia, and many other countries, often armed by the United States, bombarded their opponents with napalm to devastating effect early in the Cold War. Criticism, if it occurred at all, was fleeting.

Vietnam changed this paradigm. For the first time, napalm's horrific effects on civilians, especially children, received sustained attention in the United States. A grassroots protest movement against the incendiary and its manufacturer Dow Chemical Corporation began in northern California in 1965. It spread across the country in the late 1960s, and linked business, weapon, war, and country so effectively, and received such wide publicity, that napalm came to symbolize for many all that was objectionable about American involvement in Vietnam. In 1972, as debacle loomed for U.S. forces, "The Terror of War" photograph of nine-year-old Kim Phúc, burned naked as she ran to escape fighting, became an icon. Defeat in 1975 took napalm's reputation, and much of America's, with it. Movies, songs, artworks, poems, books, and articles produced during and especially after the Vietnam War popularized the antiwar movement's argument, and made napalm a worldwide synonym for American brutality.

International law globalized and codified this new antipathy. Diplomats and attorneys, who showed little interest in napalm for the first decades of its existence, convened conferences and drafted rules to limit its deployment starting in the late 1960s. In 1980, United Nations delegates adopted many of their proposals when they approved Protocol III of the Convention on Certain Conventional Weapons. Incendiary attacks against "concentrations of civilians" became war crimes. Most of America's allies and greatest adversaries, their way smoothed by development of alternate military technologies, endorsed the compact in relatively short order.

America refused to accept the world's judgment. Presidents Ronald Reagan and George H. W. Bush did not even submit Protocol III to the Senate for discussion. Over time, however, events changed the calculus of national advantage. Commanders in chief came to appreciate the benefits of working within a global consensus. President Bill Clinton and his successor George W. Bush changed course, and urged ratification. In 2008, in the face of multilateral alliances assembled to regulate land-mines and cluster munitions, and concern that international law to manage conventional weapons was slipping out of UN control, senators ratified the protocol. President Barack Obama signed it in 2009. A diplomatic reservation attached by the president, however, asserted that the United

States could disregard the treaty at its discretion if doing so would save civilian lives. This provision, of questionable legal validity (although no doubt valid enough in practice), suggests nostalgia for unilateralism.

In 1945 we "scorched and boiled and baked to death more people in Tokyo on that night of March 9–10 than went up in vapor at Hiroshima and Nagasaki combined," U.S. general Curtis LeMay, who directed all three attacks, wrote after the war. In 2012, however, as Bell Helicopter observed in promotional literature for its napalm-capable Cobra gunship, "the number one challenge facing armed forces on today's battlefields is the requirement to positively identify friend from foe and then be able to attack hostile targets with precision munitions so as to reduce or eliminate collateral damage to civilian personnel and property."[2]

Napalm's flames limn this arc. In 1945, it was an American hero that helped win the fight against fascism. In 1950, it held the line against communism in Korea. It served with distinction for most, or all, of the Vietnam War. Today it is a war criminal on probation, its use against concentrations of civilians banned by international covenant and its deployment against anyone else tightly restricted by the law of public opinion.

Fire's savagery as a weapon has not changed since World War II, or even since the time of Hercules. Hydrocarbon-based incendiaries, although there are alternatives, offer proven, cost-effective military solutions. What has changed in napalm's lifetime is America's defeat in Vietnam, and the rise of a global society. Incendiary gel is a symbol of the former: stigmatized to the point of monstrosity, and unmentionable for leaders. Its biography is a searing example of the authority of the latter.

Behind the broad themes of napalm's history lie poignant personal stories. Napalm's father, Louis Fieser, saw his public image damaged as opinion turned against his creation. "We thought you were a great guy, and now you're a bum," as he summarized his 1967 correspondence. His correspondents oversimplified. Teaching and research, not napalm, was Fieser's signal legacy. His textbooks, authored with his wife, explained chemistry to generations of doctors and researchers. Letters of praise from pupils fill his archive. His laboratory produced major discoveries that aided human health before and after World War II. To the end,

Fieser asserted that he envisioned that napalm would be used against things, not "babies and Buddhists." He likened his involvement to the role of a gun manufacturer, and denied culpability for unanticipated uses of his creation.[3]

Kim Phúc, for one, agreed in principle. "The rules comes from the people who are using it," she said of napalm: "A knife can be used for good, in the hands of the people who are using it. If you are using that to destroy people, it is so wrong. So terrible, so evil." Fieser's statements of principle, however, are hard to square with his personal participation in 1942 firebomb tests on Indiana farmhouses and Utah replicas of German and Japanese homes, and thorough understanding of America's operational requirements for incendiary weapons. "It is difficult to imagine what happens when 42 lbs. of burning gel is plastered all over the inside of a sturdy wooden barn: flames bursting out of the windows, blasting open the door, belching forth at the eaves and then through the roof. In a matter of minutes what remained of the structure collapsed into a burning heap," he wrote of his experiences at the Jefferson Proving Ground. In principle, this may be true. In practice, Professor Fieser knew exactly what napalm did, and how it might be used.[4]

Robert McNamara, U.S. secretary of defense from 1961 to 1968 and a top lieutenant to LeMay in World War II, was more direct. "It was a war crime," he said of the March 9, 1945, napalm attack on Tokyo. "All at once he was on the verge of weeping," wrote interviewer James Carroll.[5]

At the other end of napalm's arc, historian Bruce Cumings interviewed Korean Pak Jong Dae in Pyongyang in 1989. A direct hit from napalm almost forty years earlier caught Pak, and about twenty other members of a North Korean bridge repair crew. He was the sole survivor. Burns left him no face, just a scar stitched together by dozens of operations, one good eye, and damaged lips that slurred his words. A shrunken claw with bent fingers fused to scar tissue served for a hand. He carried himself with "a curiously proud sort of politeness and humility," Cumings wrote. Pak testified, "Everybody has his youth which is precious and important. . . . My youth has gone with thirty-six operations. I had a lot of laughter and hopes for the future. I had two hands with which I could play the accordion. All these the bomb took away from me." He concluded, "I do not think there should be any more victims like me in this world. Never again. Never in this world a victim like me." Thames Television included this statement at the end of its program when it broadcast the interview. Boston public television station WGBH edited it out, without explanation, when it showed the documentary.[6]

Kim Phúc—her name means "Golden Happiness"—became napalm's best known victim. She defected from Vietnam to Canada with her husband in 1992, settled in Toronto, and had two sons. The United Nations Educational, Scientific and Cultural Organization declared her a "living symbol of the suffering of innocent war victims" and named her a Goodwill Ambassador in 1994. She manages the Kim Foundation International to aid child victims of war. In a 2011 interview, she said the only way forward for victims of napalm is through forgiveness.[7]

She began with innocence: "As a little girl, do you think I deserved that? I was nine. I knew nothing about war. I knew nothing about pain. But then suddenly that bomb dropped." Then, she spoke of pain: "Even now, speaking with you, I still have the pain, on my back. I got really deep burns, they burned to the bone. My challenges are every day, whenever the weather changes." Hate followed: "I really hated my life, and I hated everyone who caused my suffering. Even the people who were normal, I hated them. I was envious of them. Especially other girls. I felt that I was an ugly girl. I never thought that I would get married, have a boyfriend, or a child. That is more important than that I deal with scars on my body." Her injury was profound: "The doctors and nurses mended my skin, but inside another napalm burned within me. Medication could not help. Doctors could not help. No one could help me heal my heart from hatred, from anger." She questioned: "All that suffering led me to the point that I wanted to die. But I couldn't die. But it was so hard to live with that hardship. Deep down, I was seeking to a purpose for my life: why I didn't die, and why I have to suffer. Why am I alive like that, with hatred and anger and bitterness."

Love was her only solution: "Then I found in the Bible that it said 'love thy enemy.' Finally, I turned my back to pray for my enemies who caused my suffering. The more I prayed for my enemies, the softer my heart became." She gained the strength to forgive: "I had cursed them to death. But now I am not doing that any more. I pray for them. All the hatred is gone. I just live. I count my blessings. I forgive those who caused my suffering. When I learned that lesson about forgiveness, my heart was soft. I felt like I was free. It was like heaven on earth for me."

Today she considers herself blessed: "Of course, the pain comes back very often. But in my heart, I feel there are no more scars on my heart. No more hatred. I feel so great. I got the answer, why that little girl, nine years old, is still alive. I am so grateful God has let me be alive. God has let me learn. Now I count every single minute in my life to be a blessing. Faith and forgiveness are much more powerful than napalm could ever be."[8]

Notes

Acknowledgments

Index

# Notes

Visit NapalmBiography.com for notes with links, videos, selected source materials, and revisions. Daggers † indicate additional notes online.

Prologue

1. Denise Chong, *The Girl in the Picture: The Story of Kim Phuc, the Photograph, and the Vietnam War* (Penguin Books, 1999), 53–59.
2. Tunnels: Chong, *The Girl in the Picture,* 52. Smoke signals: ibid., 59–60. Runners: ibid., 60.
3. Chong, *The Girl in the Picture,* 61–64. See Fox Butterfield, "South Vietnamese Drop Napalm on Own Troops," *New York Times,* June 9, 1972.
4. Flames: Phan Thị Kim Phúc, conversation with the author, March 17, 2012. "Too hot": Chong, *The Girl in the Picture,* 65–67. See "Picture Power: Vietnam Napalm Attack," May 9, 2005, http://news.bbc.co.uk/2/hi/asia-pacific/4517597.stm (accessed 10/7/2012).
5. Ut: Chong, *The Girl in the Picture,* 63–65. Burns: ibid., 90. Cu Chi: ibid., 71. Danh: ibid., 65–66. June 9: ibid., 76. "The Terror of War" also won World Press Photo of the Year 1972. Icon: Robert Hariman and John Louis Lucaites, "Public Identity and Collective Memory in U.S. Iconic Photography: The Image of 'Accidental Napalm,'" *Critical Studies in Media Communication* 20, no. 1 (March 2003): 39. And Hariman and Lucaites, *No Caption Needed: Iconic Photographs, Public Culture, and Liberal Democracy* (University of Chicago, 2007), 171–207. Periodicals around the world commemorated the photo's fortieth anniversary. Rob Gillies, "Woman in AP 'Napalm Photo' Honors Her Saviors," Associated Press, June 8, 2012, http://bigstory .ap.org/article/woman-ap-napalm-photo-honors-her-saviors (accessed 10/7/2012). †

Hero

1. Weather: *The Boston Globe*, July 4, 1942, p. 16. Tennis: "Test Pond with Bomb and Markers," Louis D. Fieser, *The Scientific Method: A Personal Account of Unusual Projects in War and in Peace* (Reinhold Publishing Corp., 1964), p. 38, fig. 3.2: "Test Pond with Bomb and Markers." Parapet: Harvard University Archives, Papers of Louis Frederick Fieser and Mary Peters Fieser (hereafter Fieser Papers), HUGFP 20.3 Box 4, "Scrapbook 1937–1960," n.p. See Fieser, *The Scientific Method*, 36. And James J. Bohning, "Interview with Hoyt C. Hottel at Massachusetts Institute of Technology. 18 November and 2 December 1985." Oral History Transcript #0025. 2010. Chemical Heritage Foundation, p. 34. †

2. Appearance: Fieser, *The Scientific Method*, 126, fig. 13.4; 202, fig. 20.1. Assistants: Louis Fieser to Samuel D. Robbins, March 14, 1966, in Fieser Papers, HUGFP 20.3 Box 1, Folder: "Miscellaneous Correspondence, 1949–1966." Bomb: Fieser, *The Scientific Method*, 36, 40.

3. Fieser, *The Scientific Method*, 40.

4. Battles: *The Boston Globe*, July 4, 1942, p. 1. Sugar: ibid., p. 1. Races: ibid., p. 11. Saboteurs: ibid., p. 7. Lil' Abner: ibid., p. 8.

5. *The Boston Globe*, July 4, 1942, pp. 1, 9.

6. Smell: Headquarters, Department of the Army, "Chemical Reference Handbook." *Field Manual FM 3-8*. January 6, 1967. Department of the Army, p. 17. See Fieser, *The Scientific Method*, 40.


1. Harvard's Genius

1. National Defense Research Committee (NDRC), "Status of Contract Funds," *Report of the National Defense Research Committee 6/27/40–6/28/42* [hereafter *Report*], June 30, 1941. Franklin D. Roosevelt Presidential Library and Museum Safe Files [hereafter FDR Library], Box 2, Folder: "Bush, Vannevar." Available at http://www.fdrlibrary.marist.edu/psf/box2/a13u01.html (accessed October 7, 2012). †

2. "Vannevar Bush: General of Physics," *Time,* April 3, 1944, http://www.time.com/time/covers/0,16641,19440403,00.html (accessed October 7, 2012). See OEM Defense, "Dr. Vannevar Bush, Half-Length Portrait, Seated at Desk." LC Control #2005691441, n.d. (1940–1942?). Available at http://www.loc.gov/pictures/item/2005691441/ (accessed October 7, 2012). Biography: Vannevar Bush, *Pieces of the Action* (William Morrow and Company, Inc., 1970). Youth: ibid., 74. General Electric: ibid., 243. Teaching: ibid., 244–245. See James G. Hershberg, *James B. Conant: Harvard to Hiroshima and the Making of the Nuclear Age* (Knopf, 1993), 127. World War I: G. Pascal Zachary, *Endless Frontier: Vannevar Bush, Engineer of the American Century* (The Free Press, 1997), 11–34. †

3. Bush, *Pieces of the Action*, 33–34. James Bryant Conant, *My Several Lives: Memoirs of a Social Inventor* (Harper & Row, 1970), 234. See Bush, *Pieces of the Action*, 34. †

4. Biography: June Hopkins, *Harry Hopkins: Sudden Hero, Brash Reformer* (St. Martin's Press, 1999), 14, 12–13. Grinnell College, "Mission Statement," February 2002,

http://www.grinnell.edu/aboutinfo/history/songbook/spiritofgrinnell/ (accessed October 7, 2012). Lewis C. Cobb, "Spirit of Grinnell," 1916, http://www.grinnell.edu/aboutinfo/history/songbook/spiritofgrinnell/ (accessed October 7, 2012). John Wesley: Hopkins, *Harry Hopkins,* 12. Board of Child Welfare: ibid., 110. Tuberculosis Association: Henry H. Adams, *Harry Hopkins, A Biography: The Life Story of the Man behind FDR, the New Deal and the Allied Strategy in World War II* (Putnam, 1977), 38. Red Cross: Hopkins, *Harry Hopkins,* 130. American Association of Social Workers: Hopkins, *Harry Hopkins,* 138. Relief: George McJimsey, *Harry Hopkins: Ally of the Poor and Defender of Democracy* (Harvard University Press, 1987), 46, 79. Commerce: Adams, *Harry Hopkins,* 145, 151. †

5. Language: Bush, *Pieces of the Action,* 35. Inventors: "Confer on Defense Inventions," Special to the *New York Times,* August 7, 1940. See Bush, *Pieces of the Action,* 36. OK: ibid. See Adams, *Harry Hopkins,* 165–166. †

6. Remit: Louis Johnson, Lewis Compton, Harold L. Ickes, H. A. Wallace, Harry L. Hopkins, and Frances V. Perkins (Approved: Franklin D. Roosevelt), "Order Establishing the National Defense Research Committee," June 27, 1940. FDR Library, Safe Files, Box 2, Folder: "Bush, Vannevar." Available at http://www.fdrlibrary.marist.edu/psf/box2/a13v01.html (Accessed October 7, 2012). See James Phinney Baxter III, *Scientists against Time: Official History of the Office of Scientific Research and Development* (Little, Brown and Company, 1946), 451. Council for National Defense 50 U.S.C. 1, "Creation, Purpose, and Composition of Council," August 29, 1916. Available at http://caselaw.lp.findlaw.com/casecode/uscodes/50/chapters/1/sections/section_1.html (accessed October 7, 2012). Roosevelt: Bush, *Pieces of the Action,* 36. †

7. Bush, *Pieces of the Action,* 31–32. †

8. Executives: Conant, *My Several Lives,* 234. Conant: Richard Rhodes, *The Making of the Atomic Bomb* (Simon & Schuster, 1986), 387 n. 3. NDRC, "Form of Organization: Committee Members," *Report,* June 28, 1942. FDR Library, Safe Files, Box 2, Folder: "Bush, Vannevar." Available at http://www.fdrlibrary.marist.edu/psf/box2/a13g01.html (accessed October 7, 2012). Carnegie Institute of Technology: Carnegie Mellon Engineering, Carnegie Institute of Technology, "CIT: More Than 100 Years in the Making," 2012, http://www.cit.cmu.edu/about_cit/history.html (accessed October 7, 2012). *Ex officio* and appointed positions: Louis Johnson et al., "Order Establishing the National Defense Research Committee," June 27, 1940. FDR Library, Safe Files, Box 2, Folder: "Bush, Vannevar." Available at http://www.fdrlibrary.marist.edu/psf/box2/a13v01.html (accessed October 7, 2012). Conant's responsibilities: W. A. Noyes, "The Organization of the National Defense Research Committee: General Plan," in R. Connor, D. Churchill Jr., R. H. Ewell, C. Heimsch, W. R. Kirner, G. B. Kistiakowsky, W. C. Lothrop, W. A. Noyes Jr., and E. P. Stevenson, *Chemistry: A History of the Chemistry Components of the National Defense Research Committee, 1940–1946,* ed. W. A. Noyes (Little, Brown and Company, 1948), 4.

9. Contracting: Bush, *Pieces of the Action,* 38–39. Revolution: Conant, *My Several Lives,* 236.

10. No certification: Noyes, "The Organization," 10. Theses: ibid., 8. Budgets: James Bryant Conant and Roger Adams, "Forward," in Connor et al., *Chemistry: A History,* xii.

11. NDRC, "Contractors 6/28/41," *Report,* June 28, 1941. FDR Library, Safe Files, Box 2, Folder: "Bush, Vannevar." Available at http://www.fdrlibrary.marist.edu/psf/box2 /a13t01.html (accessed October 7, 2012). NDRC, "Status of Contract Funds." ibid.

12. Goals: Conant, *My Several Lives,* 52. PhD: ibid., 23. Dual concentrations: ibid., 59. Fire: ibid., 45–46, 242. Civilian casualties: ibid., 49–50. For criticism of Conant's acceptance of racial segregation in intercollegiate athletics at the U.S. Naval Academy see Roger Angell, "Legacies: Class Report," *New Yorker,* November 17, 2008, http://www.newyorker.com/talk/2008/11/17/081117ta_talk_angell (accessed October 7, 2012).

13. Adams: Noyes, "The Organization," 4. See Conant, *My Several Lives,* 45–46, 242.

14. NDRC, *Report,* June 30, 1941. FDR Library, Safe Files, Box 2, Folder: "Bush, Vannevar." Available at http://www.fdrlibrary.marist.edu/psf/box2/a13f31.html (accessed October 7, 2012).

15. Louis Fieser, *The Scientific Method: A Personal Account of Unusual Projects in War and in Peace* (Reinhold Publishing Corp., 1964), 9.

16. Harvard University Information Systems, "Building Directory," n.d., http://www .uis.harvard.edu/harvard_directory/bldgs/bldg.php (accessed October 7, 2012). More powerful than TNT: Fieser, *The Scientific Method,* 10–11.

17. "Louis Fieser Baby Book," Harvard University Archives, Papers of Louis Frederick Fieser and Mary Peters Fieser (hereafter Fieser Papers), HUGFP 20.3 Box 1, Folder: "Louis Fieser—Baby Book." Ancestors: "Marty," Personal correspondence of Louis Fieser, May 13, 1977, in Fieser Papers, HUGFP 20.3 Box 1, Folder: "Fieser Genealogy." Motto: Fieser's translation (literally: "work conquers all"). Louis F. Fieser, "Louis F. Fieser (An Account Written for a College Fraternity Magazine)," April 15, 1958, in Fieser Papers, HUGFP 20.3 Box 1, Folder: "Louis Fieser—Autobiographical Accounts." Williams: Government of the United States, "Personnel Security Questionnaire: Employee's Declaration," April 8, 1942, in Fieser Papers, HUGFP 20.3 Box 1, Folder: "Louis Fieser—Biographical Material." Sports: "Harvard Portraits—34," *Harvard Alumni Bulletin,* n.d., 161, in Fieser Papers, HUGFP 20.3 Box 4, "Scrapbook 1937–1960," n.p. Unbeaten football team: Louis Fieser to Samuel D. Robbins, March 14, 1966, in Fieser Papers, HUGFP 20.3 Box 1, Folder: "Miscellaneous Correspondence, 1949–1966." And Fieser, "Louis F. Fieser," April 15, 1958, in Fieser Papers, HUGFP 20.3 Box 1, Folder: "Louis Fieser—Autobiographical Accounts." Post-docs: James B. Conant and Louis F. Fieser, "Free and Total Energy Changes in the Reduction of Quinones," *Journal of the American Chemical Society* 44, no. 11 (November 1922): 2480–2493.

18. Love: Louis Fieser, "Autobiographical Sketch for Members of the Williams Class of 1920," 2, Fieser Papers, HUGFP 20.3 Box 1, Folder: "Louis Fieser—Autobiographical Accounts." Harvard: Government of the United States, "Personnel Security Questionnaire: Employee's Declaration." April 8, 1942, Fieser Papers, HUGFP 20.3 Box 1, Folder: "Louis Fieser—Biographical Material." Stacey Pramer, "Mary Fieser: A Transitional Figure in the History of Women," unpublished paper for Chemistry 91r, February 1982, Fieser Papers, HUGFP 20.3 Box 1, Folder: "Mary Fieser—Biographical and Other Papers," 9. See Stacey Pramer, "Mary Fieser: A Transitional

Figure in the History of Women." *Journal of Chemical Education Volume 62 Number 3* (ACS Publications, 1985), 186. †

19. Carcinogens: "Dr. Fieser and Cancer," *Boston Herald,* September 7, 1941, in Fieser Papers, HUGFP 20.3 Box 4, "Scrapbook 1937–1960," n.p. Professor: Louis Fieser to Samuel D. Robbins, March 14, 1966, in Fieser Papers, HUGFP 20.3 Box 1, Folder: "Miscellaneous Correspondence, 1949–1966." Vitamin K: *The Nucleus,* December 1955: Fieser Papers, HUGFP 20.3 Box 4, "Scrapbook 1937–1960," n.p. Vitamin K: Louis Fieser, "The Synthesis of Vitamin K," *Science* 91, no. 2350 (January 12, 1940): 31–36. Williams: Louis Fieser to Samuel D. Robbins, March 14, 1966, in Fieser Papers, HUGFP 20.3 Box 1, Folder: "Miscellaneous Correspondence, 1949–1966." Academy: Government of the United States, "Personnel Security Questionnaire," April 8, 1942, in Fieser Papers, HUGFP 20.3 Box 1, Folder: "Louis Fieser—Bibliographic Material." Students: Fieser Papers, HUGFP 20.3 Box 1, Folder: "Louis Fieser—Autobiographical Accounts." And Gates, "Louis Frederick Fieser," National Research Council, *Biographical Memoirs Volume 65* (National Academies Press, 1994), 169.

20. Fieser, *The Scientific Method,* 11.

21. Edward R. Atkinson, "Emanuel Benjamin Hershberg," *The Nucleus Volume 70, Number 5* (Northeastern Section of the American Chemical Society, 1992), 8, in Fieser Papers, HUGFP 20.3 Box 4, "Undated Scrapbook." Fieser, *The Scientific Method,* 11.

22. Fieser, *The Scientific Method,* 11–12. †

23. Ibid., 12.

24. Ibid. See Louis F. Fieser, "Forward: War Projects—Volumes I–VI," n.d., in Fieser Papers, HUGFP 20.3 Box 1, Folder: "Louis Fieser—Autobiographical Accounts." †

25. Robert B. Woodward, "Remarks," Louis Frederick Fieser, 1899–1977 Memorial Service Program, October 7, 1977, in Fieser Papers, HUGFP 20.3 Box 1, Folder: "Louis Fieser—Biographical Materials," 2, 12. See Fieser, *The Scientific Method,* 13.

26. "Antoine-Laurent Lavoisier," *Chemical Heritage Fondation,* 2010. Available at http://www.chemheritage.org/discover/chemistry-in-history/themes/early-chemistry -and-gases/lavoisier.aspx (accessed October 7, 2012).

27. George B. Fisher, *Incendiary Warfare* (McGraw-Hill, 1946), 14–15, 25. See UN Consultant Experts on Napalm and Other Incendiary Weapons, *Napalm and Other Incendiary Weapons and All Aspects of Their Possible Use: Report of the Secretary-General, Volume 14, Issue 12* (UN, 1973) 18–19: 59–62.

28. Geoffrey Chaucer, "The Wife of Bath's Prologue," in *The Canterbury Tales,* Walter W. Skeat, ed. (Clarendon Press, 1800), 371–374. Available at http://www.gutenberg .org/files/22120/22120-h/22120-h.htm#wife (accessed October 7, 2012). Incinerated facility ruined: Fisher, *Incendiary Warfare,* 2–11, 7. Air Force ROTC Air University, *Fundamentals of Aerospace Weapons Systems* (Government Printing Office, May 1961), 133. See UN Consultant Experts, *Napalm,* 23–24: 79–80. †

29. Samson: *Bible: King James Version,* Judges 15:4–6. Available at http://http://www.bible gateway.com/passage/?search=Judges+15%3A4-6&version=KJV (accessed October 7, 2012). Assyria: Adrienne Mayor, *Greek Fire, Poison Arrows and Smoke Bombs: Biological and Chemical Warfare in the Ancient World* (Overlook Duckworth,

2003), 208. Sun Tzu, *Art of War,* trans. Lionel Giles (1910). Available at http://suntzu said.com/artofwar.php (accessed October 7, 2012). Thucydides, *History of the Peloponnesian War,* trans. Richard Crawley (1910). Available at classics.mit.edu /Thucydides/pelopwar.mb.txt (accessed October 7, 2012).

30. Hercules: Pseudo-Apollodorus, *The Library,* trans J. G. Frazer (1913). Available at http://www.theoi.com/Text/Apollodorus2.html (accessed October 7, 2012). See Perseus Project, "The Life and Times of Hercules," *Perseus Project,* n.d., http:// www.perseus.tufts.edu/Herakles/bio.html (accessed October 7, 2012). Euripides, *Medea*, trans. E. P. Coleridge (1910). Available at http://classics.mit.edu/Euripides /medea.pl.txt (accessed October 7, 2012). See Mayor, *Greek Fire,* 228, 230. Plutarch, *Life of Alexander,* trans. Barnadotte Perrin (1914), 35, 46–120. Available at http:// penelope.uchicago.edu/Thayer/E/Roman/Texts/Plutarch/Lives/Alexander*/5 .html (accessed October 7, 2012). See Mayor, *Greek Fire,* 232. †

31. Pliny the Elder, "Of Maltha," in *The Natural History,* trans. John Bostock (1855), bk. 2, ch. 108, 77–79. Available at http://perseus.tufts.edu/hopper/text?doc?=Perseus: text:1999.02.0137 (accessed October 7, 2012).

32. J. R. Partington, *A History of Greek Fire and Gunpowder* (Johns Hopkins University Press, 1999 [1960]), 21, 14. †

33. Ibid., 13, 15–16, 18, 12.

34. As described, Komnene's formula yields an inferior incendiary. Oman: Partington, *History of Greek Fire,* 15, 16, 19, 32. See Edward Gibbon, *The History of the Decline and Fall of the Roman Empire,* ed. William Smith (Harper & Brothers, 1874).

35. Grenades: Partington, *History of Greek Fire,* 14. Hama: Peter Pentz, "A Medieval Workshop for Producing 'Greek Fire' Grenades," *Antiquity* 60, no. 234 (March 1988): 89–93. See Zayn Bilkadi, "The Oil Weapons," *Saudi Aramco World* (January– February 1995). Available at http://www.saudiaramcoworld.com/issue/199501/the .oil.weapons.htm (accessed October 7, 2012). Flamethrowers: Joseph Needham with Ho Ping-Yü, Lu Gwei-Djen, and Wang Ling, *Science and Civilisation in China*, *Volume 5: Chemistry and Chemical Technology, Part 7: Military Technology: The Gunpowder Epic* (Cambridge University Press, 1986), 82–85.

36. Jean de Joinville, *The Memoirs of the Lord of Joinville,* trans. Ethel Wedgwood (E. P. Dutton and Co., 1906), 97. Available at http://etext.virginia.edu/etcbin/toccer -new2?id=WedLord.sgm&images=images/modeng&data=/texts/english/modeng/ parsed&tag=public&part=all (accessed October 7, 2012).

37. Wernher Von Braun and Frederick I. Ordway, *History of Rocketry and Space Travel* (Thomas Y. Crowell Company, 1966), 26–27.

38. William Congreve, *A Treatise on the General Principles, Powers and Facility of Application of the Congreve Rocket System, as Compared with Artillery* (Elibron Classics, 1999 [1827]), 33. See Frank H. Winter, *The First Golden Age of Rocketry* (Smithsonian Institution Press, 1990), 45. Copenhagen: Thomas Munch-Petersen, "The Politics of Pre-Emptive War: The Causes of the British Attack on Copenhagen in 1807 Revisited," lecture delivered at the University of Copenhagen, September 2, 2007. Available at http://www.thomasmunch-petersen.info/Related_Publications _files/Tom_related_publications.pdf (accessed October 7, 2012). Key: "The Car-

casses Red Glare," *National Park Service,* December 10, 2008. Available at http://www.nps.gov/fomc/historyculture/the-carcasses-red-glare.htm (accessed October 7, 2012). †

39. "The Ellipse and Treasury Park," *Mr. Lincoln's White House,* http://www.mrlincolnswhitehouse.org/inside.asp?ID=177&subjectID=4 (accessed October 7, 2012). Robert Bruce, *Lincoln and the Tools of War* (University of Illinois Press, 1989), 181–182.

40. Bruce, *Lincoln and the Tools of War,* 182, 242–244. †

41. Serpents: John W. Mountcastle, *Flame On! U.S. Incendiary Weapons, 1918–1945* (White Mane Books, 1999), 8–9. New device: Philip Noel-Baker, *The Arms Race: A Programme for World Disarmament* (Atlantic Book Publishing Company, 1958), 337. See Michael Duffy, "Weapons of War: Flamethrowers," *FirstWorldwar.com,* August 22, 2009, http://www.firstworldwar.com/weaponry/flamethrowers.htm (accessed October 7, 2012). Germans: Chemical Corps Association (CCA), *The Chemical Warfare Service in World War II: A Report of Accomplishments* (Reinhold Publishing Corp., 1948), 182. Clouds: Baxter, *Scientists against Time,* 295.

42. Psychological: Baxter, *Scientists against Time,* 295. United States: Brooks E. Kleber and Dale Birdsell, *The Chemical Warfare Service: Chemicals in Combat. United States Army in World War II: The Technical Services, Volume 3* (Center of Military History, United States Army, Government Printing Office, 1966), 514. Available at http://www.scribd.com/doc/48257221/Chemical-Warfare-Service-Chemicals-in-Combat (accessed October 7, 2012). Unsuccessful: CCA, *Chemical Warfare Service,* 182.

43. Zeppelins: Andrew Hyde, *The First Blitz: The German Bomber Campaign against Britain in the First World War* (Leo Cooper, 2002), 26. See W. Hays Parks, "The Protocol on Incendiary Weapons," *International Review of the Red Cross* 279 (November–December 1990): 535. Available at http://www.loc.gov/rr/frd/Military_Law/pdf/RC_Nov-Dec-1990.pdf (accessed October 7, 2012). And Fisher, *Incendiary Warfare,* 120. British invention of incendiary bullets: J. M. Spaight, *Air Power and War Rights,* 2nd ed. (Longmans, Green & Co, 1933), 178. Later use: ibid., 181–182. Kleber and Birdsell, *Chemical Warfare Service,* 614–615. See Mountcastle, *Flame On!,* 12–13. British incendiary bomb formulations during World War II: Jörg Friedrich, *The Fire: The Bombing of Germany, 1940–1945,* trans. Allison Brown (Columbia University Press, 2006), 15–17. And A. C. Grayling, *Among the Dead Cities: The History and Moral Legacy of the WWII Bombing of Civilians in Germany and Japan* (Walker & Co., 2006), 88–89. *Chanard*: Auguste Chanard, "Receptacle for Incendiary Aerial Bombs," Official Gazette of the United States Patent Office, 263. Available at http://books.google.com/books?id=9uSPAAAAMAAJ&lpg=PA263&ots=9qnnked1FY&dq=chanard%20incendiary%20bomb%20patent&pg=PA263#v=onepage&q=chanard%20incendiary%20bomb%20patent&f=false (accessed October 13, 2012).

44. Guernica: James S. Corum, *The Luftwaffe: Creating the Operational Air War, 1918–1940* (University of Kansas Press, 1997), 199–200. See Richard B. Frank, *Downfall: The End of the Imperial Japanese Empire* (Random House, 1999), 39. George Steer,

"The Tragedy of Guernica. Town Destroyed in Air Attack. Eye-Witness's Account," *The Times,* April 27, 1937. Germany's parliament apologized for the assault on April 24, 1998. See Marlise Simons, "Guernica Journal; Fascism's Prey: Now Healing and a Quest for Truth," *New York Times,* May 12, 1998. Shanghai: Malvern Lumsden, *Incendiary Weapons* (MIT Press, 1975), 30. On November 30, 1939, Soviet forces dropped 41,000 incendiary bombs on Finland and killed 956 Finns in another early World War II airborne incendiary attack. See Lumsden, *Incendiary Weapons,* 30.

45. Thermite (also written "thermit" and "thermate"): T. C. G. James and Sebastian Cox, *The Battle of Britain: Air Defence of Great Britain. The Classified History of Air Defence in Great Britain* (Routledge, 2000), 388, appendix 32. "Thermit": see Departments of the Army and the Air Force, "Military Chemistry and Chemical Agents," in *Technical Manual TM 3-215,* April 21, 1942, 149–150. "Electron" bomb: Fisher, *Incendiary Warfare,* 121. Gas: Noel-Baker, *The Arms Race,* 399, 338. The Blitz: see Russell Weigley, *The American Way of War* (Indiana University Press & Macmillan, 1977 [1973]), 354–355. †

46. Shanghai: John Faber, "The Baby in the Shanghai Railway Station," in Faber, *Great News Photos and the Stories behind Them* (Courier Dover Publications, 1978), 74–75. For image of baby with its rescuer see Eric Barnes, "Bloody Saturday," *Famous Pictures: The Magazine,* April 10, 2011, http://www.famouspictures.org/mag/index.php?title=Bloody_Saturday (accessed October 7, 2012). Coventry: Lumsden, *Incendiary Weapons,* 31 n. 13. 5:1: E. P. Stevenson, "Incendiary Bombs," in Connor et al., *Chemistry: A History,* 388. Navy vs. Air: Alan J. Levine, *The Strategic Bombing of Germany, 1940–1945* (Praeger, 1992), 25. On outcomes see United States Strategic Bombing Survey, *Summary Report (European War),* (Department of War, September 30, 1945). Available at http://www.anesi.com/ussbs02.htm (accessed October 7, 2012).

47. Comedian: James F. Droney, "Harvard's Soccer Field Was Proving Ground for Deadly Napalm," *Boston Sunday Herald,* June 10, 1962, n.p., in Harvard University Archives, HUG 300, "Louis Fieser Biographical File." Ready: Fieser, *The Scientific Method,* 12–13.

48. Tizard: Jennet Conant, *Tuxedo Park* (Simon & Schuster, 2003), 179–180. Bower: ibid., 184–185. Valuable: Baxter, *Scientists against Time,* 142. NDRC: Conant, *My Several Lives,* 251. Leaders: ibid., 248, 253. See Bush, *Pieces of the Action,* 42.

49. Gas: Fieser, *The Scientific Method,* 14. Bush and Conant: see Baxter, *Scientists against Time,* 452–455. Zanetti: Kleber and Birdsell, *Chemical Warfare Service,* 616.

50. Fieser, *The Scientific Method,* 14.

51. Brown and the University of Chicago: Stevenson, "Incendiary Bombs," 388. MIT and Associated Factory Mutual Fire Insurance Companies: Baxter, *Scientists against Time,* 290. Incendiary bomb designs: Stevenson, "Incendiary Bombs," 388. And "Goop and Roe," *New Yorker,* May 19, 1945, in Fieser Papers, HUGFP 20.3 Box 4, "Scrapbook 1937–1960," n.p. "Thermit": see Departments of the Army and the Air Force, "Military Chemistry and Chemical Agents," 149–150. And Noel-Baker, *The Arms Race,* 399. Flamethrowers: Mountcastle, *Flame On!,* 28. See Lewis Meyers, "Tactical Use of Flame," *Marine Corps Gazette* 29, no. 11 (November 1945), 19–22.

Available at http://pqasb.pqarchiver.com/mca-marines/access/531801931.html?dids
=531801931:531801931:531801931:531801931&FMT=ABS&FMTS=ABS:FT:TG:PAG
E&type=current&date=Nov+1945&author=Lewis+Meyers&pub=Marine+Corps+G
azette+(pre-1994)&edition=&startpage=19&desc=Tactical+Use+of+Flame (accessed
on October 7, 2012).

52. Fieser, *The Scientific Method,* 14.

53. Arnold's 1941 briefing on jelly bombs: H. H. Arnold, *Global Mission* (Harper &
Brothers, 1949), 243. Arnold's September 24, 1941, letter to Bush about magnesium:
NDRC U.S. Office of Scientific Research and Development (OSRD), "Fire Warfare:
Incendiaries and Flame Throwers," in *Summary Technical Report of Division 11,
NDRC,* vol. 3. (Columbia University Press, 1946), 8. See Baxter, *Scientists against
Time,* 294. The air force became a separate service in 1947. Approval: Fieser, *The
Scientific Method,* 14.

54. Official: NDRC U.S. OSRD, "Fire Warfare," 8. See Stevenson, "Incendiary Bombs,"
388. Objective: Baxter, *Scientists against Time,* 290. †

## 2. Anonymous Research No. 4

1. Louis Fieser, *The Scientific Method: A Personal Account of Unusual Projects in War
and in Peace* (Reinhold Publishing Corp., 1964), 16. Federal records listed the con-
tract as OEMsr-179 from December 1941. National Defense Research Committee
(NDRC) U.S. Office of Scientific Research and Development (OSRD), *Summary
Technical Report of Division 11, National Defense Research Committee, Volume 3*
(Columbia University Press, 1946), 192. †

2. Gibbs: Harvard University Information Systems, "Building Directory." (Harvard
University, 2012). Available at http://www.uis.harvard.edu/harvard_directory/bldgs
/bldg_g-o.php%23g (accessed October 7, 2012). Room-within-a-room: Fieser, *The
Scientific Method,* 16. Burning test: ibid., 18–19.

3. Fieser, *The Scientific Method,* 21–22. †

4. M-47 origins: Leo P. Brophy, Wyndham D. Miles, and Rexmond C. Cochrane, *The
Chemical Warfare Service: From Laboratory to Field. United States Army in World
War II: The Technical Services, Volume 2* (Office of the Chief of Military History,
1959), 168. M-47 specifications: United States Army, *TM 9-1904: Ammunition Inspection Guide,* March 2, 1944, pp. 671–676. Available at http://www.swf.usace
.army.mil/pubdata/fuds/5points/documents/asr/appendixc.pdf (accessed October
7, 2012). See Malvern Lumsden, *Incendiary Weapons* (MIT Press, 1975), 78. E. W.
Hollingsworth, "Use of Thickened Gasoline in Warfare," *Armed Forces Chemical
Journal* 4, no. 3 (June 1951): 32.

5. Fieser, *The Scientific Method,* 23.

6. Ibid.

7. Ibid.

8. Ibid., 24.

9. Ibid., 25. See E. P. Stevenson, "Incendiary Bombs," in R. Connor, D. Churchill Jr.,
R. H. Ewell, C. Heimsch, W. R. Kirner, G. B. Kistiakowsky, W. C. Lothrop, W. A.
Noyes Jr., and E. P. Stevenson, *Chemistry: A History of the Chemistry Components of*

*the National Defense Research Committee, 1940–1946,* ed. W. A. Noyes (Little, Brown and Company, 1948), 389. †

10. Fieser, *The Scientific Method,* 25.

11. Stevenson, "Incendiary Bombs," 389. See Fieser, *The Scientific Method,* 26.

12. Fieser, *The Scientific Method,* 25–26. See Louis Fieser, "Acceptance Address: The Scientific Method," William H. Nichols Medal Meeting, March 15, 1963, in Harvard University Archives, Papers of Louis Frederick Fieser and Mary Peters Fieser (hereafter Fieser Papers), HUGB F461.72 Box 9, pp. 28–34.

13. Fieser, "Acceptance Address," 31. See Fieser, *The Scientific Method,* 26.

14. Fieser, *The Scientific Method,* 27.

15. Ibid., 15, 28.

16. Ibid., 28.

17. Ibid., 29. See Stevenson, "Incendiary Bombs," 389.

18. Fieser, *The Scientific Method,* 29. The *Oxford English Dictionary* (Oxford University Press, 1989) defines "napalm" as "1. a. A thickening agent consisting essentially of aluminium salts of naphthenic acids and of the fatty acids of coconut oil. b. A thixotropic gel consisting of petrol and this thickening agent (or some similar agent), used in flamethrowers and incendiary bombs; jellied petrol," and cites Fieser.

19. NDRC U.S. OSRD, *Summary Technical Report,* 193.

20. "Fire Roe:" "Goop and Roe," *New Yorker,* May 19, 1945, in Fieser Papers, HUGFP 20.3 Box 4, "Scrapbook 1937–1960," n.p. Solution: Fieser, *The Scientific Method,* 31–33. †

21. Fieser, *The Scientific Method,* 36. See Fieser, "Acceptance Address," 31–32.

22. Fieser, *The Scientific Method,* 36.

23. Ibid.

24. Ibid., 40–41. See Fieser, "Acceptance Address," 32.

25. Fieser, *The Scientific Method,* 41–42.

26. Seizures: Fieser, *The Scientific Method,* 49. "Fight to the Finish": ibid., 45. Observers: ibid., 50. Disqualifications: James J. Bohning, "Interview with Hoyt C. Hottel at Massachusetts Institute of Technology. 18 November and 2 December 1985." Oral History Transcript #0025. 2010. Chemical Heritage Foundation, pp. 23–24.

27. Fieser, *The Scientific Method,* 50, 51–52. †

28. DuPont: Stevenson, "Incendiary Bombs," 392. See Baxter, *Scientists against Time,* 292. Fieser, *The Scientific Method,* 52.

29. Fagots: Volta Torrey, "How We Fight Japan with Fire: New Incendiary Bombs Packed with Gel-Gas and Pyrogel Raze the Enemy's Factories and Shipyards," *Popular Science,* May 1945, p. 100. Ejection: NDRC U.S. OSRD, *Summary Technical Report,* 70. Horizontal: Bohning, "Interview with Hoyt C. Hottel," 23. Phosphorus: Stevenson, "Incendiary Bombs," 390. James Phinney Baxter III, *Scientists against Time: Official History of the Office of Scientific Research and Development* (Little, Brown and Company, 1946), 291. See Brooks E. Kleber and Dale Birdsell, *The Chemical Warfare Service: Chemicals in Combat. United States Army in World War II: The Technical Services, Volume 3* (Center of Military History, United States Army, Government Printing Office, 1966), 628. Available at www.scribd.com/doc

/48257221/Chemical-Warfare-Service-Chemicals-in-Combat (accessed October 7, 2012). "2.6 pounds": NDRC U.S. OSRD, *Summary Technical Report,* 1, 8–9. Crane: ibid., 70, generally 70–74. †

30. Bedrooms: NDRC U.S. OSRD, *Summary Technical Report,* 74–75. Furnishings: ibid., 73, fig. 20. Firebomb placements: ibid., 74, fig. 21. On Factory Mutual Research Corporation background see "FM Global History," *FMGlobal.com,* http://www.fmglobal.com/page.aspx?id=01070000 (accessed October 7, 2012). Second-hand furniture: Bohning, "Interview with Hoyt C. Hottel," 25. Pigs: ibid., 25. †

31. Stevenson, "Incendiary Bombs," 394. See Baxter, *Scientists against Time,* 293. Just before the end of the war, Fieser received a visit from a group of distressed British officers ordered to inspect about 4 million M-69 bombs and separate the ones filled with DuPont gel, which had to be discarded, from the ones loaded with napalm that were still useful. All of the bombs looked identical. Fieser, *The Scientific Method,* 52. See Kleber and Birdsell, *Chemical Warfare Service,* 157.

32. Brookings, OR: Mary H. Williams (Compiler), *Chronology, 1941–1945. United States Army in World War II: Special Studies, Volume 4* (Office of the Chief of Military History, Department of the Army, Government Printing Office, 1960), 54. "Fu-Go": Robert C. Mikesh, *Japan's World War II Balloon Bomb Attacks on North America,* Smithsonian Annals of Flight 9 (Smithsonian Institution Press, 1973), 17. Available at http://www.sil.si.edu/smithsoniancontributions/AnnalsofFlight/pdf_lo/SAOF-0009.pdf (accessed October 7, 2012). Participants: Mikesh, *Japan's World War II Balloon Bomb Attacks,* 13, 61. Persimmon lacquer: Curtis Peebles, *The Moby Dick Project: Reconnaissance Balloons over Russia* (Smithsonian Institution Press, 1991), 63. 345 balloons: Bert Webber, *Silent Siege-III: Japanese Attacks on North America In World War II—Ships Sunk, Air Raids, Bombs Dropped, Civilians Killed* (Webb Research Group, 1992), appendixes b and c, 250–272. Fu-Go windship weapon: ibid., 173. Just three balloons landed in towns. Hanford: Webber, *Silent Siege-III,* 208–209. Three towns: ibid., 250. Mitchell: ibid., 163–170. See *On a Wind and a Prayer.* Directed by Michael White (Michael White Films, 2005). For more information see http://www.onawindandaprayer.com (accessed October 7, 2012). For 285 total incidents: Mikesh, *Japan's World War II Balloon Bomb Attacks,* 38. Only continental deaths: ibid., 68 (Japanese submarines bombarded Ellwood, California, near Santa Barbara, and Fort Stevens in Oregon, but did not cause any fatalities. Imperial troops also attacked U.S. facilities in the Aleutian Islands). †

33. Too small: Stevenson, "Incendiary Bombs," 394. Bad test: Baxter, *Scientists against Time,* 292.

34. Stevenson, "Incendiary Bombs," 392–393. See Baxter, *Scientists against Time,* 292.

35. Architects: NDRC U.S. OSRD, *Summary Technical Report,* 74, fig. 24. See "Biographical/Historical Note," Erich and Luise Mendelsohn Papers, 1894–1992. Finding Aid, n.d., Getty Research Institute. Available at http://archives2.getty.edu:8082/xtf/view?docId=ead/880406/880406.xml;chunk.id=ref13;brand=default (accessed October 7, 2012). Pegs and spruce: Bohning, "Interview with Hoyt C. Hottel," 26. Trucks: Mike Davis, *Dead Cities and Other Tales* (The New Press, 2002), 67 n. 3. Esso: Bohning, "Interview with Hoyt C. Hottel," 26. Buildings: Stevenson,

"Incendiary Bombs," 392–393. Prisoners and "watering": Davis, *Dead Cities,* 67. Road and water town: Bohning, "Interview with Hoyt C. Hottel," 26.

36. Furnishings: see E. Bartlett Kerr, *Flames over Tokyo: The U.S. Army Air Force's Incendiary Campaign against Japan, 1944–45* (Donald I. Fine, 1991), 29–32. Tatami: Bohning, "Interview with Hoyt C. Hottel," 25. Factory: James F. Droney, "One of War's Deadliest Weapons Came from a Village Built to Burn," *Boston Sunday Herald,* July 1, 1962, p. 3, in Fieser Papers, HUGFP 20.3 Box 6, "Scrapbook," n.p. Residential: the tests lasted from May 17 to September 1, 1943. Stevenson, "Incendiary Bombs," 392–393. See Davis, *Dead Cities,* 67.

37. Stevenson, "Incendiary Bombs," 33–94. Reconstructions: Davis, *Dead Cities,* 67. Follow-up: NDRC U.S. OSRD, *Summary Technical Report,* 81–82. †

38. M-1: Fieser, *The Scientific Method,* 57. City Slicker: ibid., 91. See NDRC U.S. OSRD, *Summary Technical Report,* 46–48. †

39. Fieser, *The Scientific Method,* 113, 118, 192, 202–203. The Alsos program continued until the autumn of 1945. †

40. Pooh: Fieser, *The Scientific Method,* 230. Crabgrass: Fieser Papers, HUGFP 20.3 Box 3, "Wooden Photo Album," n.p. Associated Press, "Flame Considered Best Weapon Used in Pacific," September 24, 1945, in Fieser Papers, HUGFP 20.3 Box 4, "Scrapbook 1937–1960," n.p. See "Flame Held Vital Arm: Colonel Calls It Second Only to Atomic Bomb," *New York Times,* September 25, 1945. See also "Goop and Roe," n.p. †

41. Louis Fieser, "Autobiographical Sketch for Members of the Williams Class of 1920," 5, in Fieser Papers, HUGFP 20.3 Box 1, Folder: "Louis Fieser—Autobiographical Accounts."

## 3. American Kamikazes

1. Conception: Joe Michael Feist, "Bats Away!" *American Heritage Magazine* 33, no. 3 (April/May 1982). Available at http://www.americanheritage.com/content/ii-bats-away?page=show (accessed October 7, 2012). Mail: William F. Trimble and W. David Lewis, "Lytle S. Adams, the Apostle of Nonstop Airmail Pickup," *Technology and Culture* 29, no. 2 (April 1988): 265. FDR: Jack Couffer, *Bat Bomb: World War II's Other Secret Weapon* (University of Texas Press, 1992), 5. †

2. Couffer, *Bat Bomb,* 6–7. †

3. Ibid., 25–26, 15.

4. Ibid., 20, 25–26, 42. †

5. Migration: Couffer, *Bat Bomb,* 48. Tiny bomb: Louis Fieser, *The Scientific Method: A Personal Account of Unusual Projects in War and in Peace* (Reinhold Publishing Corp., 1964), 121. See Couffer, *Bat Bomb,* 89. Parachutes: Louis Feiser, "Notes for Autobiography," 6–7, in Harvard University Archives, Papers of Louis Frederick Fieser and Mary Peters Fieser (hereafter Fieser Papers), HUGFP 20.3 Box 1, Folder: "Louis Fieser—Autobiographical Accounts."

6. Fieser, *The Scientific Method,* 121–123. †

7. Party: Fieser, *The Scientific Method,* 124. Few bats: James F. Droney, "Boston Man Part of 'Batty' War Plan," *Boston Sunday Herald,* June 17, 1962, p. 3, in Fieser Papers, HUGFP 20.3 Box 6, "Scrapbook," n.p.

8. Fieser, *The Scientific Method,* 127. Couffer, *Bat Bomb,* 105–106.

9. Fieser, *The Scientific Method,* 133. Couffer, *Bat Bomb,* 107, 110. Surgical clips: ibid., 224–225.

10. Frozen: Droney, "Boston Man." Rescheduled: Fieser, *The Scientific Method,* 127. Couffer, *Bat Bomb,* 106–108.

11. Fieser, *The Scientific Method,* 127.

12. Couffer, *Bat Bomb,* 113–114. Fieser, *The Scientific Method,* 127.

13. Couffer, *Bat Bomb,* 116.

14. Ibid., 118.

15. Bulldozer: Couffer, *Bat Bomb,* 119–120. Mistake: "Fire-Bomb Secrets Bared to Engineers," *Baltimore Evening Sun,* n.d., in Fieser Papers, HUGFP 20.3 Box 4, "Scrapbook 1937–1960," n.p.

16. X-Ray: Couffer, *Bat Bomb,* 146–147. Cave locations: ibid., 126. Bases and airplane: ibid., 150. Adams out: ibid., 203.

17. Couffer, *Bat Bomb,* 211. Fieser, *The Scientific Method,* 131.

18. Bat bomb expenses totaled about $2 million in 1944. Feist, "Bats Away!" Couffer, *Bat Bomb,* 226. See Fieser, *The Scientific Method,* 133. †

4. We'll Fight Mercilessly

1. Amos A. Fries and Clarence J. West, *Chemical Warfare* (McGraw-Hill, 1921), 352. John W. Mountcastle, *Flame On! U.S. Incendiary Weapons, 1918–1945* (White Mane Books, 1999), 28, 32. †

2. Eben Emael: Mountcastle, *Flame On!,* 34. See Simon Dunstan and Hugh Johnson, *Fort Eben Emael: The Key to Hitler's Victory in the West* (Osprey Publishing, 2005), 17. Intelligence: Brooks E. Kleber and Dale Birdsell, *The Chemical Warfare Service: Chemicals in Combat. United States Army in World War II: The Technical Services, Volume 3* (Center of Military History, United States Army, Government Printing Office, 1966), 535. Available at http://www.scribd.com/doc/48257221/Chemical -Warfare-Service-Chemicals-in-Combat (accessed October 7, 2012). E1: Mountcastle, *Flame On!,* 38.

3. M1: Mountcastle, *Flame On!,* 43. Improvements: Chemical Corps Association (CCA), *The Chemical Warfare Service in World War II: A Report of Accomplishments* (Reinhold Publishing Corp., 1948), 183. See "The M1/M1A1 Flamethrower Portable Flamethrower: The M1/M1A1 Series of Flamethrowers Saw Widespread Use by American Forces in the Pacific Theater," *MilitaryFactory.com,* July 19, 2010. Available at http://www.militaryfactory.com/smallarms/detail.asp?smallarms _id=388 (accessed October 8, 2012).

4. Japanese: CCA, *Chemical Warfare Service,* 181. Development: James Phinney Baxter III, *Scientists against Time: Official History of the Office of Scientific Research and Development* (Little, Brown and Company, 1946), 294. †

5. World War I: CCA, *Chemical Warfare Service,* 183. Five yards: National Defense Research Committee (NDRC) U.S. Office of Scientific Research and Development (OSRD), *Summary Technical Report of Division 11, National Defense Research Committee, Vol. 3.* (Columbia University Press, 1946), 97. Munda: CCA, *Chemical*

*Warfare Service,* 187–188. New Guinea: Kleber and Birdsell, *Chemical Warfare Service,* 545.

6.  E. W. Hollingsworth, "Use of Thickened Gasoline in Warfare," *Armed Forces Chemical Journal* 4, no. 3 (June 1951): 28–30. Artillery officer: E. F. Bullene, "It's Not New but Napalm is an All-Purpose Wonder Weapon," *United States Army Combat Forces Journal* (November 1952): 26.

7.  Range: Louis F. Fieser, George C. Harris, E. B. Hershberg, Morley Morgana, Frederick C. Novello, and Stearns T. Putnam, "Napalm," *Industrial & Engineering Chemistry* 38, no. 8 (August 1946): 773. NDRC U.S. OSRD, *Summary Technical Report,* 100. See Louis F. Fieser, "Forward: War Projects—Volumes I–VI," n.d., in Harvard University Archives, Papers of Louis Frederick Fieser and Mary Peters Fieser, HUGFP 20.3 Box 1, Folder: "Louis Fieser—Autobiographical Accounts," 4. Other gels: Louis Fieser, *The Scientific Method: A Personal Account of Unusual Projects in War and in Peace* (Reinhold Publishing Corp., 1964), 53. Paterson: Fieser et al., "Napalm," 773 n. 2. M1: Baxter, *Scientists against Time,* 295. †

8.  "Standard components and low moisture": Leo P. Brophy, Wyndham D. Miles, and Rexmond C. Cochrane, *The Chemical Warfare Service: From Laboratory to Field. United States Army in World War II: The Technical Services, Volume 2* (Office of the Chief of Military History, 1959), 350–352. Conveyors: Hollingsworth, "Use of Thickened Gasoline in Warfare," 27. Packaging: NDRC U.S. OSRD, *Summary Technical Report,* 194, and generally on manufacturing 193–197. Deliveries: Brophy et al., *Chemical Warfare Service,* 170.

9.  Sicily: Kleber and Birdsell, *Chemical Warfare Service,* 593, 157, 550. Flamethrowers also saw action in Italy at the Battles of Cassino and Anzio, among others, but did not prove popular. "[T]he reputation of early models was not such as to commend the weapon to combat commanders. . . . The rugged mountains encountered throughout most of Italy made it difficult, if not impossible, to man-carry the cumbersome weapon to the front line. . . . The cold, wet climate had almost the same deleterious effect as the heat and moisture of the tropics . . . [and] doctrine and training were somewhat neglected," wrote Kleber and Birdsell, *Chemical Warfare Service,* 594–595. Field mixtures: Benis M. Frank and Henry I. Saw Jr., *History of U.S. Marine Corps Operations in World War II. Volume V: Victory and Occupation* (Historical Branch, G-3 Division, Headquarters, U.S. Marine Corps, 1968), 704 n. 66. Available at http://www.ibiblio.org/hyperwar/USMC/V/index.html (accessed October 7, 2012). See Hollingsworth, "Use of Thickened Gasoline in Warfare," 31. Hill: Frank and Saw, *History of U.S. Marine Corps Operations,* 704. Pohnpei: Samuel Eliot Morrison, *History of United States Naval Operations in World War II. Volume 7: Aleutians, Gilberts and Marshalls, June 1942–April 1944* (University of Illinois Press, 2002), 287. Noyes dates the Pohnpei (or "Ponape") attack to March 1944. Baxter, *Scientists against Time,* 293. Population: *The Columbia Encyclopedia,* 6th ed. (Columbia University Press, 2004).

10.  Germany: Brophy et al., *Chemical Warfare Service,* 170–171. 40 percent: Kleber and Birdsell, *Chemical Warfare Service,* 155. "An excellent tactical weapon": ibid., 159.

11.  Beachheads, ports, expediters: Kleber and Birdsell, *Chemical Warfare Service,* 162. Diversions: ibid., 159. Resolution: ibid., 161–163.

12. Frank Wesley Craven and James Lea Cate, eds., *The Army Air Forces in World War II, Volume 3: Europe: Argument to V-E Day* (Office of Air Force History, 1983 [1953]), 233. Falaise and von Kluge: Kleber and Birdsell, *Chemical Warfare Service,* 632. See Kit C. Carter and Robert Mueller, *U.S. Army Air Forces in World War II: Combat Chronology, 1941–1945* (Center for Air Force History, 1991), 433. But note: napalm was used by the Eighth Air Force only "on a few special missions where blanket fire cover was required, notably against German strong points on the French coast in April 1945," according to Roger A. Freeman, *The Mighty Eighth War Manual* (Jane's, 1984), 226. See William C. Sylvan and Francis G. Smith Jr., *Normandy to Victory: The War Diary of General Courtney H. Hodges and the First U.S. Army* (University Press of Kentucky, 2008), 189 n. 100: "474th [Fighter] Group meanwhile put 67 out of 70 Napalm bombs on Kleinhau." On occasion Perspex, a British oil thickener, served as an alternative to napalm powder. Kleber and Birdsell, *Chemical Warfare Service,* 157. CWS: ibid., 159, 161–162. Totals: Lewis Meyers, "Tactical Use of Flame," *Marine Corps Gazette* 29, no. 11 (November 1945): 22. Available at http://pqasb.pqarchiver .com/mca-marines/access/531801931.html?dids=531801931:531801931:531801931:531 801931&FMT=ABS&FMTS=ABS:FT:TG:PAGE&type=current&date=Nov+1945 &author=Lewis+Meyers&pub=Marine+Corps+Gazette+(pre-1994)&edition=&start page=19&desc=Tactical+Use+of+Flame (accessed October 7, 2012). See Michael Clodfelter, *Warfare and Armed Conflicts, a Statistical Reference to Casualty and Other Figures, 1494–2000,* 3rd ed. (McFarland & Co., 2008), 508. Extensively employed in Europe: E. P. Stevenson, "Incendiary Bombs," in R. Connor, D. Churchill Jr., R. H. Ewell, C. Heimsch, W. R. Kirner, G. B. Kistiakowsky, W. C. Lothrop, W. A. Noyes Jr., and E. P. Stevenson, *Chemistry: A History of the Chemistry Components of the National Defense Research Committee, 1940–1946,* ed. W. A. Noyes (Little, Brown and Company, 1948), 416.

13. Enthusiasm: Carl W. Hoffman, *The Seizure of Tinian* (U.S. Marine Corps Historical Monographs, 1951), 34–35. Available at http://www.ibiblio.org/hyperwar/USMC /USMC-M-Tinian/USMC-M-Tinian-1.html (accessed October 7, 2012). Tinian: Richard Harwood, *A Close Encounter: The Marine Landing on Tinian* (History and Museums Division, Headquarters, U.S. Marine Corps, 1994), 6. Available at http:// www.ibiblio.org/hyperwar/USMC/USMC-C-Tinian/index.html (accessed October 7, 2012). See Scott Russell, *Tinian: The Final Chapter* (CNMI Division of Historic Preservation, 1995), 11. And Clive Howard and Joe Whitley, *One Damned Island after Another: The Saga of the Seventh Air Force in World War II* (University of North Carolina Press, 1946), 228. On disposable bombs see: Mountcastle, *Flame On!,* 105.

14. Kleber and Birdsell, *Chemical Warfare Service,* 635.

15. Chief Engineer: Hollingsworth, "Use of Thickened Gasoline," 30. Europeans: Kleber and Birdsell, *Chemical Warfare Service,* 607–608. See Mountcastle, *Flame On!,* 63. Lighters: Hollingsworth, "Use of Thickened Gasoline in Warfare," 30. †

16. British and Canadian machines: Baxter, *Scientists against Time,* 296. 200 yards: E. F. Bullene, "It's Not New," 26. Castle: H. Gilman Wing, "Flame," *Armed Forces Chemical Journal* 7, no. 1 (July 1953): 11. House: CCA, *Chemical Warfare Service,* 186.

17. Tanks: George F. Unmacht, "Flame Throwing Seabees," *Armed Forces Chemical Journal* 3 (July 1948): 50, reprinted from *United States Naval Institute Proceedings* (April 1948). †

18. Invincible: CCA, *Chemical Warfare Service,* 193. Range: Hollingsworth, "Use of Thickened Gasoline in Warfare," 31.

19. Broke and ran: Kleber and Birdsell, *Chemical Warfare Service,* 633. Fled: Frank Futrell, "Luzon," in Frank Wesley Craven and James Lea Cate, eds., *The Army Air Forces in World War II, Volume 5: The Pacific: Matterhorn to Nagasaki June 1944 to August 1945* (Office of Air Force History, 1953), 436. Available at http://www.ibiblio .org/hyperwar/AAF/V/AAF-V-14.html (accessed October 7, 2012). Feeble resistance: Kleber and Birdsell, *Chemical Warfare Service,* 635. †

20. Pacific: Kleber and Birdsell, *Chemical Warfare Service,* 572. Europe: Charles B. MacDonald, *The Siegfried Line Campaign* (Center of Military History, 1990), 262. Available at http://www.history.army.mil/books/wwii/Siegfried/Siegfried%20 Line/siegfried-fm.htm (accessed October 7, 2012).

21. George Feifer, *The Battle of Okinawa: The Blood and the Bomb* (Globe Pequot, 2001), 260. †

22. Kleber and Birdsell, *Chemical Warfare Service,* 635. The total number of "firebombs" deployed was 12,000 in Europe and "twice that" in the Pacific, according to Brophy et al., *Chemical Warfare Service,* 183. Of the 656,400 tons of bombs dropped by the allies during the Pacific War, 160,800 tons, or about one-quarter, fell on the home islands of Japan. In Europe, 1.36 million tons, roughly half, fell on Germany. United States Strategic Bombing Survey, *Summary Report (Pacific War)*, July 1, 1946, rev. December 7, 1999, 16. Available at http://www.anesi.com/ussbs01.htm (accessed October 7, 2012).

23. Bombsight: Max Boot, *War Made New: Technology, Warfare, and the Course of History, 1500–Today* (Gotham, 2006), 272–273. Franklin Roosevelt, "Appeal of President Roosevelt to Great Britain, France, Italy, Germany and Poland. September 1, 1939," *The French Yellow Book: Diplomatic Documents (1938–1939).* 2008. Available at http:// avalon.law.yale.edu/wwii/ylbk325.asp (accessed October 7, 2012). "We thought of air warfare in 1938 rather as people think of nuclear warfare today," Harold Macmillan later observed. James S. Corum, *The Luftwaffe: Creating the Operational Air War, 1918–1940* (University of Kansas Press, 1997), 200. Britain and France confirmed their desire to "spare civilian populations" subject to reciprocal behavior by their enemies in a joint declaration on September 2. Germany gave "unqualified agreement . . . in all circumstances to avoid bombing non-military objectives during military operations." Julius Stone, *Legal Controls of International Conflict: A Treatise on the Dynamics of Disputes- and War-Law,* 2nd rev. ed. (Stevens & Sons Ltd., 1959), 625–626.

24. Fairchild: Michael S. Sherry, *The Rise of American Air Power: The Creation of Armageddon* (Yale University Press, 1989), 55. Arnold was acting deputy chief of staff for air when these comments were published. He was later promoted to command the entire air force during World War II. Henry H. Arnold and Ira C. Eaker, *Winged Warfare* (Harper & Brothers, 1941), 133–134. See Sherry, *The Rise of American Air Power,* 93. †

25. Cologne: Alan J. Levine, *The Strategic Bombing of Germany, 1940–1945* (Praeger, 1992), 47. Hamburg: Horatio Bond, "Fire Casualties of the German Attacks," in Bond, ed., *Fire and the Air War: A Compilation of Expert Observations on Fires of the War Set by Incendiaries and the Atomic Bombs, Wartime Fire Fighting, and the Work of the Fire Protection Engineers Who Helped Plan the Destruction of Enemy Cities and Industrial Plants* (National Fire Protection Association International, 1946), 119. U.S. B-17s: Ronald Schaffer, *Wings of Judgment: American Bombing in World War II* (Oxford University Press, 1985), 64. †

26. "Tally-ho!": Frederick Taylor, *Dresden: Tuesday, February 13, 1945* (HarperCollins, 2005), 245. Deaths: Valentine Low, "German Report Says Dresden Firebomb Toll Was Exaggerated," *The Times,* March 18, 2010. See David Rising, "Dresden Bombing Killed Fewer Than Thought," Associated Press, October 1, 2008. Available at http://usatoday30.usatoday.com/news/world/2008-10-01-3057188751_x.htm (accessed October 7, 2012). See also Taylor, *Dresden,* appendix b, 443–448. Margaret Freyer, "The Bombing of Dresden, 14 February 1945," in John Carey, ed., *Eyewitness to History* (Avon Books, 1987), 609. Reservoir: Taylor, *Dresden,* 294–295. See Schaffer, *Wings of Judgment,* 97. †

27. Memo: Taylor, *Dresden,* 375–376. Withdrawn: ibid., 378. Final: ibid., 379. Harris: ibid., 377–378. Attacks: ibid., 380. Rail yards: ibid., 380–381. †

28. Radar: John E. Fagg, "Autumn Assault on Germany," in Craven and Cate, *The Army Air Forces in World War II, Volume 3,* 668, 667. Thomas R. Searle, " 'It Made a Lot of Sense to Kill Skilled Workers': The Firebombing of Tokyo in March 1945," *The Journal of Military History* 66, no. 1 (January 2002): 109. Sherry asserts "blind bombing" guided three-fourths of missions. Sherry, *The Rise of American Air Power,* 261. One-third: Craven and Cate, *The Army Air Forces in World War II, Volume 3,* 667: "For the last three months of 1944 the percentage of Eighth Air Force bombs that fell within 1,000 feet of the target was 38, 25 and 25, respectively; in the same months the Fifteenth Air Force score was 40, 36, and 36." †

29. Schaffer, *Wings of Judgment,* 83–84. See Conrad C. Crane, *Bombs, Cities, and Civilians: American Airpower Strategy in World War II* (University Press of Kansas, 1993), 106.

30. Schaffer, *Wings of Judgment.* 95, 97–98, 92.

31. Ibid., 99–100, 94. See Crane, *Bombs, Cities, and Civilians,* 116–117.

32. Mitchell: Sherry, *The Rise of American Air Power,* 58. See Richard B. Frank, *Downfall: The End of the Imperial Japanese Empire* (Random House, 1999), 48. Marshall: Robert Sherrod, "Secret Conference with General Marshall," in David Brown and W. Richard Bruner, eds., *I Can Tell It Now* (E. P. Dutton & Co., 1964), 42. See Sherry, *The Rise of American Air Power,* 109. Charles Longstreth McNichols and Clayton D. Carus, "One Way to Cripple Japan: The Inflammable Cities of Osaka Bay," *Harper's,* June 1942, pp. 29–36. Available at http://harpers.org/archive/1942/06/0020300 (accessed October 7, 2012).

33. United States Strategic Bombing Survey, *Summary Report (Pacific War),* 16. Air Force Historical Studies Office, "24 November 1945," *U.S. Army Air Forces in World War II: Combat Chronology. November 1944,* n.d. See Robert Morgan with

Ron Powers, *The Man Who Flew the Memphis Belle: Memoir of a WWII Bomber Pilot* (Dutton, 2001), 309. †

34. Robert Guillain, *I Saw Tokyo Burning: An Eyewitness Narrative from Pearl Harbor to Hiroshima*, trans. William Byron (Doubleday & Company), 178–179.

35. Curtis E. LeMay with MacKinlay Kantor, *Mission with LeMay: My Story* (Doubleday & Company, 1965), 343.

36. Ibid., 321, 343.

37. Schaffer, *Wings of Judgment*, 110–119.

38. Hankow/Wuhan: LeMay with Kantor, *Mission with LeMay*, 351. Tonnage: Frank, *Downfall*, 51. Norstad: James Lea Cate and James C. Olson, "Precision Bombardment Campaign," in Craven and Cate, *The Army Air Forces in World War II, Volume 5*, 564. †

39. Cate and Olson, "Precision Bombardment Campaign," 564.

40. Firefighting: A total of fifty-seven B-29s reached the city. The bombs burned 140,000 square feet (3.2 acres). Kenn Rust, *Twentieth Air Force Story . . . in World War II* (Historical Aviation Album, 1979), 23–24. See Cate and Olson, "Precision Bombardment Campaign," 565.

41. Morgan with Powers, *The Man Who Flew the Memphis Belle*, 302.

42. Guam: Cate and Olson, "Precision Bombardment Campaign," 565, 567–568. Musashino: Rust, *Twentieth Air Force Story*, 24. Musashino was "not destroyed by a damn sight," Hansell told correspondents. St. Clair McKelway, "A Reporter with the B-29s II: The Doldrums, Guam, and Something Coming Up," *New Yorker*, June 16, 1945, 30. Command: LeMay with Kantor, *Mission with LeMay*, 340–348.

43. Morgan with Powers, *The Man Who Flew the Memphis Belle*, 298. LeMay suffered from Bell's palsy: St. Clair McKelway, *Reporting at Wit's End: Tales from* The New Yorker (Bloomsbury, 2010), 177–178: "He had had serious sinus trouble. . . . A muscle normally used to lift and spread the corners of the mouth became partially paralyzed."

44. LeMay with Kantor, *Mission with LeMay*, 16, 19, 23.

45. Ibid., 27–33.

46. Ibid., 35–60.

47. Frank, *Downfall*, 57.

48. Nagoya: Rust, *Twentieth Air Force Story*, 25–26. See Frank, *Downfall*, 58. See Cate and Olson, "Precision Bombardment Campaign," 568. And Robert Trumbull, "New Air Tactics Used in Reduction of Japan; Low-Level Attacks with Incendiaries Raze Many 'Shadow Factories,'" *New York Times*, April 1, 1945. Zeros: Morgan with Powers, *The Man Who Flew the Memphis Belle*, 298, 302.

49. Photos: Schaffer, *Wings of Judgment*, 125. Arnold: Craven and Cate, *The Army Air Forces in World War II, Volume 5*, 572. "Big firecrackers": "The M-69 Goes to Work," *IMPACT* 3, no. 4 (April 1945): 19, in James Parton, ed., "The Eve of Triumph," Vol. 8, *Impact: The Army Air Forces' Confidential Picture History of World War II: Declassified and Now Published for the General Public for the First Time, with Fourteen New Retrospective Essays by World War II Leaders and Journalists* (National Historical Society, 1989). Tokyo: Guillain, *I Saw Tokyo Burning*, 180–181. Raleigh, NC,

as comparable meteorological site: Horatio Bond and James K. McElroy, "Some Observations and Conclusions," in Bond, ed. *Fire and the Air War*, 243–244. Snow and rain decreased effectiveness by about 20 percent: Air Force ROTC Air University, *Fundamentals of Aerospace Weapons Systems*, 132. See UN Consultant Experts on Napalm and Other Incendiary Weapons, *Napalm and Other Incendiary Weapons and All Aspects of Their Possible Use: Report of the Secretary-General, Volume 14, Issue 12* (UN, 1973), 23–24: 79–80. And E. Bartlett Kerr, *Flames over Tokyo: The U.S. Army Air Force's Incendiary Campaign against Japan, 1944–45* (Donald I. Fine, 1991), 139–142. First U.S. area incendiary bombing: "Tokyo in Flames," *New York Times*, March 12, 1945. Mutually assured destruction: Jimmy Carter, "Presidential Directive/NSC-59, Nuclear Weapons Employment Policy," July 25, 1980. Available at http://www.fas.org/irp/offdocs/pd/pd59.pdf (accessed October 7, 2012). Armageddon and modernity: Jonathan Schell, *The Fate of the Earth* (Knopf, 1982).

50. Twentieth Air Force historian Kenn Rust attributes the initial conception of the low-level night attacks without defensive armaments to Thomas Power. "Following the 25th February strike at Tokyo, Brig. Gen. Power . . . wondered what results would have been obtained if there had been more B-29s and they had flown the entire mission at lower altitudes where they would use less fuel and thus be able to carry a considerably greater load of incendiary bombs." Rust, *Twentieth Air Force Story*, 30. "The Cigar": St. Clair McKelway, "A Reporter with the B-29s III: The Cigar, the Three Wings, and the Low-Level Attacks," *New Yorker*, June 23, 1945, p. 30. LeMay with Kantor, *Mission with LeMay*, 59–60. Japanese pilots: United States Strategic Bombing Survey, *Summary Report (Pacific War)*, 9: "Average flying experience fell off throughout the war, and was just over 100 hours, as contrasted to 600 hours for United States pilots, at the time of surrender." LeMay with Kantor, *Mission with LeMay*, 348. See Crane, *Bombs, Cities, and Civilians*, 131. Frank, *Downfall*, 65. B-17F: Freeman, *The Mighty Eighth War Manual*, 153. B-17G: ibid., 159.

51. Morgan with Powers, *The Man Who Flew the Memphis Belle*, 309. McKelway, "A Reporter with the B-29s III," p. 32.

52. Target information sheet: Searle, "'It Made a Lot of Sense to Kill Skilled Workers,'" 121. Morgan with Powers, *The Man Who Flew the Memphis Belle*, 306, 278. Arthur Harris, *Bomber Offensive* (Collins, 1947), 264. †

53. LeMay with Kantor, *Mission with LeMay*, 383–384. McKelway, "A Reporter with the B-29s III," p. 36. †

54. Deniability: LeMay with Kantor, *Mission with LeMay*, 342. See McKelway, "A Reporter with the B-29s III," p. 30; Kerr, *Flames over Tokyo*, 156–166; Morgan with Powers, *The Man Who Flew the Memphis Belle*, 317; Craven and Cate, *The Army Air Forces in World War II, Volume 5*, 614; and generally Mark Clodfelter, *Beneficial Bombing: The Progressive Foundations of American Air Power, 1917–1945* (University of Nebraska Press, 2010), 221–226. Idiot: Thomas M. Coffey, *Iron Eagle: The Turbulent Life of General Curtis LeMay* (Crown, 1986), 162. Norstad: Kerr, *Flames over Tokyo*, 165–166. Show: Craven and Cate, *The Army Air Forces in World War II, Volume 5*, 614.

## 5. The American Century

1. Gordon Daniels, "The Great Tokyo Air Raid, 9–10 March 1945," in W. G. Beasley, ed., *Modern Japan: Aspects of History, Literature and Society* (University of California Press, 1975), 122. See Robert Guillain, *I Saw Tokyo Burning: An Eyewitness Narrative from Pearl Harbor to Hiroshima,* trans. William Byron (Doubleday & Company), 181: "almost as violent as a spring typhoon." But see also National Defense Research Committee (NDRC) U.S. Office of Scientific Research and Development (OSRD), *Summary Technical Report of Division 11, National Defense Research Committee, Vol. 3.* (Columbia University Press, 1946), 92: "It is generally believed that the effect of natural ground wind on fire propagation during these attacks was negligible in comparison with the tremendous draft created by the fires. . . . Never in the history of the Tokyo weather observatory had there been a wind over 55 mph during that month." †

2. Edwin P. Hoyt, *Inferno: The Firebombing of Japan, March 9–August 15, 1945* (Madison Books, 2000), 11. See Ronald Schaffer, *Wings of Judgment: American Bombing in World War II* (Oxford University Press, 1985), 130–131.

3. Pathfinders: Richard B. Frank, *Downfall: The End of the Imperial Japanese Empire* (Random House, 1999), 66. Flaming cross: Hoyt, *Inferno,* 11. M-47: U.S. War Department, *Ammunition Inspection Guide: War Department Technical Manual TM 9-1904,* March 2, 1944, p. 674. Incendiary bombs in general: ibid., 677–695. Available at http://www.ibiblio.org/hyperwar/USA/ref/TM/pdfs/TM9-1904.pdf (accessed October 8, 2012). M-47: "M47A1 Napalm Incendiary bomb," *TimeMoneyand Blood.com.* Available at http://www.timemoneyandblood.com/HTML/museums /palm-springs/incendiary-bomb-m47.html (accessed October 8, 2012). Four miles by three: James Lea Cate and James C. Olson, "Urban Area Attacks," in Frank Wesley Craven and James Lea Cate, eds., *The Army Air Forces in World War II, Volume 5: The Pacific: Matterhorn to Nagasaki June 1944 to August 1945* (Office of Air Force History, 1953), 615. Target information sheet: Thomas R. Searle, "'It Made a Lot of Sense to Kill Skilled Workers': The Firebombing of Tokyo in March 1945," *The Journal of Military History* 66, no. 1 (January 2002): 121. See Schaffer, *Wings of Judgment,* 131. And Mark Selden, "A Forgotten Holocaust: US Bombing Strategy, the Destruction of Japanese Cities and the American Way of War from World War II to Iraq," *Japan Focus,* May 2, 2007, Available at http://www.japanfocus.org/-Mark -Selden/2414 (accessed October 8, 2012). (Citing for population density statistics Cary Karacas, "Imagining Air Raids on Tokyo, 1930–1945," paper presented at the Association for Asian Studies Annual Meeting, Boston, March 23, 2007, pp. 2–5.) Manhattan: New York City Commission on Congestion and Pollution, *Report,* February 28, 1911 (166.1 people per acre, 640 acres per square mile). "Master of Ceremonies": James Lea Cate and James C. Olson, "Precision Bombardment Campaign," in Craven and Cate, *The Army Air Forces in World War II, Volume 5,* 564. See Ronald W. Clark, *The Role of the Bomber* (Crowell, 1977), 119. And Thomas S. Power with Albert A. Arnhym, *Design for Survival* (Coward-McCann, 1965), 28.

4. Hundreds of miles: Robert Morgan with Ron Powers, *The Man Who Flew the Memphis Belle: Memoir of a WWII Bomber Pilot* (Dutton, 2001), 309: "more than 300

miles." See Power, *Design for Survival*, 27: "some 1,700 tons of fire bombs." And E. P. Stevenson, "Incendiary Bombs," in R. Connor, D. Churchill Jr., R. H. Ewell, C. Heimsch, W. R. Kirner, G. B. Kistiakowsky, W. C. Lothrop, W. A. Noyes Jr., and E. P. Stevenson, *Chemistry: A History of the Chemistry Components of the National Defense Research Committee, 1940–1946*, ed. W. A. Noyes (Little, Brown and Company, 1948), 401. Glittering blue: Guillain, *I Saw Tokyo Burning*, 182, 184. On p. 188 Guillain asserts 700,000 bombs fell on Tokyo on March 9. Streamers: Volta Torrey, "How We Fight Japan with Fire: New Incendiary Bombs Packed with Gel-Gas and Pyrogel Raze the Enemy's Factories and Shipyards," *Popular Science*, May 1945, p. 100. The United States dropped about 1,900 tons of incendiaries in total on Tokyo on March 9–10, 1,753 tons of them clusters of napalm-packed M-69 bombs. James Phinney Baxter III, *Scientists against Time: Official History of the Office of Scientific Research and Development* (Little, Brown and Company, 1946), 98, 295. Each cluster weighed 425 pounds and contained thirty-eight individual bombs. NDRC U.S. OSRD, *Summary Technical Report*, 1. See "The M-69 Goes to Work," *IMPACT* 3, no. 4 (April 1945): 19, in James Parton, ed. "The Eve of Triumph," Vol. 8, *IMPACT: The Army Air Forces' Confidential Picture History of World War II: Declassified and Now Published for the General Public for the First Time, with Fourteen New Retrospective Essays by World War II Leaders and Journalists* (National Historical Society, 1989). And E. Bartlett Kerr, *Flames over Tokyo: The U.S. Army Air Force's Incendiary Campaign against Japan, 1944–45* (Donald I. Fine, 1991), 140–141. And Barrett Tillman, *Whirlwind: The Air War against Japan, 1942–1945* (Simon & Schuster, 2010), 139–140 (on M-69, M-74, and M-76 napalm bombs). U.S. airplanes did attack Nagoya with over 1 million napalm bombs on May 14, 1945. J. M. Spaight, *Air Power and War Rights*, 2nd ed. (Longmans, Green & Co, 1933), 219 n. 4.

5. Firestorm: Departments of the Army and the Air Force, "Field Behavior of Chemical, Biological, and Radiological Agents," in *Technical Manual TM 3-240*, April 15, 1969, p. 40. See UN Consultant Experts on Napalm and Other Incendiary Weapons, *Napalm and Other Incendiary Weapons and All Aspects of Their Possible Use: Report of the Secretary-General, Volume 14, Issue 12* (UN, 1973), 25: 84. Pine trees: Baxter, *Scientists against Time*, 98. Lanterns: Guillain, *I Saw Tokyo Burning*, 184. Lasting impression: Power with Arnhym, *Design for Survival*, 28.

6. Quoted and paraphrased from Hoyt, *Inferno*, 15.

7. Shelters: U.S. Strategic Bombing Survey, *Summary Report (Pacific War)*, July 1, 1946, p. 20. Available at http://www.ibiblio.org/hyperwar/AAF/USSBS/PTO-Summary.html (accessed October 8, 2012). See Guillain, *I Saw Tokyo Burning*, 174. And Daniels, "The Great Tokyo Air Raid," 123. Toshiko: quoted and paraphrased from Hoyt, *Inferno*, 12–13. A visual representation: Miyairi Keijiro, "My Family—Trying to Escape the Flames," in "That Unforgettable Day—The Great Tokyo Air Raid through Drawings," *Japan Focus*, 2004. Available at http://www.japanfocus.org/site/view/3470 (accessed October 8, 2012).

8. Quoted and paraphrased from Hoyt, *Inferno*, 33, 30–31.

9. Quoted and paraphrased from Hoyt, *Inferno*, 31, 21.

10. Walls of humanity: Guillain, *I Saw Tokyo Burning*, 186. Boiling canals: Craven and Cate, *The Army Air Forces in World War II, Volume 5*, 617 n. 37.

11. Hoyt, *Inferno,* 28, 32–33. Obata survived despite being left for dead.

12. Morgan with Powers, *The Man Who Flew the Memphis Belle,* 309, 310. See Frank, *Downfall,* 65.

13. Morgan with Powers, *The Man Who Flew the Memphis Belle,* 311–313.

14. Turbulence: Robert Nathans, "Making the Fires That Beat Japan," in Horatio Bond, ed., *Fire and the Air War: A Compilation of Expert Observations on Fires of the War Set by Incendiaries and the Atomic Bombs, Wartime Fire Fighting, and the Work of the Fire Protection Engineers Who Helped Plan the Destruction of Enemy Cities and Industrial Plants* (National Fire Protection Association International, 1946), 145–146. See Martin Sheridan, "GIANT TOKYO FIRES BLACKENED B-29'S; Correspondent in One Reports Soot and Smoke Reached Planes High in Skies," *New York Times,* March 11, 1945. Roasting flesh: Morgan with Powers, *The Man Who Flew the Memphis Belle,* 311–313. †

15. Australian Broadcasting Corporation, "Transcript," *Radio Eye: Tokyo's Burning,* 1995. Available at http://www.abc.net.au/radionational/programs/radioeye/tokyos-burning -1995/3276086 (accessed October 8, 2012).

16. Horde: Morgan with Powers, *The Man Who Flew the Memphis Belle,* 312. Bomb bays: Sheridan, "GIANT TOKYO FIRES BLACKENED B-29'S." Glow: Bruce Rae, "RECORD AIR ATTACK; B-29's Pour over 1,000 Tons of Incendiaries on Japanese Capital. BOMBS RAIN 1½ HOURS; Tremendous Fires Leap Up in Thickly Populated Center of Big City. Enemy Is Surprised," *New York Times,* March 10, 1945 (glow visible for eighty-five miles). Curtis E. LeMay with MacKinlay Kantor, *Mission with LeMay: My Story* (Doubleday & Company, 1965), 353 (glow visible for 150 miles).

17. 325 started, fourteen lost: LeMay with Kantor, *Mission with LeMay,* 353. 279 reached Tokyo: Baxter, *Scientists against Time,* 98. See Frank, *Downfall,* 66. No damage from fighters: Brooks E. Kleber and Dale Birdsell, *The Chemical Warfare Service: Chemicals in Combat. United States Army in World War II: The Technical Services, Volume 3* (Center of Military History, United States Army, Government Printing Office, 1966), 630. Available at http://www.scribd.com/doc/48257221 /Chemical-Warfare-Service-Chemicals-in-Combat (accessed October 8, 2012).

18. Higher death tolls exceed the number of words in this book. Baxter, *Scientists against Time,* 99, 293. See Schaffer, *Wings of Judgment,* 132. Richard Rhodes, *The Making of the Atomic Bomb* (Simon & Schuster, 1986), 599 (more than 100,000 deaths). Hoyt, *Inferno,* 97. Morgan with Powers, *The Man Who Flew the Memphis Belle,* 313. Cate and Olson, "Urban Area Attacks," 617. See Corbis-Bettman Archive, "Tokyo Bombing Damage," in *About Japan: A Teacher's Resource,* October 1, 2007. Available at http:// aboutjapan.japansociety.org/content.cfm/tokyo_bombing_damage (accessed October 8, 2012). Fire and police estimates: Mark Selden, "A Forgotten Holocaust," in Yuki Tanaka and Marilyn B. Young, eds., *Bombing Civilians: A Twentieth-Century History* (The New Press, 2009), 84. See Baxter, *Scientists against Time,* 84–85.

19. Kubota: Hoyt, *Inferno,* 41. Disease: ibid., 43. The destruction wrought on Tokyo was greater than Nero's Roman conflagration of AD 64, when ten of fourteen wards in a much smaller city burned. It was also much larger than any of the greatest peacetime urban fires: London 1666 (436 acres or .68 square miles, 13,200 build-

ings); Moscow 1812 (38,000 buildings); Chicago 1871 (21,188 buildings); and San Francisco 1906 (four square miles, 21,188 buildings). Cate and Olson, "Urban Area Attacks," 617. See Tacitus, *The Annals*, 56-c.117: 15:40. Available at http://penelope .uchicago.edu/Thayer/E/Roman/Texts/Tacitus/Annals/15B*.html (accessed October 8, 2012).

20. Hoyt, *Inferno*, 47.

21. Arnold: LeMay with Kantor, *Mission with LeMay*, 353. Power: Ronald Schaffer, *Wings of Judgment*, 132. See Power, *Design for Survival*, 27. Selden, "A Forgotten Holocaust," 84: "[P]robably more persons lost their lives by fire at Tokyo in a 6-hour period than at any time in the history of man," concluded the United States Strategic Bombing Survey. See Baxter, *Scientists against Time*, 98. And Cate and Olson, "Urban Area Attacks," 617. LeMay: Michael S. Sherry, *The Rise of American Air Power: The Creation of Armageddon* (Yale University Press, 1989), 288. See James Carroll, *House of War: The Pentagon and the Disastrous Rise of American Power* (Houghton Mifflin Co., 2006), 96. Arnold: LeMay with Kantor, *Mission with LeMay*, 353: "A study of the Tokyo attack of March 10 and the knowledge of the fact that by July 1 you will have nearly a thousand B-29s under your control, leads one to conclusions which are impressive even to old hands at bombardment operations. Under reasonably favorable conditions you should then have the ability to destroy whole industrial cities should that be required," Arnold forecast on March 21. See Herman S. Wolk, *Cataclysm: General Hap Arnold and the Defeat of Japan* (University of North Texas Press, 2010), 129.

22. 1,000 tons, Japanese government: Rae, "RECORD AIR ATTACK." Fifteen square miles: Warren Moscow, "CITY'S HEART GONE; Not a Building Is Left Intact in 15 Square Miles, Photos Show a MILLION HOMELESS. LeMay Says Purpose Is Won if B-29's Shortened War by One Day," *New York Times*, March 11, 1945.

23. Japan radio: "TOKYO PUT IN PANIC BY B-29 FIRE BOMBS; Tass Correspondent Tells of Mad Exodus—Asahi Says High Wind Whipped Flames Tokyo Frightened into Mad Panic by B-29 Bomb Rain in High Wind Many Hunt Kin Amid Ruins Transportation Inadequate Faces Blackened by Hot Winds," *New York Times*, March 16, 1945. Residential areas: Robert Trumbull, "B-29'S TURN JAPAN INTO CHAOTIC LAND; Domestic Broadcasts Reveal Refugees in Millions," *New York Times*, March 23, 1945. Japanese and U.S. casualties: Warren Moscow, "51 Square Miles Burned Out in Six B-29 Attacks on Tokyo; LeMay Backs Figures with Photos of Havoc—1,000,000 Japanese Are Believed to Have Perished in Fires," *New York Times*, May 30, 1945.

24. Ten days: Craven and Cate, *The Army Air Forces in World War II, Volume 5*, 618. Nagoya: LeMay with Kantor, *Mission with LeMay* 353. St. Clair McKelway, "A Reporter with the B-29s IV: People," *New Yorker*, June 30, 1945.

25. Thirty-one square miles: Cate and Olson, "Urban Area Attacks," 623. See U.S. Strategic Bombing Survey, *Summary Report (Pacific War)*, 17. Scalding chemicals: LeMay with Kantor, *Mission with LeMay*, 368–369. See Cate and Olson, "Urban Area Attacks," 614–627 (esp. the list on pp. 624–625); and James Lea Cate and James C. Olson, "The All-Out B-29 Attack," in Craven and Cate, *The Army Air Forces in World War II, Volume 5*, 674–675, table 1.

26. "Wonderful": Schaffer, *Wings of Judgment,* 138. Greatest damage: "JAPAN'S 8-DAY LOSS TO B-29'S A RECORD; General Norstad Says Damage Was Probably Greatest Ever Inflicted in Like Period Heavy Loss in Production," *New York Times,* March 24, 1945. Rushed direct: LeMay with Kantor, *Mission with LeMay,* 370. America dropped over 40,000 tons of M-69 bombs on Japan, each of which weighed 6.2 pounds and contained 2.6 pounds of napalm, a total of 80 million pounds of bombs, 12.9 million individual shells, and 33.5 million pounds of napalm. Between January 3 and June 19, 1945, napalm-filled AN-M-69 bombs comprised 53 percent of all bombs dropped on Japanese cities (AN-M47: 25.4%, AN-M50: 19.1%, AN-M76 2.1%, M74 0.4%). Thick palls of smoke rose over firebombed cities and made accuracy for following bombers a misnomer. Totals: NDRC U.S. OSRD, *Summary Technical Report,* 1. Bomb breakdown: ibid., 90, table 8. Supply ship: ibid., p. 91, para. 4. Accuracy: ibid., 91–94. †

27. LeMay: Cate and Olson, "Urban Area Attacks," 626. Ronald Reagan with Richard G. Hubler, *Where's the Rest of Me?* (Duell, Sloan and Pearce, 1965), 119. Atom bombs: U.S. Strategic Bombing Survey, *Summary Report (Pacific War),* 24. See Michael D. Gordin, *Five Days in August: How World War II Became a Nuclear War* (Princeton University Press, 2007), 7: "the issue of military justification [for nuclear weapons] is moot."

28. Burning deaths: U.S. Strategic Bombing Survey, *Summary Report (Pacific War),* 20. Sixty-six cities: Baxter, *Scientists against Time,* 99. Cate and Olson, "Urban Area Attacks," 643 (six primary cities attacked) and Cate and Olson, "The All-Out B-29 Attack," 674–675 (sixty secondary cities attacked). Leaflets: U.S. Strategic Bombing Survey, *Summary Report (Pacific War),* 21. Tokyo: LeMay with Kantor, *Mission with LeMay,* 355. †

29. Losses: Frank, *Downfall,* 69. LeMay with Kantor, *Mission with LeMay,* 367: "We lost exactly 0.9 percent of all those who participated in the March fire attacks," LeMay wrote. Cate and Olson put the total lost in seventeen "maximum-effort incendiary attacks" at 136, an average of 1.9 percent of all sorties. Cate and Olson, "Urban Area Attacks," 644. Big finale: James Lea Cate and Wesley Frank Craven, "Victory," in Craven and Cate, eds. *The Army Air Forces in World War II, Volume 5,* 732–733. Half were M-69s: Baxter, *Scientists against Time,* 294. †

30. Suzuki: Cate and Craven, "Victory," 756. U.S. Strategic Bombing Survey, *Summary Report (Pacific War),* 26. Some have criticized the report's conclusions. OSRD: Baxter, *Scientists against Time,* 98. Saburō Ienaga, *The Pacific War 1931–1945: A Critical Perspective on Japan's Role in World War II,* trans. Frank Baldwin (Pantheon, 1978), 200. †

31. 80 million pounds: NDRC U.S. OSRD, *Summary Technical Report,* 193. "Best weapon": "Flame Considered Best Weapon Used in Pacific," Associated Press, September 24, 1945, in Harvard University Archives, Papers of Louis Frederick Fieser and Mary Peters Fieser, HUGFP 20.3 Box 4. "Scrapbook 1937–1960," n.p. See "Flame Held Vital Arm: Colonel Calls It Second Only to Atomic Bomb," *New York Times,* September 25, 1945. See Baxter, *Scientists against Time,* 289. On Germany see Bond, ed. *Fire and the Air War,* 80: "[P]hoto studies of damage indicated incendiaries were 4.8 times as effective as high explosive bombs on residence areas and

against the smaller industrial and mercantile properties." Costs for atomic bombs presumably would have declined significantly if they were mass-produced in World War II. "The Costs of the Manhattan Project," *Brookings*, 2002, Available at http://www.brookings.edu/about/projects/archive/nucweapons/manhattan (accessed October 8, 2012). †

Soldier

1. Orders not received: Isaac Kidd et al., "Findings of Fact," in *U.S. Navy Court of Inquiry to Inquire into the Circumstances of the Armed Attack on USS* Liberty *(AGTR-5) on 8 June 1967* (Department of the Navy, Office of the Chief of Naval Operations, 1968), 1, items 7–9. Available at http://www.thelibertyincident.com/docs/FindingsOfFact.pdf (accessed October 8, 2012). el-Arīsh minaret: W. L. McGonagle, *Log of Liberty AGTR-5* (U.S. Navy, June 8, 1967). Available at http://www.thelibertyincident.com/docs/Logs1-24.pdf (accessed October 8, 2012).

2. Identifications: Israel Defense Forces (IDF) History Department, Research and Instruction Branch, *The Attack on the "Liberty" Incident, June 8, 1967* (June 1982), 8, 20. Available at http://www.thelibertyincident.com/docs/israeli/IDF-history-report-en.pdf (accessed October 8, 2012). See William D. Gerhard and Henry W. Millington, *Attack on a Sigint Collector, the U.S.S.* Liberty (National Security Agency/Central Security Service, 1981), 40–41. Available at http://www.thelibertyincident.com/docs/nsa/NSAreport.pdf (accessed October 8, 2012).

3. Sea attacks: IDF History Department, Research and Instruction Branch, *The Attack on the "Liberty,"* 21.

4. Audiotapes: Jay A. Cristol, *The Liberty Incident: The 1967 Israeli Attack on the U.S. Navy Spy Ship* (Brassey's Inc., 2002), appendix 2. See ibid., 48–49 for diagrams. And James Scott, *The Attack on the Liberty: The Untold Story of Israel's Deadly 1967 Assault on a U.S. Spy Ship* (Simon & Schuster, 2009), 215–216. IDF History Department, Research and Instruction Branch, *The Attack on the "Liberty,"* 13.

5. James M. Ennes Jr., *Assault on the Liberty: The True Story of the Israeli Attack on an American Intelligence Ship* (Random House, 1979), 67.

6. Ibid., 68, 70. McGonagle described "firefly-like pieces of napalm flying around inside the pilot house." Bulkheads: Scott, *The Attack on the Liberty*, 62.

7. Kidd et al., "Findings of Fact," 5, item 26. See Clark Clifford, "The Israeli Attack on the USS *Liberty*," unpublished memorandum to W. W. Rostow, July 18, 1967, pp. 3–5. Available at http://www.thelibertyincident.com/clifford.html (accessed October 8, 2012).

8. William Beecher, "Israel, in Error, Attacks U.S. Ship: 10 Navy Men Die, 100 Hurt in Raids North of Sinai," *New York Times,* June 9, 1967, p. 1. Ted Sell, "Israel Attacks U.S. Navy Ship in Error; 10 Die," *Los Angeles Times,* June 6, 1967, p. 1. Louis Dombrowski, "Israel Offers to Pay Reparations to U.S.," *Chicago Tribune,* June 11, 1967, p. 10. Neil Sheehan, "Sailors Describe Attack on Vessel: Israelis Struck So Suddenly U.S. Guns Were Unloaded," *New York Times,* June 11, 1967, p. 27. See Scott, *The Attack on the Liberty*, 2–5. Apology: Ennes, *Assault on the Liberty*, 284–288. See Ram Ron, *Israel Defense Force Inquiry Commission Report,* June 16, 1967,

pp. 9–16. Available at http://thelibertyincident.com/docs/israeli/ram-ron-report. pdf (accessed October 8, 2012). See also Gerhard and Millington, *Attack on a Sigint Collector,* 63–64. †

6. Freedom's Furnace

1. Louis F. Fieser, George C. Harris, E. B. Hershberg, Morley Morgana, Frederick C. Novello, and Stearns T. Putnam, "Napalm," *Industrial & Engineering Chemistry* 38, no. 8 (August 1946): 772–773. Fieser assigned his rights to the secretary of war: "Louis D. Fieser, assignor to the United States of America as represented by the Secretary of War. Incendiary Gels. United States Patent Office No. 2,606,107. 5 August 1952." Available at http://patimg1.uspto.gov/.piw?Docid=02606107&homeurl =http%3A%2F%2Fpatft.uspto.gov%2Fnetacgi%2Fnph-Parser%3FSect1%3DPTO2 %2526Sect2%3DHITOFF%2526p%3D1%2526u%3D%25252Fnetahtml%25252 FPTO%25252Fsearch-adv.htm%2526r%3D1%2526f%3DG%2526l%3D50%2526d%3 DPALL%2526S1%3D02606107%25260S%3DPN%2F02606107%2526RS%3DPN% 2F02606107&PageNum=&Rtype=&SectionNum=&idkey=NONE&Input=View +first+page (accessed October 8, 2012).

2. See United Nations (UN) Consultant Experts on Napalm and Other Incendiary Weapons, *Napalm and Other Incendiary Weapons and All Aspects of Their Possible Use: Report of the Secretary-General, Volume 14, Issue 12* (UN, 1973), 51: 178. †

3. Griswold: Lawrence S. Wittner, *American Intervention in Greece, 1943–1949* (Columbia University Press, 1982), 243 and n. 49. See Howard Jones, *"A New Kind of War": America's Global Strategy and the Truman Doctrine in Greece* (Oxford University Press, 1989), 290 n. 22. Fourteen bombs: ibid., 293 n. 3. Operation Torch, and surrenders: Wittner, *American Intervention in Greece,* 251. A. C. Sedgwick, "Greek Army Opens Grammos Assault; Advance to Albanian Border Is Made on North in Drive in Last Main Rebel Zone," *New York Times,* August 26, 1949. Win: Wittner, *American Intervention in Greece,* 251. †

4. North Korean army: John Halliday and Bruce Cumings, *Korea: The Unknown War* (Viking, 1988), 73. Weekend leave: Callum MacDonald, *Korea: The War before Vietnam* (The Free Press, 1986), 30.

5. Twenty-four-hours: Earle J. Townsend, "They Don't Like 'Hell Bombs,'" *Armed Forces Chemical Journal* 4, no. 3 (January 1951), n.p. See Robert Frank Futrell, *The United States Air Force in Korea, 1950–1953* (Duell, Sloan and Pearce, 1961), 29. Townsend, "They Don't Like 'Hell Bombs,'" n.p.

6. Richard J. Johnson, "Jets Destroy 60-100 Tanks, Nearly Half of Red's Force," *Boston Herald-N.Y. Times Dispatch,* July 9, 1950, Harvard University Archives, Papers of Louis Frederick Fieser and Mary Peters Fieser (hereafter Fieser Papers), HUGFP 20.3 Box 4, "Scrap Book: 1937–1960," n.p. Fifty-yards-square: Roy E. Appleman, *South to the Naktong, North to the Yalu (June–November 1950)* (Government Printing Office, 1961), 379 n. 9. See E. F. Bullene, "It's Not New but Napalm Is an All-Purpose WONDER WEAPON," *United States Army Combat Forces Journal* (November 1952): 25–26: "A belly-tank load of napalm will splatter a hell of roaring flames over an area as big as a football field, and any tank caught in it is likely to have

its crew killed, its gasoline burned and its ammunition exploded." And Donald Bode, "Napalm Bombs in Korea" [an interview conducted by the Historical Office, Office of the Chief Chemical Officer, on March 1, 1951], in John G. Westover, *Combat Support in Korea* (Combat Forces Press, 1955), 82. †

7. Napalm Day: Townsend, "They Don't Like 'Hell Bombs,'" n.p. See Walt Sheldon, *Hell or High Water: MacArthur's Landing at Inchon* (Macmillan, 1968), 16. No. 1: C. B. Allen, "Napalm, the No. 1 Weapon in Korea," *New York Herald Tribune,* October 15, 1950, p. 2, sect. 2–4. Tank and ordnance officers: Townsend, "They Don't Like 'Hell Bombs,'" n.p. "Cooking oil": Walter Karig, Malcolm W. Cagle, and Frank A. Manson, *Battle Report: The War in Korea, Prepared from Official Sources* (Rinehart and Company, 1952), 423. See Keystone-France, "Napalm Bombs in Corea 1951," *GettyImages.com,* January 20, 1951, Available at http://www.gettyimages.com/detail /news-photo/some-allied-soldiers-unloading-some-napalm-bombs-somewhere -news-photo/106498743 (accessed October 8, 2012). †

8. That's napalm: René Cutforth, *Korean Reporter* (Wingate, 1952), 172. Forty yards: Roy E. Appleman, *East of Choisin: Entrapment and Breakout in Korea, 1950* (Texas A & M University Press, 1987), 213. Not every close strike was successful. A U.S. captain recalled that in December 1950 a South Korean soldier who took cover from a nearby napalm hit "came up out of the drainage, took three faltering steps toward me and collapsed and died on the road. He had inhaled the heat blast as it traveled down the drainage" (Appleman, *East of Choisin,* 210). Disoriented: Karig et al., *Battle Report,* 258.

9. Paul Freeman: Rudy Tomedi, *No Bugles, No Drums: An Oral History of the Korean War* (John Wiley & Sons, 1994), 119, 121. Screams: Stanley Sandler, *The Korean War: No Victors, No Vanquished* (University Press of Kentucky, 1999), 80. Napalm was also useful against dug-in personnel: "When the bomb lands, the burning napalm spreads out and drops down into foxholes," reported Eighth Army chemical officer Donald Bode (Bode, "Napalm Bombs in Korea," 82). Futrell cataloged some offensive successes: a supply depot was 95 percent destroyed, firebombs killed nearly 300 soldiers when airplanes surprised a sleeping battalion, and a company of troops attacked at supper was said to have been wiped out. Futrell, *The United States Air Force in Korea,* 2nd ed. (Office of Air Force History, 1983), 518. See Allen S. Whiting, *China Crosses the Yalu: The Decision to Enter the Korean War* (Stanford University Press, 1960), 71 (quoting Chinese military commentators on tactical effectiveness of napalm). †

10. Immediately scatter: D. M. Giangreco, *War in Korea, 1950–1953* (Presidio, 1990), 261. Two episodes: Townsend, They Don't Like 'Hell Bombs,'" n.p. Prisoners in one instance asserted they feared napalm only when it was dropped directly on their positions and ran from it as a maneuver, but this approach does not appear to have been the norm. Futrell, *The United States Air Force in Korea,* 1st ed., 331. See "Napalm Jelly Bombs Prove a Blazing Success in Korea," *All Hands,* April 1951, p. 17: "If you were to ask Communist troops in Korea which weapons they most fear, the majority would say napalm." Available at http://www.navy.mil/media/allhands/acrobat /ah195104.pdf (accessed October 8, 2012).

11. Tiger tanks: H. Gilman Wing, "Flame," *Armed Forces Chemical Journal* 7, no. 1 (July 1953): 12. Psychological factor: Bullene, "It's Not New," 27.

12. Seoul bombing: *New York Herald Tribune,* September 23, 1950. Seoul flame tanks: Jerry Ravino and Jack Carty, *Hearts of Iron: The Epic Struggle of the 1st Marine Division Flame Tank Platoon, Korean War 1950–1953* (Turner Publishing, 2003), 10. See http://www.flamedragons.info/FlamePlatoon.html (accessed October 8, 2012).

13. Basements: Wing, "Flame," 12. *This Is Korea!* Directed by John Ford (United States Navy, Republic Pictures, 1951). Available at http://www.youtube.com/watch ?v=hrn3VaDI2qk (accessed October 8, 2012). Carrier crews loading napalm belly tank bombs: 28'57". Close support strikes: 35'00", 39'00"–40'52", 45'00"–45'55"). See Halliday and Cumings, *Korea: The Unknown War,* 166.

14. Offensive use of flamethrowers proved dangerous in the relatively static war that followed. Of ninety-seven systems used by one division in October and November 1951, "65 were lost through enemy action or were abandoned so the operator could escape. Six operators were killed," the unit's chemical officer reported. This account was typical: "A rifle bullet instantly killed one of the operators. . . . The second operator managed to get off one short burst before the machine malfunctioned" (Walter G. Hermes, *United States Army in the Korean War, Volume 2: Truce Tent and Fighting Front* (Government Printing Office, 1966), 387.

15. Fougasses: Wing, "Flame," 12. Spring 1951: Bullene, "It's Not New," 25, 26. †

16. Futrell, *The United States Air Force in Korea,* 1st ed., 41.

17. I. F. Stone, *The Hidden History of the Korean War* (Little, Brown, 1989), 312. See Malvern Lumsden, *Incendiary Weapons* (MIT Press, 1975), 45. And Futrell, *The United States Air Force in Korea,* 1st ed., 42.

18. Pyongyang proposal: Futrell, *The United States Air Force in Korea,* 1st ed., 42, 194. Vandenburg: MacDonald, *Korea: The War before Vietnam,* 234.

19. Robert F. Futrell, "Tactical Employment of Strategic Air Power in Korea," *Airpower Journal* (Winter 1988). Available at http://www.airpower.au.af.mil/airchronicles/apj /apj88/win88/futrell.html (accessed October 8, 2012).

20. Stone, *The Hidden History of the Korean War,* 312. †

21. Dean Acheson, *Present at the Creation: My Years in the State Department* (Norton, 1969), 463. See MacDonald, *Korea: The War before Vietnam,* 234: "Population centers behind enemy lines were assumed to hold troops, and all movement on roads was defined as military. Only family groups with children were to be spared."

22. Authorization: Acheson, *Present at the Creation,* 464. Shinŭiju, Hoeryŏng, North West area: Bruce Cumings: *The Origins of the Korean War, Volume 2: The Roaring of the Cataract 1947–1950* (Princeton University Press, 1990), 753: "550 tons of incendiary bombs" on Shinŭiju. 85,000 bombs: Townsend, "They Don't Like 'Hell Bombs,'" n.p. (dating Shinŭiju attack to January 10). Some officials denied a change in policy had occurred. "The cities of North Korea are highly inflammable and would make ideal incendiary targets. Docks, supply bases, railroad yards, and bridges, however, are legitimate targets," Bullene wrote in November 1952. Bullene, "It's Not New," 28.

23. Pyongyang 1950–1951: Cumings, *The Origins of the Korean War, Volume 2,* 753. Burned like a furnace: Futrell, *The United States Air Force in Korea,* 2nd ed., 278. 4,000 feet: ibid., 518. Seoul: "Official Reports Describing the Day's Operations

in Korea; Reds Advance South of Seoul and Threaten U.N. Flank," *New York Times,* January 6, 1951.

24. Smart: Futrell, *The United States Air Force in Korea,* 2nd ed., 516–517. 23,000 gallons: Hermes, *United States Army in the Korean War, Volume 2:* 324–325. See MacDonald, *Korea: The War before Vietnam,* 234: "2,300 gallons [*sic*]." †

25. Every fighter: Townsend, "They Don't Like 'Hell Bombs,'" n.p. Navy rules required pilots to drop napalm bombs before they returned to carriers. See Allen, "Napalm, the No. 1 Weapon in Korea." 21,000 gallons: Futrell, *The United States Air Force in Korea,* 2nd ed., 371 (asserting 7.8 million gallons of napalm in first year of war). Bode, Plastic $40, Korean facilities: Westover, *Combat Support in Korea,* 81. Japan manufacturers: Harry G. Summers Jr. "Napalm," *Korean War Almanac* (Facts on File, 1990), 196. And Stephen Lyon Endicott and Edward Hagerman, *The United States and Biological Warfare* (Indiana University Press, 1998), 117. 32,357 tons: Futrell, *The United States Air Force in Korea,* 1st ed., 645. †

26. Douglas MacArthur, "Casualties in Korea." Committee on Armed Services and the Committee on Foreign Relations, United States Senate, *Military Situation in the Far East: Hearings to Conduct an Inquiry Into the Military Situation in the Far East and the Facts Surrounding the Relief of General of the Army Douglas MacArthur from his Assignments in that Area* (Government Printing Office, 1951), part 1 (May 3, 1951), n.p. At least half of eighteen cities: Bruce Cumings, *The Korean War: A History* (Modern Library, 2010), 160. Pyongyang: Jon Halliday, "The North Korean Enigma," *New Left Review* 127 (May–June 1981): 29. Halliday notes that North Korea has not released total casualty figures, but an estimate based on a Soviet source asserts 11.5 to 15 percent of the population was killed: more than in the USSR during World War II. Curtis E. LeMay with MacKinlay Kantor, *Mission with LeMay: My Story* (Doubleday & Company, 1965), 382. See Richard Rhodes, *Dark Sun: The Making of the Hydrogen Bomb* (Simon & Schuster, 1995), 443 (quoting LeMay: "we killed off—what—twenty percent of the population of Korea as direct casualties of war, or from starvation and exposure?"). O'Donnell: Stone, *The Hidden History of the Korean War,* 312.

27. Cutforth, *Korean Reporter,* 174. Vomit: Karig et al., *Battle Report,* 111.

28. Donald Knox, *The Korean War, an Oral History: Pusan to Chosin* (Harcourt Brace Jovanovich, 1985). Tanyang Cave: Choe Sang-Hun, "South Korea Says U.S. Killed Hundreds of Civilians," *New York Times,* August 3, 2008. But note that in 1952 U.S. Army chief chemical officer E. F. Bullene asserted, "It is untrue that napalm 'can kill by sucking all of the oxygen out of the air.' A man can live for some time in air containing less oxygen than is required to burn gasoline." In instances where napalm did not kill by burning, "Death, it seems, may come from a combination of heat, shock, dearth of oxygen, and possibly fumes, but not necessarily from any one of them alone." Bullene, "It's Not New," 26.

29. George Barrett, "Radio Hams in U.S. Discuss Girls, So Shelling of Seoul Is Held Up," *New York Times,* February 9, 1951. See Stone, *The Hidden History of the Korean War,* 258–259. Dean Acheson demanded censors stop this kind of "sensationalized reporting." Cumings, *The Origins of the Korean War, Volume 2,* 755. †

30. Predominantly civilian: "M.P.'S AGAIN SCORE NAPALM BOMB USE; Both Labor and Conservatives Raise Question of Drops on Civilian Areas in Korea," Special to the *New York Times,* May 22, 1952. Reuters, "NAPALM BOMB DE-NOUNCED; Archbishop of York Urges Use of Weapon Be Outlawed," *New York Times,* April 28, 1952, p. 2. Methodist and Free Church of Scotland leaders also objected. MacDonald, *Korea: The War before Vietnam,* 234. Monstrous: Austin Stevens, "U. S. Counters Red Charges Napalm Is Used on Civilians; U.N. Leaflets Warning North Koreans of Bombing U. S. Counters Reds on Napalm Bombs," Special to the *New York Times,* August 19, 1952.

31. Pentagon denials: Stevens, "U. S. Counters Red Charges Napalm Is Used on Civilians." Churchill: M. L. Dockrill, "The Foreign Office, Anglo-American Relations, and the Korean Truce Negotiations, July 1951–July 1953," in James Cotton and Ian Neary, eds., *The Korean War in History* (Humanities Press International, 1989), 108. Britain's chiefs of staff justified "a modern development of flame-throwing weapons which had long been used in warfare."

32. J. M. Spaight, "Napalm," *Journal of the Royal United Services Institute for Defence Studies* 98, no. 589 (February 1953), 82, 83, 84. See Brett Holman, "J. M. Spaight," *Airminded: Airpower and British Society, 1908–1941 (Mostly),* n.d. Available at http://airminded.org/biographies/j-m-spaight (accessed October 8, 2012).

33. Stephen R. Shalom, *The United States and the Philippines: A Study of Neocolonialism* (Institute for the Study of Human Issues, 1981), 82.

34. Verano: Hugh Thomas, *Cuba: The Pursuit of Freedom* (Harper & Row, 1971), 998. See Lumsden, *Incendiary Weapons,* 49. Bay of Pigs: Howard Jones, *The Bay of Pigs* (Oxford University Press, 2008), 114–115. †

35. " 'Napalm Bombs' on Peru Guerrillas," *The Times,* September 20, 1965, p. 8. Special Forces: Lumsden, *Incendiary Weapons,* 68.

36. "Bolivia Uses Napalm in Fight On Guerrillas in Southeast," *New York Times,* March 28, 1967, p. 3. Associated Press, "Bolivians Pressing Drive on Guerrillas," *New York Times,* March 30, 1967, p. 12. Guevara: Donald R. Selvage, "The Final Days July 7–October 8, 1967," in *Che Guevara in Bolivia* (paper presented at a seminar, Marine Corps Command and Staff College, April 1, 1985). Available at http://www.globalsecurity.org/military/library/report/1985/SDR.htm (accessed October 8, 2012). See Peter Kornbluh, *The Death of Che Guevara: Declassified.* National Security Archive Electronic Briefing Book No. 5. n.d. Available at http://www.gwu.edu/~nsarchiv/NSAEBB/NSAEBB5/ (accessed October 8, 2012). †

37. 1956 Egypt: Derek Varble, *The Suez Crisis 1956* (Osprey, 2003), 39 (with France), 49, http://books.google.com/books?id=MrP3kgd4sf8C&lpg=PP1&vq=napam&pg=PA49%23v=onepage&q=napalm&f=false (accessed October 8, 2012). And Lumsden, *Incendiary Weapons.* 63. 1964 Syria: Brigadier General Ezer Weizmann, commander of the Israeli air force: "The Israeli jets, he declared, used napalm (jellied gasoline) and rockets." W. Granger Blair, "Israeli Jets Rake Syrians in Battle," *New York Times,* November 14, 1964, p. 1. 1967 Syria (Six Day War): Eric Britter, "Demand to Stop Syria Battle: UN Reports Use of Napalm," *The Times,* June 10, 1967, p. 1. See Michael Clodfelter, *Warfare and Armed Conflicts, a Statistical Reference to Casualty and Other Figures, 1494–2000,* 3rd ed. (McFarland & Co., 2008), 613:

"The Israeli Army also had . . . 4,000 pounds of bombs or napalm." And Charles Bonnay, "Egyptian Soldier Burned by Israeli Napalm," http://www.gettyimages .com/detail/news-photo/egyptian-soldier-burned-by-israeli-napalm-during-arab -news-photo/506745231969. Lebanon: Geoffrey Sumner, "Israel Raiders Accused of Using Napalm," *The Times*, February 26, 1969, p. 6. 1969 Egypt: Confirmed by Israeli defense minister Moshe Dayan. Lumsden, *Incendiary Weapons*, 64. Associated Press, "Israeli Planes Strafe, Drop Napalm on Egypt," *Spartanburg Herald*, February 13, 1970, http://news.google.com/newspapers?id=mTssAAAAIBAJ&sjid =BswEAAAAIBAJ&pg=3703,2159531 (accessed October 8, 2012). 1972 Lebanon: "TERRORISM: And Now, Mail-a-Death," *Time*, October 2, 1972: "[T]he hills were still afire from napalm airstrikes." 1973 Syria (Yom Kippur War): "The War of the Day of Judgment," *Time*, October 22, 1973: "Finally, Israeli armored units, closely supported by Phantoms and Skyhawks whooshing in to splatter napalm on the forward Syrian units, halted the Syrian drive and turned the Arabs back." And Gabriel Duval, "The Body of a Syrian Soldier, Burned by Israeli Napalm Shell," *GettyImages.com*, October 17, 1973. Available at http://www.gettyimages.com/detail /news-photo/the-body-of-a-syrian-soldier-burned-by-israeli-napalm-shell-news -photo/51425419 (accessed October 8, 2012). See Tony Summers, "Egypt's Deputy Premier Accuses the United States of Supplying Israel with Napalm for Use in Syria," *BBC*, October 14, 1973. Available at http://www.itnsource.com/shotlist// RTV/1973/10/16/BGY509030328/?s=napalm (accessed October 8, 2012). Egypt: John Pike, Ed. "Napalm in War." 2012: http://www.globalsecurity.org/military /systems/munitions/napalm-war.htm (accessed October 8, 2012). †

38. Clyde H. Farnsworth, "64 Planes in Raid; Greek Cypriotes Put Casualties at 300— Warn of Reprisal. Jets Continue Attacks on Cyprus as Nicosia Reports Landings by Turkish Troops. Bombers Batter Greek Positions. Planes Seek to Blunt Drives on a Turkish Stronghold in Island's Northwest," Special to the *New York Times*, August 10, 1964. Zenon Rossides: "Excerpts from Speeches in the U.N. Security Council Debate on the Cyprus Crisis," *New York Times*, August 10, 1964. Satan: Lumsden, *Incendiary Weapons*, 65. Austrians: "Austrian Protest at Napalm Attack on U.N. Car," *The Times*, August 16, 1974, p. 8, col. B. See Lumsden, *Incendiary Weapons*, 65.

39. "Bombes spéciales": L. M. Chassin, *Aviation Indochine* (Amiot-Dumont, 1954), 97. Viet Minh: Bernard Fall, *Street without Joy* (Schocken, 1972 [1961]), 39. Tactics: Chassin, *Aviation Indochine*, 239. American forces later followed his advice, without success. Operation Sherwood Forest, in late March 1965, used magnesium bombs to burn the jungle. It was a failure. Operation Hot Tip, in January 1966, added napalm, destroyed 17.5 percent of the forest canopy, and was considered "encouraging," but ultimately insufficient, by U.S. Department of Agriculture experts. Operation Sherwood Forest and Operation Hot Tip: GlobalSecurity.org. "Operation Sherwood Forest, Operation Hot Tip," December 2, 2012, http://www.globalsecurity .org/military/ops/sherwood-forest.htm (accessed October 8, 2012). "Encouraging" results from Hot Tip: Mutch et al. "Operation Pink Rose: Final Report." May 1967: U.S. Department of Agriculture—Forest Service. 6. (Pink Rose used magnesium bombs). Available at http://www.dod.mil/pubs/foi/International_security_affairs /vietnam_and_southeast_asiaDocuments/801.pdf. See Malvern Lumsden, *Napalm*

*and Incendiary Weapons: Legal and Humanitarian Aspects* (Stockholm International Peace Research Institute, 1972), 75.

40. Mau-Mau: Robert Conley, " 'Gray Men' Leave Kenya's Jungles; Ex-Mau Mau Bands Taking Advantage of Amnesty; Official Explains Pardon; Britain Sent Troops," *New York Times,* December 2, 1963. Portugal: Reuters, "Angola Terror Seen: British Cleric Lays Atrocities to Portuguese Troops," *New York Times,* July 23, 1961. Henry Tanner, "Portugal Battles Elusive Enemy and Ever-Present Angola Jungle; Troops Grope through Difficult Terrain, Capturing Villages but Almost Never Catching a Glimpse of Rebel Foe," *New York Times,* August 27, 1961. Lloyd Garrison, "Angolans Fleeing into Congo Again; 200 Crossing Border Daily from Areas in Revolt," *New York Times,* April 17, 1962. Lawrence O'Kane, "Victory by Lisbon in Africa Doubted; U.N. Panel Says Angolans Gain Despite Repression Reform Efforts Futile," *New York Times,* November 21, 1962. See Barry Hatton, "Film Wakens Portugal to an Unsettling Past; TV Series Reveals Africa War Atrocities," *Washington Post,* December 30, 2007, p. A18. Resolution 2918: UN General Assembly Resolution 2918 (XXVII). Question of Territories under Portuguese Administration, November 14, 1972. Available at http://daccess-dds-ny.un.org/doc /RESOLUTION/GEN/NR0/269/48/IMG/NR026948.pdf?OpenElement (accessed October 8, 2012). †

41. Yemen: Lumsden, *Incendiary Weapons,* 65. Kashmir: Thomas F. Brady, "Scars of Battle Evident at Kashmir Truce Line," *New York Times,* September 24, 1965. India: "Red Cross Told That Napalm Has Been Used," *The Times,* December 11, 1971, p. 5, col. G. Kurds: Lumsden, *Incendiary Weapons,* 65. See Don Shannon, " 'Hottest War' Raging in Iraq, Kurd Declares," *Los Angeles Times,* June 8, 1974, p. A9. Nigeria: GlobalSecurity.org, "Napalm in War," 2012. Available at http://www.global security.org/military/systems/munitions/napalm-war.htm (accessed October 8, 2012). Brazil: Reuters, "Napalm Used on Brazilian Rebel Hideouts," *Los Angeles Times,* April 29, 1970, p. 21. †

7. Vietnam Syndrome

1. Associated Press, "Two Planes Bomb Palace in Saigon; Diem Keeps Rule; Leader Is Unhurt. Attack Believed Made by Dissident Pilots—Building Afire," *New York Times,* February 27, 1962. Trained by the United States: Homer Bigart, "Saigon Discounts Pilots' Raid on Presidential Palace; Diem Appears Calm," *New York Times,* February 28, 1962. Diem was assassinated in 1963. Independence Palace reopened in 1966. North Vietnamese conquerors renamed it Reunification Palace in 1975.

2. McNamara: Homer Bigart, "McNamara Asks Vietnam Chief to Alter Tactics in Struggle; U.S. Is Showing Impatience over Lag on Mekong Delta Pacification Plan American Pilot Is Wounded," *New York Times,* May 11, 1962. American strike: Associated Press, "Heavy Air Strike Rips Vietnam Reds in a New Offensive," *New York Times,* February 9, 1963. South Vietnamese attacks: Homer Bigart, "Vietnamese Slay 300 Reds in Clash; U. S. Forces Fly Troops to Attack South of Saigon—Two Copters Downed Planes Find Guerrillas," *New York Times,* May 13, 1962. Caravelle

view: Hedrick Smith, "The Unreality of Saigon; Capital Continues to Gossip and Shop under New Regime as under the Old," *New York Times,* December 7, 1963.

3. Burned baby: "U.S. Admits Use of Napalm," *The Times,* March 30, 1964. North Vietnam: United States Department of Defense, *The Pentagon Papers: The Defense Department History of United States Decisionmaking on Vietnam, Volume 3.* Senator Gravel edition (Beacon Press, 1971), 278. Available at http://www.mtholyoke .edu/acad/intrel/pentagon3/pent6.htm (accessed October 8, 2012). See Eric Prokosch, *The Technology of Killing: A Military and Political History of Antipersonnel Weapons* (Zed Books, 1995), 119. And Jack Raymond, "U.S. Fliers Using Napalm in Raids; Air Strikes in North Vietnam Aided by Fire Bombs," *New York Times,* March 20, 1965.

4. Three kinds of napalm: Departments of the Army and the Air Force, *Military Chemistry and Chemical Agents, Technical Manual TM 3-215, Air Force Manual 355-7,* December 1963, 40–41. Equipment: Departments of the Army and the Air Force, *Bombs and Bomb Components, Technical Manual TM 9-1325-200,* April 1966, 2-33–2-55. Available at http://www.scribd.com/doc/59235651/TM-9-1325-200-Bombs -and-Bomb-Components-USA-1966 (accessed October 8, 2012). See Seymour M. Hersh, *Chemical and Biological Warfare: America's Hidden Arsenal* (The Bobbs-Merrill Company, 1968), 64. Phosphorus fragments could smolder for extended periods in the bodies of victims. Frank Harvey, "The Air War in Vietnam," *Flying,* November 1966, p. 54. Malvern Lumsden, *Napalm and Incendiary Weapons: Legal and Humanitarian Aspects* (Stockholm International Peace Research Institute, 1972), 55. †

5. Tom Wells, *The War Within: America's Battle over Vietnam* (University of California Press, 1994), 88.

6. South Vietnamese forces used unknown additional quantities of napalm. See Malvern Lumsden, *Incendiary Weapons* (MIT Press, 1975), 50, table 1.1., and Lumsden, *Napalm and Incendiary Weapons,* 84, table II.8. Other sources offer different totals: 1,500 tons per month: "Napalm—A Useful but Not a Pretty Weapon," *New York Times,* December 10, 1967 (agrees with Lumsden if referring to 1965); 25,000 tons per month: Hersh, *Chemical and Biological Warfare,* 64. THOR, the Theater History of Operations Reports, may provide more precise data when it becomes publicly available. See Bryan Bender, "Bomb database useful for past, present wars," *Boston Globe,* July 30, 2012. Burned to death: see "Napalm—A Useful but Not a Pretty Weapon." †

7. How it feels: Harvey, "The Air War in Vietnam," 43. See "Napalm—A Useful but Not a Pretty Weapon."

8. "The War: The Massacre of Dak Son," *Time,* December 15, 1967.

9. Departments of the Army and the Air Force, "Incendiary Bombs" and "Firebombs," in *Technical Manual TM 9-1325-200,* April 1966, pp. 2-33 and 2-40 respectively. Department of the Army Headquarters, "Combat Flame Operations," in *Army Field Manual FM 20-33,* 1970, pp. 7-1, 7-3, 7-5. See Headquarters, Department of the Army, *Flame Fuels: Technical Manual TM 3-366,* June 14, 1971, p. 3: "Flame fuel is a thick, jellylike substance which ranges in consistency from a pourable liquid to a

rubbery, very thick gel. . . . [I]t is used in both portable and mechanized flame-throwers as well as fire bombs and flame field expedients." †

10. Bob Parker, "Chemicals and People Sniffers," in Matthew Brennan, ed., *Hunter-Killer Squadron: Aero-Weapons, Aero-Scouts, Aero-Rifles, Vietnam 1965–1972* (Presidio, 1990), 237. "Choi Hoi" literally means "Oh, my God!" See Department of the Army Headquarters, "Combat Flame Operations," 7-6. †

11. 1972: "The Air War: To See Is to Destroy," *Time,* April 17, 1972. †

12. Graham Greene, *The Quiet American* (Penguin, 2004 [1955]), 143. Robert Gorham Davis, "In Our Time No Man is a Neutral; Graham Greene's Controversial New Novel Deals with America's Role in Indochina," *New York Times,* March 11, 1956. Bertrand Russell, "Letters to the *Times*: Vietnam Policy Protested Russell Holds Our Aim Is to Block Economic Reform," *New York Times,* April 8, 1963. "Lord Russell's Letter," *New York Times,* April 8, 1963. †

13. Guerrillas or farmers: Associated Press, "U.S. Combat Instructors Learn as They Teach in South Vietnam," *New York Times,* July 8, 1962. Georges Penchenier, "Close-up of the Vietcong in Their Jungle; A French Reporter Held Captive by Guerrillas in South Vietnam Here Reports on What He Saw of the Vietcong—the Men, Their Morale, Their Methods," *New York Times,* September 13, 1964. Augustine Nguyen Lac Hoa: United Press International, "Saigon's Tactics Scored by Priest; Fighter against Reds Says Cruelty Costs Popularity," *New York Times,* September 1, 1964. Neil Sheehan, "Vietnam Peasants Are Victims of War," *New York Times,* February 15, 1966.

14. Jack Langguth, "Air Power Put to Test in Vietnam," *New York Times,* March 7, 1965.

15. Emily Rosdolsky, "Remark on Napalm," *New York Times,* March 16, 1965. House: Clyde H. Farnsworth, "War-Gas Debate Stirs Commons; Wilson Parries Criticism—Many Nations Aroused," *New York Times,* March 24, 1965. Jack Langguth, "Air Power Wins Vietnam Battle; Beleaguered Troops Saved by Strikes of U.S. Planes," *New York Times,* May 15, 1965.

16. Charles Mohr, "Air Strikes Hit Vietcong—and South Vietnam Civilians," *New York Times,* September 5, 1965.

17. H. Bruce Franklin, *Vietnam and Other American Fantasies* (University of Massachusetts Press, 2000), 75. Franklin later became a professor of English and American Studies at Rutgers University. H. Bruce Franklin. "Curriculum Vitae of H. Bruce Franklin." No date: http://andromeda.rutgers.edu/~hbf/cv.html (accessed October 8, 2012). On "thoughtful, committed citizens" see Institute for Intercultural Studies, "What Is the Source of the 'Never doubt . . .' Quote?" Available at http://www.interculturalstudies.org/faq.html#quote (accessed October 8, 2012).

18. Winter protests: Prokosch, *The Technology of Killing,* 127. See Eric Prokosch, "Making a Napalm Scrapbook," *Stanford Daily,* May 26, 1966. Secret tip: Franklin, *Vietnam and Other Fantasies,* 74–75.

19. Napalm B: Franklin, *Vietnam and Other Fantasies,* 74–75. Original napalm formulations burned at 800–1,200°C (1,472–2,152°F). Later formulations burn at 1,500–2,000°C (2,732–3,632°F). See Gilbert Dreyfus, "Napalm and Its Effects on Human Beings," *International War Crimes Tribunal—1967,* December 1, 1967,

http://www.vietnamese-american.org/b1.html (accessed October 8, 2012). Masahiro Hashimoto, "The Napalm Bomb," *International War Crimes Tribunal—1967,* December 1, 1967. Available at http://www.vietnamese-american.org/b2.html (accessed October 8, 2012). Polystyrene: "Napalm-B to Use Huge Amount of Polystyrene," *Chemical and Engineering News,* March 14, 1966. Later formulations used 20 percent benzene, 43 percent polystyrene, and 37 percent gasoline. George W. Mushrush, Erna J. Beal, Dennis R. Hardy, and Janet M. Hughes, "Use of Surplus Napalm as an Energy Source," *Energy Sources* 22, no. 2 (2000): 147. See Ogden Air Logistics Center, United States Air Force, "Military Specification MIL-N-38645: NAPALM B," December 4, 1968. Available at http://engineers.ihs.com/document /abstract/TJXMDAAAAAAAAAAA (accessed October 8, 2012). 1965 production: E. N. Brandt, *Growth Company: Dow Chemical's First Century* (Michigan State University Press, 1997). Bids: ibid., 356. Mixing line: ibid., 352. (Brandt finished a lengthy Dow career as director of public relations.) †

20. Franklin. *Vietnam and Other Fantasies,* 74–76, 77.

21. Ibid., 78.

22. Ibid., 80.

23. UTC contract: "Napalm-B to Use Huge Amount of Polystyrene." See Prokosch, *The Technology of Killing,* 127. Franklin, *Vietnam and Other Fantasies,* 82. Facility: Rent was $327 per month. James F. Colaianni, "Napalm: Made in U.S.A., a Small-town Diary," *Ramparts* 5 (August 1966), 47. †

24. Franklin, *Vietnam and Other Fantasies,* 82.

25. Franklin ejected, adjournment: Franklin, *Vietnam and Other Fantasies,* 83. Greene: Lawrence E. Davies, "Napalm Foes Petition for Vote to Bar Factory in Coast City," *New York Times,* April 17, 1966. First protest: Wallace Turner, "Pacifists Balked in Napalm Fight: Judge Rejects a Plan That Would Shut Coast Plant," *New York Times,* May 21, 1966. †

26. Davies, "Napalm Foes." Newsletter: Redwood City Committee against Napalm, *Napalm Newsletter,* 1966 [author's collection]. Mailed to all voters: Eric Prokosch, correspondence with author, April 2, 2012.

27. Colaianni: Davies, "Napalm Foes." UTC: Hersh, *Chemical and Biological Warfare,* 258. "Decision Belongs at a National Level," *Palo Alto Times,* April 20, 1966. NBC, CBS: Franklin, *Vietnam and Other Fantasies,* 84–85. Colaianni, "Napalm: Made in U.S.A.," 48. See Eric Prokosch (rev. H. Bruce Franklin), "History of the Redwood City Campaign against Napalm," 1967, unpublished manuscript.

28. Economic boom, roasted alive: Colaianni, "Napalm: Made in U.S.A," 47. "Climate Best by Government Test": Prokosch, *The Technology of Killing,* 128. †

29. 3,761: Franklin, *Vietnam and Other Fantasies,* 85. 2,416: "Let Voters Decide the Napalm Issue," *Redwood City Tribune,* April 5, 1966. See Daryl Lembke, "Protests Force City to Vote on Napalm Factory," *Los Angeles Times,* April 17, 1966, p. 1-B. Lawsuit: Turner, "Pacifists Balked in Napalm Fight." In New York, anti-napalm protesters picketed Witco's annual meeting. See Brandt, *Growth Company,* 353.

30. Production: Prokosch, *The Technology of Killing,* 129–130. Tchaikovsky: ibid., 130. Empty cases, Manganiello: Franklin, *Vietnam and Other Fantasies,* 85. See Eric

Prokosch, "Napalm Arrests," *Stanford Daily,* May 17, 1966. And Eric Prokosch as Emanuel Gordon, "Napalm Foes Arrested, Decision Expected," *Stanford Daily,* May 18, 1966.

31. Turner, "Pacifists Balked in Napalm Fight." †

32. Ibid. †

33. Dow: Prokosch, *The Technology of Killing,* 131. Signs: Tom Wicker, "New Left on Coast, Like Radical Right, Denounces Liberalism," *New York Times,* May 29, 1966. See Tom Wicker, "In the Nation; People and Trucks," *New York Times,* May 23, 1989. *Tribune:* Colaianni, "Napalm: Made in U.S.A.," 50. †

34. Douglas Robinson, "Dow Chemical Office Picketed for Its Manufacture of Napalm," *New York Times,* May 29, 1966. See Brandt, *Growth Company,* 253. Torrance: Brandt, *Growth Company,* 354. †

35. Brandt, *Growth Company,* 354. See David Maraniss, *They Marched into Sunlight: War and Peace Vietnam and America October 1967* (Simon & Schuster, 2004), 70.

36. *The War at Home.* Directed by Glenn Silber and Barry Alexander Brown (Catalyst Media, 1979), at 13′43″.

37. Memo: Maraniss, *They Marched into Sunlight,* 71. Staff: Brandt, *Growth Company,* 253. Wakefield: Robinson, "Dow Chemical Office Picketed." Doan: Herbert D. Doan, "Why Does Dow Chemical Make Napalm?" *Wall Street Journal,* December 8, 1967, p. 18. †

38. Kennedy: William F. Pepper, "The Children of Vietnam," *Ramparts* 5, no. 7 (January 1967), 58–59. Splashing: Brandt, *Growth Company,* 352. See Robert S. McNamara in Doan, "Why Does Dow Chemical Make Napalm?" p. 18. †

39. Protests subsided: Hersh, *Chemical and Biological Warfare,* 261. Opening day of school: Wells, *The War Within,* 85 n. 53. But see Fred W. McDarrah, "Balloon Happening in Grand Central," *GettyImages.com,* January 8, 1967. Available at http://www.gettyimages.com/detail/news-photo/view-of-signs-suspended-from-balloons-in-grand-central-news-photo/103094001 (accessed October 8, 2012).

40. Committee of Responsibility for Treatment in the United States of War-Burned Vietnamese Children: Pepper, "The Children of Vietnam," 87. See Wells, *The War Within,* 87. Two patients: Neil Sheehan, "Grim Sidelight of Vietnamese War: Civilian Hospital at Cantho," *New York Times,* June 6, 1966. Peace march: Nancy Zaroulis and Gerald Sullivan, *Who Spoke Up? American Protest against the War in Vietnam, 1963–1975* (Doubleday & Co., 1984), 91. †

## 8. Seeing Is Believing

1. *Ramparts* circulation: "Magazines: A Bomb in Every Issue," *Time,* January 6, 1967. *Ladies Home Journal* circulation: Robert E. Bedingfeld, "Curtis Publishing Sells 2 Magazines; Downe Paying $5.4-Million in Stock," *New York Times,* August 15, 1968. *Redbook* circulation: Kathleen L. Endres and Therese L. Lueck, eds. *Women's Periodicals in the United States: Consumer Magazines* (Greenwood Press, 1995), 303–304.

2. Pepper was also executive director of the Commission on Human Rights based in New Rochelle, New York. William F. Pepper, "The Children of Vietnam," *Ramparts* 5, no. 7 (January 1967), 46, 55, 58, 59, 60. †

3. Martha Gellhorn, "Suffer the Little Children . . . ," *Ladies Home Journal,* January 1967, p. 108. †

4. Ibid., 108–109. See Nancy Zaroulis and Gerald Sullivan, *Who Spoke Up? American Protest against the War in Vietnam, 1963–1975* (Doubleday & Co., 1984), 108.

5. Gellhorn, "Suffer the Little Children," 108.

6. Bewildered eyes: Richard E. Perry with Robert J. Levin, "Where the Innocent Die," *Redbook,* January 1967, p. 103. †

7. Howard A. Rusk, "Vietnam Tour I; Reports of Many Children Burned by American Napalm Are Challenged," *New York Times,* March 12, 1967. See Howard A. Rusk, "Vietnam Tour II; Effects of American Medical Effort on Health Service and Disease Assayed," *New York Times,* March 19, 1967. David Maraniss, *They Marched into Sunlight: War and Peace Vietnam and America October 1967* (Simon & Schuster, 2004), 72–74. E. N. Brandt, *Growth Company: Dow Chemical's First Century* (Michigan State University Press, 1997), 357–358. Malvern Lumsden, *Napalm and Incendiary Weapons: Legal and Humanitarian Aspects* (Stockholm International Peace Research Institute, 1972), 49, 49–52. †

8. King: David J. Garrow, *Bearing the Cross: Martin Luther King, Jr., and the Southern Christian Leadership Conference* (William Morrow, 1986), 543. McNamara's office: Zaroulis and Sullivan, *Who Spoke Up?,* 103.

9. Wisconsin: The first antiwar protests took place in mid-October 1963, according to Paul Soglin. See *The War at Home.* Directed by Glenn Silber and Barry Alexander Brown (Catalyst Media, 1979), at 5'35". Haslach: ibid., at 33'30". Bailed out: Maraniss, *They Marched into Sunlight,* 235–235. Over 1,000: ibid., 487. See Zaroulis and Sullivan, *Who Spoke Up?,* 106. †

10. *Daily Collegian:* Kenneth J. Heineman, *Campus Wars: The Peace Movement at American State Universities in the Vietnam Era* (New York University Press, 1993), 157. Not fade away: ibid., 180. V.C. acne: Silber and Brown, *The War at Home,* at 33'30". †

11. Jack McGuire, "Napalm Sunday," *WIN Peace & Freedom thru Nonviolent Action* magazine, April 7, 1967, p. 2. See Eric Prokosch, *The Technology of Killing: A Military and Political History of Antipersonnel Weapons* (Zed Books, 1995), 131.

12. Spiritual death: Martin Luther King, "Beyond Vietnam—A Time to Break Silence," April 4, 1967. Available at http://www.americanrhetoric.com/speeches/mlkatimeto breaksilence.htm (accessed October 13, 2012). "Let Us Have Peace": Grant Monument Association, "Grant's Tomb: An Overview. Relief Design," *Grant's Tomb,* http://www.grantstomb.org/ov3.html (accessed October 13, 2012). Denounced: Neal Conan and Tavis Smiley, "The Story of King's 'Beyond Vietnam' Speech," *Talk of the Nation,* March 30, 2010. Available at http://www.npr.org/templates /story/story.php?storyId=125355148&ft=1&f=1045 (accessed October 13, 2012). Peasant-cooking facility: "Fortunes Cookieless," *WIN Peace & Freedom thru Nonviolent Action* magazine, May 12, 1967, p. 13. See Prokosch, *The Technology of Killing,* 132. †

13. Mike Truman, "Dow Run Out of Town," *New Left Notes,* May 1, 1967, p. 2. See Prokosch, *The Technology of Killing,* 131.

14. Truman, "Dow Run Out of Town," 2. †

15. Brandt, *Growth Company,* 356–357. See Prokosch, *The Technology of Killing,* 130. †

16. Physicians for Social Responsibility, "History of Accomplishments," *PSR.org,* http://www.psr.org/about/history-of-accomplishments.html (accessed October 13, 2012). †

17. Peter Reich and Victor W. Sidel, "Napalm," *New England Journal of Medicine* 277, no. 2 (July 13, 1967): 87. "Smoldering": Frank Harvey, "The Air War in Vietnam," *Flying,* November 1966, p. 54. †

18. Victor Sidel, interview with the author, September 3, 2009. †


9. Indicted

1. Inductees: Selective Service System, "History/Records: Induction Statistics," *SSS.gov,* http://www.sss.gov/induct.htm (accessed October 14, 2012). International Voluntary Service: Frances Fitzgerald, *Fire in the Lake: The Vietnamese and the Americans in Vietnam* (Vintage, 1972), 482.

2. *The War at Home.* Directed by Glenn Silber and Barry Alexander Brown (Catalyst Media, 1979), at 36'–43'. David Maraniss, *They Marched into Sunlight: War and Peace Vietnam and America October 1967* (Simon & Schuster, 2004), 363–369. Injuries: "Ire against Fire," *Time,* November 3, 1967. First use of tear gas on a U.S. college campus: Nancy Zaroulis and Gerald Sullivan, *Who Spoke Up? American Protest against the War in Vietnam, 1963–1975* (Doubleday & Co., 1984), 106. Number of articles about Dow: Maraniss, *They Marched Into Sunlight,* 487. †

3. Best weapon: "Flame Considered Best Weapon Used in Pacific," Associated Press, September 24, 1945, in Harvard University Archives, Papers of Louis Frederick Fieser and Mary Peters Fieser (hereafter Fieser Papers), HUGFP 20.3 Box 4, "Scrapbook 1937–1960," n.p.. Commentary: See the transcript of *Two Days in October.* Directed by Robert Kenner (Robert Kenner Films, 2005). Available at http://www.pbs.org/wgbh/amex/twodays/filmmore/pt.html (accessed October 14, 2012). †

4. Protests: "Napalm: Dow Bows Out," *Newsweek,* December 1, 1969, p. 78. Universities: Gerd Wilcke, "Dow Will Ignore Campus Protests: Napalm Maker Reports Its Recruiting Unaffected," *New York Times,* October 27, 1967. Forty-six protests: Anthony Ripley, "Napalm Protests Worrying Dow, though Company Is Unhurt," *New York Times,* December 11, 1967. Fifty-five protests in 1966–1967 to 133 in 1967–1968: E. N. Brandt, *Growth Company: Dow Chemical's First Century* (Michigan State University Press, 1997), 355–356. Dow reported 133 protests in the 1967–1968 school year and twenty-nine in the 1968–1969 school year. Jerry Flint, "Napalm Bid Lost, Dow Still Target; It Expects Further Protests Despite Contract End," *New York Times,* November 23, 1969. 339 campus visits in 1967–1968: "Napalm: Dow Bows Out," 78. In 1970, Dow chairman Carl Gerstacker said the company had faced "221 major anti-Dow demonstrations" on U.S. campuses since 1967: 217 in 1967–1969 and four that year. Robert J. Cole, "'Keep Your Cool,' Dow Advises Targets of Antiwar Protesters," *New York Times,* June 4, 1970. Maraniss says there "had been more than 100 campus protests against Dow in the year since" October 1966. Maraniss, *They Marched into Sunlight,* 487. Zaroulis and Sullivan counted twenty cam-

pus demonstrations in 1967, most led by local chapters of Students for a Democratic Society. Zaroulis and Sullivan, *Who Spoke Up?*, 106. †

5. Wilcke, "Dow Will Ignore Campus Protests." Doan: see "Ire against Fire."

6. 0.5 percent: Wilcke, "Dow Will Ignore Campus Protests." See "Ire against Fire." Absolute production: Wilcke, "Dow Will Ignore Campus Protests." †

7. Leaflets: "Students Will Protest Dow Chemical Today," *Harvard Crimson,* October 25, 1967, http://www.thecrimson.com/article/1967/10/25/students-will-protest-dow-chemical-today/ (accessed October 14, 2012). "Genocide": W. Bruce Springer, "300 Stage Sit-In at Mallinckrodt Hall to Halt Dow Chemical Recruitment: Glimp Warns 'Severance' Is Possible for Leaders," *Harvard Crimson,* October 26, 1967, http://www.thecrimson.com/article/1967/10/26/300-stage-sit-in-at-mallinck rodt-hall/ (accessed October 14, 2012). Laboratories: Harvard University, "Conant Chemistry Laboratory" and "Converse Chemistry Laboratory," http://www.uis .harvard.edu/harvard_directory/bldgs/bldg.php (accessed October 14, 2012). Demonstration: Springer, "300 Stage Sit-In." Longest ordeal: Brandt, *Growth Company,* 361. "Dow has become anathema to anti-war groups because of its production of napalm. The substance is intended to burn out jungle overgrowth, but it falls all too often on Vietnamese civilians," the editorial board wrote. "A Justified Demonstration," *Harvard Crimson,* October 26, 1967, http://www.thecrimson.com/article /1967/10/26/a-justified-demonstration-pyesterdays-sit-in-demonstration/ (accessed October 14, 2012). A minority opinion signed by fourteen staff members appeared on October 27: "But the protest was irrelevant and inappropriate since a change in Dow's policies will not stop the war or even obstruct the use of napalm. If Dow suddenly refused to manufacture napalm, there are dozens of companies that would vie for the government contract to carry on production." Boisfeuillet Jones Jr. et al., "The Wrong Way to Peace: On the Other Hand," *Harvard Crimson,* October 27, 1967. †

8. Delegation: "Napalm Inventor Discounts 'Guilt': Harvard Chemist Would 'Do It Again' for the Country," *New York Times,* December 27, 1967. Adams for U.S. Senate Committee, Citizens Campaign against Napalm (Brooklyn N.Y.), Student Nonviolent Coordinating Committee (SNCC), Students for a Democratic Society, Massachusetts Political Action for Peace (PAX), "Can You Support Naplam Used against Children?" in Fieser Papers, HUGFP 20.3 Box 7.

9. E. J. Corey, "Remarks," *Louis Frederick Fieser 1899–1977,* pamphlet, October 7, 1977, in Fieser Papers, HUGFP 20.3 Box 1, Folder: "Louis Fieser—Bibliographic Material," p. 10. See Walter Sullivan, "Cigarettes Peril Health, U.S. Report Concludes; 'Remedial' Action Urged: Cancer Link Cited, Smoking Is Also Found 'Important' Cause of Chronic Bronchitis," *New York Times,* January 12, 1964, in Fieser Papers, HUGFP 20.3 Box 6, "Scrapbook," n.p. And Marjorie Hunter, "U.S. Names Panel to Study Smoking," *New York Times,* October 28, 1962, in Fieser Papers, HUGFP 20.3 Box 6, "Scrapbook," n.p. †

10. President Harry Truman, "Certificate of Merit . . . for outstanding fidelity and meritorious conduct in aid of the war effort against the common enemies of the United States and its allies in World War II," March 1, 1948, Medal for Merit Board, in Fieser

Papers, HUGFP 20.3 Box 4, "Scrapbook 1937–1960," n.p. Letters: "The Professors," *Time,* January 5, 1968. Bum: see "Napalm Inventor Discounts 'Guilt.'" †

11. Bright line: John Lannan, "Napalm Inventor Honored at Harvard: Fieser 'Couldn't forsee its use against babies'" [no publication listed], November 1967, in Fieser Papers, HUGFP 20.3 Box 7. Folder: "Louis Fieser—Retirement Dinner, 1967." Unforseeable: see "Napalm Inventor Discounts 'Guilt.'" No judging: see "The Professors." Napalm plans: Louis Fieser, "Comments about the Day (My Day, Nov. 10, 1967)," November 10, 1967, in Fieser Papers, HUGFP 20.3 Box 1, Folder: "Louis Fieser— Retirement Dinner, 1967." Silenced: James J. Bohning, "Interview with Hoyt C. Hottel at Massachusetts Institute of Technology. 18 November and 2 December 1985." Oral History Transcript #0025. 2010. Chemical Heritage Foundation, p. 19.

12. Hometown newspaper: "Louis Fieser Retires from Harvard Faculty," *Belmont Citizen,* July 27, 1967, in Fieser Papers, HUGFP 20.3 Box 7. Williams: "Neilson Chair at Smith for Harvard Chemist," *Williams Alumni Review,* February 1968, Fieser Papers, HUGFP 20.3 Box 7. Eulogies: *Louis Frederick Fieser, 1899–1977,* October 7, 1977, in Fieser Papers, HUGFP 20.3 Box 1, Folder: "Louis Fieser—Biographical Materials," p. 14. Zeal: Corey, "Remarks," 9. Bibliography: Marshall Gates, "Louis Frederick Fieser, April 7, 1899–July 25, 1977: A Biographical Memoir," in *Biographical Memoirs, Volume 65* (National Academy Press, 1994), 165. Available at http:// books.nap.edu/openbook.php?record_id=4548&page=169 (accessed October 14, 2012). Laboratory: President and Fellows of Harvard College, "Moving to the Head of the Class: Renovation Project Creates World-Class Chemistry Lab for Students," *Harvard University Gazette,* December 12, 1996. See Robert D. Simoni, Robert L. Hill, Martha Vaughan, and Herbert Tabor, "Contributions of Organic Chemists to Biochemistry: Louis F. Fieser, Mary Fieser, and Max Tishler," *The Journal of Biological Chemistry* 278 (December 26, 2003): e4–e6. And Fieser Papers, HUGFP 20.3 Box 1, Folder: "Fieser Laboratory Dedication Correspondence, 1996." †

13. Publication continued until March 25, 1969. Brandt, *Growth Company,* 355. See E. N. Brandt, *Chairman of the Board: A Biography of Carl A. Gerstacker* (Michigan State University Press, 2003), 97.

14. Howard Zinn, *Dow Shalt Not Kill* (Boston University/B.U. News rpt., n.d.), in Southern Student Organizing Committee, *The New South Student,* December 1967, 3, 4, 6. Zinn dropped napalm bombs on the town of Royan in German-occupied France in April 1945. Howard Zinn, Mike Konopacki, and Paul Buhle, *A People's History of American Empire: A Graphic Adaptation* (Henry Holt & Co., 2008), 129– 132. Petition: "House Committee on Armed Services, Records of the Committee on Armed Services, 80th–90th Congresses (1947–68). RG 233. 4.95." *National Archives and Records Administration,* http://www.archives.gov/legislative/guide/house /chapter-04-armed-services.html (accessed October 14, 2012). †

15. Watson: "Napalm—a Useful but Not a Pretty Weapon; Arsenal of Weapons," *New York Times,* December 10, 1967. Alumni: See Seymour M. Hersh, *Chemical and Biological Warfare: America's Hidden Arsenal* (The Bobbs-Merrill Company, 1968), 262. Pickets: Pam Belluck, "Napalm Disposal Plan Dissolves under Debate, but Shipment Rolls On," *New York Times,* April 15, 1998.

16. "Cal State, SFV and Dow," *New Left Notes,* December 18, 1967, p. 3. †

17. Image: Hersh, *Chemical and Biological Warfare,* 261. Creative men: Ripley, "Napalm Protests Worrying Dow." Quality: Hersh, *Chemical and Biological Warfare,* 261. Gas: Nathaniel Freedland, "How Now, Dow?" *Los Angeles Times,* January 14, 1968, p. B8. Bidding high: Hersh, *Chemical and Biological Warfare,* 261. Clarification: "Dow Seeks to Deny It Might Get Out of Napalm Business," *New York Times,* November 23, 1967.

18. "Napalm Protest," *The Times,* May 9, 1968. Kenneth C. Field, "Dow Chemical Meeting Backs Production of Napalm; Antiwar Protestors Rebuffed," *Wall Street Journal,* May 9, 1968, p. 4. Brandt says 300 protesters gathered. Brandt, *Chairman of the Board,* 99.

19. Field, "Dow Chemical Meeting Backs Production of Napalm," p. 4. See Brandt, *Growth Company,* 358–360. And Brandt, *Chairman of the Board,* 99.

20. Homemade napalm: Daniel Berrigan, *The Trial of the Catonsville Nine* (Beacon Press, 1970), vii. See "Clergy: The Berrigan Brothers: They Rob Draft Boards," *Time,* June 7, 1968. Field, "Dow Chemical Meeting Backs Production of Napalm," p. 4. †

21. Actions: Marilyn Julius, *Fire and Faith: The Catonsville Nine File* (Enoch Pratt Free Library, 2005). See Andrea Seabrook, "Fire Sparked Push to End Vietnam War," *All Things Considered,* May 17, 2008, *NPR.org,* http://www.npr.org/templates/story /story.php?storyId=90433944 (accessed October 14, 2012). Testimonials: Berrigan, *The Trial of the Catonsville Nine,* 33, 44–45, 65–66, 93. Denouement: The brothers appeared on the cover of *Time* magazine in June 1971. Daniel Lewis, "Philip Berrigan, Former Priest and Peace Activist in the Vietnam War Era, Dies at 79," *New York Times,* December 7, 2002. A judge found the protesters guilty on each of three counts—destruction of U.S. property, destruction of Selective Service records, and interference with the Selective Service Act of 1967—and sentenced them to prison terms of between two and three years. Berrigan, *The Trial of the Catonsville Nine,* vii. See Joe Tropea, "Hit and Stay: The Catonsville Nine and Baltimore Four Actions Revisited," *Baltimore City Paper,* May 14, 2008. And Joe Tropea and Skizz Cyzyk, "Five Minute Work-in-Progress Trailer," *Hit & Stay.* Available at http:// www.HitAndStay.com/ (accessed October 14, 2012). Dow D.C. offices: "5 Priests among 9 Seized in Dow Protest in Capital," *New York Times,* March 23, 1969. "9 Dow Protesters Charged in Capital," *New York Times,* March 25, 1969. Zaroulis and Sullivan, *Who Spoke Up?,* 107. Papers four inches deep: Brandt, *Growth Company,* 360. 91 percent: ibid., 351. †

22. Brandt, *Growth Company,* 203–204. †

23. Announcement: "Dow Declares It Has Stopped Production of Napalm for U.S," *New York Times,* November 15, 1969. Jerry Flint, "Napalm Bid Lost, Dow Still Target," *New York Times,* November 23, 1969. American Electric: Robert A. Wright, "New Napalm Pact Stirs Coastal Town: Homeowners and War Foes Protesting Production," *New York Times,* December 2, 1969. City Investing: "Dow Drops Napalm," *Time,* November 28, 1969. Denials: see "Napalm: Dow Bows Out," 78. †

24. Notre Dame: see "Dow Drops Napalm." Flint, "NAPALM BID LOST." See Troy Kehoe, "Vietnam Era Protesters Return to Notre Dame to Mark Solemn Anniversary," *WSBT,* November 18, 2009. *Crimson:* Brandt, *Growth Company,* 360; and Robert

J. Cole, "'Keep Your Cool,' Dow Advises Targets of Antiwar Protesters," *New York Times,* June 4, 1970. Shareholders: Brandt, *Growth Company,* 361. †

25. Vilified: John S. DeMott, "Welcome, America, to the Baby Bust," *Time,* February 23, 1987. See John Bussey, "Softer Approach: Dow Chemical Tries to Shed Tough Image and Court the Public—It Pushes Its Ad Campaign, Gives Data to Regulators, Backs Ecological Moves—But Has It Really Changed?" *Wall Street Journal,* November 20, 1987: "Dow still gets questions about napalm, even though it stopped making the flammable gel 17 years ago." Most hated: "America's Most-Hated Companies: A Roll-Call of Commercial Vilification," *Economist,* December 24, 2005. War machine: Tom Engelhardt, "Tomgram: Nick Turse, Back to the Future with the Complex?" *TomDispatch.com,* December 15, 2008, http://www.tomdispatch .com/post/175014 (accessed October 14, 2012). See Justin Engel, "'Mad Men' again References Dow Corning, Napalm . . . or Did They?" *MLive,* June 4, 2012, http:// www.mlive.com/entertainment/saginaw/index.ssf/2012/06/mad_men_again_refer ences_dow_c.html (accessed October 14, 2012).

26. Homeowners lost: Robert A. Wright, "New Napalm Pact Stirs Coastal Town: Homeowners and War Foes Protesting Production," *New York Times,* December 2, 1969. †

27. Tom Wells, *The War Within: America's Battle over Vietnam* (University of California Press, 1994), 532.

28. Fox Butterfield, "South Vietnamese Drop Napalm on Own Troops," *New York Times,* June 9, 1972.

29. Danh's nine-month-old brother died six weeks later from his injuries. These were the only civilian fatalities from the napalm strike. Denise Chong, *The Girl in the Picture: The Story of Kim Phuc, the Photograph, and the Vietnam War* (Penguin Books, 1999), 75, 83. See "Vietnam Napalm," *ITN.* Available at http://www.you tube.com/watch?v=Ev2dEqrN4i0&feature=related (accessed October 14, 2012), at 1'14".

30. Chong, *The Girl in the Picture,* 78–79.

31. Ibid., 83–84. Barsky: David W. Dunlap, "Dr. Arthur Barsky Dies at 83; a Plastic Surgeon in Vietnam," *New York Times,* February 11, 1982. Miller: "Tom Miller," *Milwaki.com,* http://milwaki.com/our-staff/attorneys/tom-miller/ (accessed October 14, 2012). Journalists Christopher Wain and Michael Blakey also helped transfer Kim from the First Children's Hospital. Chong, *The Girl in the Picture,* 79–80. See Annick Cojean, "'La fille de la photo' sort du cliché," *M le magazine du Monde,* June 17, 2012. And Rob Gilles, "Woman in AP 'Napalm Photo' Honors Her Saviors," Associated Press, June 8, 2012.

32. Chong, *The Girl in the Picture,* 95. See Associated Press, "Napalmed Girl Recovering in Saigon," *New York Times,* August 9, 1972.

33. Chong, *The Girl in the Picture,* 104–105. Elizabeth Omara-Otunnu, "Napalm Survivor Tells of Healing after Vietnam War," *University of Connecticut Advance,* November 8, 2004. †

34. Failing war: David Neiman, Producer. "Battlefield: Vietnam. Timeline 1969–1972." *Battlefield: Vietnam* n.d., http://www.pbs.org/battlefieldvietnam/timeline/index3.html (accessed October 14, 2012). Earlier photos: As Robert Hariman and John Louis

Lucaites, professors of rhetoric and communications, respectively, observed, "Indeed, by 1972 the public had seen burned skin hanging in shreds from Vietnamese babies." Hariman and Lucaites, "Public Identity and Collective Memory in U.S. Iconic Photography: The Image of 'Accidental Napalm,' " *Critical Studies in Media Communication* 20, no. 1 (March 2003), 40, 44.

35. Last troops: David Neiman, "Battlefield: Vietnam. Timeline 1973–1975." *Battlefield: Vietnam,* n.d. http:// www.pbs.org/battlefieldvietnam/timeline/index4.html (accessed October 14, 2012). Fallbrook: Belluck, "Napalm Disposal Plan Dissolves under Debate." 34,653 canisters: Gidget Fuentes, "Navy Prepares New Life for Napalm Storage Site," *North County Times,* April 5, 2001 (67 acres). Defeat: Joseph Treaster, "U. S. Forces out of Vietnam; Hanoi Frees the Last P.O.W.; War Role Is Ended after Decade of Controversy," *New York Times,* March 30, 1973.

## Pariah

1. Gross revenues: "Apocalypse Now," *Box Office Mojo,* September 15, 2012. Available at http://boxofficemojo.com/movies/?id=apocalypsenow.htm (accessed October 14, 2012). †

2. John Milius and Francis Ford Coppola, *Apocalypse Now.* Directed by Francis Ford Coppola (American Zoetrope, 1979).

3. John Milius and Francis Ford Coppola, *Apocalypse Now Redux.* Directed by Francis Ford Coppola (American Zoetrope, 2001).

4. Enemy on the bombed hill "slipped out in the night," according to the script. John Milius and Francis Ford Coppola, *Apocalypse Now,* December 3, 1975, pp. 44–99. Available at www.dailyscript.com/scripts/apocolypse.html (accessed October 14, 2012).

## 10. Baby Burners

1. Many other commenters in countries around the world offered contemporaneous criticisms of napalm. See, for example, Bettina L. Knapp, "Reviewed Work(s): *Napalm* by André Benedetto," *Books Abroad* 43, no. 4 (Autumn 1969): 557. Perversions: J. G. Ballard, *Love and Napalm: Export U.S.A.* (Grove Press, 1972 [1969]), 132–133. See Paul Theroux, *"Love and Napalm; Export U.S.A.* by J. G. Ballard. Preface by William S. Burroughs," *New York Times,* October 29, 1972. †

2. Golub: Grace Glueck, "Art Review; A Hostile Witness to the Inhumanity of the Human Condition," *New York Times,* May 25, 2001. See Leonard Golub, "Napalm Head," oil on canvas, 1969, Smithsonian American Art Museum, http://americanart .si.edu/collections/search/artwork/?id=9266 (accessed October 14, 2012); "Napalm V," acrylic on canvas, http://americanart.si.edu/collections/search/artwork/?id=74688 (accessed October 14, 2012); "Napalm I," acrylic on linen, 1969, Ronald Feldman Fine Arts, http://www.artnet.com/artwork/424482952/373/leon-golub-napalm-i .html (accessed October 14, 2012). Baranik: Roberta Smith, "Rudolf Baranik Dies at 77; Artist and a Political Force," *New York Times,* March 15, 1998.

3. Mark Lane, "The Covered Wagon: Finding the Power to Affect our Destinies," in Covered Wagon Musicians, "Liner Notes," *We Say No to Your War!* (Paredon Records, 1972). Available at http://folklife-media01.si.edu/liner_notes/paredon/PAR01015.pdf (accessed October 14, 2012).

4. John Boychuck, "Napalm Sticks to Kids," in Covered Wagon Musicians, *We Say No to Your War!* †

5. McCarthy: Richard Corliss, "Eugene McCarthy: 1916–2005," *Time,* December 12, 2005. Williams: "Human Beings Fused Together," *Time,* October 23, 1972. See Christopher Lydon, "G.I.'s Regret Stuns a M'Govern Rally; Tape by a Vietnam Veteran Played by Democrat for Minnesota Students," *New York Times,* October 13, 1972.

6. Bob Parker, "Chemicals and People Sniffers," in Matthew Brennan, ed. *Hunter-Killer Squadron: Aero-Weapons, Aero-Scouts, Aero-Rifles, Vietnam 1965–1972* (Presidio, 1990), 245.

7. Philip Caputo, *A Rumor of War* (Henry Holt and Company, 1996 [1977]), 4. Robert Yeo, *And Napalm Does Not Help* (Heinemann Educational Books [Asia], 1977), 6.

8. Over thirty albums: See "Napalm Death Discography," http://en.wikipedia.org /wiki/Napalm_Death_discography (accessed October 14, 2012). See *Napalm Death,* http://napalmdeath.org (accessed October 14, 2012). Choosing the name: Albert Mudrian and John Peel, *Choosing Death: The Improbable History of Death Metal and Grindcore* (Feral House, 2004), 27. Mark "Barney" Greenway, "NAPALM DEATH bandname," correspondence with the author, July 17, 2012. Corporations: Nicholas Bullen, Napalm Death, "Multinational Corporations," *Rock Lyrics,* http://www.rockalyrics.com/125-1237-14390/napalm-death/death-by-manipula tion/multinational-corporations-lyrics.html (accessed October 14, 2012). Portland: "Wehrmacht (band)," http://en.wikipedia.org/wiki/Wehrmacht_(band) (accessed October 14, 2012). Wehrmacht, "Napalm Shower," *LyricsTime,* http://www.lyrics time.com/wehrmacht-napalm-shower-lyrics.html (accessed October 14, 2012). See "Wehrmacht Napalm Shower Live at The Dynamo 2010," http://www.youtube .com/watch?v=SXO=BoMLQkA (accessed October 14, 2012). "About Us," *Napalm Records,* www.napalmrecords.com/napalm_bio.php?osCsid=fad7f797fa15446e34 866a7398c6d0a3 (accessed October 14, 2012).

9. "Nay-pom": William Boyd, *On the Yankee Station: Stories by William Boyd* (William Morrow and Company, 1984), 123. Bruce Weigl, *Song of Napalm: Poems* (Atlantic Monthly Press, 1988), 34–35. †

10. "Mentions of 'Napalm' 1945–2010." 2011: http://Query.NYTimes.com (accessed June, 2011). *Los Angeles Times,* "Mentions of 'Napalm' 1945–2010." 2011: *Los Angeles Times.* http://ProQuest.UMI.edu (accessed June, 2011). There was no peak in the 1950s, which suggests that the *New York Times* covered napalm usage in Korea more closely than most. Google NGram Viewer. "napalm." 2012. http://books.google.com /ngrams/graph?content=napalm&year_start=1940&year_end=2012&corpus =0&smoothing=3 (accessed October 14, 2012). †

11. Douglas Day Stewart, *An Officer and a Gentleman,* 28. Available at http://www .dailyscript.com/scripts/officerandgentleman.pdf (accessed October 14, 2012). Gross

revenues: "An Officer and a Gentleman," *Box Office Mojo,* 2012, http://www.boxof ficemojo.com/movies/?id=officerandagentleman.htm (accessed October 14, 2012). Worldwide revenue figures are not available and are estimated at approximately twice domestic revenues. Naomi Foner Gyllenhaal, *Running on Empty.* Directed by Sidney Lumet (Warner Brothers, 1988). †

12. Gross revenues: "Platoon," *Box Office Mojo,* 2012, http://www.boxofficemojo.com /movies/?id=platoon.htm (accessed October 14, 2012). Worldwide revenue figures are not available and are estimated at approximately twice domestic revenues. Audience estimated at $5 in revenue per viewer. *Flight of the Intruder,* a 1991 thriller about a Vietnam War bomber pilot directed by *Apocalypse Now* coauthor John Milius also included a climactic napalm strike at the end of the film but showed the fire cloud only from above and without particular commentary. Robert Dillon and David Sha-ber, *Flight of the Intruder.* Directed by John Milius (Paramount Pictures, 1991).

13. Eric Roth and Winston Groom, *Forrest Gump.* Available at http://www.imsdb.com /scripts/Forrest-Gump.html (accessed October 14, 2012). Gross revenues: "Forrest Gump," *Box Office Mojo,* 2012, http://www.boxofficemojo.com/movies/?id=forrestgump .htm (accessed October 14, 2012). †

14. Jack Kelley, "Stash of Napalm Has Met Its Match," *USA Today,* May 21, 1993. †

15. Film: Jim Uhls, *Fight Club.* Directed by David Fincher (20th Century Fox, 1999). The script uses slightly different language. Jim Uhls, *Fight Club.* Available at http:// www.imsdb.com/scripts/Fight-Club.html (accessed October 14, 2012). Book: Chuck Palahniuk, *Fight Club* (Henry Holt and Company, 1996), 11–13. †

16. Kissing: Michiko Kakutani, "Books of the Times; The Unconventional and the Unloved in an Urban Mosaic," *New York Times,* June 29, 2001. Napalm Stars: Ste-gall established the band in 2000. The line came from a song by UK band The Clash on their 1980 album *Sandinista!:* "Charlie don't surf for his hamburger mama/ He's gonna be a napalm star." Ronnie, "Napalm Stars," *Ear Candy,* http://members.tri pod.com/earcandy_mag/napalmstars.htm (accessed October 14, 2012).

17. Gloves coming off: Cofer Black, director of the Central Intelligence Agency's Counterterrorist Center 1999–May 2002, testimony before the Joint Investigation into September 11th: Fifth Public Hearing, September 26, 2002—Joint House/Sen-ate Intelligence Committee Hearing. *FAS,* http://www.fas.org/irp/congress/2002 _hr/092602black.html (accessed October 14, 2012). Randall Wallace, *We Were Sol-diers.* Directed by Randall Wallace (Paramount Pictures, 2002). Loblollying: Har-old G. Moore and Joseph L. Galloway, *We Were Soldiers Once . . . and Young: Ia Drang—The Battle that Changed the War in Vietnam* (Ballantine Books, 2004 [1992]), 175, 127. †

18. Moore and Galloway, *We Were Soldiers Once,* 282. Gross revenues: "We Were Sol-diers," *Box Office Mojo,* 2012, http://boxofficemojo.com/movies/?id=weweresoldiers .htm (accessed October 14, 2012).

19. Museum: "Introduction," *The Center of the Tokyo Raid and War Damages,* http:// www.tokyo-sensai.net/english_page/index.html (accessed October 14, 2012). See Jonathan Rauch, "Firebombs over Tokyo," *Atlantic Monthly,* July–August 2002. How-ard W. French, "Tokyo Journal; 100,000 People Perished, but Who Remembers?"

*New York Times,* March 14, 2002. Mari Yamaguchi, "Museum Recalls Tokyo Fire-bombing," Associated Press, March 10, 2002. †

20. John F. Mullins, *Napalm Dreams: A Men of Valor Novel* (Pocket Books, 2004), 68, 67, 69.

21. Jonathan Lemkin, *Shooter.* Directed by Antoine Fuqua (Paramount Pictures, 2007). Gross revenues: "Shooter," *Box Office Mojo,* http://boxofficemojo.com/movies/?id=shooter.htm (accessed October 14, 2012). Rafe Telsch, "DVD Sales: Shooter Knocks Out Competition," *CinemaBlend.com,* http://www.cinemablend.com/dvd news/DVD-Sales-Shooter-Knocks-Out-Competition-5070.html (accessed October 14, 2012).

22. Avant Research: "About Us." http://web.archive.org/web/20091124200716/http://avantresearch.com/about (accessed October 14, 2012). Napalm: http://web.archive.org/web/20100325084642/http://avantresearch.com/products/napalm (accessed October 14, 2012). Nomination: http://web.archive.org/web/20091123134102/http://avantresearch.com/node/47 (accessed October 14, 2012). See AvantLabs.com (accessed October 14, 2012). †

23. Napalm Orange and other colors: "News." (Special Effects, LLC., 2002 rev. 2008), www.specialeffectsusa.com/news.html (accessed October 14, 2012). Testimonials: "Special Effects Napalm Orange Hair Dye," http://www.amphigory.com/se_napalm_orange.html (accessed October 14, 2012).

24. Roger Ebert, "Death Race," *Chicago Sun-Times,* August 21, 2008. Robert Koehler, "Death Race," *Variety,* August 21, 2008. Peter Hartlaub, "Death Race a Bloody Wreck," *San Francisco Chronicle,* August 22, 2008. Gross receipts: "Death Race," *Box Office Mojo,* 2012, http://boxofficemojo.com/movies/?id=deathrace.htm (accessed October 14, 2012). †

25. Thanh Tran, *Napalm.net,* http://www.napalm.net/index.html (accessed October 14, 2012). "Napalm," *Fiastarta.com,* http://www.fiastarta.com/NAPALM/ (accessed October 14, 2012). See "Killzone 2: Napalm & Cordite Pack," Amazon.com, 23 July, 2009, http://www.amazon.com/Killzone-Napalm-Cordite-Add-Playstation-3/dp/B002N2YL8K (accessed October 14, 2012). Rob Taylor, "Mercenaries 2: World in Flames," *CVG.com,* March 14, 2008, http://www.computerandvideogames.com/184801/previews/mercenaries-2-world-in-flames/ (accessed October 14, 2012).

26. Facebook: "NAPALM Fun Club," June 25, 2012, http://www.facebook.com/pages/NAPALM/89993485334?sid=770e6fa1dd0ef56707b789f6828447of&ref=s (accessed October 14, 2012) (4,102 likes). "Napalm," June 25, 2012, http://www.facebook.com/pages/Napalm/4572820241?ref=ts (accessed October 14, 2012) (1,719 likes). Clips change frequently. For the most recent list see http://www.youtube.com/results?search_type=videos&search_query=how+to+make+napalm (accessed October 14, 2012). †

27. *Playboy*: Rob Tannenbaum, "*Playboy* Interview: John Mayer," March 2010. Twitter: CowboyKush, "Results for napalm," February 13, 2010: https://twitter.com/search?q=napalm&src=typd (accessed October 14, 2012). See Ernie S. Irwin, *Cooking with Napalm* (CreateSpace Independent Publishing Platform, 2011); website: http://www.cookwithnapalm.com (accessed October 14, 2012). †

28. "Napalm Dreams," *Amazon.com,* June 12, 2011, http://www.amazon.com/Napalm -Dreams-Men-Valor-Novel/dp/0743477677/ref=sr_1_1?ie=UTF8&s=books&qid =1269636953&sr=1-1 (accessed October 14, 2012).

29. See E-Rick, "The Making of 'The Girl in the Picture' November (Flying Snowman Productions, April 15, 2004). http://www.flyingsnowman.com/modules/news/arti cle.php?storyid=3 (accessed October 14, 2012).

30. Walter Goodman, "'Kim Phuc' and 'Sanctuary' in Double Bill," *New York Times,* December 11, 1985. While a South Vietnamese pilot dropped the napalm that burned Kim, the gel was paid for by the U.S., made in California, dispatched by an American controller, and delivered by a U.S. Douglas Aircraft Company airplane.

31. Disney ranked sixth among all U.S. brands and all brands worldwide in 2004, according to Interbrand. MacDonald's was seventh in both categories. "Best Global Brands: 2004 Ranking of the Top 100 Brands," *Interbrand,* http://www.interbrand .com/en/best-global-brands/previous-years/best-global-brands-2004.aspx (accessed October 14, 2012).

## 11. Trial of Fire

1. 106 states parties to Protocol III: United Nations Office at Geneva (UNOG), "States parties and Signatories," *The Convention on Certain Conventional Weapons* (UNOG, 26 July 2012). Available at http://www.unog.ch/__80256ee600585943 .nsf/(httpPages)/3ce7cfc0aa4a7548c12571c00039cb0c?OpenDocument&Expand Section=2%2C3%2C1%23_Section1#_Section2 (accessed October 14, 2012). †

2. Venture: "La Compagnie génévoise des colonies suisses de Sétif," *CercleAlgerian- iste.asso.fr,* May 24, 2010, http://www.cerclealgerianiste.asso.fr/contenu/autres31 .htm (accessed October 14, 2012). Stiviere: "Biography: Henry Dunant," *NobelPrize .org,* http://www.nobelprize.org/nobel_prizes/peace/laureates/1901/dunant-bio.html (accessed October 14, 2012).

3. Battle: Henry Dunant, *A Memory of Solferino* (ICRC, 1986 [1862]), 4–5. Worse: ibid., 11. Worms: ibid., 14–15. No regard to nationality: ibid., 17. Thousands of beds: ibid., 20.

4. Weary: Dunant, *A Memory of Solferino,* 24. A little relief: ibid., 28. †

5. International Committee of the Red Cross (ICRC), "State Parties," *Convention for the Amelioration of the Condition of the Wounded in Armies in the Field. Geneva, 22 August 1864* (ICRC, 2005). Available at http://www.icrc.org/ihl.nsf/WebSign? ReadForm&id=120&ps=P (accessed October 14, 2012). See "Biography: Henry Dunant." See Dunant, *A Memory of Solferino,* 2, 30. †

6. Gorchakov: D. Schindler and J. Toman, "Introduction: Declaration Renouncing the Use, in Time of War, of Explosive Projectiles under 400 Grammes Weight. Done at Saint Petersburg, 29 November [Gregorian 11 December] 1868," in Schindler and Toman, eds. *The Laws of Armed Conflicts* (Martinus Nihjoff, 1988), 102. Available at http://www.icrc.org/ihl.nsf/FULL/130?OpenDocument (accessed October 14, 2012). Declaration: International Military Commission, *Declaration Renouncing the Use, in Time of War, of Explosive Projectiles under 400 Grammes*

*Weight. Saint Petersburg, 29 November [Gregorian 11 December] 1868,* in Schindler and Toman, *The Laws of Armed Conflicts,* 102. Available at http://www.icrc.org/ihl .nsf/FULL/130?OpenDocument (accessed October 14, 2012). †

7. "A Brief History of the American Red Cross," *RedCross.org,* http://www.redcross .org/about-us/history (accessed October 14, 2012).

8. Five Years: First Peace Conference of The Hague, 1899. *Declaration (IV,1), to Prohibit, for the Term of Five Years, the Launching of Projectiles and Explosives from Balloons, and Other Methods of Similar Nature. The Hague, 29 July 1899* (International Peace Conference, 1899), in Schindler and Toman, *The Laws of Armed Conflicts,* 202–204. Available at http://www.icrc.org/ihl.nsf/FULL/160?OpenDocument (accessed October 14, 2012). "Belligerents": First Peace Conference of The Hague, 1899. *Convention (II) with Respect to the Laws and Customs of War on Land and its annex: Regulations concerning the Laws and Customs of War on Land. The Hague, 29 July 1899* (International Peace Conference, 1899), Art. 22, in Schindler and Toman, *The Laws of Armed Conflicts,* 69–93. Available at http://www.icrc.org /ihl.nsf/FULL/150?OpenDocument (accessed October 14, 2012). "Superfluous injury": ibid., Art. 23(e). Bombardment: ibid., Art. 25. See Philip Noel-Baker, *The Arms Race: A Programme for World Disarmament* (Atlantic Book Publishing Company, 1958), 335. †

9. First Peace Conference of The Hague, *Convention (II) with Respect to the Laws and Customs of War on Land.* "First Peace Conference of The Hague, 1899. *Convention (II) with Respect to the Laws and Customs of War on Land and its Annex: Regulations Concerning the Laws and Customs of War on Land. The Hague, 29 July 1899* (International Peace Conference, 1899). Forty-nine states: Second Peace Conference of The Hague, 1907. *Convention (IV) respecting the Laws and Customs of War on Land and its Annex: Regulations Concerning the Laws and Customs of War on Land. The Hague, 18 October 1907,* Art. 23(e). 36 Stat. 2277. Bevans, *Treaties and Other International Agreements,* 631: "[I]t is especially forbidden. . . . To employ arms, projectiles, or material calculated to cause unnecessary suffering." Available at http://www.icrc.org/ihl.nsf/FULL/195?OpenDocument (accessed October 14, 2012). "Superfluous injury" and "unnecessary suffering" now deemed synonymous: W. Hays Parks, "Means and Methods of Warfare," *George Washington International Law Review* 38 (2006), 516 n. 19. Reiteration of prohibition on balloon bombardments: Second Peace Conference of The Hague, 1907. *Declaration (XIV) Prohibiting the Discharge of Projectiles and Explosives from Balloons. The Hague, 18 October 1907* (International Peace Conference, 1907). In Schindler and Toman, *The Laws of Armed Conflicts,* 202–205. Available at http://www.icrc.org/ihl.nsf/FULL /245?OpenDocument (accessed October 14, 2012). †

10. J. M. Spaight, *Air Power and War Rights,* 2nd ed. (Longmans, Green & Co, 1933), 179. See Frits Kalshoven, *Reflections on the Law of War: Collected Essays* (Koninklijke Brill, 2007), 339–341. †

11. Versailles: "Articles 159–213: Military, Naval and Air Clauses," Richard Hacken and Jane Plotke, eds., *World War I Document Archive* (Brigham Young University, March 26, 2001). Available at http://net.lib.byu.edu/~rdh7/wwi/versa/versa4.html (accessed October 14, 2012). "Table No. II: Tabular Statement of Armament Estab-

lishment for Maximum of Seven Infantry Divisions, Three Cavalry Divisions, and Two Army Corps Headquarter Staffs," ibid. Available at http://net.lib.byu.edu /~rdh7/wwi/versa/chart1.gif (accessed October 14, 2012). Saint-Germain-en-Laye: Australian Department of Foreign Affairs and Trade, *Treaty of Peace between the Allied and Associated Powers and Austria; Protocol, Declaration and Special Declaration (St. Germain-en-Laye, 10 September 1919).* Australian Treaty Series 1920 No. 3. Available at http://austlii.edu.au/au/other/dfat/treaties/1920/3.html (accessed October 14, 2012). Neuilly-sur-Seine and Trianon: "Article 82," *Treaty of Peace between the Allied and Associated Powers and Bulgaria, and Protocol and Declaration signed at Neuilly-sur-Seine, 27 November 1919.* Hacken and Plotke, eds. *World War I Document Archive.* Available at http://wwi.lib.byu.edu/index.php/Treaty_of_Neuilly (accessed October 14, 2012). "Article 119," *Treaty of Peace between the Allied and Associated Powers and Hungary and Protocol and Declaration, Signed at Trianon June 4, 1920.* ibid. Available at http://wwi.lib.byu.edu/index.php/Part_IX_-_X (accessed October 14, 2012). †

12. Proposal: "Article XVIII" (bullets) and "Article XXII" (bombardment), *The Hague Rules of Air Warfare: The Hague, December, 1922–February, 1923.* ibid. Available at http://wwi.lib.byu.edu/index.php/The_Hague_Rules_of_Air_Warfare (accessed October 14, 2012). See Spaight, *Air Power and War Rights,* 42. Malvern Lumsden, *Incendiary Weapons* (MIT Press, 1975), 23. Kalshoven, *Reflections on the Law of War,* 341. †

13. Cruelty: Noel-Baker, *The Arms Race,* 336. Adopted: Lumsden, *Incendiary Weapons,* 24. See Kalshoven, *Reflections on the Law of War,* 343–344. †

14. Germany abandoned the League of Nations the week after it left the disarmament conference. See "Disarmament Conference," in *The Columbia Encyclopedia,* 6th ed. (Columbia University Press, 2000). Also at http://encyclopedia.com/topic/Dis armament_Conference.aspx (accessed October 14, 2012). See "Geneva Conference 1932–1934," *GlobalSecurity.org,* http://www.globalsecurity.org/military/world/na val-arms-control-1932.htm (accessed October 14, 2012). And Spaight, *Air Power and War Rights,* 244–248.

15. Julius Stone, *Legal Controls of International Conflict: A Treatise on the Dynamics of Disputes- and War-Law.* 2nd rev. ed. (Stevens & Sons Ltd. 1959), 43–44. †

16. Guernica: Stone, *Legal Controls of International Conflict,* 625 n. 117. China: ibid. Cranborne, Bodenschatz: Spaight, *Air Power and War Rights,* 271, 270. See Stone, *Legal Controls of International Conflict,* 626. "One might almost say that it has been found necessary to reverse the process by which the Chinese arrived at the secret of roast pork. The cooking could be done, after all, by the burning of the house down," Spaight averred. Spaight, *Air Power and War Rights,* 271. †

17. Precision: United Nations Secretariat (UNS), *Respect for Human Rights in Armed Conflict: Existing Rules of International Law concerning the Prohibition or Restriction of Use of Specific Weapons, Survey Prepared by the Secretariat.* November 7, 1973. UN Doc, A/9215 (Vol. I), 146: 86, 141–142: 72, 146: 86. See Kalshoven, *Reflections on the Law of War,* 148 n. 5. See Malvern Lumsden, *Napalm and Incendiary Weapons: Legal and Humanitarian Aspects* (Stockholm International Peace Research Institute, 1972), 28: "napalm would have stayed outside the proposed definition." †

18. "During the Korean War, the Security Council and the General Assembly tolerated the use of these munitions [including napalm] by the United Nations forces," international legal scholar Henry Meyrowitz wrote in 1969. UNS, *Respect for Human Rights in Armed Conflict,* 142. "Incendiary weapons and napalm in particular were not mentioned in the debate," Dutch scholar Frits Kalshoven observed of the signal 1957 International Red Cross Conference at New Delhi. Kalshoven, *Reflections on the Law of War,* 349.

## 12. The Third Protocol

1. United Nations Secretariat (UNS), *Respect for Human Rights in Armed Conflict: Existing Rules of International Law concerning the Prohibition or Restriction of Use of Specific Weapons, Survey Prepared by the Secretariat.* November 7, 1973. UN Doc. A/9215 (Vol. I), 142: 72. †

2. Teheran: UN, "Organization of the Conference," *Final Act of the International Conference on Human Rights, Teheran, 22 April to 13 May 1968.* 1968. UN Doc. A/ CONF. 32/41, 2:9–14. Available at http://untreaty.un.org/cod/avl/pdf/ha/fatchr/Final _Act_of_TehranConf.pdf (accessed October 14, 2012). See UN, "Annex I: List of Participants," in *Final Act of the International Conference on Human Rights, Teheran,* 21–34. Johnson: Lyndon Johnson, "Message from the President of the United States," in *Final Act of the International Conference on Human Rights, Teheran,* 39. UN, *Resolution XXIII adopted by the International Conference on Human Rights, Teheran, 12 May 1968.* 1968. UN Doc. A/CONF.32/41, 18. See D. Schindler and J. Toman, eds., *The Laws of Armed Conflicts* (Martinus Nihjoff, 1988), 261–262. Available at http://www.icrc.org/ihl.nsf/FULL/430?OpenDocument (accessed October 14, 2012). Richard R. Baxter, "Conventional Weapons under Legal Prohibitions," *International Security* 1, no. 3 (Winter 1977): 45. UN General Assembly (UNGA), *U.N. General Assembly Resolution 2444 (XXIII).* December 19, 1968. United Nations. Available at http://daccess-dds-ny.un.org/doc/RESOLUTION/GEN/NR0 /244/04/IMG/NR024404.pdf?OpenElement (accessed October 14, 2012). †

3. UN Secretary-General, *Respect for Human Rights in Armed Conflicts: Report of the Secretary-General.* November 20, 1969. UN Doc. A/7720, 62–63: 200. The other reports, all with the same title, are UN Docs. A/8052 (September 18, 1970), A/8370 (1971), A/8781 (September 20, 1972), and A/9215 (November 7, 1973). See Baxter, "Conventional Weapons under Legal Prohibitions," 46. And UN Secretary-General, *Respect for Human Rights in Armed Conflicts: Report of the Secretary-General.* September 18, 1970. UN Doc. A/8052, 41: 126.

4. UNGA, *U.N. General Assembly Resolution 2852 (XXVI). Respect for human rights in armed conflicts.* December 20, 1971. Available at http://daccess-dds-ny.un.org /doc/RESOLUTION/GEN/NR0/328/68/IMG/NR032868.pdf?OpenElement (accessed October 14, 2012). See UNGA, *U.N. General Assembly Resolution 2674 (XXV). Respect for human rights in armed conflicts.* December 9, 1970. Available at http:// daccess-dds-ny.un.org/doc/RESOLUTION/GEN/NR0/349/39/IMG/NR034939 .pdf?OpenElement (accessed October 14, 2012). (Air bombardments: 77 in favor, 2

against, 36 abstentions.) And UNGA, *U.N. General Assembly Resolution 2677 (XXV). Respect for human rights in armed conflicts.* December 9, 1970. Available at http:// daccess-dds-ny.un.org/doc/RESOLUTION/GEN/NR0/349/42/IMG/NR034942 .pdf?OpenElement (accessed October 14, 2012). (International law: 111 in favor, 0 against, 4 abstentions.) And Malvern Lumsden, *Incendiary Weapons* (MIT Press, 1975), 84–86, appendix 1C.

5. Experts: Rolf Björnerstedt, "Introductory Note," in UN Consultant Experts on Napalm and Other Incendiary Weapons, *Napalm and Other Incendiary Weapons and All Aspects of Their Possible Use: Report of the Secretary-General, Volume 14, Issue 12* (UN, 1973), iv. J. Ashley Roach, "Certain Conventional Weapons Convention: Arms Control or Humanitarian Law?" *Military Law Review* 105: 10 n. 22. See Robert Alden, "U.N. Committee Urges a Ban on Napalm," *New York Times,* October 18, 1972. Report: Rolf Björnerstedt, "Letter of Transmittal," in UN Consultant Experts, *Napalm,* v. †

6. UN Consultant Experts, *Napalm,* 54: 185, 50: 176, 55: 187. See Sydney D. Bailey, "Book Review," *Survival: Global Politics and Strategy* 15, no. 4: 203 (incendiaries are in general "A major weapon for both tactical and strategic warfare.") †

7. UN Consultant Experts, *Napalm,* 50: 176. †

8. Ibid., 52–53: 183.

9. "Nowadays the meaning of the word 'napalm' has broadened to include . . . all types of thickened hydrocarbons used as incendiary agents," the experts wrote. They did not specify what the narrower definitions might have been. UN Consultant Experts, *Napalm,* 10–11: 31, 51–52: 180, 54: 184. See Louis Fieser, *The Scientific Method: A Personal Account of Unusual Projects in War and in Peace* (Reinhold Publishing Corp., 1964), 29. (The term napalm was "now seen to be nondescriptive": a generic for any incendiary made from thickened petroleum.)

10. UN Consultant Experts, *Napalm,* 55: 190, 56: 193. The report did not specifically mention Vietnam. Alden, "U.N. Committee Urges a Ban on Napalm." †

11. "U.N. Unit Deplores the use of Napalm," *New York Times,* November 17, 1972. †

12. A final provision required the secretary-general to circulate the report among member states and present their comments to the General Assembly the following year. This ensured napalm remained a subject of discussion. UNGA, *Resolution 2932 (XXVII). General and complete disarmament.* November 29, 1972. Available at http:// daccess-dds-ny.un.org/doc/RESOLUTION/GEN/NR0/269/62/IMG/NR026962 .pdf?OpenElement (accessed October 14, 2012). UN, *Respect for Human Rights in Armed Conflict: Existing Rules of International Law,* 145: 82. †

13. See Second Peace Conference of The Hague, *Convention (IV) respecting the Laws and Customs of War on Land and its annex: Regulations concerning the Laws and Customs of War on Land. The Hague, 18 October 1907,* Art. 23(e) in D. Schindler and J. Toman, *The Laws of Armed Conflicts* (Martinus Nijhoff, 1988), pp. 69–93. Available at http://www.icrc.org/ihl.nsf/FULL/195?OpenDocument (accessed October 14, 2012). "[I]t is especially forbidden . . . to employ arms, projectiles, or material calculated to cause unnecessary suffering." Baxter, "Conventional Weapons under Legal Prohibitions," 48. †

14. UN, *Respect for Human Rights in Armed Conflict: Existing Rules of International Law,* November 7, 1973, UN Document A/9215, Vol. I, 145: 82–83.

15. International Committee of the Red Cross (ICRC), *International Review of the Red Cross* 153 (December 1973): 627, 654. Available at http://www.loc.gov/rr/frd/Military_Law/pdf/RC_Dec-1973.pdf (accessed October 14, 2012). Baxter, "Conventional Weapons under Legal Prohibitions," 50.

16. The resolution was adopted on November 15, 1973. ICRC, *International Review of the Red Cross* 153 (December 1973), 627, 654. †

17. UNGA, *Napalm and Other Incendiary Weapons and All Aspects of their Possible Use: 3076 (XXVIII).* December 6, 1973. Available at http://daccess-dds-ny.un.org/doc/RESOLUTION/GEN/NR0/281/48/IMG/NR028148.pdf?OpenElement.

18. ICRC, "Resolution 22: Follow-up regarding Prohibition or Restriction of Use of Certain Conventional Weapons," in *Resolutions of the Diplomatic Conference of Geneva of 1974–1977.* June 9, 1977 (ICRC, Geneva). Available at http://www.icrc.org/ihl.nsf/WebART/480-770006?OpenDocument (accessed October 14, 2012).

19. U.S. participation: Baxter, "Conventional Weapons under Legal Prohibitions," 50. ICRC, *Conference of Government Experts on the Use of Certain Conventional Weapons (Lucerne, 24.9–18.10.1974): Report.* 1975 (ICRC, Geneva), 27: 85. Hereafter *Lucerne.* Available at http://www.loc.gov/rr/frd/Military_Law/pdf/RC-conf-experts-1974.pdf (accessed October 14, 2012). †

20. ICRC, *Lucerne,* 31: 101–102.

21. Nature of the target: ICRC, *Lucerne,* 31–32: 103–104. Thing of the past: ibid., 19: 57. Discriminate use: ibid., 31: 104. See Frits Kalshoven, *Reflections on the Law of War: Collected Essays* (Koninklijke Brill, 2007), 163: "[napalm] contrary to popular belief, can be delivered with great accuracy." †

22. Complete prohibition: ICRC, *Lucerne,* 33: 109. Population centers: ibid., 34: 112. Specific weapons: ibid., 34: 114.

23. ICRC, *Lucerne,* 33: 108. See Kalshoven, *Reflections on the Law of War,* 164–165.

24. Vote: Baxter, "Conventional Weapons under Legal Prohibitions," 49. Resolution: UNGA, *Resolution 3255 (XXIX): Napalm and Other Incendiary Weapons and all Aspects of their Possible Use.* December 9, 1974. Available at http://daccess-dds-ny.un.org/doc/RESOLUTION/GEN/NR0/738/57/IMG/NR073857.pdf?OpenElement (accessed October 14, 2012). Interestingly, the *New York Times* did not mention the declaration.

25. ICRC, *Conference of Government Experts on the Use of Certain Conventional Weapons (Second Session—Lugano, 28.1–26.2.1976): Report.* 1976 (ICRC, Geneva), 106. Hereafter *Lugano.* Available at http://www.loc.gov/rr/frd/Military_Law/pdf/RC-conf-experts-1976.pdf (accessed October 14, 2012).

26. Norway made a similar proposal. ICRC, *Lugano,* 184, 192, 206, 176, 181–182 (Document COLU/207: revision proposed by the United States and others to allow attacks on "specific military objectives" within a concentration of civilians subject to certain limitations); 182 (Document COLU/205 Annex A: revision proposed by Indonesia for a presumption of civilian status in case of doubt). See Baxter, "Conventional Weapons under Legal Prohibitions," 54. †

27. ICRC, *Lugano,* 109–110: 30, 110: 31. Canada: Eric Prokosch, *The Technology of Killing: A Military and Political History of Antipersonnel Weapons* (Zed Books, 1995), 156.

28. Korea: ICRC, *Lugano,* 110: 32. General purpose bombs: ibid., 110: 33. Other experts: ibid., 111: 34. "Copes": U.S. Delegation, *Report on the Lugano Conference Submitted to U.S. Secretary of State 9 August 1976.* Correspondence from Eric Prokosch, April 2012, in author's collection. †

29. ICRC, *Lugano,* 104: 6(c), 106: 13(d), 104: 6(d), 106: 13(e).

30. Ibid., 128–129.

31. U.S. argument: W. Hays Parks, "Means and Methods of Warfare," *George Washington International Law Review* 38 (2006), 515. Conclusions: Articles 36 ("New weapons") and 55 ("Protection of the natural environment") in Additional Protocol I are the only provisions that discuss means and methods of warfare. Office of the United Nations High Commissioner for Human Rights (OHCHR), *Protocol Additional to the Geneva Conventions of 12 August 1949, and relating to the Protection of Victims of International Armed Conflicts (Protocol 1).* June 8, 1977 (entry into force December 7, 1979). Available at www2.ohchr.org/english/law/protocol1.htm (accessed October 14, 2012). OHCHR, *Protocol Additional to the Geneva Conventions of 12 August 1949, and relating to the Protection of Victims of Non-International Armed Conflicts (Protocol II).* June 8, 1977 (entry into force December 7, 1978). Available at http://www.unhcr.org/refworld/docid/3ae6b37f40.html (accessed October 14, 2012). The United States has not signed the 1977 Additional Protocols. ICRC, *State Parties to the Following International Humanitarian Law and Other Related Treaties as of 10-Oct-2012.* October 10, 2012. †

32. ICRC, "Resolution 22." Resolution 22 was supported in particular by Sweden, Egypt, Mexico, the Netherlands, Norway, Switzerland, Austria, and Yugoslavia. Parks, "Means and Methods of Warfare," 517.

33. Ibid., 516 n. 21. See Baxter, "Conventional Weapons under Legal Prohibitions," 60 n. 45. The United States is one of six states with a formal weapons review process. Parks, "Means and Methods of Warfare," 516.

34. Parks, "Means and Methods of Warfare," 517 n. 25.

35. Carter: David Binder, "Issue and Debate; Comprehensive U. S. Arms Sale Policy Seen as Means of Restraining Other Suppliers," *New York Times,* March 8, 1977. Memorandum 12: Bernard Gwertzman, "Carter Is Studying Arms Sale Controls; Approval Expected on Proposals for Tightened Restraints on Export of U.S. Weapons," *New York Times,* April 25, 1977. (The Bureau of Political-Military Affairs is the Department of State's principal link to the Department of Defense. See "Bureau of Political-Military Affairs (PM)," *U.S. Department of State,* www.state.gov/t/pm/ (accessed October 14, 2012). Leaked: "Summit at Downing Street," *Time,* May 9, 1977. See Don Oberdorfer, "$1 Billion in Arms Sales Bids Refused in 1977, U.S. Says," *Washington Post,* May 20, 1978, p. A3 (sale of fuses for napalm bombs not allowed). U.S. arsenal: Andrew H. Malcolm, "For a Busy U.S. General in Korea, Pullout Is Later, Readiness Now," *New York Times,* April 21, 1977 (napalm used in training exercises in Korea).

36. Headquarters, Department of the Army, "66-MM Rocket Launcher: M202A1," *Training Circular TC-23.2*. April 1978, p. 1-2: item 1-3. Available at www.scribd.com/doc/3218834/TC23-2-66MM-ROCKET-LAUNCHER-M202A1#page=3 (accessed October 14, 2012). See Gary W. Cooke, "M202A1 Flame Assault Shoulder Weapon (Flash)," *Gary's U.S. Infantry Weapons Reference Guide*, February 14, 2008, http://www.inetres.com/gp/military/infantry/flame/M202.html (accessed October 14, 2012). Other alternatives to napalm cataloged by SIPRI in 1972 included "fragmentation bombs and rockets, cluster bombs, fuel-air explosives, gunships which fire 18,000 rounds a minute, use of strategic bombers in tactical support, etc." Malvern Lumsden, *Napalm and Incendiary Weapons: Legal and Humanitarian Aspects* (Stockholm International Peace Research Institute, 1972), 39. America's 1990 *Field Manual FM 3-11, Flame Field Expedients*, which superseded *FM 20-33, Combat Flame Operations*, does not discuss flamethrower tactics. William C. Schneck, "Review: *Flame On! U.S. Incendiary Weapons, 1918–1945*," *Engineer: The Professional Bulletin for Army Engineers*, April 2000. †

37. Parks, "Means and Methods of Warfare," 521. Yves Sandoz, "A New Step Forward in International Law: Prohibitions or Restrictions on the Use of Certain Conventional Weapons," *International Review of the Red Cross* 220 (January–February 1981), 13. †

38. W. Hays Parks, "The Protocol on Incendiary Weapons," *International Review of the Red Cross* 279 (November–December 1990): 539–540. Available at http://www.loc.gov/rr/frd/Military_Law/pdf/RC_Nov-Dec-1990.pdf (citing U.S. Strategic Bombing Survey). †

39. Parks, "The Protocol on Incendiary Weapons," 539, 541. †

40. UNOG, *Convention on Prohibitions or Restrictions on the Use of Certain Conventional Weapons Which May Be Deemed to Be Excessively Injurious or to Have Indiscriminate Effects as Amended on 21 December 2001*. December 21, 2001. Available at http://www.unog.ch/80256EDD006B8954/(httpAssets)/40BDE99D98467348C12571DE0060141E/$file/CCW+text.pdf (accessed October 14, 2012). UNOG. "Protocol on Prohibitions or Restrictions on the Use of Incendiary Weapons." *The Convention on Certain Conventional Weapons* (10 October 1980), Article 1.1(b). Available at http://www.icrc.org/ihl.nsf/FULL/515 (accessed October 14, 2012). †

41. UNOG, *Convention on Prohibitions*. Protocol III, Article 1. †

42. Ibid., Article 2.2, 2.3, 2.4. †

43. USSR: "Soviet Accepts Curb on Bombing; The Treaty and Protocols," *New York Times*, October 8, 1980. Convention: "The Convention on Certain Conventional Weapons." UNOG.ch. "The Convention on Prohibitions or Restrictions on the Use of Certain Conventional Weapons Which May Be Deemed to Be Excessively Injurious or to Have Indiscriminate Effects as Amended on 21 December 2001 (Convention on Certain Conventional Weapons, also Inhumane Weapons Convention: C.C.W.)," *The Convention on Certain Conventional Weapons* (United Nations, n.d.). Available at http://www.unog.ch/80256EE600585943/(httpPages)/4F0DEF093B4860B4C1257180004B1B30?OpenDocument (accessed October 14, 2012). See Bernard D. Nossiter, "U.N. Members Sign Treaty on Napalm and Land Mines," *New York Times*, April 11, 1981. And Arms Control Association, "Convention on

Certain Conventional Weapons (C.C.W.) at a Glance," *ArmsControl.org,* n.d., http://www.armscontrol.org/factsheets/CCW (accessed October 14, 2012). †

44. "Accord on Rules of War Is Completed; Another Parley May Be Convened," *New York Times,* October 10, 1980. Nossiter, "U.N. Members Sign Treaty." †

45. "CCW: Ratification Summary." Treaty Compliance, Office of the Under Secretary of Defense for Acquisition, Technology and Logistics (Department of Defense, n.d.). Available at http://www.acq.osd.mil/tc/treaties/ccwapl/ratifsum.htm (accessed October 14, 2012). See "States Parties and Signatories." Available at http://www .unog.ch/__80256ee600585943.nsf/(httpPages)/3ce7cfc0aa4a7548c12571c00039cb 0c?OpenDocument&ExpandSection=2%2C3%2C1%23_Section1#_Section2 (accessed October 14, 2012). †

## 13. Judgment Day

1. "In my considered opinion, no such general prohibition on the use of napalm can be distilled from the law in force," law of war authority and Henry Dunant Medal holder (the highest International Committee of the Red Cross honor) Professor Frits Kalshoven wrote in his 2007 *Reflections on the Law of War: Collected Essays* (Koninklijke Brill, 2007), 347.

2. Ethiopia: "A Land of Anarchy and Bloodshed," *Time,* May 31, 1976. Alexander De Waal, *Evil Days: 30 Years of War and Famine in Ethiopia* (Human Rights Watch, 1991), 79. Edward W. Desmond, "Ethiopia a Forgotten War Rages On," *Time,* December 23, 1985. Rhodesia and Angola: John Burns, "Rhodesia Invoking Harsher Measures to Stem Guerrillas; Church Sources Provide Some Data Killing of Teacher Described 5,000 Civilians Reported Dead Military Courts Cause Concern," *New York Times,* December 28, 1977: "Napalm has been widely used." †

3. Afghanistan: Drew Middleton, "Soviet Troops Said to Test New Weapons in Afghanistan; Military Analysis New Weapons Used by Soviets," *New York Times,* July 10, 1980: "American sources said that the Soviets had used napalm widely." Robert Schultheis and Ken Olsen, "War of a Thousand Skirmishes," *Time,* May 18, 1987: "napalm and high explosives fell wide of the mark." Thailand: Neil Kelly, "Thais Drop Napalm on Vietnamese," *The Times,* April 6, 1983, p. 1. See Reuters, "Thais Ready to Order New Strikes on Vietnamese," *New York Times,* April 7, 1983. Iraq: Paul von Zielbauer, "Kurds Tell of Gas Attacks by Hussein's Military," *New York Times,* August 23, 2006: "fiery napalm canisters dropped on villages from Iraqi military jets and helicopters."

4. El Salvador: Wayne Biddle, "Salvador Officer Said to Have Told of Napalm Use," *New York Times,* October 9, 1984. In 1984, U.S. ambassador Thomas R. Pickering confirmed the country had stocks of napalm. Wayne Biddle, "Salvador Military Has Napalm Bomb Stocks," *New York Times,* September 30, 1984. Falklands: Christopher Chant, *Air War in the Falklands 1982* (Osprey Publishing, 2001), 67. See Walter F. DeHoust, *Offensive Air Operations of The Falklands War,* April 2, 1984. Marine Corps Development and Education Command, p. 70. Available at http://globalsecurity.org/military/library/report/1984/DWF.htm (accessed October 14, 2012) Henry Stanhope and Stewart Tendler, "Napalm Stocks Found. Argentina

Lost 250 Men at Goose Green," *The Times,* June 2, 1982, p. 1, col. B. See R. W. Apple, "Britain Reports Seizing Key Hills Outside Stanley," *New York Times,* June 2, 1982. Richard Evans, "Napalm Found Also at Stanley Airfield," *The Times,* July 2, 1982, p. 6, col. D.

5.  Western Sahara: "Polisario Guerrillas Charge French Attack in West Sahara," *New York Times,* December 19, 1977. Jonathan Kandell, "French Jets Have Apparently Joined Sahara Fighting," *New York Times,* December 23, 1977. East Timor: Henry Kamm, "War-Ravaged Timor Struggles Back from Abyss," *New York Times,* January 28, 1980. Debbie Elliott, "Death Tally May Rattle E. Timor-Indonesia Ties," *All Things Considered,* NPR, January 21, 2006, *NPR.org,* http://www.npr.org/templates/story/story.php?storyId=5166959 (accessed October 15, 2012): "The report also charges that Indonesia used napalm and chemical weapons to poison food and water." Colum Lynch and Ellen Nakashima, "E. Timor Atrocities Detailed; At Least 100,000 Died, Report to U.N. Says," *Washington Post,* January 21, 2006, p. A12. Chad: Alan Cowell, "Pilot Presented by Chad as Libyan Asserts Planes Dropped Napalm," *New York Times,* August 9, 1983; "Libyan Warplanes Pound Chad Desert Post with Bombs and Napalm." *The Times,* August 10, 1983, p. 4, col. A. Chad made similar allegations when fighting broke out again in 1987. Associated Press, "Chad Says Libyans Used Napalm," *New York Times,* January 4, 1987. James Brooke, "Chad Reports 4th Day of Attacks by Libyan Planes," *New York Times,* August 13, 1987. Angola: Ray Kennedy, "Pretoria Denies Napalm Raid on Angola Town," *The Times,* August 16, 1983, p. 5, col. A. And Aquiles Ngonguela, "Political and Ethnic Cleansing in Central Angola," *FAS.org,* http://www.fas.org/irp/world/para/docs/unita/en0610991.htm (accessed October 14, 2012) "the MPLA has resorted to indiscriminate air bombing raids, using prohibited napalm and phosphorous bombs on the civilian population." Chechnya: Lally Weymouth, "Chechnya's Resolve," *Washington Post,* January 30, 1995, p. A15. †

6.  Britain/United States: "How the Allies Might Retaliate," *Time,* February 25, 1991. George J. Church, "The Battleground," *Time,* March 11, 1991. Iraq: Howard G. Chua-Eoan, "Defeat and Flight," *Time,* April 15, 1991: "In some cases targeted with napalm and phosphorus, thousands of civilians streamed toward the southern sector of the country occupied by U.S. troops." †

7.  "Bosnia . . . Napalm Attacks," *Time,* November 18, 1994. No injuries: "Serb Jets Raid 'Safe Area' in Bosnia; Rebels Use Napalm," *Los Angeles Times,* November 19, 1994, p. 10. Chuck Sudetic, "Napalm and Cluster Bombs Dropped on Bosnian Town," *New York Times,* 19 November 1994: "No one was injured, said Maj. Koos Sol, a United Nations military spokesman here. 'They were lucky,' he said, referring to the people of Bihać. 'All three bombs landed in the center of town within 100 meters of one another.'" †

8.  United Nations Security Council, *Security Council Resolution S/RES/958 (1994) Resolution 958 (1994) Adopted by the Security Council at Its 3461st Meeting, on 19 November 1994.* 19 November 1994. Available at http://www.un.org/ga/search/view_doc.asp?symbol=S/RES/958(1994) (accessed October 14, 2012). † Roger Cohen, "NATO, Expanding Bosnia Role, Strikes a Serbian Base in Croatia," *New York*

*Times,* November 22, 1994. "NATO Punishes Serbs for Napalm Attack," *Time,* November 21, 1994.

9. Vegetation, forest fires, and ice: [author unknown], "Chemical Warfare Discoveries Will Be Used in Peace: To Aid War against Harmful Insects and Aquatic Vegetation," n.d., in Harvard University Archives, Papers of Louis Frederick Fieser and Mary Peters Fieser, HUGFP 20.3 Box 4, "Scrapbook 1937–1960," n.p. Shampoo: "Napalm Will Be Made into G-I Liquid Soap," *Science News-Letter* 49, no. 14 (April 6, 1946), 219. See "War's Napalm May Fill Numerous Peacetime Roles," *Baltimore Sun,* September 28, 1952, p. L7. The story suggests "resilient, non-breakable plastic products. Disks, the size of a quarter, to start up the logs in your fireplace without paper or kindling."

10. Happy Camp: Associated Press, "Napalm Used on Forest Fire," *New York Times,* July 24, 1982. See Allan Parachini, "Napalm Used in Battle against Brush Fire Risk," *Los Angeles Times,* January 6, 1984, p. F1. Colorado: Iver Peterson, "Forest Regeneration by Fire Fizzles in Its Colorado Test," *New York Times,* June 5, 1985. *Exxon Valdez*: Malcolm W. Browne, "Oil on Surface Covers Deeper Threat," *New York Times,* March 31, 1989. †

11. Robert Rabin, "Navy Drops Napalm on Vieques." US/Puerto Rico Solidarity Network Trans. (Vieques Historical Archives, 1992). Available at http://www.hartford-hwp.com/archives/43/023.html (accessed October 14, 2012). Rolland Girard and Ron Richards, "Puerto Rican Youth Demand U.S. Military Leave Vieques Island," *The Militant* 62, no. 15 (April 20, 1998). Available at http://www.hartford-hwp.com/archives/43/073.html (accessed October 14, 2012). Karl Ross, "Death at Navy Bombing Range Resonates through Puerto Rico; Island Officials Seek Lasting Cease-Fire," *Washington Post,* August 19, 1999, p. A10. See Juan Figueroa, "Step In on Vieques," *New York Times,* January 18, 2001: "Studies already document that Navy-launched napalm, uranium and cluster bombs have caused increasing cancer and infant mortality rates and have collapsed the island's fishing, agriculture and tourism industries." See also "Vieques, Puerto Rico Overview," December 8, 2011. http://www.atsdr.cdc.gov/sites/vieques/overview.html (accessed October 15, 2012). And Ronald O'Rourke, "Vieques, Puerto Rico Naval Training Range: Background and Issues for Congress," *Congressional Research Service Report for Congress* (Congressional Research Service, December 17, 2001). Available at http://www.history.navy.mil/library/online/vieques.htm (accessed October 15, 2012). †

12. Oyster beds: "Oregon Oyster Growers Say Spill Perils Harvest," *Washington Post,* February 14, 1999, p. A05. "359,000 gallons of fuel oil and 37,400 gallons of diesel fuel": Environment News Service, "Grounded Cargo Ship Spilling Oil on Oregon Coast," February 9, 1999, http://www.ens-newswire.com/ens/feb1999/1999-02-09-03.asp (accessed October 15, 2012). Kim Murphy, "Navy Team Fails to Ignite Fuel Oil on Grounded Ship," *Los Angeles Times,* February 11, 1999. See Jeff Barnard, Associated Press, "Cargo Ship Still Stuck in Oregon; Demolitions Experts Turn to Napalm," *Durant Daily Democrat,* February 11, 1999: "After a brief flash and a plume of oily black smoke, a smoldering glow in two of the ship's cargo holds was all there was to show for eight hours of preparations." Mary Curtius and Lynn

Marshall, "Spectacular Blasts Ignite Oil Aboard Grounded Ship," *Los Angeles Times,* February 12, 1999. "400 pounds": Rene Sanchez, "Oil Burn on Grounded Ship Called Success; Mild Weather Helped Contain Fuel; Little of 400,000 Gallons Likely to Reach Beaches," *Washington Post,* February 13, 1999, p. A02.

13. Knight: Curtius and Marshall, "Spectacular Blasts." "I got burned": Rene Sanchez, "Experts Ignite Blast in 2nd Bid to Burn Off Mired Ship's Fuel," *Washington Post,* February 12, 1999, p. A03.

14. Twenty-five miles: Sanchez, "Oil Burn on Grounded Ship." Good fire: Curtius and Marshall, "Spectacular Blasts." See "Fighting Mire with Fire," *Time,* February 22, 1999. †

15. Firecon, Inc. of Ontario, Oregon, manufactured Terra Torches. See "Gel Fuel Terra Torch Model 1400," *Terra-Torch.com,* http://www.terra-torch.com/Products /1400_Terra_Torch.htm (accessed October 15, 2012). Carcasses: Advanstar Communications, "Napalm Sparks Interest Overseas," *DVM, The Newsmagazine of Veterinary Medicine,* Vol. 32, No. 5 (May 2001), p. 6. United Kingdom: Marina Murphy, "Funeral Pyre," *New Scientist,* March 21, 2001. Health officials ultimately killed millions of animals. See "Timeline: Foot-and-Mouth Cases," *BBC. co.uk,* October 19, 2001. Available at http://news.bbc.co.uk/2/hi/uk_news/1207 463.stm (accessed October 15, 2012). MP Dalyell: Sir Thomas Dalyell Loch, 11th Baronet, "Hansard (House of Commons Daily Debates) – Archive," *Bound Volume Hansard – Debate.* April 23, 2001. Available at http://www.publications.parlia ment.uk/pa/cm200001/cmhansrd/vo010423/debtext/10423-09.htm (accessed October 15, 2012), col. 32. No inhibitions: ibid.

16. Hugh-Jones: Murphy, "Funeral Pyre." Anderson: Advanstar Communications, "Napalm Sparks Interest Overseas." Don D. Jones, Stephen Hawkins, and Daniel R. Ess, "Non-Traditional and Novel Technologies," in *Carcass Disposal: A Comprehensive Review* (National Agricultural Biosecurity Center Consortium, August 2004), 20. Available at http://fss.k-state.edu/FeaturedContent/CarcassDisposal /PDF%20Files/Preface.pdf (accessed October 15, 2012). Their judgment of napalm's popular image was widely held. "[A]mong civilians, fire weapons are considered inhumane. The fuel for flamethrowers is basically napalm, and napalm has never recovered from its Vietnam reputation for awfulness," Slate.com military affairs correspondent Scott Shuger, for example, wrote in a 2001 column that urged the United States to consider deploying flamethrowers in Afghanistan. Scott Shuger, "Fire When Ready: Why We Should Consider Using Flamethrowers in Afghanistan," *Slate.com,* October 31, 2001. Available at http://www.slate.com/articles/news _and_politics/war_stories/2001/10/fire_when_ready.html (accessed October 15, 2012).

17. Steve Connor, "Foot-And-Mouth Crisis: Incineration—Ministry May Use Napalm to Burn Animal Carcasses," *Independent,* March 27, 2001, p. 5. "Napalm Could Aid Carcass Disposal," *BBC.co.uk,* April 24, 2001, Available at http://news.bbc.co .uk/2/hi/uk_news/1293925.stm (accessed October 15, 2012). See David Montgomery, "Epidemic Raises Issues for Future," *Scotsman,* April 2, 2001, p. 4: "A MAFF spokeswoman said it had no plans to use napalm."

18. In 1992, California state environmental officials fined the navy $191,500 for keeping some napalm in an open paper bag, and failing to post required "No Smoking"

signs, among other infractions. Lily Dizon, "State EPA Cites Navy for Waste at Seal Beach," *Los Angeles Times,* May 9, 1992. By 1994, a total of 1,774 canisters had leaked and had to be repaired, removed, or incinerated. "Apocalypse Then," *New York Times,* January 15, 1995. A 1998 analysis by the Fuels Section of the Naval Research Laboratory estimated the size of the total U.S. napalm stockpile at 3.4 million gallons. See George W. Mushrush, Erna J. Beal, Dennis R. Hardy, and Janet M. Hughes, "Use of Surplus Napalm as an Energy Source," *Energy Sources* 22, no. 2 (2000): 147. "Napalm Park Nickname": Richard Ross, "Discarded Napalm Bombs," 1994, *CorbisImages.com,* http://www.corbisimages.com/stock-photo /rights-managed/CH001040/discarded-napalm-bombs (accessed October 15, 2012). "Honey-like": Navy Napalm Media Task Force, "Description of Canisters and Materials," *Napalm Project Information Sheet* (Department of the Navy, December 1998). Available at http://www.toddmargrave.com/NapalmProjectFacts_Dec1998 .pdf (accessed October 15, 2012). Kangaroo rats: Tony Perry, "Relegating Napalm to Its Place in History," *Los Angeles Times,* April 1, 2001. See "National News Briefs; Navy Reaches Deal for Burning Napalm," *New York Times,* January 6, 1999. Disposal: Southwest Division, NAVFACENGCOM, "Recycled Napalm Successfully Converted to Industrial Use," *RMP News,* Fall 2001. See Pam Belluck, "Napalm Disposal Plan Dissolves under Debate, but Shipment Rolls On," *New York Times,* April 15, 1998.

19. Sales: Southwest Division, NAVFACENGCOM, "Recycled Napalm." See Belluck, "Napalm Disposal Plan": " 'There were efforts at one time to actually sell it,' said Commander Smith. 'Those did not work.' " Palm Enterprises: "Fallbrook Naval Weapons Station," *GlobalSecurity.org,* http://www.globalsecurity.org/military /facility/fallbrook.htm (accessed October 15, 2012). Much of the supply was "Napalm B": 20 percent benzene, 43 percent polystyrene, and 37 percent gasoline. "Due to the high concentration of polystyrene, napalm itself could not be burned directly as a fuel because the spray nozzles of practically all injectors in combustors would plug," Naval Research Laboratory investigators wrote in 1998. Mushrush et al., "Use of Surplus Napalm," 148. Williams: Orange County Register, "Critics Fume at Navy's Attempt to Dispose of Old Napalm Bombs," *Wilmington Morning Star,* November 24, 1995, p. 13A. Battelle Memorial Institute: "About Us," *Battelle.org,* http://www.battelle.org/aboutus/index.aspx (accessed October 15, 2012). Rick Lyman, "Much-Repudiated Napalm Finds Wary Acceptance, If Not Warm Welcome, in Texas," *New York Times,* August 10, 1998. See Mushrush et al., 150: "The huge amount of surplus napalm possessed by the military is too large to simply ignore or destroy by destructive methods such as incineration. . . . The energy content of the surplus napalm was calculated to be 18,383 Btu/pound." Belluck, "Napalm Disposal Plan."

20. Belluck, "Napalm Disposal Plan."

21. Image, straw: Belluck, "Napalm Disposal Plan." Kilgore: Mike Dorning, "Congressmen Getting Political Mileage Out of Napalm Train," *Chicago Tribune,* April 19, 1998.

22. Dorning, "Congressmen Getting Political Mileage." T. Shawn Taylor and Stanley Ziemba, "Napalm Shipment on Train to Nowhere," *Chicago Tribune,* April 15, 1998. KKK Rally: Belluck, "Napalm Disposal Plan." See Hon. Robert B. Pirie, Jr.

"Testimony at Hearings Before a Subcommittee of the Committee on Appropriations, House of Representatives, One Hundred Fifth Congress, Second Session, Subcommittee on Military Construction Appropriations" (Government Printing Office, 1998). Available at http://www.gpo.gov/fdsys/pkg/CHRG-105hhrg48548/html /CHRG-105hhrg48548.htm (accessed October 15, 2012).

23. Belluck, "Napalm Disposal Plan": "Campbell said, he felt like he had come 'full circle,' because he started his career working for Dow Chemical and remembers looking outside his Rockefeller Center window when protesters were picketing against that company for manufacturing napalm." Taylor and Ziemba, "Napalm Shipment on Train to Nowhere."

24. Holy Saturday commemorates the day between Good Friday and Easter Sunday when the body of Jesus Christ lay in its tomb, according to Christian tradition. See Henri Leclercq, "Holy Saturday," *The Catholic Encyclopedia,* vol. 7 (Robert Appleton Company, 1910). Available at http://www.newadvent.org/cathen/07424a.htm (accessed October 15, 2012). Kenneth H. Bacon, "DoD News Briefing," *FAS.org,* April 14, 1998. http://www.fas.org/man/dod-101/sys/dumb/t04141998_t0414asd-4 .html (accessed October 15, 2012). Sneaking, General Accounting Office investigation demanded: Belluck, "Napalm Disposal Plan." "Dead of night": Michael Leland, "Napalm Train," *Voice of America,* April 15, 1998. Transcript available at http://www .fas.org/man/dod-101/sys/dumb/980415-napalm.htm (accessed October 15, 2012).

25. GNI: Lyman, "Much-Repudiated Napalm." Delay: Eric Lichtblau, "Long-Delayed Disposal of Napalm Is Set to Begin," *Los Angeles Times,* July 11, 1998.

26. Briefest flurry: Lyman, "Much-Repudiated Napalm." "10,000 gallons": "National News Briefs; Texas Company to Begin Recycling U.S. Napalm," *New York Times,* July 14, 1998. See Eric Anderson, KBPS, "Vietnam Era Napalm," *Morning Edition,* July 14, 1998. Available at http://www.npr.org/templates/story/story.php?storyId =1025638 (accessed October 15, 2012). Katherine Blake, "Napalm Train: Last Stop, Texas," *CBS News,* July 14, 1998, http://www.cbsnews.com/stories/1998/07/14/na tional/main13882.shtml (accessed October 15, 2012). Reeves: Lyman, "Much-Repudiated Napalm." Saunders: Lichtblau, "Long-Delayed Disposal." Assistant Navy Secretary Robert B. Pirie Jr. visited Deer Park to try to ease the concerns of residents, in a sign of the extent of the public relations campaign the Navy was forced to mount. Blake, "Napalm Train" (date displayed by website may vary). Yocum: Lyman, "Much-Repudiated Napalm."

27. Anderson, Starns: Lyman, "Much-Repudiated Napalm." Crabtree: Lichtblau, "Long-Delayed Disposal."

28. The GNI Group, Inc., "Results of Operations—Fiscal 2000 Third Quarter Compared with Fiscal 1999 Third Quarter." Securities and Exchange Commission Form 10-Q, May 15, 2000. Available at http://google.brand.edgar-online.com/display filinginfo.aspx?FilingID=614064-1244-51197&type=sect&TabIndex=2&companyid =29088&ppu=%2fdefault.aspx%3fcompanyid%3d29088 (accessed October 15, 2012). GNI filed for bankruptcy on September 12, 2000. "The GNI Group Files for Bankruptcy Protection," *Houston Business Journal,* September 14, 2000. Available at http://www.bizjournals.com/houston/stories/2000/09/11/daily22.html (accessed

October 15, 2012. Rhodia: Shoshana Hebshi, "Napalm Removal Project Wrapping Up," *North Country Times,* February 4, 2001. "National News Briefs; Navy Reaches Deal For Burning Napalm," *New York Times,* January 6, 1999 (Baton Rouge). Additional supplies went to Chem Waste Management based in Port Arthur, Texas. Greg Harman, "WCS Still Pursuing Napalm Contract," *Odessa American,* April 9, 1999. Available at http://www.texasradiation.org/andrews/OA-WCSNapalmContract .html (accessed October 15, 2012). See Mushrush et al., "Use of Surplus Napalm," 155: "Napalm can be safely handled and used as an energy source if it is used in the presence of cosolvents. . . . This solution could provide a viable energy resource that can be used in commercial applications such as electrical power generation, central heating plants, or industrial processes that require heat."

29. Last canisters: Michael Taylor, "Military Says Goodbye to Napalm. Pentagon Recycles Remaining Stock of a Notorious Weapon," *San Francisco Chronicle,* April 4, 2001. See Eric Anderson, "Napalm Clean-Up," *Morning Edition,* April 4, 2001, http://www.npr.org/templates/story/story.php?storyId=1120992 (accessed October 15, 2012). Good riddance: Gidget Fuentes, "Navy Prepares New Life for Napalm Storage Site," *North Country Times,* April 5, 2001.

30. Definition: Fieser deemed napalm a generic or chemically "nondescriptive" term that identified any incendiary made from thickened petroleum. Louis Fieser, *The Scientific Method: A Personal Account of Unusual Projects in War and in Peace* (Reinhold Publishing Corp., 1964), 29. "Napalm" in the *Oxford English Dictionary* (Oxford University Press, 1989) is defined as: "1. . . . b. A thixotropic gel consisting of petrol and this thickening agent (or some similar agent), used in flamethrowers and incendiary bombs; jellied petrol." As Hoyt Hottel, chief of the National Defense Research Council's World War II incendiary weapons program, observed of napalm in a 1995 interview, "that name was invented early and the composition is entirely different today, but the name is still used." James J. Bohning, "Interview with Hoyt C. Hottel at Massachusetts Institute of Technology. 18 November and 2 December 1985." Oral History Transcript #0025. 2010. Chemical Heritage Foundation, 22. See "Hoyt Hottel Dies at 95; Was Expert on Energy, Combustion," *MIT News,* September 26, 1998. Available at http://web.mit.edu/newsoffice/1998/hottel-0926.html (accessed October 15, 2012). Franks: See "Napalm," *GlobalSecurity.org,* http://www.globalsecurity.org /military/systems/munitions/napalm.htm (accessed October 15, 2012). †

## 14. The Weapon That Dare Not Speak Its Name

1. SS *Cape Jacob*: U.S. Department of Defense (DoD), "Sailors Offload Ammo for U.S. Marines," *Defend America: U.S. Department of Defense News About the War on Terrorism,*" February 2, 2003, http://www.defendamerica.mil/archive/2003-02 /20030212.html (accessed October 15, 2012). See "T-AK 5029 Cape Jacob," *Federation of American Scientists,* 2011, http://www.fas.org/programs/ssp/man/usw pns/navy/sealift/tak5029.html (accessed October 15, 2012). Twenty-four-hour shifts: W. A. Napper Jr., "Ammunition Finds Its Way from Kuwait Port to Marines' Hands," *USMC News,* February 2, 2003. Available at http://www.globalsecurity

.org/military/library/news/2003/02/mil-030211-usmc02.htm (accessed October 15, 2012). Planning: "Transcript of Powell's U.N. Presentation," *CNN.com,* February 5, 2003, http://articles.cnn.com/2003-02-05/us/sprj.irq.powell.transcript_1_genuine -acceptance-iraq-one-last-chance-disarmament-obligations?_s=PM:US (accessed October 15, 2012). Eric Schmitt and Thom Shanker, "War Plan Calls for Precision Bombing Wave to Break Iraqi Army Early in Attack," *New York Times,* February 2, 2003.

2. "President Bush Addresses the Nation," March 19, 2003. Office of the Press Secretary, the White House. http://georgewbush-whitehouse.archives.gov/news/releases /2003/03/20030319-17.html (accessed October 15, 2012). "Operation Iraqi Freedom: Major Combat Operations 'Dash to Baghdad,'" *GlobalSecurity.org,* May 7, 2011. http://www.globalsecurity.org/military/ops/iraqi_freedom-mco.htm (accessed October 15, 2012).

3. 1991 cease-fire: Steve Coll and Guy Gugliotta, "Iraq Accepts All Cease-Fire Terms," *Washington Post,* March 4, 1991. See Stephen A. Bourque, "Incident at Safwan," *Armor,* January–February 1999, 30. Available at http://www.benning.army.mil/armor /armormagazine/content/Issues/1999/ArmorJanuaryFebruary1999web.pdf (accessed October 15, 2012). Howitzers: Lindsay Murdoch, "Dead Bodies Are Everywhere," *Sydney Morning Herald,* March 22, 2003.

4. Murdoch, "Dead Bodies Are Everywhere." Martin Savidge, "Savidge: Protecting Iraq's Oil Supply," *CNN.com,* March 22, 2003, http://edition.cnn.com/2003/WORLD /meast/03/21/otsc.irq.savidge/ (accessed October 15, 2012).

5. Murdoch, "Dead Bodies Are Everywhere."

6. Laura McClure (Compiler), "War of Words," *Salon.com,* March 22, 2003, http:// http://www.salon.com/2003/03/22/world21/ (accessed October 15, 2012). Amy Harmon, "A NATION AT WAR: Weblogs; Facts Are in, Spin Is Out," *New York Times,* March 25, 2003; corrected March 26, 2003.

7. James W. Crawley, "Officials Confirm Dropping Firebombs on Iraqi Troops: Results Are 'remarkably similar' to Using Napalm," *San Diego Union-Tribune,* August 5, 2003.

8. "Fuel-gel mixture": Ben Cubby, "New, Improved and More Lethal: Son of Napalm," *Sydney Morning Herald,* August 8, 2003. "Firebombs": Crawley, "Officials Confirm Dropping Firebombs." On Mark-77 firebombs see "MK77 750lb Napalm. MK78 500lb Napalm. MK79 1000lb Napalm," *FAS.org,* http://www.fas.org /man/dod-101/sys/dumb/mk77.htm (accessed October 15, 2012) And "Firebombs," *Ordnance.org,* http://www.ordnance.org/firebomb.htm (accessed October 15, 2012). For video see: "Mk 77 Fire Bomb Drop," *YouTube,* http://www.youtube.com /watch?v=3iXTYJ8YpP4 (accessed October 15, 2012). "Mk77 Firebomb," *YouTube,* http://www.youtube.com/watch?v=hr92t1IDDJg&feature=plcp (accessed October 15, 2012). Vernacular: Cubby, "New, Improved and More Lethal: Son of Napalm." Confusingly, a 1999 navy public affairs document cited by the *Herald* in the same piece reported that "the US Marine Corps has a requirement and uses it [napalm] at ranges at Yuma and Twenty-Nine Palms." Environment: Crawley, "Officials Confirm Dropping Firebombs."

9. Andrew Buncombe, "US Admits It Used Napalm Bombs in Iraq," *Independent,* August 10, 2003. Pike: "John E. Pike—Director," *GlobalSecurity.org,* http://www .globalsecurity.org/org/staff/pike.htm (accessed October 15, 2012). See Crawley, "Officials Confirm Dropping Firebombs." And Michele Norris, "Pentagon Defends Use of Toxic Agent in Iraq," *All Things Considered,* November 18, 2005. Available at http://www.npr.org/templates/story/story.php?storyId=5019073 (accessed October 15, 2012).

10. John Goetz and Georg Restle/MONITOR 507, "Heavy Reproaches against US Pentagon: Napalm Bombs in the Iraq War," *InformationClearingHouse.info,* August 7, 2003, http://www.informationclearinghouse.info/article4395.htm (accessed October 15, 2012). Buncombe, "US Admits It Used Napalm Bombs in Iraq."

11. Buncombe, "US Admits It Used Napalm Bombs in Iraq."

12. Harry Cohen, "Written Answers to Questions," *Bound Volume Hansard – Written Answers,* 11 January 2005, col. 374W. Available at http://www.publications.parlia ment.uk/pa/cm200405/cmhansrd/vo050111/text/50111w01.htm#50111w01.html _sbhd3 (accessed October 15, 2012). War opponent: "Mr Harry Cohen MP, Leyton and Wanstead voted *strongly against* the policy: Iraq 2003 – For the invasion," *The Public Whip,* http://www.publicwhip.org.uk/mp.php?mpid=1684&dmp=1049 (accessed October 15, 2012). Adam Ingram, "Written Answers to Questions," *Bound Volume Hansard – Written Answers,* 11 January 2005, col. 373W.

13. "Blair Sets 5 May as Election Date," *BBC.co.uk,* April 5, 2005, http://news.bbc .co.uk/2/hi/uk_news/politics/4409935.stm (accessed October 15, 2012). Adam Ingram, "Written Answers to Questions." *Bound Volume Hansard – Written Answers.* 28 June 2005, col. 1396W. Available at http://www.publications.parliament.uk/pa /cm200506/cmhansrd/vo050628/text/50628w03.htm#50628w03.html_sbhd4 (accessed October 15, 2012). Reelected: Michael White and Alan Travis, "Labour's Majority Slides Away," *Guardian,* May 6, 2005. See "Blair Wins Historic Third Term – Majority of 66," *BBC.co.uk,* May 5, 2005; rev. September 9, 2005, http:// news.bbc.co.uk/2/hi/uk_news/politics/vote_2005/constituencies/default.stm (accessed October 15, 2012) (35.3 to 32.3 percent). Key issue: David Cowling, "Opinion Polls: Movement on the Issues?" *BBC.co.uk,* May 3, 2005, http://news.bbc.co.uk/2 /hi/uk_news/politics/vote_2005/issues/4506035.stm (accessed October 15, 2012). See Harold Clarke, David Sanders, Marianne Stewart, and Paul Whiteley, "2005 British General Election," *American Political Science Association,* http://www .apsanet.org/content_15008.cfm (accessed October 15, 2012).

14. Adam Ingram, "Letter to Linda Riordan, MP," *Rai News 24,* June 13, 2005, http:// www.rainews24.rai.it/ran24/inchiesta/foto/documento_ministero.jpg (accessed October 15, 2012). See discussion of U.S. deployment of MK-77 bombs and napalm in Iraq in Susie Myatt, "Letter to Michael Lewis: Request for Information – Notification of Excess Cost," July 15, 2005. UK Ministry of Defence. Ref. 25-04-2005-094904-004. Available at http://www.iraqanalysis.org/local/647_25042005-094904-004RFIRE SPONSEMK77-1.pdf (accessed October 16, 2012).

15. Months later, the Ministry of Defence explained the debacle as follows: "A UK official working in Baghdad contacted the Baghdad Combined Operations Centre asking for

clarification of whether MK 77 Firebombs had been used in Iraq. A US Officer working in that centre provided the assurance that they had not. We understand that
the assurance was given orally. That information was conveyed back to the UK
by telephone conversation." Susie Myatt, "Letter to Michael Lewis: Request for
Information – Incendiary Bombs," August, 2005. UK Ministry of Defence. Ref.
18-07-2005-122443-007, p. 1. Available at http://www.iraqanalysis.org/local/657
_18-07-2005-122443-007-RFI-ResponseClarification-MK77bombs-.pdf (accessed
October 15, 2012). See Colin Brown, "US Lied to Britain over Use of Napalm in Iraq
War," *Independent,* June 17, 2005. Not napalm: "Minister Slammed on Napalm Error,"
*BBC.co.uk,* June 24, 2005, http://news.bbc.co.uk/2/hi/uk_news/politics/4116262
.stm (accessed October 15, 2012).

16. See "Minister Slammed on Napalm Error."

17. Jonathan Holmes, "The Legacy of Fallujah," *Guardian,* April 4, 2007. Jane Perlez,
"An Assault in Iraq, a Stage Hit in London," *New York Times,* May 29, 2007.

18. Fairness and Accuracy in Reporting (FAIR), "Incendiary Weapons Are No 'Allegation,'" *FAIR.org,* June 11, 2007, http://www.fair.org/index.php?page=3114 (accessed October 15, 2012). U.S. authorities first asserted white phosphorus had been
used only for illumination at Fallujah, but later, when confronted with contradictory
evidence from one of the military's own publications, admitted it had been used to
drive enemy fighters from cover in a tactic nicknamed "shake and bake." "Shake and
Bake," *New York Times,* November 29, 2005. General Peter Pace, chairman of the
Joint Chiefs of Staff, perhaps added to the confusion, and underlined how critical
fine distinctions of nomenclature have become under intense public scrutiny, when
he observed at a press briefing in response to the *New York Times* editorial "Shake
and Bake": white phosphorus, he said, "is not a chemical weapon, it is an incendiary" (but not, briefers elaborated, an incendiary weapon as defined by Protocol III
of the Convention on Certain Conventional Weapons [CCW]), U.S. DoD, "Press
Briefing (Nov. 29, 2005)," quoted in American Society of International Law, "U.S.
Defends Use of White Phosphorus Munitions in Iraq," *The American Journal of
International Law* 100, no. 2 (April 2006): 487. See FAIR, "Incendiary Weapons
Are No 'Allegation.'" In a follow-up alert, FAIR distinguished between napalm and
white phosphorus—"WP [white phosphorus] is not napalm at all, which FAIR did
not argue. Rather, the point was that a chemical agent with potentially lethal effects
was used in a battle in a major Iraqi city"—but repeated its claim that the matter was
a "slender technicality." FAIR, "NY Times Responds on Fallujah Weapons," *FAIR.
org,* July 20, 2007, http://www.fair.org/index.php?page=3141 (accessed October 15,
2012).See W. Hays Parks, "Means and Methods of Warfare," *George Washington
International Law Review* 38 (2006), 521–522 ("Thermite (or thermate) munitions,
flame throwers, and napalm are incendiary weapons, but weapons with incidental
incendiary effects, such as white phosphorus and small arms tracer ammunition,
are not.") RAI News: Sigfrido Ranucci and Maurizio Torrealta, "Fallujah, the Hidden Massacre," *RAI News 24,* November 8, 2005, http://www.youtube.com
/watch?v=UwrsNRoyblE (accessed October 15, 2012). See George Monbiot, "Behind the Phosphorus Clouds Are War Crimes within War Crimes," *Guardian,* November 22, 2005. Some news outlets, including the mass-circulation UK newspaper

the *Sunday Mirror* on November 28, 2004, even reported that U.S. troops in Iraq had used "napalm gas," an unknown substance. State Department officials published an excruciatingly detailed refutation of "a number of widespread myths including false charges that the United States is using chemical weapons such [as] napalm and poison gas" in response—but had to correct it twice over the next eleven months as additional information came to light. U.S. Department of State (DoS), "Is the U.S. Using 'Illegal' Weapons in Fallujah?" *USEmbassy.gov,* December 9, 2004, rev. January 27, 2005, rev. November 10, 2005. January revision available at http://www.globalsecurity.org/military/library/report/2005/050127-fallujah.htm (accessed October 15, 2012). Revision history: "Did the U.S. Use 'Illegal' Weapons in Fallujah?" *RAI News 24,* November 10, 2005, http://www.rainews24.rai.it /ran24/inchiesta/en/illegal_weapons.asp (accessed October 15, 2012). Clark Hoyt, "Was There Napalm in Fallujah?" *New York Times,* July 18, 2007. Hoyt ultimately rejected FAIR's assertion and supported Perlez's assessment. Clark Hoyt, "Was There Napalm in Fallujah? Part II," *New York Times,* July 24, 2007.

19. "Napalm Recipe Posted Online," *Internet Terror Monitor,* May 18, 2009, http:// www.cbsnews.com/8301-502684_162-5023379-502684.html (accessed October 15, 2012). CBS did not report that the 1969 U.S. Army Special Forces *Improvised Munitions Handbook,* which provides detailed instructions for making "gelled flame fuels" from gasoline mixed with soap, egg whites, animal blood, and other thickeners, supplemented by amateur recipes for napalm on numerous websites, was also available online in 2009. Headquarters, Department of the Army, *Improvised Munitions Handbook, TM 31-210 Department of the Army Technical Manual,* 1969: Sec. V, No. 4.1–4.7, pp. 159–170. Available at http://www.scribd.com/doc/14108872 /US-Army-Improvised-Munitions-Handbook-TM-31210#page=159 (accessed October 15, 2012). "Napalm case": Thyrie Bland, "Details Emerge in Napalm Case: Man Charged in Meth Lab Bust Works for Defense Contractor," *Pensacola News Journal,* March 3, 2012, p. C1.

20. Mary Hill, U.S. Army Field Support Command, Rock Island, IL. "13 – MK77 Mod 5 Firebomb, NSN: 1325-01-286-3586; P/N: 923AS652; Approximately 993 Each." Sources Sought Notice, Solicitation Number W52P1J04-R-0077, January 13, 2004, Available at http://www.iraqanalysis.org/local/644_MK77procurementnotice.pdf (accessed October 15, 2012). See Mary Hill, U.S. Army Field Support Command, Rock Island, IL, "Amendment of Solicitation No. W52P1J-04-R-0077." Solicitation Number W52P1J04-R-0077 Mod. 0005, June 4, 2004, http://www.iraqanalysis .org/local/645_fedprocure0005.pdf (accessed October 15, 2012). Bell Helicopter, "The Bell AH-1Z Zulu-Features," *Bell Helicopter, A Textron Company,* 2011, http:// www.bellhelicopter.com/en_US/Military/AH-1Z/AH_1Z.html#/?tab=features-tab (accessed October 15, 2012).

21. Warren Christopher, "Letter of Submittal," in *Message from the President of the United States Transmitting Protocols to the 1980 Convention on Prohibitions or Restrictions on the Use of Certain Conventional Weapons . . .* Senate Treaty Document 105-1, 105th Congress, 1st Session, January 7, 1997. Available at http://www .gpo.gov/fdsys/pkg/CDOC-105tdoc1/html/CDOC-105tdoc1.htm (accessed October 15, 2012). America accepted revisions to the CCW and Protocols I and II on March

24, 1995; Christopher referred to this later date in his message. U.S. DoS, "Article-by-Article Analysis of the Protocol on Prohibitions or Restrictions on the Use of Incendiary Weapons Annexed to the Convention on Prohibitions or Restrictions on the Use of Certain Conventional Weapons Which May Be Deemed to Be Excessively Injurious or to Have Indiscriminate Effects (Protocol III)," in *Message from the President . . .* , 30). As recently as May 12, 1994, Clinton wrote to the Senate, "there are concerns about the acceptability of Protocol III from a military point of view that require further examination." William J. Clinton, "Letter of Transmittal," in *Message from the President . . .*

22. Iraq inspections: United Nations (UN) Special Commission, "Chronology of Main Events," December 1999, *UN.org,* http://www.un.org/Depts/unscom/Chronology /chronologyframe.htm (accessed October 15, 2012). See Dan Smith, "On Protocol III of the C.C.W.," *The Quakers' Colonel,* November 24, 2008, http://quakerscolo nel.blogspot.com/2008/11/on-protocol-iii-of-ccw.html (accessed October 15, 2012). Exceptions: Clinton, "Letter of Transmittal," *Message from the President . . .* Christopher's conclusion may have been premature. "The precise wording of this condition, however, continued to undergo military review, in order to ensure that the United States was able to retain its ability to employ incendiaries against high-priority military targets," DoS legal advisor John Bellinger told the Senate in 2008. He did not provide further details. John B. Bellinger, "Prepared Statement of Hon. John B. Bellinger, Legal Adviser, Department of State, Washington, D.C.," in Annex II: Treaty Hearing of April 15, 2008, *An Amendment and Three Protocols to the 1980 Conventional Weapons Convention: Report of the Committee on Foreign Relations,* September 11, 2008. U.S. Senate Exec. Report 110-22, p. 24. Hereafter Report 110-22. Available at http://www.fas.org/irp/congress/2008_rpt/protocols .pdf (accessed October 15, 2012). "By filing this reservation, the United States essentially rejected Protocol III, Article 2," opined Matthew Dunham, air force deputy staff judge advocate. Matthew Dunham, "The Fate of Cluster Munitions," *The Reporter* 37, no. 1 (Spring 2010): 28, n. 14.

23. Department attorneys favored the term "proportionality": "The United States must retain its ability to employ incendiaries to hold high-priority military targets such as these at risk in a manner with the principle of proportionality which governs the use of all weapons under existing law." U.S. DoD, Office of the Under Secretary of Defense for Acquisition, Technology, and Logistics, "Tab (B). The Article-by-Article Analysis of Incendiary Weapons Protocol," *Message from the President . . .* , 32–33: 3–4. Also at U.S. DoD, Office of the Under Secretary of Defense for Acquisition, Technology, and Logistics, "Article-by-Article Analysis of the Protocol on Prohibitions or Restrictions on the Use of Incendiary Weapons Annexed to the Convention on Prohibitions or Restrictions on the Use of Certain Conventional Weapons Which May Be Deemed to Be Excessively Injurious or to Have Indiscriminate Effects (Protocol III)," *Treaty Compliance,* n.d., http://www.acq.osd.mil/tc/treaties /ccwapl/artbyart_pro3.htm (accessed October 15, 2012). As Parks observed in 1990, under certain circumstances commanders barred from using incendiary weapons may be forced to "employ artillery fire or an air-delivered high explosive munition that would be less accurate or more destructive than an air-delivered incendiary

weapon, resulting in greater collateral civilian casualties or damage to civilian objects. Only time will tell whether the prohibition contained in Article 2(2) has increased protection for innocent civilians near military objectives." W. Hays Parks, "The Protocol on Incendiary Weapons," *International Review of the Red Cross* 279 (November–December 1990): 548.

24. The U.S. Constitution requires that the Senate ratify treaties submitted by the president by a two-thirds vote. Chairs: "History of the Committee," *U.S. Senate Committee on Foreign Relations,* http://www.foreign.senate.gov/about/history/ (accessed October 15, 2012). Office of U.S. Senator Barack Obama, "Committee Assignments," December 9, 2006, http://web.archive.org/web/20061209190827/obama .senate.gov/committees/ (accessed October 15, 2012).

25. John B. Bellinger, "Prepared Statement," 25.

26. International Campaign to Ban Landmines, "Ban History," http://www.icbl.org /index.php/icbl/Treaty/MBT/Ban-History (accessed October 15, 2012), "States Parties," http://www.icbl.org/index.php/icbl/Universal/MBT/States-Parties (accessed October 15, 2012), "About us," http://www.icbl.org/index.php/icbl/About-Us (accessed October 15, 2012).

27. Convention on Cluster Munitions, "Ratifications," *ClusterConvention.org,* http:// www.clusterconvention.org/ratifications-and-signatures/ (accessed October 15, 2012). See Cluster Munition Coalition (CMC), "111 States on Board the Convention on Cluster Munitions," *StopClusterMunitions.org,* August 1, 2010, http://www.stopcluster munitions.org/treatystatus/ (accessed October 15, 2012). Valerie Pacer, "Cluster Munitions Treaty Enters into Force," *Arms Control Today* 40 (September 2010). Available at http://www.armscontrol.org/act/2010_09/Cluster (accessed October 15, 2012). Model: CMC, "A Model for Making Change Globally," http://www .stopclustermunitions.org/the-solution/change-globaly/ (accessed October 15, 2012). Countries that held a majority of the world's cluster munitions did not participate. Jeff Abramson, "107 Countries Approve Cluster Munitions Treaty," *Arms Control Today* 38 (July/August 2008). Available at http://www.armscontrol.org/act/2008 _07-08/cluster (accessed October 15, 2012). †

28. Priority: Jeffrey Berger, Assistant Secretary of State for Legislative Affairs, U.S. DoS, "Letter to the Honorable Joseph R. Biden, Jr., Chairman, Committee on Foreign Relations, United States Senate," February 7, 2007. Available at http://www .state.gov/documents/organization/116355.pdf (accessed October 15, 2012). American Bar Association (ABA): Armando Lasa-Ferrer, "Letter to the Honorable Joseph R. Biden, Jr., Chairman, Committee on Foreign Relations, U.S. Senate," October 31, 2007. Available at http://apps.americanbar.org/intlaw/leadership/policy /300implementation_letter.pdf (accessed October 15, 2012). "U.S. ratification . . . technologies": Robert P. Casey, "Opening Statement," in Report 110-22, p. 17. The ABA, with almost 400,000 members, is "the largest voluntary professional association in the world." Its Governmental Affairs Office lobbies Congress to support the association's priorities. See "History of the American Bar Association," American Bar Association, http://www.americanbar.org/utility/about_the_aba/history.html (accessed October 15, 2012). Foreign Relations Committee: Casey, "Opening Statement," 17. Biden and Lugar: ibid., 19.

29. "[O]ur uniformed military officers strongly support these treaties and believe they are consistent with U.S. national security interests. . . . The Department of Defense, including our combatant commands, already complies with, and fulfills in practice, the norms contained in all five of these law of war treaties," the Pennsylvania senator said. Casey, "Opening Statement," 18. See "Treaties," *U.S. Senate Committee on Foreign Relations,* April 15, 2008, http://www.foreign.senate.gov/hearings/hearing/?id=b526cb54-fc05-981d-dfb0-d6bea459dfed (accessed October 15, 2012). John Bellinger, "Prepared Statement," 8, http://www.foreign.senate.gov/imo/media/doc/BellingerTestimony080415p.pdf (accessed October 15, 2012). Charles Allen, "Statement of Charles A. Allen, Deputy General Counsel (International Affairs) Department of Defense before the Senate Committee on Foreign Relations Law of Armed Conflict Treaties,"4, http://www.foreign.senate.gov/imo/media/doc/AllenTestimony080415p.pdf (accessed October 15, 2012). Bellinger also suggested that a further "understanding" that "U.S. military personnel cannot be judged on the basis of information that subsequently comes to light" be attached to the protocol. "[A]ny decision by any military commander, military personnel, or any other person responsible for planning, authorizing or executing military action shall only be judged on the basis of that person's assessment of the information reasonably available to the person at the time the person planned, authorized, or executed the action under review, and shall not be judged on the basis of information that comes to light after the action under review was taken," read his proposed text (Report 110-22, pp. 10, 13).

30. Casey, "Opening Statement," 18. Bellinger, "Prepared Statement," 20, 21, 38.

31. Bellinger and Allen, "Responses of Legal Adviser John Bellinger and Deputy General Counsel Charles Allen to Questions Submitted for the Record by Senator Casey," Report 110-22, p. 42. Allen on utility: Allen, "Statement of Charles A. Allen," 2. Michelle Johnson, "Statement of BG Michelle D. Johnson, Deputy Director for the War on Terrorism and Global Effects, J-5 Strategic Plans and Policy Directorate, Joint Staff, Washington, D.C.," Report 110-22, p. 37. †

32. Senators also required that the president include Allen's proposed understanding about U.S. troop liability, and a declaration that "This Protocol does not confer private rights enforceable in United States courts." Christopher Dodd, "XI. Resolutions of Advice and Consent to Ratification," Report 110-22, pp. 12–13, 9.

33. U.S. Senate, "Incendiary Weapons Protocol," *Congressional Record,* S9332-33, September 23, 2008. Available at http://www.gpo.gov/fdsys/pkg/CREC-2008-09-23/pdf/CREC-2008-09-23-pt1-PgS9328.pdf#page=5 (accessed October 15, 2012). Largest number of treaties since 1910: Dick Jackson, "Law of War Treaties Pass the Senate," *Army Lawyer,* January 1, 2009, p. 56 n. 10. See Duncan Hollis, "A Treaty-Happy Senate?" *Opinio Juris,* September 28, 2008. http://opiniojuris.org/2008/09/28/a-treaty-happy-senate/ (accessed October 15, 2012).

34. Charles J. Brown, "Most Underreported Story of the Week: C.C.W.," *Undiplomatic.net,* January 30, 2009, http://www.undiplomatic.net/2009/01/30/most-underreported-story-of-the-week-ccw/ (accessed October 15, 2012). The CCW has 114 states parties and five signatories. Cameroon, Israel, Morocco, South Korea, Turkey, and Turkmenistan have approved the convention but reject Protocol III. United Nations Office at Geneva (UNOG), "States parties and Signatories," *The Conven-*

*tion on Certain Conventional Weapons* (UNOG, 26 July 2012). Available at http://
www.unog.ch/__80256ee600585943.nsf/(httpPages)/3ce7cfc0aa4a7548c12571c000
39cb0c?OpenDocument&ExpandSection=2%2C3%2C1%23_Section1#_Section2
(accessed October 15, 2012). A total of seventy-four countries have not signed. UNOG,
"States Not Parties," http://www.unog.ch/__80256ee600585943.nsf/(httpPages)
/3ce7cfc0aa4a7548c12571c00039cb0c?OpenDocument&ExpandSection
=4%2C1%23_Section1#_Section4 (accessed October 15, 2012). †

35. Vienna Convention: *Vienna Convention on the Law of Treaties,* United Nations
Treaty Series, Vol. 1155, p. 331 (United Nations, May 23, 1969, entered into force January 27, 1980), Article 20(5). Available at http://untreaty.un.org/ilc/texts/instruments
/english/conventions/1_1_1969.pdf (accessed October 15, 2012). †

36. National positions: Jeff Abramson, "U.S. Incendiary-Weapons Policy Rebuffed,"
*Arms Control Today* 40 (April 2010). Available at http://www.armscontrol.org/act
/2010_04/Incendiary (accessed October 15, 2012).

Epilogue

1. John Winthrop, "A Modell of Christian Charity," n.d., http://www.hks.harvard
.edu/fs/phall/03.%20winthrop,%20Christian%20Cha.pdf, p. 6 (accessed October
11, 2012). See "Ye are the light of the world. A city that is set on an hill cannot be
hid." Gospel of Matthew, King James trans. (1611), 5:14. Available at http://www
.biblegateway.com/passage/?search=Matthew+5%3A14-16&version=KJV (accessed
October 11, 2012).

2. Curtis E. LeMay with MacKinlay Kantor, *Mission with LeMay: My Story* (Doubleday & Company, 1965), 387. "Pocket Guide: Bell AH-1Z," *Bell Helicopter* (collection of
the author, 2006), n.p., http://www.bellhelicopter.com/Military/AH-1Z/1291148375494.
html#/?tab=highlights-tab (accessed June 2012, later removed). But see Chalmers
Johnson, *Nemesis: The Last Days of the American Republic* (Metropolitan Books,
2006), 32–33 (on Iraqi civilian casualties after U.S. invasion).

3. "Napalm Inventor Discounts 'Guilt:' Harvard Chemist Would 'Do It Again' for the
Country," *New York Times,* December 27, 1967.

4. Kim Phúc: interview with the author, April 28, 2011. Louis Fieser, *The Scientific
Method: A Personal Account of Unusual Projects in War and in Peace* (Reinhold Publishing Corp., 1964), 50–51.

5. James Carroll, "Interview with Robert McNamara" [February 2003], in Carroll,
*House of War: The Pentagon and the Disastrous Rise of American Power* (Houghton
Mifflin Co., 2006), 97. "If we lose the war we'll be tried as war criminals," LeMay
said in 1945, according to McNamara. "I think he was right. We would have been,"
the secretary wrote in the *Los Angeles Times* of August 3, 2003 (quoted in Carroll,
*House of War,* 97 n. 233). See *The Fog of War.* Directed by Errol Morris (Sony Pictures Classics, 2003).

6. Bruce Cumings, *War and Television* (Verso, 1992), 223. See Sven Lindqvist, *A History of Bombing,* Linda Haverty Rugg, trans. (New Press, 2003).

7. "History," n.d., http://www.kimfoundation.com/modules/contentpage/index.php
?file=story.htm&ma=10&subid=101 (accessed October 11, 2012). The contact details

of the foundation are: P.O. Box 31025, 15 Westney Road North, Ajax ON L1T 3V2, Canada. Tel.: (905) 426-5860. See "Kim Phuc," *Nzone Tonight,* September 24, 2008. Available at http://www.youtube.com/watch?v=Xhz2gCnhr-I (accessed October 11, 2012). Goodwill Ambassador: "Kim Phuc Phan Thi," n.d., http://www.unesco.org/new/en/unesco/about-us/who-we-are/goodwill-ambassadors/kim-phuc-phan-thi/ (accessed October 11, 2012).

8. Kim Phúc, interview with the author, April 28, 2011. See Kim Phúc, "The Long Road to Forgiveness," *This I Believe,* June 30, 2008, http://www.npr.org/templates/story/story.php?storyId=91964687 (accessed October 11, 2012). And Elizabeth Omara-Otunnu, "Napalm Survivor Tells of Healing after Vietnam War," *University of Connecticut Advance,* November 8, 2004. Available at http://www.advance.uconn.edu/2004/041108/04110803.htm (accessed October 11, 2012).

# Acknowledgments

A book is a team in print. My greatest thanks are to my wife, Maixuan, who supported this project from its earliest days. My children, Marco and Sophia, leavened an often difficult assignment with irrepressible cheer. They also reminded me of the infinite stakes behind the bland term "civilians." My father, Dr. Robert Neer, and my stepmother, Ann Eldridge, offered critiques of immense value and exquisite grammatical accuracy. My brother, Professor Richard Neer, sets a stellar academic example.

Joyce Seltzer, my editor, Susan Wallace Boehmer, editor-in-chief, Brian Distelberg, Christine Thorsteinsson, Margaux Leonard, and the rest of the team at Harvard University Press, and Melody Negron and Paul Vincent at Westchester Book Group's word forge, define publishing excellence. I am grateful to my anonymous reviewers for their advice and suggestions, which I have done my best to follow. Sandy Dijkstra and Elise Capron, agents provocateurs, piloted me through the world of publishers with verve and excellent judgment.

Columbia University in the City of New York is a superlative place to study American history. My teachers and colleagues there inspire me: Herb Sloan, Ken Jackson, Sam Moyn, Carol Gluck, Eric Foner, Alan Brinkley, Anders Stephanson, Mark Mazower, Alice Kessler-Harris, Richard Bushman, and Pamela Smith, among many others, from the history faculty; Barbara Black, from the law school; and John Witt, from Yale Law School. Sharee Nash, J. T. Denicola, and Maritza Colón guided me to a landing. Nathan Perl-Rosenthal, Bryan Rosenblithe, Elizabeth Kai Hinton, Sarah Kirshen, Nick Osborne, Valerie Paley, Jared Manasek, Daniel Immerwahr, Stephen Wertheim, Ruben Savizky, Abigail Struhl, and many others taught me the power of academic collegiality. Brittany Edmoundson got me to the finish line.

Libraries are the heart of scholarship. Michael Ryan and Eric Wakin proved the point to me at Columbia. Butler Library's reference staff, and the elves who administer the Interlibrary and Borrow Direct loan services, delivered critical materials as if by magic. Barbara Meloni and Kate Bowers cataloged the Fieser Papers at Harvard's Archives and helped me immensely. All quotations from the papers are courtesy of the archives, and with their permission. New York's Public Library, perhaps the most beautiful in the world, was of great assistance.

"History should be written as philosophy," Voltaire wrote. I agree. My time teaching Contemporary Civilization and other classes at Columbia College profoundly influenced this treatise. "Empire of Liberty: A Global History of the U.S. Military," a summer seminar I taught for the History Department, put my ideas in context. My undergraduate and graduate students—best, as they know, of all possible students—kept my spirits high, and my feet on the ground. Matt Jones, Roosevelt Montas, Philip Kitcher, Michael Stanislawski, and Kathryn Yatrakis opened the door for me, and taught me much about philosophy. David Ratzan and Megan Doherty stood by my side. Lavinia Lorch, Michael Dunn, Kristin Gager, Jennifer Thompson, Sarah Dziedzic, Maria Baquero, Dehlia Hannah, and Nandi Theunissen encouraged me every step of the way.

Many experts gave me crucial insights, provided source materials I would otherwise have missed, and answered questions, in particular Phan Thị Kim Phúc, Eric Prokosch, Malvern Lumsden, H. Bruce Franklin, W. Hays Parks, Elly Rose, Bruce Cumings, Jon Halliday, ever-patient Denise Chong, Marsh Carter, exacting Sheldon M. Finkelstein, Jonathan Beard, and Jim Dingeman. Banksy, Perry Kretz, Vitalii S. Latov, the Harvard University Archives, the National Archives, the U.S. Army, Navy, Coast Guard, and Air Force, Dr. William F. Pepper, Caleb Stone and Avant Research, and the University of Wisconsin, among others, contributed images. Speaking opportunities at the New York Military Affairs Symposium, the Saltzman Institute of War and Peace Studies at Columbia's School of International and Public Affairs, Arizona State University, and the George Washington University-London School of Economics-University of California at Santa Barbara International Graduate Student Conference on the Cold War helped me organize my thoughts and generated useful feedback.

David Kravitz offered piercing legal analysis, a wooded retreat, and best friendship. Ned Hodgman's Russian was flawless. Daniella Zalcman was eloquent beyond words. Maureen and Eileen Marzano, Alexandra Dalferro, Phyllis Ma, and Alyssa Markert gave me peace of mind. Macallan K. Nein helped me choose this topic, and was closer to its exposition than anyone.

I owe my education to a long procession of teachers that started with my mother, Eva J. Neer, MD, professor of medicine and biochemistry at Harvard Medical School, and includes friends and fellow students at Harvard College, the National University of Singapore, and schools around the world, as well as Columbia. This book carries their contributions in every word.

# Index